SCHOOLS
OF
ASCETICISM

LUTZ KAELBER

SCHOOLS
OF
ASCETICISM

Ideology and
Organization in
Medieval Religious
Communities

The Pennsylvania State University Press
University Park, Pennsylvania

Library of Congress Cataloging-in-Publication Data

Kaelber, Lutz.
    Schools of asceticism : ideology and organization in medieval
religious communities / Lutz Kaelber.

        p.   cm.
    Includes bibliographical references and index.
    ISBN 0-271-01754-6 (cloth : alk. paper)
    ISBN 0-271-01755-4 (pbk. : alk. paper)
    1. Church history—Middle Ages, 600–1500.   2. Asceticism.
3. Monasticism and religious orders—History—Middle Ages,
600–1500.   4. Waldenses.   5. Albigenses.   I. Title.
BR270.K34   1998
306.6'4847'0902—dc21   97-33621
                                                                              CIP

Published by The Pennsylvania State University Press,
University Park, PA 16802-1003

It is the policy of The Pennsylvania State University Press to use acid-free
paper for the first printing of all clothbound books. Publications on uncoated
stock satisfy the minimum requirements of American National Standard for
Information Sciences-Permanence of Paper for Printed Library Materials,
ANSI Z39.48–1992.

CONTENTS

ACKNOWLEDGMENTS

One of the pleasures that derive from writing a book is the opportunity to thank those without whom the task could never have been accomplished. My greatest debt is to David Zaret, who introduced me to the intricacies of studying history from a sociological perspective. First as my teacher and then as the supervisor of the dissertation that formed the point of departure for this book, he encouraged me to merge sociological analysis with historical inquiry. In many ways, his work has inspired my own, and it continues to do so. I am equally indebted to Leah Shopkow, who constantly reminded me that a critical analysis of primary sources and original documents is at the heart of the historian's enterprise. I wish to thank her for being a major source of support and encouragement. Tom Gieryn and Jim Wood read several earlier versions of the manuscript and provided detailed commentary. I am grateful to both of them for this undertaking. Some parts of this book have been read by other scholars who have provided me with helpful criticism; among them are Robert Lerner, Guenther Roth, Dyan Elliott, John Mundy, Walter Wakefield, Kent Redding, Pam Walters, David James, and Richard Moye. I wish to thank all of them, and also my new colleagues Al Toborg, Allen Yale, Leighton Hazlehurst, and Bob Dixon, who have made my stay in a new academic environment a very pleasurable one.

Support for the writing of this book came from Indiana University graduate fellowships and grants of the College of Arts and Sciences and of the Political Economy Workshop, from the Association for the Sociology of Religion and the Comparative Historical Sociology section of the American Sociological Association via the Robert McNamara award and the Reinhard Bendix award, and from a travel grant from Lyndon State College. I am indebted to the librarians at Indiana University and at Lyndon State College, as well as to Dr. Michael Stoller, Butler Library, Columbia University, all of whom have been invaluable in obtaining materials. As my research assistants, Jennifer Emery and Sara Quinn worked with me on the final revision of the manuscript, for which they provided much help. Peter J. Potter of Penn State Press has been a supportive, skillful, and responsive editor and a pleasure to work with. I wish to thank them all.

Finally, this book may well not have reached completion without the help of Ellen Arapakos and the cheerful company of our two children, Amadeus and Cecilia. They helped me come back from the past and experience the joys of the present. I dedicate this book to them.

INTRODUCTION

In the second half of the twelfth century, new heresies began to spring up in many places in the medieval West. They appealed to the common man and woman, and some enjoyed continued popular support. For the largest heretical groups, the Waldensians and the Cathars, there was in fact so much support that in some areas the representatives of orthodox religious life took unusual measures to stem the rise of heresy. Dealing with Cathars and Waldensians in southern France, Catholic preachers agreed to a series of public debates with some whom they had *defined* as heretics.[1] In one somewhat peculiar instance, the debates carried on in front of large audiences for about two weeks, after which period the winner was to be determined by a panel of judges the parties had agreed on. However, the verdict and the outcome—the judges ultimately refused to render a judgment, and the debates did little to sway many supporters of either side—were much less significant than the fact that such a debate, or rather a whole series of them, took place at all. What a testament to the power and influence of the heretics that, at least in this case, they could successfully demand to make religious righteousness a matter of public consideration and judgment.[2]

What was it that made Waldensianism and Catharism appealing, so much so that, within a few decades after these public disputations had taken place, some Waldensians and Cathars would rather burn at the stake than renounce their affiliation with heresy? The answer to this vexed question, which has occupied medieval historians for many decades now, may lie in the public demonstration of certain behavior. The banner of the Cathars' and the Waldensians' religious convictions was a frugal

---

1. For a discussion of the changes in definitions of heresy over the centuries, see Jeffrey Burton Russell, *Dissent and Order in the Middle Ages: The Search for Legitimate Authority* (New York: Macmillan, 1992). See also Lester R. Kurtz, *The Politics of Heresy* (Berkeley and Los Angeles: University of California Press, 1986), 12–16, on the social construction of heresy.

2. For detailed accounts of the events described in this paragraph, see Marie-Humbert Vicaire, *Histoire de Saint Dominique: Un homme évangélique*, 2 vols., 2d ed. (Paris: Cerf, 1982), 1:196–97, 206–27, 274–79; Élie Griffe, *Le Languedoc cathare de 1190 à 1210* (Paris: Letouzey et Ané, 1971), 218–22, 251–61.

lifestyle among their leaders and most devoted followers. This lifestyle consisted in physical austerity, poverty, and preaching, and even abstention from certain foods (in the case of the Cathars). As a highly visible expression of asceticism, it struck a chord with many people at the time. What was the direction of Waldensian and Cathar asceticism? In what ways did it derive from their religious ethics and the social organization of their religious communities? How did heterodox asceticism contrast with asceticism in orthodox religious life? And what were the effects of asceticism, both in its orthodox and heterodox forms, on social life?

These are the questions addressed in this book. However, before sketching out some of the answers, I wish to point out that the questions themselves are not quite as novel as they might appear. The same or similar questions were asked almost one hundred years ago, in a different context, by a German social scientist who had just recovered from a debilitating and career-threatening nervous disorder. The context was the Reformation and the rise of Protestantism in the early modern period, and the scientist was Max Weber. The answers Weber proposed have preoccupied generations of sociologists ever since, but for the themes developed in this book, more important than the answers themselves is how Weber arrived at them. Weber was interested in religious asceticism because he traced religion's potential as an ordering, rationalizing force in life to its capacity to generate active ascetic conduct. He may have taken a hint from his contemporary Friedrich Nietzsche, who wrote in one of his most famous essays: "The ascetic treats life as a wrong road on which one must finally walk back to the point where it begins, or as a mistake that is put right by deeds—that we *ought* to put right: for he *demands* that one go along with him; where he can he compels acceptance of *his* evaluation of existence." To which Nietzsche added, "'Triumph in the ultimate agony': the ascetic ideal has always fought under this hyperbolic sign."[3]

In his writings in the sociology of religion, Weber stripped these thoughts of their pathos and emphasized the great transformative potential of the ascetic. Asceticism, which has its etymological origin in the Greek ἄσχησις, meaning "exercise" or "training," entails two aspects.[4]

---

3. Friedrich Nietzsche, *On the Genealogy of Morals*, in *Basic Writings of Nietzsche*, ed. and trans. Walter Kaufmann (New York: Modern Library, 1992), 3d essay, sec. 11. Weber considered this a "brilliant essay" ("The Social Psychology of the World Religions," in Max Weber, *From Max Weber*, ed. Hans H. Gerth and C. Wright Mills [New York: Oxford University Press, 1958], 270).

4. See H. Strathmann, "Askese I (nichtchristlich)," in *Reallexikon für Antike und Christentum*, ed. Theodor Klauser (Stuttgart: Hiersemann, 1950), vol. 1, cols. 749–58; Johannes Leipoldt, *Griechische Philosophie und frühchristliche Askese* (Berlin: Akademie, 1961), especially 3–5.

One is restraint and abstention: the ascetic attempts to block all distractions that tend to interfere with a plan for action. The other is the systematic pursuit of this plan. The outcome of the combination of both aspects is methodical self-control, expressed in a continuous and stringent discipline aimed at a certain end. Ascetic discipline and control can be a decisive stimulus from within, guiding people toward rationalized patterns of conduct that may have an impact on, and change, social and natural environments. It was this potential for an ascetic structuring of society and personality that Weber, when he wrote to Adolf von Harnack, bemoaned as lacking in Germany's modern history and in himself: "That our nation never went through the hard school of asceticism in *any* form . . . is the source of everything that I find hateful in it (as well as in myself)."[5] He, together with his longtime friend and colleague Ernst Troeltsch, found such schools of asceticism, instead, in the religious communities of early modern ascetic Protestantism.

This book, too, deals with schools of asceticism. It explores the Weberian theme of religious asceticism in the context of medieval religion. Its topic is forms and directions of ascetic behavior in orthodox religion and in heresy. It analyzes how the ideology and social organization of religious groups shaped rational ascetic conduct of their members, and how the different forms of asceticism affected cultural and economic life. Combining a sociological approach to the analysis of medieval history with an original analysis of primary sources, the book bridges the neighboring disciplines of comparative historical and theoretical sociology, medieval history, and religious studies. It develops a Weberian framework for the exploration of the relationship between religion and ascetic behavior, and applies this framework in an analysis of orthodox

5. Max Weber, *Briefe 1906–1908*, ed. M. Rainer Lepsius and Wolfgang J. Mommsen in collaboration with Birgit Rudhard and Manfred Schön (Tübingen: Mohr, 1990), 33 (emphasis in original); the letter is dated 5 February 1906. This view led Weber to adopt the ascetic motif on a secular foundation, particularly in his later speeches "Science as a Vocation" and "Politics as a Vocation" (in *From Max Weber*, 77–156; newly edited in Max Weber, *Wissenschaft als Beruf: 1917/1919; Politik als Beruf: 1919*, ed. Wolfgang J. Mommsen and Wolfgang Schluchter in collaboration with Birgitt Morgenbrod [Tübingen: Mohr, 1992]; see also Wolfgang Schluchter's cogent commentary, 40–43). The topic of the differences and similarities between Weber's and Nietzsche's views of the social importance of ascetic ideals has triggered considerable interest. See the recent discussion in Hartmann Tyrell, "Worum geht es in der 'Protestantischen Ethik'? Ein Versuch zum besseren Verständnis Max Webers," *Saeculum* 41 (1990): 154–61; Hubert Treiber, "Im Westen nichts Neues: Menschwerdung durch Askese: Sehnsucht nach Askese bei Weber und Nietzsche," in *Religionswissenschaft und Kulturkritik*, ed. Hans Gerhard Kippenberg and Brigitte Luchesi (Marburg: Diagonal, 1991), 283–323; David Owen, "Autonomy and 'Inner Distance': A Trace of Nietzsche in Weber," *History of the Human Sciences* 4 (1991), particularly 82–84.

and heretical religious groups. It therefore studies an old topic from a new perspective, and it arrives at new conclusions.

The book is divided into two major parts. The first part contains the theoretical framework and a study of orthodox religion; the second part addresses heresy. Chapter 1 deals with the relations between ideology, organization, and ascetic conduct from a theoretical point of view. It begins with an analysis of Weber's and Troeltsch's writings on religion, asceticism, and rationalism. Weber's studies in the sociology of religion addressed how ethical and institutional factors in religions brought about or inhibited different kinds of ascetic behavior in the context of larger social, cultural, and economic developments. Although his comparative historical studies covered ancient Judaism, Buddhism, Hinduism, and Confucianism, Weber planned to extend his most famous work, *The Protestant Ethic and the Spirit of Capitalism*,[6] stepping back in time. He wanted to study the historical development of methodical rational ways of life preceding the Reformation. The chapter provides a detailed study of Weber's views on medieval religion as they evolved over the years between the publication of the original version of *The Protestant Ethic* and his later writings, which were intended to provide a comparative typology and historical analysis of religious rationalizations in the major world religions, including medieval Christianity. I also analyze Troeltsch's writings, which not only complemented those of Weber, but have remained a major contribution to the field of ecclesiastical history in their own right. The analysis shows that medieval religion played a much more pertinent role in Weber's research program than previously acknowledged. The cornerstones of a sociology of medieval religion, addressing monasticism and orthodox and heterodox lay spirituality, had already been laid in the original version of *The Protestant Ethic*. Subsequently, Troeltsch carried out some, but not all, of the research envisioned by Weber. Building on Troeltsch in turn, Weber then expanded his research to a larger thematic context and employed a wider methodological perspective. He retained his interest in monasticism and lay spirituality, but the accent in his research program shifted toward an inquiry about lay heterodox movements as precursors of Calvinist inner-worldly asceticism. While regarding orthodox lay religion as an impediment to religious rationalization, Weber pointed out the existence of precursors of Calvinist ascetic rationalism in fringe and heterodox religious movements.

Chapters 2 and 3 address this theme by focusing on asceticism in orthodox religious life. Monastic asceticism is the subject of Chapter 2.

---

6. Max Weber, *The Protestant Ethic and the Spirit of Capitalism*, trans. T. Parsons (New York: Charles Scribner's Sons, 1976).

Most sociologists and many historians following in the footsteps of Weber and Troeltsch accepted Weber's thesis of a close relationship between monasticism and ascetic rationalism; more recently, some have even claimed that medieval nuns and monks were European civilization's first inner-worldly ascetics. I evaluate this claim, together with Weber's and Troeltsch's more guarded theses, by looking, first, at the normative foundation of monastic conduct in the sixth-century Rule of St. Benedict. Then the analysis shifts to the ways in which specific organizational and historical contexts mediated the linkages between ideology and behavior, and how they influenced the types, directions, and stringency of monastic asceticism over the following centuries. The conclusions of this analysis differ from the arguments made in the sociological and historical litera-ture. Over the course of the earlier Middle Ages, monasticism increas-ingly specialized in providing religious services for the nobility, while the performance of manual labor shifted to monastic affiliates. This monastic division of spiritual and manual labor continued in the later Middle Ages, when monasticism took a significant turn toward the world in combining preaching with austerity in the mendicant orders. Yet, and most important, mendicant austerity was modeled on prece-dents in lay spirituality. Thus, it was religious movements composed of laity in the High Middle Ages that became the harbingers and foremost carriers of asceticism. This argument goes against the trend in existing scholarship on monastic asceticism to center on the mendicants as initiators, not imitators, of worldly ascetic practices.

Chapter 3 turns to asceticism in lay orthodox religion. In the sociological literature, Weber set the tone for the exploration of lay religious asceticism in arguing that the laity's involvement in magical practices impeded the development of lay asceticism until the Reformation.[7] Historians who have taken up this argument are engaged in a lively debate about its merits in the context of early modern religion. What is missing, however, is an exploration of this issue for the

7. For example, in Robert Bellah's evolutionary scheme, medieval Christianity is classified as a "historic religion." Bellah notes that in the transition from historic religion to the next stage, termed "early-modern religion," in Europe much "of the cosmological baggage of medieval Christianity is dropped as superstition," including "a fundamentally ritualist interpretation of the sacrament of the Eucharist" ("Religious Evolution," *American Sociological Review* 29 [1964]: 369). Here medieval religion is seen as an enchanted realm when compared to more enlightened early modern religious beliefs and practices. See also Wolfgang Schluchter, "The Paradox of Rationalization: On the Relation Between Ethics and World," in Guenther Roth and Wolfgang Schluchter, *Max Weber's Vision of History: Ethics and Methods* (Berkeley and Los Angeles: University of California Press, 1979), 32–45.

Middle Ages. This chapter provides this exploration by discussing the role of magic as an impediment to rationalized action. It also addresses the acceptance of magical beliefs and practices among the laity as a substitute for ascetic action. The analysis shows that, indeed, for laity the boundaries between religion and magic were often blurry. The Catholic Church, increasingly supportive of the employment of proto-magical objects, encouraged reliance on the performance of rituals, rather than ascetic practices, as proper means to salvation. However, magic rituals did not supplant asceticism in all groups of laity. Disenchantment was not a process that started with the Reformation. Much neglected in existing scholarship, important exceptions to the prevalence of magic as a means to salvation arose in lay religious movements in the eleventh and twelfth centuries. The emergence of lay rationalism in this period was tied to new religious prophecies, the rejection of protomagical ecclesiastical rituals, the expansion of literacy, and new organizational forms to enhance religious knowledge among the laity. Lay rationalism expressed itself in ascetic patterns of action. These developments preceded, and were the basis for, the advent of more stringently ascetic types of life conduct in heterodox movements. These findings set the stage for Part Two of the book.

Part Two consists of an in-depth study of perhaps the most important heresies in the High Middle Ages, Waldensianism and Catharism. Chapter 4 deals with the religious ethics, organization, and ascetic behavior of medieval Waldensians. The Waldensians attempted to emulate the life of early Christian communities by emphasizing preaching, poverty, and austerity. Three stages in the development of Waldensianism, which differ significantly enough to treat them as distinct cases, can be distinguished: early, later, and Austrian Waldensianism. Based on the exploration of primary sources, the comparative historical analysis demonstrates that asceticism in early and later Waldensianism was other-worldly and confined to Waldensian itinerant preachers. Among the Austrian Waldensians, however, asceticism not only extended to lay congregations, but was also oriented toward the secular world. For the Austrian Waldensians, the world was a task, and had to be mastered through inner-worldly asceticism. In some ways, their rationalized conduct was a precursor of the type of asceticism found among some Protestant communities centuries later.

Chapter 5 turns to medieval Catharism. Having argued in Chapter 4 that the types and directions of Waldensian asceticism can be explained by reference to the interplay of ethical and organizational features, I now develop a similar argument for the Cathars. The analysis begins with Cathar ethics. In regard to their theological premises, the ethical precepts of Cathar religion were in strong contrast with Catholic divinity. Founded upon metaphysical dualism, Catharism posited a radical distinction between the good, spiritual realm and the evil realm of matter. This antagonism to the world and all material things imbued the leading circles of Catharism, the perfects, with a strong other-worldly asceticism. Judging by references to Cathar conduct in a variety of sources, the Cathar perfects surpassed their monastic and Waldensian counterparts in austerity. Yet the Cathar religious ethic was not indifferent to secular society, nor did Cathars avoid all contact with it. The relations between Cathar religion and its social environments hinged on the relations between Cathar perfects, their supporters, and their surrounding communities. I explore such relations by analyzing mediating organizational contexts, the networks of artisan shops run by Cathar perfects for the purpose of training apprentices in handicraft professions, as well as in the religious vocation of a perfect. I strengthen the argument that Catharism's tenacity depended on an organizational network of supportive establishments by demonstrating that the deterioration in organizational support was closely linked to the decline of the Bolognese Cathars late in the thirteenth century and of Catharism in southern France in the early fourteenth century.

The conclusion then summarizes the central arguments in this book. It discusses some implications for sociological scholarship on Weber and the Weberian theme of religion and rationalization, comparative historical sociology, and historical scholarship on medieval heresy.

Part One

A SOCIOLOGY
OF MEDIEVAL
RELIGION

Weber, Troeltsch, and Beyond

1

─────═⟫◉⟪═─────

MEDIEVAL RELIGION AND THE ROOTS OF RATIONALISM

Weber's Lacuna

Few works in twentieth-century social thought have received as much attention as Max Weber's *Protestant Ethic and the Spirit of Capitalism* (PE), which appeared in its original form in 1904–5.[1] In the wake of this study, Weberian scholars and critics have focused on the links between religion and the modern economy, but have overlooked an important component of Weber's study: medieval religion. Analyzing the cultural significance of modern ascetic rationalism, Weber initially wanted to extend the PE, stepping back in time, and to study the historical

A shortened version of this chapter was published as "Weber's Lacuna: Medieval Religion and the Roots of Rationalization," *Journal of the History of Ideas* 57 (1996): 465–85. I am grateful to an anonymous referee for that journal for a suggestion regarding the title, which I partially adopted for this chapter.

1. Max Weber, "Die protestantische Ethik und der 'Geist' des Kapitalismus, I: Das Problem," *Archiv für Sozialwissenschaft und Sozialpolitik* 20 (1904): 1–54 (cited hereafter as PE I and *Archiv*); "Die protestantische Ethik und der 'Geist' des Kapitalismus, II: Die Berufsidee des asketischen Protestantismus," *Archiv* 21 (1905): 1–110 (cited hereafter as PE II). It is customary to date Weber's publications, as is done here, to the time of their distribution by the publisher; the dates are given in Martin Riesebrodt, "Bibliographie zur Max Weber-Gesamtausgabe," in *Prospekt der Max Weber Gesamtausgabe*, ed. Horst Baier, M. Rainer Lepsius, Wolfgang J. Mommsen, Wolfgang Schluchter, and Johannes Winckelmann (Tübingen: Mohr, 1981), 16–32.

development of methodical rational ways of life preceding the Reformation. Between publication of the PE and his death in 1920, Weber specified his research agenda and elaborated on his earlier views. First these specifications and elaborations were made as a response to a series of writings by Ernst Troeltsch, particularly *The Social Teaching of the Christian Churches*,[2] and later, while preparing his study *The Christianity of the Occident* as part of his *Collected Essays in the Sociology of Religion*. This chapter provides a detailed analysis of Weber's views on medieval religion as they evolved between 1904–5 and 1920, and shows how Weber linked his explorations of medieval religion to his larger intellectual agenda, appropriating and transcending ideas current in contemporary historical and religious scholarship.

Furthermore, I hope to demonstrate that the conclusions of the few existing studies of Weber's views on this topic should be revised. His remarks on medieval religion were not confined to the conceptualization of structural transformations in the Middle Ages,[3] nor did they contain the notion of medieval Christianity as a step backward in the course of Western rationalization.[4] On the contrary, Weber was interested in religious contributions and impediments to an ascetic empowerment of the self in different groups and movements in the Middle Ages, and while he mostly saw impediments in orthodox lay religion, he presumed the existence of precursors of Calvinist ascetic rationalism in fringe and heterodox religious movements.

In the development of his thought, Weber's interest in this topic ran through three phases: first, the years 1904–5, when the PE was published, containing the cornerstones of a sociological treatment of medieval religion; second, the years between 1906 and 1910, when Ernst Troeltsch's analyses supplemented Weber's treatment and elicited his response; and third, the years between 1910 and 1920, when Weber began to put medieval Christianity in the context of a comparative typology and historical analysis of religious rationalizations in the major world religions.

2. Troeltsch's magnum opus first appeared as "Die Soziallehren der christlichen Kirchen und Gruppen" in the *Archiv* in 1908–10 and was published, revised and expanded, as a book under the same title in 1912. My references are to the English translation, *The Social Teaching of the Christian Churches*, trans. O. Wyon (New York: Macmillan, 1956).

3. Randall Collins, "The Weberian Revolution of the High Middle Ages," in *Weberian Sociological Theory* (Cambridge: Cambridge University Press, 1986), 45–76. Nuanced, but still focused on institutional aspects, is Wolfgang Schluchter, *Paradoxes of Modernity: Culture and Conduct in the Theory of Max Weber*, trans. Neil Solomon (Stanford: Stanford University Press, 1996), chap. 4.

4. Ralph Schroeder, *Max Weber and the Sociology of Culture* (London: Sage, 1992), 84–96.

The Protestant Ethic of 1904–1905

Ascetic Rationalism and the Empowerment of the Self

In the PE[5] Weber set out to provide an "illustration of the manner by which *ideas* become effective factors in history."[6] For this task Weber chose the early modern period, analyzing how religious factors contributed to the historical development of one constitutive component of modern culture: rational behavior on the basis of the idea of a "calling."[7] Analytically, his exploration focused on the influence of core doctrines and dogmas and their practical-psychological consequences on patterns of social action.[8] In its emphasis on the effects of ideas, the PE was from the beginning a narrowly focused study with a set of conceptual tools correspondingly chosen for its purpose. The study's narrow focus derived from Weber's reliance on a Kantian epistemology that conceived reality as a "tremendous confusion of interdependent influences" of historical factors such as ideas, material conditions, and organizational settings.[9] In this view the analysis of historical events from any one angle was in principle as legitimate as from any other, though in practice heuristic constraints often necessitated the choice of a particular point of view. For the PE, Weber chose an idealistic angle, and material

5. Despite calls for a closer examination of the original version (e.g., Friedrich H. Tenbruck, "The Problem of Thematic Unity in the Works of Max Weber," in *Reading Weber*, ed. Keith Tribe [London: Routledge, 1989], 49; Dirk Käsler, *Max Weber: An Introduction to his Life and Work*, trans. P. Hurd [Cambridge: Polity Press, 1988], 220 n. 5), the only existing account, which fails to address medieval religion, is Gottfried Küenzlen, *Die Religionssoziologie Max Webers: Eine Darstellung ihrer Entwicklung* (Berlin: Duncker & Humblot, 1980), 18–26. Wolfgang Schluchter's eminent reconstruction of the development of Weber's sociology of religion begins with Weber's writings around 1910 (*Rationalism, Religion, and Domination: A Weberian Perspective*, trans. Neil Solomon [Berkeley and Los Angeles: University of California Press, 1989], 411–32).

6. PE I, 53 (my translation, as are all subsequent translations unless otherwise noted).

7. PE I, 54; PE II, 104–5, 107.

8. PE II, 3–4, 23 n. 36, 25 n. 48, 106.

9. PE I, 54. Cf. Max Weber, "'Objectivity' in Social Science and Social Policy," in *The Methodology of the Social Sciences*, ed. and trans. Edward A. Shils and Henry A. Finch (Glencoe, Ill.: Free Press, 1949), 72, 78, 81, 84, 105, 111. On Weber's relationship to Southwest German neo-Kantianism, see Dieter Henrich, *Die Einheit der Wissenschaftslehre Max Webers* (Tübingen: Mohr, 1952); Thomas Burger, *Max Weber's Theory of Concept Formation: History, Laws, and Ideal Types*, 2d, enlarged ed. (Durham, N.C.: Duke University Press, 1987); Guy Oakes, *Weber and Rickert: Concept Formation in the Social Sciences* (Cambridge: MIT Press, 1988); Peter-Ulrich Merz, *Max Weber und Heinrich Rickert: Die erkenntniskritischen Grundlagen der verstehenden Soziologie* (Würzburg: Königshausen & Neumann, 1990).

and organizational factors remained at the periphery of his study and were mentioned only in passing.[10]

Yet Weber's intellectual interest in ascetic Protestantism in 1904–5 went beyond the topic of religious contributions to the emergence of modern capitalism in the early modern era. The overarching issue was the cultural significance of Protestantism's "ascetic rationalism," which was to be studied for both later and earlier periods, particularly the centuries preceding the Reformation.[11] In delineating the meaning of this concept, Weber was careful to point out that ascetic rationalism of a religious providence was just one among many empirical forms the generic concept of rationalism could designate: "One can very well 'rationalize' life according to very different ultimate points of view and in different directions; 'rationalism' is a historical concept that encompasses a world of differences."[12] It was therefore necessary to provide a specification of the term, for which Weber took a cue from the economist Werner Sombart.

In 1902 Sombart published his *Modern Capitalism*, in which he identified the central and distinguishing characteristic of the modern capitalist economy as thorough "calculability" (*Rechenhaftigkeit*). Calculability denotes the precise, encompassing structuring of means for the achievement of capitalist profit. Weber found Sombart's characterization highly accurate.[13] But he also differed from Sombart in two important aspects. First, he viewed calculability as an important manifestation of a larger underlying process: ascetic rationalism. For Weber, ascetic rationalism manifested itself in the thorough calculability of all social spheres; it was not merely an institutional characteristic of the economy, as Sombart had defined it. Ascetic rationalism designated the combination of a mental outlook and a pattern of social action—the methodical and sober mastery of life as a normative principle. The penetration of ascetic rationalism and its particular calculability into not only the modern economy, which Sombart had described, but all secular spheres

10. Cf. Weber's characterization of the PE as "a sort of 'spiritualistic' construction of the modern economy" (letter to Heinrich Rickert, dated 2 April 1905; quoted in Marianne Weber, *Max Weber: A Biography*, trans. Harry Zohn [New Brunswick, N.J.: Transaction, 1988], 356). For an investigation of materialist aspects in the PE, though taken from the revised version, see Michael Löwy, "Weber Against Marx? The Polemic with Historical Materialism in the *Protestant Ethic*," *Science and Society* 53 (1989): 71–83. For references to organizational factors, see notes 25 and 26 below.

11. PE I, 12; PE II, 6, 109.

12. PE I, 35.

13. Werner Sombart, *Der moderne Kapitalismus*, 2 vols. (Leipzig: Duncker & Humblot, 1902), 1:198, 207, 395; PE I, 34; PE II, 77 n.7.

rested firmly on what Weber called a principled, value-based way of life, or permanent habitus—*Lebensführung*.[14]

For such a permanent habitus, or life conduct, of calculability to emerge, it was not plausible to assume, as Sombart had done, that its origins lay in an autochthonous rise in the urge to make money. What kinds of goals in life existed and how stringently the means were organized to achieve them had historically been determined in part by value systems capable of emanating such goals and of providing psychological incentives to achieve them. To a significant extent, religions constituted such value systems, but the directions in which and the degrees to which religions rationalized life conduct varied. The historical contribution of ascetic Protestantism, Weber argued, was that it brought about a prevalent form of life conduct that engendered inner-worldly ascetic rationalism. Such a religiously co-conditioned life conduct denoted an "empowerment of the self," putting all aspects of existence consistently and stringently under ethical prerogatives. Given certain institutional conditions, this empowerment of the self provided the means with which individuals could methodically permeate all spheres of society with ascetic practices.[15]

To examine the emergence and effects of the ascetic Protestant empowerment of the self that manifested itself in a certain life conduct of calculability was to assess ascetic rationalism's cultural significance. The "cultural significance" of a historical phenomenon refers to its causal influence on other social phenomena that follow it, the relationship between this phenomenon and other contemporary aspects of society and culture, and the contribution of social factors to its emergence and development. Therefore, to assess ascetic rationalism's cultural significance was to broaden the narrow focus of the PE in order to analyze (1) the contribution of religious and other social factors in earlier periods to the historical emergence of inner-worldly asceticism

14. PE I, 35; PE II, 77 n.7, 91–92, 98. Cf. Friedrich Lenger, *Werner Sombart, 1863–1941: Eine Biographie* (Munich: Beck, 1994), 129–35.

15. See Harvey S. Goldman, *Max Weber and Thomas Mann: Calling and the Shaping of the Self* (Berkeley and Los Angeles: University of California Press, 1988), 131–68; idem, *Politics, Death, and the Devil: Self and Power in Max Weber and Thomas Mann* (Berkeley and Los Angeles: University of California Press, 1992), 9–18; idem, "Weber's Ascetic Practices of the Self," in *Weber's "Protestant Ethic": Origins, Evidence, Contexts*, ed. Hartmut Lehmann and Guenther Roth (Cambridge: Cambridge University Press, 1993), 161–77; Wolfgang J. Mommsen, "Personal Conduct and Societal Change: Toward a Reconstruction of Max Weber's Concept of History," in *Max Weber, Rationality, and Modernity*, ed. Scott Lash and Sam Whimster (London: Allen & Unwin, 1987), 35–51. I am less inclined than Goldman and Mommsen, however, to view the empowerment of the self as the exclusive domain of charismatic or otherwise extraordinary personalities.

and the modern capitalist ethic, and (2) the relation of asceticism and capitalism to other contemporary developments, and their effect on spheres other than religion and the economy.[16]

Weber's Research Program

An important part of Weber's investigation of the cultural significance of ascetic rationalism was to step back in time and analyze the contributions of religion and other factors to its emergence. Weber addressed this in his research program at the end of the PE:

> Now, the task is . . . to show the significance of ascetic rationalism, only touched upon in the foregoing sketch, for the contents of the socioeconomic ethic, that is, for the type of organization and the functions of the social organizations from the conventicle to the state. Then, its [ascetic rationalism's] relationship to humanist rationalism and its ideals of life and cultural influence, as well as to the development of philosophic and scientific empiricism, and to technological development and to the spiritual values of our culture, has to be analyzed. Then, finally, its development is to be traced, from the *medieval beginnings of inner-worldly asceticism*, through its dissolution into sheer utilitarianism, historically and through the various areas of ascetic religiosity's dissemination. Only in this way can the cultural significance of ascetic Protestantism in relation to other formative elements of modern culture be revealed. In doing so, [the analysis has to] reveal the manner in which Protestant asceticism was in turn influenced in its emergence and its peculiar features by the entirety of the cultural conditions in society, especially economic ones.[17]

Following up on all these possible extensions of the PE would be a demanding task and in some cases go beyond the area of interest covered by the *Archiv*.[18] Nevertheless, with reference to ascetic

16. Similar to my argument is that of Künzlen, *Die Religionssoziologie Max Webers*, 46 n.10. For further elaboration on Weber's notion of cultural significance, see Henrich, *Die Einheit der Wissenschaftslehre*, 72–83; Johannes Weiß, *Max Webers Grundlegung der Soziologie* (Munich: Verlag Dokumentation, 1975), 33–45.

17. PE II, 109–10 (my emphasis).

18. PE II, 110 n. 86: "Whether, by the way, one or the other of the more general problems outlined above can be dealt with within the limits of *this* journal is not certain

Protestantism's cultural significance Weber had conceived three major avenues of research: (1) to analyze the effect of ascetic rationalism on the modern economy after the period covered in the PE, and on other social spheres; (2) to widen the narrow focus of the PE, taking into consideration material and organizational factors, in order to address the development of ascetic Protestantism and its relevance for the spirit of modern capitalism; and (3) to elaborate on a sociology of medieval religion already contained in the existing essay.[19]

The first avenue of research would involve an investigation of ascetic rationalism after the "heroic epoch of capitalism," that is, in an era when utilitarian motives had come to reign.[20] This could be complemented with an analysis of the impact of methodical life conduct based on the notion of a calling on other social spheres, such as science or politics, social policies, and the state.[21] Second, Weber wanted to complement the idealistic focus in the PE essays with a materialist analysis even before he faced critics' accusations of idealistic reductionism. "For those whose conscience regarding causality is not appeased without economic ('materialist,' as it is unfortunately still called) interpretation, it may be remarked hereby that I consider the influence of economic development on the destiny of religious thoughts to be very significant and that I shall attempt to set forth later how in our case the mutual processes of adaptation and relationships between the two took shape."[22] Such an investigation of the material underpinnings of the motives of

in view of the tasks it is dedicated to. I am not very inclined to writing thick books that would have to follow other (theological and historical) works to such a great extent as would be the case here." The *Archiv* was dedicated to the analysis of the economic and sociocultural implications of modern capitalism, but not to the exploration of religion, culture, or technology per se. See note 22 below.

19. Cf. Hartmann Tyrell's comment: "The question arises: what did Weber have in mind regarding further studies [on the theme of the PE]? It appears to me that it is a pivotal task to address this issue in future studies on the work history of the 'Protestant Ethic'" ("Protestantische Ethik—und kein Ende," *Soziologische Revue* 17 [1994]: 399). Previous research has shed little light on this. See Küenzlen, *Die Religionssoziologie Max Webers*, 44–46; Wolfgang Schluchter, *The Rise of Western Rationalism: Max Weber's Developmental History*, trans. G. Roth (Berkeley and Los Angeles: University of California Press, 1981), 147; Tenbruck, "The Problem of Thematic Unity," in *Reading Weber*, ed. Tribe, 58–60; Stephen P. Turner, *The Search for a Methodology of Social Science: Durkheim, Weber, and the Nineteenth-Century Problem of Cause, Probability, and Action* (Dordrecht: Reidel, 1986), 201–3.

20. PE II, 92, 104.

21. Cf. Weber's comments on science (PE II, 53 n. 108, 97 n. 59) and on politics, social policies, and the state (PE II, 15 n. 21a, 23 n. 36, 42 n. 78, 61, 66 n. 130, 71–72).

22. PE II, 101 n. 69. Upon becoming a coeditor of the *Archiv* early in 1904, Weber drafted (according to Marianne Weber) and signed a collective statement by the new

ascetic Protestants—the "class relationships" and "class conditioning" of Protestant asceticism[23]—also entailed a closer look at affinities between Reformation religiosity and the cities, that is, ascetic Protestantism's support from aspiring urban middle-class strata.[24] Furthermore, a materialist analysis could be combined with one that paid more attention to ascetic Protestantism's social organization, its "ecclesiastical constitution,"[25] employing the ideal types of church and sect.[26] Third, with regard to periods before the Reformation, Weber suggested that the contribution of humanist thought might be relevant for the emergence of ascetic rationalism. Even more important, he thought, were manifestations of inner-worldly asceticism in the Middle Ages. In the final footnote in the PE, Weber noted that "the period of capitalist development previous to the one we have looked at was co-conditioned everywhere by Christian influences—impeding as well as conducive ones."[27] The groundwork for such an expansion of the PE into the Middle Ages Weber had already laid in the essay itself, addressing medieval religion's potential for an ascetic empowerment of the self in the context of medieval monasticism, lay spirituality, mysticism, and heterodox groups.

An Early Sociology of Medieval Religion

Medieval Monasticism

Around the turn of the century, Weber appears to have developed a special interest in medieval monasticism. Books on the history,

---

editors declaring that the publishing activity of the journal "is based, and has to be based, upon a rather specific perspective: that of the economic conditioning of cultural phenomena" (Werner Sombart, Max Weber, and Edgar Jaffé, "Geleitwort," *Archiv* 19 [1904]: v). Cf. Marianne Weber, *Max Weber*, 278; Gangolf Hübinger, "Max Weber und die historischen Kulturwissenschaften," in *Deutsche Geschichtswissenschaft um 1900*, ed. Notker Hammerstein (Stuttgart: Steiner, 1988), 275. See also Weber's remarks in "'Objectivity' in Social Science and Social Policy" (69–70), where he notes that, regarding the economic interpretation of history, "following a period of boundless overestimation, the danger now almost exists that its scientific value will be underestimated."

23. PE II, 69 n. 69, 79 n. 14, 101 n. 69.

24. PE I, 2–3, 26 n. 1; PE II, 78 n. 14, 93 n. 52.

25. PE II, 2 n. 2, 5 n. 4, 33, 46.

26. Weber introduced the distinction between church and sect briefly in "'Objectivity' in Social Science and Social Policy" (93). In the PE the application of these concepts was largely confined to Quaker religious life, whereas other groups—Calvinists, Lutherans, and the medieval church—were mentioned only in passing. See PE II, 61–68, especially 63–64.

27. PE II, 110 n. 86 (emphasis removed).

constitution, and economy of medieval monasteries and orders made up some of Weber's pastime reading in Rome during his recuperation from his nervous breakdown between fall 1901 and Easter 1902.[28] Medieval monasticism was a topic he apparently had not explored previously,[29] at least not before 1898.[30] Weber's interest in medieval monasticism stemmed from two considerations. First, monks or nuns had elite status in medieval Catholicism. They were the foremost carriers of orthodox ethics. Second, as religious virtuosos members of monastic orders were most directly confronted with a principal problem in all systematized belief systems that put strong ethical demands on the secular spheres: the tension between ethics and the world. How did medieval monasticism deal with the basic incommensurability between lofty ethical ideals and practical contingencies of secular life?[31] The distinguished Protestant theologian Adolf von Harnack had provided an authoritative answer to this question, and his views set the tone for Weber.[32]

28. See Marianne Weber, *Max Weber*, 250–55, 326.

29. Marianne Weber (ibid., 253, 326) reports Weber's intensive study of this literature (which he "absorbed"). Her assessment that these studies may have been a preliminary to the PE essay is reasonable in light of the fact that the essay contains an abundance of (undocumented) references to monastic developments and achievements in the Middle Ages.

30. Weber's *Grundriss zu den Vorlesungen über Allgemeine ("theoretische") Nationalökonomie* (Outline to the lectures on general ("theoretical") economics) (Tübingen: Mohr, [1898] 1990), which around April 1898 he had distributed to his students in Heidelberg for the summer semester, represents the latest extant document on the state of his thoughts on economic and social development in history before his incapacitating "descent to hell" (see Marianne Weber, *Max Weber*, 237 and, more generally, 235–50). The *Outline* lists over five hundred books and journal contributions, but does not include a single reference to medieval monasticism, and no chapter or section is devoted to this topic. Hence it is quite unlikely that Weber took up his inquiries into medieval monasticism earlier than fall 1901.

31. This was to become a central aspect in Weber's later religious writings. See Max Weber, "Religious Rejections of the World and Their Directions," in *From Max Weber*, 323–59; idem, *Economy and Society*, ed. Claus Wittich and Guenther Roth (Berkeley and Los Angeles: University of California Press, 1978), 576–610.

32. Adolf von Harnack, *Das Mönchtum: Seine Ideale und seine Geschichte*, 4th ed. (Giessen: Ricker'sche Buchhandlung, 1895). Although Weber makes no reference to his sources on monasticism, he undoubtedly knew the contents of Harnack's book. On Weber's respect for Harnack, see Harry Liebersohn, *Fate and Utopia in German Sociology*, 1870–1923 (Cambridge: MIT Press, 1988), 88. Other theological informants of Weber are discussed in Küenzlen, *Die Religionssoziologie Max Webers*, chap. 3; Friedrich Wilhelm Graf, "The German Theological Sources and Protestant Church Politics," in *Weber's "Protestant Ethic,"* ed. Lehmann and Roth, 27–50; Hans Gerhard Kippenberg, "Max Weber im Kreise von Religionswissenschaftlern," *Zeitschrift für Religions- und Geistesgeschichte* 45 (1993): 348–66.

Harnack described the principal ideal of monasticism as world flight (*Weltflucht*) or world abnegation (*Weltentsagung*). The spearhead of Catholic religion, monasticism contributed to major reforms of the Western Church in the sixth (the Rule of Saint Benedict), the eleventh (Cluny and the Gregorian reform), and the thirteenth centuries (the mendicant orders), but could ultimately not avoid becoming entangled in the secular sphere and bringing forth less stringent and more secularized forms of spirituality.[33] Weber followed Harnack in his principal argument, yet concentrated on early monastic developments in the West and stressed more than Harnack the ascetic achievements and rationalization in monastic life, which produced the "first human being (in the Middle Ages) to live according to a time schedule."[34] In Weber's view, the church was successful in channeling haphazard world flight and self-tormenting doubts into systematized and methodical, hence rationalized, forms of asceticism:

> In the Rule of St. Benedict, even more so in the case of the monks of Cluny and the Cistercians . . . , [Christian asceticism] has become a systematically developed method of rational life conduct, with the goal to overcome the *status naturae*, to free man from the power of irrational impulses and his dependence on the world and nature, to bring him under the supremacy of purposive volition, to subject his action to constant self-control and the consideration of the ethical consequences [of his deeds], and thus to train the monk—objectively—to be a worker in the service of the Kingdom of God, and thereby also—subjectively— to assure him of the salvation of his soul. . . . The empowerment to live a conscientious and alert life in the light . . . was the end, the destruction of the unmeditated state of impulsive enjoyment the most important task, to bring order into the life conduct of the adherents the most important means, of asceticism. All these decisive aspects manifest themselves in the rules of Catholic monasticism just as strongly as in the Calvinist principles of life conduct.[35]

One of the most significant characteristics of monasticism's asceticism was an emphasis on the methodical and systematic performance of labor. Collective systematic work according to a stringent schedule was

---

33. Harnack, *Das Mönchtum*, 7–8, 35–62.
34. PE II, 78 n. 11.
35. PE II, 28–30 (emphasis removed).

a distinctive feature of Occidental monasticism.[36] At the same time, the church integrated its religious virtuosos into its body by declaring subservience to the church an ascetic virtue.[37] However, the monastic ethic applied to but a few, not the masses, and in its other-worldly orientation it did not stipulate secular rationality: "Christian asceticism, at first fleeing from the world into solitude, had . . . mastered the world outside of the cloister in renouncing it. But it had, on the whole, left worldly conduct in everyday life in its natural ingenuous condition."[38]

The Orthodox Laity

The other side of monasticism's historical legacy lay in its contribution to the relaxation of ethical demands in lay orthodox spirituality. The "moral contentedness"[39] of lay Catholicism derived from a dualist ethical system and the means by which the laity could compensate for ethical shortcomings. Whereas medieval nuns and monks were held to the higher ethical standards of the evangelical counsels expressed in the monastic vows (poverty, chastity, and obedience), the laity were under less demanding ethical obligations. Weber poignantly described this as a two-tiered system of morals, consisting of (in the terminology he used in a letter to Else Jaffé after the publication of the PE) an "ethic of the average" for the laity and an "ethic of heroes" for the monastics.[40] A general willingness to follow these commands and to defer to the church's authority sufficed to assure individuals adhering to the "ethic of the average" of their salvation. The church provided ample means to "make up" for ethical lapses, such as in the thesaurus of merits accumulated by the saints.[41] Consequently, direct and unequivocal ethical incentives for a systematic rationalization according to

36. PE II, 28.
37. PE II, 66 n. 130.
38. PE II, 73.
39. PE II, 30.
40. "One can divide all 'ethics,' regardless of their material contents, into two major groups according to whether they make principal demands on a person that he is generally unable to live up to, except in the great heyday of his life, [and] that point the way as guideposts in his striving in infinity: 'ethic of heroes.' Or whether they [the ethics] are modest enough to accept his mundane 'nature' as the maximum requirement: 'ethic of the average'" (*Briefe 1906–1908*, 399; the letter is dated 13 September 1907). Later Weber used the terms "ethics of virtuosos" and "ethics of the masses" with the same connotations, denoting differences in the ethical or religious qualification of people. See Schluchter, *Paradoxes of Modernity*, 57–63.
41. PE I, 41; PE II, 25, 28 n. 53, 30, 73, 94.

ethical ideals were comparatively weak: "With regard to ethics, the medieval Catholic lives in a way 'from hand to mouth.' Above all, he fulfills his traditional duties conscientiously. His 'good works' above and beyond those [duties] are, however, usually a planless series of individual acts, performed to make up for concrete sins or under guidance of pastoral advice or at the end of his life, so to speak, as a payment toward insurance [against damnation]."[42] The ideal-typical Catholic layperson was therefore at best a conscientious observer of a system of religious duties, and at worst an indifferent bystander. Since this moral economy "lastly counteracted tendencies toward systematic inner-worldly asceticism,"[43] Weber turned to late medieval mysticism and heterodox groups for traces of inner-worldly asceticism preceding the Reformation.

Mysticism

A crucial difference between medieval Catholicism and ascetic Protestantism was the latter's attribution of an ultimate ethical value to the pursuit of worldly trades.[44] In the PE, Weber devoted a section to the emergence of the notion of a calling, or "the valuation of the fulfillment of duty *within* worldly professions as the *highest* form that the moral activity of the individual could assume."[45] The search for precursors of this notion led Weber to consider an unlikely candidate: mysticism.

In the 1880s the influential Lutheran theologian Albrecht Ritschl published his seminal *History of Pietism*. Ritschl posited a sharp distinction between the relative backwardness of (late) medieval spirituality and the enlightened features of Protestantism. The former he associated with mystical currents in popular religious devotion, which to him represented a more or less sentimental backdrop to rational Lutheran-Protestant conceptions. Because of its contemplative nature, Ritschl argued, mysticism avoided all engagement with the world.[46] Weber, while critical of Ritschl's unequivocal identification of religious and cultural progress with Lutheran Protestantism (a view Weber shared with prominent authors of the PE's theological sources), accepted Ritschl's views on the traditional and nonrational character of some

42. PE II, 26–27.

43. PE II, 31.

44. PE II, 26–35, 87 n. 35.

45. PE I, 35–54 (the quote is from 41).

46. Albrecht Ritschl, *Geschichte des Pietismus*, 3 vols. (Bonn: Marcus, 1880–86), 1:46–61.

mystical currents in the Middle Ages.[47] But Weber rejected Ritschl's claim that a mystic was interested only in avoiding secular affairs. On the contrary, "[m]ystical contemplation and rational vocational asceticism do not preclude each other."[48] Although mysticism promoted inwardness in its striving for rest in God, Weber credited medieval mystics like Johannes Tauler with an increased valuation of secular vocations. He even saw an emergent notion of perseverance of faith (*Bewährung*) in conduct, because mysticism attached a particular significance to methodically controlled ways of life.[49] Still, these were largely notions of medieval German theologians, which, however influential or popular, operated on an intellectual plane and may not have permeated practical conduct.[50]

Heterodox Asceticism

Weber finally turned to ascetic rationalism in heterodox religious groups. His initial cue likely came again, as in his treatment of mysticism, from Ritschl, who had drawn attention to the mendicants' attempt to diminish "the difference between the Christian perfection of monasticism and the merely passive Christian life of the laity" by seeking to "introduce ascetic life conduct into civic society."[51] Weber echoed Ritschl's assessment with a reference to the tertiary order of the Franciscans, asserting that the preaching of the mendicants and fringe groups like the Humiliati and Beguines helped to lay the foundation for the type of ascetic lay morality that later prevailed in Calvinism.[52] However, Weber was skeptical about these groups' capacity to extend such morality to the laity. His theological informants were again Harnack and Troeltsch.

Harnack's *History of Dogma* included a treatment of the proliferation of lay spiritual groups in the Middle Ages. The way in which the

47. See PE II, 21 n. 33, 34 n. 69, 41 n. 76, 57 n. 114a. On Ritschl's influence, see Graf, "The German Theological Sources," in *Weber's "Protestant Ethic,"* ed. Lehmann and Roth, 41–47; Liebersohn, *Fate and Utopia in German Sociology*, 45–49; J. R. Ward, "Max Weber and the Lutherans," in *Max Weber and His Contemporaries*, ed. Wolfgang J. Mommsen and Jürgen Osterhammel (London: Allen & Unwin, 1987), 205–7.

48. PE II, 21 n. 33. Cf. Ritschl's statement in *Geschichte in Pietismus*, 1:28.

49. PE I, 37 n. 2, 41, 43 n. 2, 48 n. 2, 50; PE II, 21 n. 33.

50. Weber made no mention of Romance mysticism, as did some leading German theological works. See, e.g., Reinhold Seeberg, *Thomasius' Dogmengeschichte des Mittelalters und der Neuzeit* (Erlangen: Deichert'sche Verlagsbuchhandlung, 1889), 274–90.

51. Ritschl, *Geschichte des Pietismus*, 1:14, 15.

52. PE II, 30–31, 63 n. 123. Cf. 30: "It is not as though within Catholicism the 'methodical' life had been restricted to the cloister cells. This was not at all the case in theory, and also not in practice."

Catholic Church incorporated these groups Harnack described as "monastization of the laity"—a process by which vanguard elements of lay religious groups were channeled into orthodox religion and cloistered types of life by adjoining them to monastic orders.[53] This corresponded to Ernst Troeltsch's thesis of a "relatively unitary culture of the Middle Ages," one of the central tenets of his later work. In Troeltsch's view, the medieval Catholic Church succeeded in preserving a general cultural unity in its spheres of influence and in keeping heterodox elements at bay, integrating fringe elements with force into the body of the church.[54] Weber echoed the Harnack-Troeltsch thesis in the PE:

> The historical fact was rather that the official Catholic Church regarded the *inner*-worldly asceticism of the laity, wherever it went as far as the formation of conventicles, with utmost suspicion and attempted to direct it toward the formation of orders, thus *out* of the "world," or at least adjoined it as asceticism of secondary status to the mendicant orders and subjected it to the control of the church. Where this [integration of these groups and taking control over them] did not succeed, the church equally sensed the danger that the cultivation of subjectivist ascetic morality might lead to the denial of authority and to heresy.[55]

This view may explain Weber's brevity in alluding to fringe lay groups in the Middle Ages. Not allowed to carry on their religious life as they would have liked, they were channeled into semimonastic ways of life and thereby removed from the centers of social life. This consideration applies less to heretical sects, which were not subject to a monastization

53. Adolf von Harnack, *Lehrbuch der Dogmengeschichte*, 3 vols. (Tübingen: Mohr, 1894–97), 3:402–9 (the quote is from 403).

54. In one of his earliest academic writings, Troeltsch wrote: "In negating the world for the sake of salvation, the church dominates the world for the purpose of the preservation and implementation of salvation, as a state has never before ruled. All spheres of life are taken under its wings. . . . Where this is not achieved in reality, the church lays claim to it and preserves this claim for more favorable times" ("Religion und Kirche," *Preußische Jahrbücher* 81 [1895]: 233–34). By early 1900, Troeltsch used the phrases "unity of the Christian church" and "accomplishment of a unitary Christian-scientific culture" in this context explicitly (review of *Lehrbuch der Dogmengeschichte: Zweite Hälfte: Die Dogmengeschichte des Mittelalters und der Neuzeit*, by R. Seeberg, *Göttingische gelehrte Anzeigen* 163 [1901]: 15, 20–21).

55. PE II, 62 n. 123. In his essay "'Objectivity' in Social Science and Social Policy" (96) Weber states that "the Church of the Middle Ages was certainly able to bring about a unity of belief and conduct to a particularly high degree."

of lay religious life and were more likely to provide a moral setting conducive to asceticism: "Only positive religions—or more precisely expressed: dogmatically bound sects—are able to confer on the content of cultural values the status of unconditionally valid ethical imperatives."[56] Major heretical groups such as the Waldensians and Cathars, however, were not mentioned at all in the PE.

Weber's emergent sociology of medieval religion was therefore still in a preliminary stage. Its major theme, religious contributions to the ascetic empowerment of the self in different religious groups, was unevenly developed. Medieval monasticism, and with it other-worldly asceticism, had received the most attention, while religious life in fringe and heterodox groups, likely the most relevant cases of pre-Protestant inner-worldly asceticism, received the least. Also, Weber had not yet discussed the role of Catholicism as a classic representation of sacramental or semimagical attainment of grace. In the original version of the PE, the major comparative cases were Calvinism (ascetic Protestantism) and Lutheranism (nonascetic Protestantism), rather than Catholicism; references to a "magical interpretation of the sacraments" or a "dependence on a sacramental mediation of grace" were made in the context of Lutheran, not Catholic, spirituality. Similarly, the role of confession in relieving religious doubts about proper behavior and thus in inhibiting methodical life conduct was also discussed with reference to early modern Lutheranism.[57] If Weber was inclined to follow up with a study on the relationship between religion and society before the Reformation, one could therefore have expected in his future studies a stronger delineation of orthodox medieval religious life from Calvinism and a more detailed account of its fringe and heterodox elements. Events that significantly influenced Weber with regard to both aspects followed in the next period, between mid-1905 and 1910.

Weber's "Dark Years" and Ernst Troeltsch's *Social Teaching*

The years between 1905 and 1910 have been called the "dark years" in Weber's biography due to the paucity of information on his religious studies, but more information has become available with the publication, in the *Max Weber Gesamtausgabe*, of some of his works and

56. Weber, "'Objectivity' in Social Science and Social Policy," 57.
57. PE II, 37 n. 74, 51, 60, 66 (grace and sacraments), 50–51, 55 n. 111 (confession).

correspondence from this period, notably his letters written between 1906 and 1910.[58] Besides responding to his critics H. Karl Fischer and Felix Rachfahl, Weber authored the essay "'Churches' and 'Sects,'" though no other writings on religious topics in these years.[59] Around 1910, he turned to his comparative historical studies on the relationship between religion and society in all world religions. This has led some to conclude that Weber's original research program "do[es] not [do] much to illuminate the projects Weber ultimately undertook,"[60] while others affirm the opposite, that Weber steadily continued to work on religious topics relating to his original plans until 1910 and then extended his religious studies to religions other than early modern Christianity.[61]

My analysis in this section comes to a different set of conclusions. Between 1905 and 1910, (1) Weber widened the focus of the original PE and addressed how the social organization of early modern religious groups and their later secular derivatives contributed to the rationalization of conduct; (2) he took up parts of his research program dealing with industrial sociology, which together with his involvement in other projects led him away from religious topics; and (3) a series of publications by Ernst Troeltsch changed Weber's plans to address religion in centuries before the Reformation. Troeltsch's sociology of medieval

58. Küenzlen, *Die Religionssoziologie Max Webers*, 46; Weber, *Briefe 1906–1908*; idem, *Briefe 1909–1910*, ed. M. Rainer Lepsius and Wolfgang J. Mommsen in collaboration with Birgit Rudhard and Manfred Schön (Tübingen: Mohr, 1994).

59. Max Weber, "'Kirchen' und 'Sekten,'" *Frankfurter Zeitung*, 13 April 1906, 1, and 15 April 1906, 1; slightly expanded as "'Kirchen' und 'Sekten' in Nordamerika: Eine kirchen- und sozialpolitische Skizze," *Die christliche Welt* 20, no. 24 (14 June 1906): cols. 558–62, and no. 25 (21 June 1906): cols. 577–83 (translated by C. Loader as "'Churches' and 'Sects' in North America: An Ecclesiastical Socio-Political Sketch," *Sociological Theory* 3 [1985]: 7–13); H. Karl Fischer, "Kritische Beiträge zu Professor Max Webers Abhandlung 'Die protestantische Ethik und der Geist des Kapitalismus'" [1907], in Max Weber, *Die protestantische Ethik, II: Kritiken und Antikritiken*, ed. Johannes Winckelmann, 5th ed. (Gütersloh: Mohn, 1987), 11–26; Max Weber, "Kritische Bemerkungen zu den vorstehenden 'Kritischen Beiträgen'" [1907], in ibid., 27–37; H. Karl Fischer, "Protestantische Ethik und 'Geist des Kapitalismus': Replik auf Herrn Professor Max Webers Gegenkritik" [1908], in ibid., 38–43; Max Weber, "Bemerkungen zu der vorstehenden 'Replik'" [1908], in ibid., 44–56; Felix Rachfahl, "Kalvinismus und Kapitalismus" [1909], in ibid., 57–148; Max Weber, "Antikritisches zum 'Geist' des Kapitalismus" [1910], in ibid., 149–87; Felix Rachfahl, "Nochmals Kalvinismus und Kapitalismus" [1910], in ibid., 216–82; Max Weber, "Antikritisches Schlußwort zum 'Geist des Kapitalismus'" [1910], in ibid., 283–346 (partly translated by W. Davis as "Anticritical Last Word on *The Spirit of Capitalism*," *American Journal of Sociology* 83 [1978]: 1110–30).

60. Turner, *The Search for a Methodology of Social Science*, 204.

61. Küenzlen, *Die Religionssoziologie Max Webers*, 47.

religion went far beyond Weber's preliminary explorations in the PE, but did not preclude a separate analysis of this topic by the latter. At the end of the period, Weber restated the major directions in his research program with new emphases in regard to medieval religion.

Weber's New Projects: From the "'Churches' and 'Sects'" to the *Handbook of Political Economy*

In Weber's own words, his essay "'Churches' and 'Sects'" in 1906 was a "continuation" of the work begun with the PE.[62] Based on his experiences while visiting the United States in 1904, Weber showed that the effects of religion on economic life, and culture in general, could be observed well beyond the era when early modern capitalism had gone hand in hand with religious fervor.[63] Modern sectarian associations in religious and secular form (such as clubs and lodges) continued to shape public morality and economic life in the United States, even though the original religious motivations for membership were increasingly giving way to utilitarian ones. Sects and sectarian associations derive their capacity for shaping conduct from the way in which they control members and allow them to participate in group life. Membership is conferred and retained according to how well an individual lives up to a sect's criteria for appropriate personal conduct, and discipline is upheld through mutual control. The internal life of sects is strengthened by their organization in congregations, which, if not necessarily democratic, are characterized by a high degree of lay involvement in social and moral matters, including communal control of leaders, and thus entail a collective responsibility for achieving common goals.[64]

Weber therefore shifted his emphasis from the effects of religious ideas and their practical consequences to the influence of social organization—that is, the structure of, and interaction in, sects and congregations—on patterns of social action. This he explored, in a

---

62. Letter to his publisher Paul Siebeck, dated 2 April 1907 (Weber, *Briefe 1906–1908*, 276). See also Jeffrey C. Alexander and Colin Loader, "The Cultural Grounds of Rationalization: Sect Democracy Versus the Iron Cage," in Jeffrey C. Alexander, *Structure and Meaning: Rethinking Classical Theory* (New York: Columbia University Press, 1989), 101–22.

63. Wolfgang J. Mommsen, "Die Vereinigten Staaten von Amerika," in *Max Weber: Gesellschaft, Politik und Geschichte* (Frankfurt: Suhrkamp, 1974), 72–96; now superseded by Hans Rollmann's magnificent essay "'Meet Me in St. Louis': Troeltsch and Weber in America," in *Weber's "Protestant Ethic,"* ed. Lehmann and Roth, 357–83.

64. Weber, "'Churches' and 'Sects,'" 8–11.

somewhat impressionistic manner, solely for the early modern and the contemporary period, though he could have employed his conceptual elaborations on sects and congregations in analyses of other periods. But Weber took up other research. In his second reply to Fischer (published in January 1908), he commented, in a footnote, on "the direction of further explorations in the future to supplement, interpret, and further evaluate" his PE thesis:

> That I am not able to provide them [these explorations] yet is not due to difficulties with the topic, but in part to personal circumstances . . . , in part to some (as anyone knows who has looked into the *Archiv*) other remote works, and, finally, in part to the fact that in the meantime my colleague and friend E. Troeltsch had taken up a whole set of problems, which I had wanted to address, from his perspective in the most fruitful way. I wanted to avoid useless parallel research (for which he is endowed with greater expertise). Yet I hope that I shall be able to take up this work again during this current year and, for the time being, edit the [PE] essays for a separate [book] edition until spring.[65]

This account alludes not only to Troeltsch's contributions, but also to Weber's involvement in a variety of inquiries following the publication of the PE. Between late spring 1905 and early fall 1906, Weber dedicated himself to studies on the revolutionary events in Russia in 1905, which resulted in two monumental "chronicles" of Russia's political situation and a near physical and mental breakdown.[66] Besides writing additional essays on methodological issues, providing newspaper commentary on political events, and authoring two, albeit brief, replies to Fischer,[67] Weber labored in the fall of 1907 on an article "Agrarian Conditions in Antiquity" as his contribution to the third edition of the

65. Weber, "Bemerkungen," in *Die Protestantische Ethik, II*, ed. Winckelmann, 48, 54 n. 3. Cf. similar remarks in the revision of the PE (Weber, *The Protestant Ethic and the Spirit of Capitalism*, 284 n. 119), and by Marianne Weber (*Max Weber*, 331).

66. See Max Weber, *Zur Russischen Revolution von 1905: Schriften und Reden 1905–1912*, ed. Wolfgang J. Mommsen in collaboration with Dittmar Dahlmann (Tübingen: Mohr, 1989). On Weber's physical and mental condition, see his letters (*Briefe 1906–1908*, 108, 118, 143) to his brother Alfred (dated 8 July 1906), Ulrich Stutz (dated 22 July 1906), and Werner Sombart (dated 20 August 1906). He regularly relied on sedatives and sleep-inducing drugs to calm down and find sleep.

67. For Weber's other writings during and after his work on Russia, see Riesebrodt, "Bibliographie zur Max Weber-Gesamtausgabe," in *Prospekt der Max Weber Gesamtausgabe*, ed. Baier et al., 22–23.

Handwörterbuch der Staatswissenschaften,[68] which he turned into, as Marianne Weber put it, a "a sort of sociology of antiquity," covering three thousand years of history and such divergent political and geographical entities as Mesopotamia, Egypt, Israel, Greece, and the Roman Empire.[69] While his overall interest in this work in "the origin of the distinctiveness of the late medieval and modern economic constitution, in the end: of modern capitalism," was compatible with questions raised in the PE, and included a comparison of the ancient polis and the medieval city in the West,[70] his thematic focus differed. He now explored the development of ancient (and, to some degree, medieval) capitalism in terms of economic and political influences, not its religious underpinnings. The analysis had shifted from the "spirit" of capitalism to its "form."[71]

Thereafter Weber turned to more contemporary aspects of modern capitalism in investigating the physical and mental aspects of modern industrial labor as part of a larger project commissioned by the Verein für Sozialpolitik. Weber was actively involved in planning the project and for his part observed labor processes and their psychological consequences in the Oerlinghausen textile-manufacturing company his wife had inherited from her grandfather.[72] Another, even larger project that appeared on the horizon was a new edition of an encyclopedia of political economy initially intended to replace Schönberg's *Handbook of Political Economy* (*Handbuch der politischen Ökonomie*). Weber had been in contact with the editor of the previous edition, Paul Siebeck, since April 1905, and over the next few years his position evolved from mere consultant to Siebeck on candidates for future editor to de facto

68. Max Weber, "Agrarverhältnisse im Altertum" [1909], in *Gesammelte Aufsätze zur Sozial- und Wirtschaftsgeschichte* (Tübingen: Mohr, 1988), 1–288 (translated by R. I. Frank in *Agrarian Sociology of Ancient Civilizations* [London: Verso, 1988], 35–386). The first and second editions of the *Handwörterbuch*, which had appeared in 1897 and 1898, contained much shorter contributions by Weber under the same title.

69. Marianne Weber, *Max Weber*, 329.

70. Weber, *Agrarian Sociology of Ancient Civilizations*, 336–66 (the quote is from 348; translation altered).

71. On this distinction, see PE I, 25–28; Weber, "Antikritisches zum 'Geist' des Kapitalismus," in *Die protestantische Ethik, II*, ed. Winckelmann, 164, 170–72. As in his previous work on Russia, Weber totally devoted himself to the task. He called it "a horrible work of duty" and a "drudgery," relied heavily on drugs, and was burned out afterward. See his letters (*Briefe 1906–1908*, 426, 430, 478) to Oskar Siebeck (dated 26 December 1907), Marie Baum (dated 4 February 1908), and Robert Michels (dated 24 March 1908).

72. See Max Weber, *Zur Psychophysik der industriellen Arbeit: Schriften und Reden 1908–1912*, ed. Wolfgang Schluchter in collaboration with Sabine Frommer (Tübingen: Mohr, 1995).

mastermind behind the new edition. In May 1909 Weber finished drawing up a preliminary sketch of the topics and assigned contributors, which he then revised and sent out as *Plan for the Division of Topics* (*Stoffverteilungsplan*) by May 1910.[73] The *Plan* contained numerous topics Weber had committed himself to cover. These topics ranged from the relationship between the economy and society, to methodological considerations, to the legal and technological foundations of modern capitalism.[74] Yet the only part for which Weber could possibly have envisioned incorporating reflections on religion was a subsection of his main assignment ("Economy and Society") entitled "Economy and Culture (Critique of Historical Materialism)." Consequently, at the time, as Wolfgang Schluchter has noted, "one is not yet able to discover Weber's subsequent program in the sociology of religion."[75]

Hence, between 1905 and 1910 Weber's involvement in studies on politics and antiquity, his work in industrial sociology, and his responsibilities for the reedition of the *Handbook* steadily led him away from his religious studies. These works, together with a still impaired mental and physical condition, left little time and energy for other projects. By 1909, Weber had also finally given up plans to revise the PE for a separate edition.[76] Then, there were also the writings of Ernst Troeltsch.

73. See Johannes Winckelmann, *Max Webers hinterlassenes Hauptwerk: Die Wirtschaft und die gesellschaftlichen Ordnungen und Mächte* (Tübingen: Mohr, 1986), 5–10; Schluchter, *Rationalism, Religion, and Domination*, 433–36. For Weber's extensive correspondence with Siebeck regarding the reedition of the *Handbook*, see Weber, *Briefe 1906–1908*, 92–93, 95, and passim; idem, *Briefe 1909–1910*, 15–17 and passim. Weber's original sketch of the *Plan* (1909) is lost. The other big project for Weber in these years was his involvement in the foundation and organization of the Deutsche Gesellschaft für Soziologie.

74. The *Plan* is printed in Winckelmann, *Max Webers hinterlassenes Hauptwerk*, 151–55, and in Weber, *Briefe 1909–1910*, 766–74; the relevant sections are translated in Schluchter, *Rationalism, Religion, and Domination*, 466.

75. Schluchter, *Rationalism, Religion, and Domination*, 415. Schluchter gives 1909 as the year for which this is the case, but one can safely extend Schluchter's assessment to 1910, since neither the *Plan* of May 1910 (on which Schluchter bases his assessment) nor Weber's letters give any indication of Weber's interest in a study on a religious topic. There is nothing to support Küenzlen's argument that Weber's "Critique of Historical Materialism" was "basically a work in the sociology of religion," and that Weber focused on religion in the period between 1905 and 1910 (*Die Religionssoziologie Max Webers*, 51, 53).

76. At first Weber responded favorably to Siebeck's inquiry about such an edition. Intending to revise the original essays and to append the essay "'Churches' and 'Sects,'" Weber promised the revision for about summer 1907. After that date had passed, he continued to give indications of a future publication (*Briefe 1906–1908*, 119, 273, 276, 279–80, 285, 300, 426, 435, 609; idem, "Bemerkungen," in *Die Protestantische Ethik, II*, ed. Winckelmann, 54 n. 3; idem, *Briefe 1906–1908*, 609), and during a vacation in the

Troeltsch, a close friend and colleague of Weber at the time,[77] complemented Weber's preliminary exploration of medieval religious life in the PE with his own accounts of early, medieval, and early modern Christian religion in the West—a contribution significant enough not only to become a standard theological-historical treatment of the period, but also, as Weber wrote by 1908, to settle a "whole set of problems" he himself had wanted to address "in the most fruitful way."[78]

The Contributions of Ernst Troeltsch

A series of major contributions by Troeltsch, prompting Weber to make this judgment, began in 1906 with Troeltsch's lecture "The Significance of Protestantism for the Rise of the Modern World" at the annual meeting of German historians. Addressing the implications of Protestant theology and ethics for different social spheres, Troeltsch stressed the contribution of Protestantism to the emergence of an individualized, autonomous personality free from dependence on the sacramental provision of grace by a priest. Early Protestantism remained medieval, however, in that it retained the notion of a sole encompassing church with claim to a unified Christian culture.[79] Troeltsch followed up on this in his "Protestant Christianity and Church in the Modern Period" of the same year, where he dealt with the history of Western Christianity from the continuance of medieval Catholicism's founding ideas in early Lutheranism and Calvinism to the emancipation of modern (German) society and secular culture from (Protestant) theology. Here again early

---

Netherlands in August 1907 he visited some Dutch libraries, where he looked into additional literature on Dutch Calvinism (letters to Marianne Weber, dated 17 August 1907, and to Alfred Weber, dated 3 September 1907, in *Briefe 1906–1908*, 361, 381; idem, "Kritische Bemerkungen," in *Die Protestantische Ethik, II*, ed. Winckelmann, 30). Yet Weber's letters of 1909–10, beyond his replies to Rachfahl, contain no indication of any further study on this topic.

77. See Friedrich Wilhelm Graf, "Friendship Between Experts: Notes on Weber and Troeltsch," in *Max Weber and His Contemporaries*, ed. Mommsen and Osterhammel, 215–33; idem, "Max Weber und die protestantische Theologie seiner Zeit," *Zeitschrift für Religions- und Geistesgeschichte* 39 (1987): 133–37; Hans-Georg Drescher, *Ernst Troeltsch: His Life and Work*, trans. J. Bowden (Minneapolis: Fortress Press, 1993), 122–26.

78. See page 28 above.

79. Ernst Troeltsch, "Die Bedeutung des Protestantismus für die Entstehung der modernen Welt," *Historische Zeitschrift* 97 (1906): 1–66 (translated by W. Montgomery from a later, revised and expanded version as *Protestantism and Progress: A Historical Study of the Relation of Protestantism to the Modern World* [Boston: Beacon Press, 1966]). Weber had originally been scheduled as lecturer.

Protestantism appeared in its fundamental principles as a remnant of medieval ideas.[80] Troeltsch then further developed this theme in his articles for the *Archiv*, published between 1908 and 1910, "The Social Teachings of the Christian Churches and Groups."[81]

For Troeltsch, the specific character of medieval Christianity derived from a deep mutual penetration of church, state, and culture after the Gregorian reforms, which stood in stark contrast to earlier developments. The earliest Christian groups were founded upon messianic hopes and focused on religious, not social, issues. The missionary efforts of Saint Paul turned Christianity into a mass movement, but it remained conservative in its social and cultural agenda. The assimilation to the secular sphere was paralleled by the development of the church into an institution that regarded as its main priority the dispensation of grace, in the form of sacraments, by its priests, while it left the quest for higher forms of perfection to monastics, who came to excel in literary production, agricultural labor, and ethical instruction. The role of the church in society further expanded with the ascent of the Carolingians, who placed the church in the service of the state and made use of monastic achievements in agriculture and literacy. With cultural and social policies added to its agenda, the church legitimated the existing political system of domination while enjoying the protection of secular rulers.[82]

The reaction to this development, the Gregorian reforms, brought about the centralization of the church under the papacy, with a crucial change in the relationship between the church and state. The Gregorian church not only established its independence from the state and its rulers, but also demanded the principal deference of secular rule and culture to its authority. Based on the church's experience that "[t]he full freedom and independence of the Church was only reached when the temporal powers were subordinate to the Church, conditioned by her in their very nature, and directed by her in all matters pertaining to salvation," all domains of

80. Ernst Troeltsch, "Protestantisches Christentum und Kirche in der Neuzeit," in *Die Kultur der Gegenwart*, ed. Paul Hinneberg (Berlin: Teubner, 1906), pt. 1, sec. 4, 253–458; see especially 257. His major argument was, as in earlier publications, directed against Ritschl. Cf. Wolfhart Pannenberg, "Reformation und Neuzeit," in *Troeltsch-Studien*, vol. 3, *Protestantismus und Neuzeit*, ed. Horst Renz und Friedrich Wilhelm Graf (Gütersloh: Mohn, 1984), 21–34; Hermann Fischer, "Die Ambivalenz der Moderne: Zu Troeltschs Verhältnisbestimmung von Reformation und Neuzeit," in ibid., 54–77.

81. These articles did not cover Calvinism. Since my references are to the book, I verified that the following themes were contained in the articles. See also Troeltsch's *Augustin, die christliche Antike und das Mittelalter* (Aalen: Scientia Verlag, [1915] 1963), in which he elaborated on the differences between ancient and medieval ecclesiastical ideas.

82. Troeltsch, *The Social Teaching*, 23–223.

life became subordinate to its demands. This claim to primacy even in secular spheres, first established in the central period of the Middle Ages and upheld until the early modern era, was what Troeltsch meant by the "relative unitary culture" of the Middle Ages.[83]

It was not merely a prescriptive ideal. The penetration of the world by religious ethics was rooted in the "sacramentalism" of the church:

> [I]t was essential to develop the methods of spiritual and ethical control. Although the priesthood was designed in the first place to secure the religious idea and tradition which affects and determines the whole structure, yet, even in the Early Church, far more important than this guarantee or than the teaching office, was the sacramental power, which, indeed, had become also in dogma the priestly power, or *potestas ordinis*. . . . As time went on, the more the securing of orthodoxy in doctrine became a matter for the highest courts, all the more preemptory became the need to surround and include the whole life of the faithful with sacramental grace.[84]

Corollaries of this focus on ethical control (in the sacraments) were, first, a more repressive ecclesiastic system than in earlier periods. The unitary culture of the Middle Ages was not based on a tolerant coexistence of church with individuals and groups in society. On the contrary, it was a culture of authority and compulsion.[85]

Second, the locus of accountable moral action shifted from the individual to the ecclesiastical institution, as the sacrament of penance became an important means of controlling conscience: "Out of it [the sacrament of penance] there develops the whole Christian ethic of the Church—as self-examination and direction of conscience, as absolution, and as the key to the whole system of satisfactions and merits, as the unification of all ethical problems and inconsistencies by the authority of the Church, which removes the responsibility for the unification of the duties of life from the individual, and takes it on to its own shoulders."[86]

---

83. Ibid., 229–30; see generally 201–5, 229–30, 235–37. See also Schluchter, *Paradoxes of Modernity*, 206–12; Ulrich Köpf, "Die Idee der Einheitskultur des Mittelalters," in *Troeltsch-Studien*, vol. 6, *Ernst Troeltschs Soziallehren: Studien zu ihrer Interpretation*, ed. Friedrich Wilhelm Graf and Trutz Rendtorff (Gütersloh: Mohn, 1993), 103–21.

84. Troeltsch, *The Social Teaching*, 232.

85. Ibid., 235. See also Troeltsch, "Protestantisches Christentum," in *Die Kultur der Gegenwart*, ed. Hinneberg, 256.

86. Troeltsch, *The Social Teaching*, 233. See also the excellent analysis in Schluchter, *Rise of Western Rationalism*, 166–69.

Third, in order to be applicable to all members of the church and to all spheres of life, the system of ecclesiastical ethics worked with several levels of ethical standards. Grounded in scholastic notions of an organic social ethic and relativized natural law, ethical duties and expectations were graded according to individual abilities and positions in society. At the top were the extraordinary ascetic yet transcendent (*überweltliche*) morals and deeds of the monastics; below this were the more lenient expectations and prescriptions imposed on the ordinary mass of believers. These different elements of Christian society made for a harmonic fit in that "it [the medieval period] ensured the supernatural through asceticism, while at the same time it appointed to people living in the world a life which only approximated to asceticism, and united both classes as complementary elements in the organism of the Church."[87]

Fourth, while Catholicism prescribed to its ordinary members sacraments provided by priests, rather than asceticism, as the path to salvation, the reaction to this practice, which could be interpreted as compromising the rigors of the Gospels, came in the form of fringe and heterodox movements. These movements rejected the relativization of divine ethics and instead emphasized "pure" asceticism. Given the church's intolerance, this inevitably meant heresy and separation from the church.[88]

Troeltsch followed up on the last point by applying Weber's concepts of "church" and "sect" to medieval orthodoxy and heterodoxy to discuss how differences in their structure related to differences in religious ethics and behavior. The post-Gregorian church was a prototypical "church." Its members were born into it, based on an objective deed (baptism) rather than a voluntary decision, and its priests dispensed sacramental grace according to the objective performance of the sacraments irrespective of their own subjective imperfections. The church was set up to embrace all Christians; its universalist character required a relative affirmation of the world (*Weltbejahung*) and a modest dose of religious requirements. In contrast, medieval "sects" of laymen were small, exclusive associations that rejected compromises with the secular spheres and stressed the individual's direct, personal relationship to the deity and his obligations contrived in absolute natural law. Demands on conduct in heterodoxy were thereby more stringent than in orthodoxy, and they guided it in a different direction. Unlike the Catholic laity, medieval sect members based their spirituality on ascetic deeds rather

87. Troeltsch, *The Social Teaching*, 243; see also 257–328; idem, *Augustin*, 160–70.
88. Troeltsch, *The Social Teaching*, 237, 245.

than the performance of rituals. But their asceticism was neither rooted in worldly indifference, as in early Christian groups (whose ascetic demands were lower), nor aimed at transcending the world, as in monasticism. It was motivated instead, as Troeltsch clarified in the book version of *The Social Teaching*, by abstention from, or antagonism to, the world (*Weltenthaltung, Weltfeindschaft*).[89]

Against the background of this notion of sectarian abstention from the world Troeltsch addressed various heterodox associations of laity. Though noting the ascent of lay religious movements in the eleventh and twelfth centuries in conjunction with the rise of the cities and the diffusion of the Bible in the vernacular, Troeltsch limited his discussion of religious groups in the High Middle Ages to terse characterizations mainly of the Waldensians and Cathars.[90] The Waldensians were "the most significant and influential sect of all" for the religious equality among their members and the substitution of subjective personal deeds and religious achievements for sacramental grace. The Cathars were important for the harsh asceticism of their leaders, doctrinally grounded in Manichaean dualism, their abrogation of civil and orthodox ecclesiastical duties, and the closeness of their circles, based on lay preaching.[91] Yet not these groups but the Lollards and Hussites of the later Middle Ages "did a good deal to prepare the way for Protestantism,"[92] by which Troeltsch arguably meant a Calvinist, rather than Lutheran, type of spirituality. For the Lollards this function derived from Wyclif's ideas of predestination, which led to a limitation of the role of the sacraments as mediators of grace and to the notion of a (numerically small) church of believers whose predestined salutary status had to be proved on practical-ethical grounds. Factions of the Hussites then drew more radical consequences from Wyclif's religious thought. While the most ecclesiastically conservative of these factions, the Utraquists, did not question the mediating role of (Catholic) priests and sacraments, the Taborites and the "Moravian Brethren" went further. Among the Taborites the individual member of the congregation,

89. Ibid., 328–49 (the clarification is on 332). Troeltsch also saw elements of early Christian universalism (religious brotherhood) in the sects, but it was generally limited to those who were religiously qualified, that is, sect members (ibid., 330, 336–37).

90. Ibid., 349–58, 371. Troeltsch relied heavily on the Italian church historian Gioacchino Volpe (*Movimenti religiosi e sette ereticali nella società medievale italiana (secoli XI–XIV)*, 5th ed. [Florence: Sansoni, (1922) 1977]).

91. Troeltsch, *The Social Teaching*, 354–55 (Waldensians; the quote is from 354), 350–51 (Cathars). He also mentions the Pataria, followers of hermit preachers like Peter of Bruys or Henry of Toulouse, the Spiritual Franciscans, and the Beguines and Beghards.

92. Ibid., 358. Besides these two late medieval groups, Troeltsch also mentions the Brethren of the Common Life (ibid., 371).

not a sacrament or priest, was responsible for his salvation; major elements of Catholic spirituality—such as indulgences, worship of host and saints, or belief in purgatory—were rejected. Uncompromising with regard to worldly necessities and the existing secular order, they propagated the subordination of secular and religious spheres to a type of "individualistic-communistic Christian socialism" through means of violence.[93]

For Troeltsch, the ultimate failure of the radical elements in Hussitism confirmed his general thesis that asceticism in medieval sects was engendered by abstention from the world. Although the stress on personal achievement and sanctification introduced a notion of perseverance, or proof, of faith in religious conduct to the moral economy of the sect, the underlying current of its spirituality did not allow for the application of this notion to secular spheres. Unlike the Calvinists, who persevered in their economic callings, medieval sectarian groups were limited to proving themselves in following the ethical tenets of the Gospels; yet their radical notions of natural law and ethical individualism were ultimately linked to a progressive detachment from this world and not to its mastery. The heroic personal achievement of only a few, sectarian ascetic behavior did not find an inner-worldly conduit and thereby remained medieval.[94]

Implications of Troeltsch's Research for Weber's Medieval Studies

Weber's 1910 replies to his critic Rachfahl contain indirect responses to Troeltsch's major contributions.[95] An important response is included in a restatement of Weber's research plans:

93. Ibid., 358–69 (the quote is from 365).

94. Ibid., 337, 362, 368–69, 433 n. 164. In later parts of *The Social Teaching*, Troeltsch expands on Weber's work by addressing how Protestantism, or, more precisely, Calvinism, overcame this limitation and directed asceticism into inner-worldly channels by linking religious sanctification to an active engagement in secular spheres, most notably the economy. See ibid., 576–990. For an earlier treatment of Calvinism, see idem, "Protestantisches Christentum," in *Die Kultur der Gegenwart*, ed. Hinneberg, 269–300, revised and expanded for the second edition of 1909.

95. Wilhelm Hennis's claim that Troeltsch's work "must have irritated Weber" (*Max Weber: Essays in Reconstruction*, trans. K. Tribe [London: Allen & Unwin, 1988], 205 n. 87) remains an unfounded conjecture. Overall, Weber had few reservations about Troeltsch's seminal work, noting explicitly: "I do not see any decisive issues where I would have reason to object to his presentation" ("Antikritisches zum 'Geist' des Kapitalismus," in *Die protestantische Ethik, II*, ed. Winckelmann, 151).

[T]o me, the most pressing questions lie . . . first, in the different influences of Calvinist, Baptist, and Pietist ethics on life conduct, differences that have to be explored in much more detail. Furthermore, in a thorough investigation of the beginnings of similar developments [of ascetic rationalism] in the Middle Ages and in ancient Christianity, insofar as the works of Troeltsch still leave some room here. This, however, demands the most intensive collaboration with specialists in theology. Then, in the analysis, from the economic side, . . . of the affinity of the bourgeoisie [*Bürgertum*] for certain aspects of religious life conduct, specifically (but not only) of the kind that has been displayed most consistently in ascetic Protestantism.[96]

Weber's restated research agenda includes a more detailed account of the differences between Protestant groups in terms of the relationship between ethics and actual behavior, corresponding to the original plans to explore further the "various areas of ascetic religiosity's dissemination" and its "dissolution into sheer utilitarianism."[97] Here Weber could build on Troeltsch's extensive analysis of a full spectrum of Protestant religious groups and the impact of their ethics on economic behavior, politics and the state, the family, and other social issues.[98] As a second topic, the affinity between civic strata and ascetic rationalism deserved a closer exploration. This would expand the ideational inquiry of the PE into an analysis that took account of material factors in a historical-developmental analysis. Troeltsch's depiction of the class basis of ascetic Protestantism added little to Weber's statements in the PE.[99] Without

96. Weber, "Antikritisches Schlußwort," in *Die protestantische Ethik, II*, ed. Winckelmann, 321–22. For the following, cf. *Schluchter, Rationalism, Religion, and Domination*, 36; idem, *Paradoxes of Modernity*, 107–9.

97. See page 16 above.

98. Troeltsch, with whose work Weber was intimately familiar throughout this period, had begun to take on these issues in his "Protestantisches Christentum" in 1906. In 1909 he started working on the chapter on "Calvinism" for his *Social Teaching*, which he probably concluded in mid-1910. See Friedrich Wilhelm Graf, "'Endlich große Bücher schreiben': Marginalien zur Werkgeschichte der 'Soziallehren,'" in *Ernst Troeltschs Soziallehren*, ed. Graf and Rendtorff, 40; for references to Weber's involvement in Troeltsch's work, see Graf, "Max Weber," 137 n. 52. Insofar as Troeltsch explorations addressed themes previously dealt with by Weber, their differences were minor; for example, Troeltsch made a stronger distinction between Calvin's ideas and Calvinism (Troeltsch, *The Social Teaching*, 894 n. 344). Otherwise, Troeltsch relied heavily on Weber with regard to central concepts in the PE such as calling, perseverance, and inner-worldly asceticism (185 n. 61, 346 n. 165c, 420 n. 136, 474 n. 205, 585 n. 316, 609–11, 849 n. 230, 891).

99. Troeltsch, *The Social Teaching*, 466–67, 681, 914–15 n. 387.

the exploration of the influence of economic conditions on the emergence of a modern vocational ethic—the other side of the causal relation—Weber stressed, the PE essays remained incomplete.[100] For the medieval period, Troeltsch briefly highlighted (under Weber's influence) some of the contributions of urban life to a lay religious culture and vocational system more independent from the Catholic Church and feudal authority,[101] whereas Weber, in a complementary vein, stressed in his "Agrarian Conditions" of 1909 the development of new opportunities for practical, rational economic conduct in medieval towns without reference to religious implications.[102]

A sociology of the bourgeoisie and its affinity for practical rationalism could include a third topic, the study of religious precursors of ascetic rationalism in the Middle Ages and in ancient Christianity. In his restated research agenda Weber acknowledged the indebtedness of a future sociological investigation of medieval religion to the contributions of theologians (like Troeltsch), but his qualifying remark about the effect of Troeltsch's studies on his own research agenda with regard to medieval religion should not be read as implying that Weber had given up completely. It is true that Weber commented that he himself did not want to become involved in studies requiring useless research parallel to Troeltsch's.[103] However, there were still differences between Weber and Troeltsch that allowed for Weber's own studies. First, Weber's and Troeltsch's cognitive interests differed. Troeltsch chose the title of his articles and book conscientiously: the social *teachings* of Christianity. The purpose of his work was "to inquire into the sociological idea of Christianity proper, and its structure and organization," which he thought to contain a blueprint for relationships in religious communities and even society. However, his analysis of religious ideas and ideals did not necessarily address "the actual effects of the sociological religious

---

100. Weber, "Antikritisches zum 'Geist' des Kapitalismus," in *Die protestantische Ethik, II*, ed. Winckelmann, 172, 183 n. 34.

101. Troeltsch, *The Social Teaching*, 254–56, 295, 376–78. Some of this may go back to a 1905 lecture Troeltsch gave before the Eranos circle, "Relationship of Protestantism to the Middle Ages," in which he dealt with the development of lay religious culture in the towns of the twelfth and thirteenth centuries. See Graf, "Marginalien," in *Ernst Troeltschs Soziallehren*, ed. Graf and Rendtorff, 49–50.

102. Weber, *Agrarian Sociology of Ancient Civilizations*, 339–52.

103. See page 28 above. Misreading his sources, Wilhelm Hennis has argued recently that Troeltsch was allegedly intent on convincing Weber that the latter's research program was not feasible. According to Hennis, had Weber carried out his program, it would have amounted to "repetitive boredom" anyway. See Wilhelm Hennis, *Max Webers Wissenschaft vom Menschen: Neue Studien zur Biographie des Werks* (Tübingen: Mohr, 1996), 67.

scheme [of ideas and ideals] on other spheres of life, what influence in effect the churches had thereby on social phenomena, and, in turn, what influences from socio-political formations a religious community was subjected to."[104] Weber, in contrast, was less interested than Troeltsch in religious ideals and ideas and more in their actual practical consequences. In practice, this meant that Troeltsch's analyses dealt mostly with doctrines and dogmas, to some extent with their religious-psychological implications, and little with behavioral consequences. Weber placed far more emphasis on the latter.[105]

Second, with regard to heterodox medieval groups, Troeltsch had concluded that their doctrinally grounded abnegation of the world ultimately precluded their members from methodical rational engagement in the world. Weber apparently did not share Troeltsch's view on the other-worldly direction or world-indifferent nature of the sects. "With respect to their civic conduct the rational-ascetic sects or sect-type associations of the Middle Ages regularly display ways very similar to those of the Baptist sects."[106] In other passages, Weber referred to the "economic achievements of certain sects in the Middle Ages," and cited the late twelfth-century Italian Humiliati (whom he had mentioned in the PE before) as an example of "heretical carriers of a civic spirit of business" in the Middle Ages.[107] "Singular developments of a practical vocational ethic of this sort [existed] in the Middle Ages—I have explicitly reserved an explication of this issue to myself."[108] Compared to his comments in the PE, Weber's statements here were more specific in proposing to explore the relevance of practical rational conduct by medieval ascetic sects for secular life and vocations. This involved

104. Troeltsch, *The Social Teaching*, 34 (translation altered).

105. Each clearly stated the difference in his cognitive interest and affirmed the independence of his work. See Weber, "Antikritisches zum 'Geist' des Kapitalismus," in *Die protestantische Ethik, II*, ed. Winckelmann, 149–51; Ernst Troeltsch, "Die Kulturbedeutung des Calvinismus" [1910], in ibid., 189–92; Weber, "Antikritisches Schlußwort," in ibid., 288–89, 332 n. 8; Troeltsch, *The Social Teaching*, 986 n. 510; Weber, *The Protestant Ethic*, 188 n. 1; Ernst Troeltsch, "Meine Bücher," in *Gesammelte Schriften*, vol. 4, *Aufsätze zur Geistesgeschichte und Religionssoziologie*, ed. Hans Baron (Tübingen: Mohr, 1925), 12. Troeltsch was of course not exclusively interested in doctrines. See, for example, his own reply to Rachfahl, where he declared himself competent to assess both the dogmatic *and* the religious-psychological issues involved ("Kulturbedeutung," 192–93).

106. Weber, "Antikritisches zum 'Geist' des Kapitalismus," in *Die protestantische Ethik, II*, ed. Winckelmann, 153–54.

107. Weber, "Antikritisches Schlußwort," in *Die protestantische Ethik, II*, ed. Winckelmann, 321, 292.

108. Ibid., 319.

analyzing how sectarian ethics and new structural opportunities shaped behavior in the context of developing opportunities for rationalism in urban market economies in the High Middle Ages.[109] Troeltsch's work was therefore not the last word on extending the PE to medieval heretical groups and to the study of ascetic rationalism and the empowerment of the self in this period.

Third, Troeltsch discussed medieval monasticism in the context of the historical development of a separate tier of higher morals and ascetic achievements in areas like the economy and culture. Asceticism for him connoted abstention from pleasure and subjugation to ideals of austerity.[110] Weber, by contrast, used a more specific concept of asceticism. Focusing on the transformative potential of the monastic empowerment of the self, he was interested mostly in forms of asceticism that were based on the methodical training of the self for a transcendental purpose. He was interested in "rationalized" asceticism, in contradistinction to "planless world flight" and "merely sensual asceticism" (*Gefühlsaskese*). In his responses to Rachfahl, Weber also delineated in a more straightforward manner than in the PE the similarities between ascetic Protestantism and medieval monasticism in this regard, with the basic distinction being that the former was inner-worldly and the latter other-worldly oriented. Here, Troeltsch had little new to offer, as was true for his treatment of mysticism.[111]

---

109. At the first annual meeting of the German Sociological Society in October 1910, Ferdinand Tönnies gave a speech in which he treated the new religious ethics and conduct in the High Middle Ages as derivative of structural changes, particularly in medieval cities. Weber rejected this view in his follow-up speech, pointing to the support for Catholicism and new forms of orthodox spirituality in urban settings. See Deutsche Gesellschaft für Soziologie, *Verhandlungen des Ersten Deutschen Soziologentages* (Tübingen: Mohr, 1911), 192–202.

110. For Troeltsch, monastic asceticism was "a method of revival, a method of controlling and subduing sensuality, a hardening process in preparation for the ecclesiastical vocation, a way of practice in virtue and in the cultivation of the religious temper, a way of heroism and special excellence" (*The Social Teaching*, 244). See also 102–20, 162–64, 220, 237–45.

111. Weber, "Antikritisches zum 'Geist' des Kapitalismus," in *Die protestantische Ethik, II*, ed. Winckelmann, 155; idem, "Antikritisches Schlußwort," in ibid., 314–16. Even though his main types of religious organization were church, sect, and mysticism, Troeltsch treated medieval mysticism as a form of absolute individualism, and thus as socially inconsequential (*The Social Teaching*, 377, 737–40). He made a single reference (with Weber as his source) to the "occasional union of mysticism with the ethic of the 'calling' as a means of discipline" (815 n. 513). Medieval mysticism was a topic that Troeltsch wanted to develop further in a revision of the *Social Teaching*. See Graf, "Marginalien," in *Ernst Troeltschs Soziallehren*, ed. Graf and Rendtorff, 47; Arie L. Molendijk, *Zwischen Theologie und Soziologie: Ernst Troeltschs Typen der christlichen*

However, Troeltsch's work did suggest an important change in case selection if the themes in the PE were to be addressed in a wider context. In the PE Weber had mainly stressed the difference between strands of Lutheranism and Calvinism in terms of their contributions to the modern capitalist ethic. Troeltsch had effectively argued the inner workings of Lutheranism still mirrored in important ways the moral economy of medieval Catholicism. Calvinism and medieval Catholicism now appeared as the major comparative cases, and Troeltsch's depictions of ecclesiastical sacramentalism as the path to salvation, of the compulsive nature of membership in the Catholic Church, and of the church's emphasis on deriving religious righteousness from external acts based on a graded system of ethical duties were the main elements of a sociology of medieval Catholicism. This work extended and superseded Weber's initial explorations in the PE, while still leaving some room to analyze the relationship between doctrines and their psychological consequences and practical implementations in lay orthodox spirituality. Weber certainly recognized this, and in the second reply to Rachfahl he discussed the morally relaxing consequence of confession as a periodical relief of ethical and soteriological anxieties in the context of medieval Catholicism instead of Lutheranism.[112]

Religion and Rationalism: Preliminaries to *The Christianity of the Occident*

Themes and Contexts

Around 1911, as Marianne Weber observed, Weber "now wanted to investigate the relationship of the five great world religions to economic

---

Gemeinschaftsbildung: Kirche, Sekte, Mystik (Gütersloh: Gütersloher Verlagshaus, 1996), especially 66–76. For Weber's continuing unwillingness to equate mysticism with impulsive, unorganized behavior and withdrawal from the world into the self, see his letters to Karl Vossler (*Briefe 1906–1908*, 559, dated 5 May 1908) and his sister Lili (in Marianne Weber, *Max Weber*, 456, dated 20 September 1910).

112. Weber, "Antikritisches Schlußwort," in *Die protestantische Ethik, II*, ed. Winckelmann, 307–8. See also idem, "Antikritisches zum 'Geist' des Kapitalismus," in ibid., 175, where Weber acrimoniously told Rachfahl that he (Weber) had selected Calvinism as "the 'most consistent' antithesis to (Catholicism and) Lutheranism," making a reference to a specific page (36) in the second PE essay. There, however, Weber had only dealt with the differences between Lutheranism and Calvinism—without mentioning Catholicism.

ethics.[113] This was an enormous expansion, in terms of thematic focus and methodological concerns, of his originally far more limited religious studies. The new inquiries were "comparative studies on the *universal-historical* relationships between religion and society," intended to take the themes developed in the original PE "out of their isolation and to put them in the context of the cultural development in its entirety."[114] Weber first specified their subject matter in 1913 in a letter to Paul Siebeck, the publisher of the *Outline of Social Economics* (the former *Handbook of Political Economy*), to which Weber was to provide several contributions. The part on economy and religion (later to become a part of Weber's *Economy and Society*) comprised "all religions of the world: a sociology of teachings on salvation and of religious ethics—what Troeltsch did, [but] now for *all* religions, if much briefer. . . . *[N]othing* of the kind has ever been written, not even as a 'precursor.'"[115] Weber delineated the scope of his comparative religious studies when he offered his essays "Economic Ethics of the World Religions" to Siebeck in another letter in 1915. These essays, which were meant to complement the part on religion for the *Outline of Social Economics* and which had "been lying here since the beginning of the war," dealt with "Confucianism (China), Hinduism and Buddhism (India), Judaism, Islam, Christianity."[116]

Weber eventually published only parts of these announced studies in the *Archiv* between 1915 and 1920, namely, those on Confucianism, Hinduism and Buddhism, and ancient Judaism. A revision of the existing essays, together with the parts yet to be published, were to appear in his *Collected Essays in the Sociology of Religion*. Weber himself explained the contents and set purpose of the collection in an announcement of the *Collected Essays* in 1919. They were to include Weber's initial religious studies on the PE and on the "Protestant Sects," followed by his *Archiv* essays on the economic ethics of the world religions (Hinduism, Buddhism, Confucianism, Judaism). These studies were then to be "expanded by a short depiction of the Egyptian, Mesopotamian, and Zoroastrian religious ethics, and especially by a sketch devoted to the development of

---

113. Marianne Weber, *Max Weber*, 331. With regard to what here follows, see also the seminal exploration in Schluchter, *Rationalism, Religion, and Domination*, 34–38, 44–48, 411–32.

114. Weber, *The Protestant Ethic*, 284 n.119 (translation altered).

115. Weber to Siebeck, dated 30 December 1913; quoted in Winckelmann, *Max Webers hinterlassenes Hauptwerk*, 36.

116. Weber to Siebeck, dated 22 June 1915; quoted in Helwig Schmidt-Glintzer, "Editorischer Bericht," in Max Weber, *Die Wirtschaftsethik der Weltreligionen: Konfuzianismus und Taoismus: Schriften 1915–1920*, ed. Helwig Schmidt-Glintzer in collaboration with Petra Kolonko (Tübingen: Mohr, 1989), 35–36.

the social distinctiveness of the Occident, [that is, a sketch] of the development of the European *Bürgertum* in antiquity and the Middle Ages. . . . A third volume will contain the depiction of early Christianity, Talmudic Judaism, Islam, and Oriental Christianity. A concluding [fourth] volume will address the Christianity of the Occident." All parts were intended to deal with a central question: "What is the basis of economic and social *distinctiveness* of the Occident, how did it arise, and, especially, how is it related to the development of religious ethics?"[117]

Medieval Religion in the Context of a Typology and Sociology of Rationalism

The designation of a complete volume (no. 4) of his *Collected Essays* to Christianity, arguably covering late antiquity, the Middle Ages, and the post-Reformation period (early Christianity was scheduled for volume 3), is evidence of Weber's continued interest in a study of medieval religion.[118] In the announcement of 1919 Weber also mentioned a related topic previously included in his amended research program of 1910: the analysis of civic strata in antiquity and the Middle Ages. Insofar as religion contributed to the affinity between the *Bürgertum* and practical rational conduct, this theme was to be included in his religious studies. The overall cognitive interest guiding these religious studies was no longer, as it had been in the PE, the contribution of religious factors to one significant element of modern capitalism, that is, rational method-ical conduct on the basis of a calling. The central theme of his *Collected Essays* was now wider: a "typology and sociology of rationalism."[119]

The typology of rationalism involved the comparison of rational-izations in different geocultural areas, with two goals in mind. The first, immediate goal of this comparison was to identify those features that were unique to Western rationalism. This refers to institutional rational-izations in the early modern period—economic, scientific, bureaucratic-

117. Reprinted in Weber, *Die Wirtschaftsethik der Weltreligionen*, 28. The announce-ment appeared on 25 October 1919.

118. See also Marianne Weber's preface to the third volume of the *Collected Essays* on ancient Judaism: at least with regard to early Christianity, "the preliminaries had long been made" ("Vorwort zum dritten Band," in Max Weber, *Gesammelte Aufsätze zur Religionssoziologie*, vol. 3 [Tübingen: Mohr, (1921) 1988]).

119. Weber, "Religious Rejections," in *From Max Weber*, 324. See also Schluchter, *Rise of Western Rationalism*, 9–12; idem, *Rationalism, Religion, and Domination*, 34–38, 44–48, 99; Guenther Roth, "Rationalization in Max Weber's Developmental History," in *Max Weber, Rationality, and Modernity*, ed. Lash and Whimster, 75–91.

juridical, technical—that Weber outlined in his "Prefatory Remarks"[120] to the *Collected Essays* and have more recently been addressed under the rubric of the "rise of the West."[121] Weber was and remained convinced, however, that institutional rationalizations could not account for the distinctiveness of Western rationalism entirely. For him, institutional rationalizations in the Western sphere were complemented by a rationalization of life conduct—a rationalization of conduct that, to a significant extent, happened from within, rooted in personal values and worldviews. And internally conditioned rationalizations of life conduct had their origins partly in ethical or religious developments, so that religion played, or might have played, an important historical role in influencing the course of social action in many geocultural areas of the world, obstructing or being conducive to the ethical rationalization of behavior. To specify precisely which of the ideational and institutional elements in the world's major religions had a conducive or obstructive function was the second, ultimate goal of the typology of rationalism.[122]

Therefore, Weber's sociology and typology of rationalism in his religious studies incorporated a sociology and typology of religiously influenced rationalizations of life conduct. In the historical-developmental component of his *Collected Essays*, Weber wanted to trace religious influences on the rationalization of life conduct over time. The part on *The Christianity of the Occident* would have provided Weber with the opportunity to relate medieval Christianity to his central comparative case, ascetic Protestantism, and the type of social action it

---

120. Translated as "Author's Introduction," in Weber, *The Protestant Ethic*, 13–31. See also Benjamin Nelson, "Max Weber's 'Author's Introduction' (1920): A Master Clue to His Main Aims," *Sociological Inquiry* 44 (1974): 269–78.

121. See, e.g., Eric L. Jones, *The European Miracle: Environments, Economies, and Geopolitics in the History of Europe and Asia*, 2d ed. (Cambridge: Cambridge University Press, 1987); Daniel Chirot, "The Rise of the West," *American Sociological Review* 50 (1985): 181–95; John A. Hall, *Powers and Liberties: The Causes and Consequences of the Rise of the West* (Berkeley and Los Angeles: University of California Press, 1986). For a critique of these views, including some of Weber's, see Janet Abu-Lughod, *Before European Hegemony: The World System, A.D. 1250–1350* (New York: Oxford University Press, 1989); James M. Blaut, *The Colonizer's Model of the World: Geographical Diffusionism and Eurocentric History* (New York: Guilford Press, 1993).

122. Weber, "Author's Introduction," in *The Protestant Ethic*, 26–27; idem, *Economy and Society*, 562; idem, *The Religion of India: The Sociology of Hinduism and Buddhism* [1916–17], ed. and trans. Hans H. Gerth and Don Martindale (Glencoe, Ill.: Free Press, 1960), 4; idem, *The Religion of China: Confucianism and Taoism* [1915], ed. and trans. Hans H. Gerth (New York: Free Press, 1964), 240, 243; idem, *General Economic History* [1923], trans. F. Knight (New Brunswick, N.J.: Transaction, 1981), 313–14, 352–69. See also Stephen Kalberg, "The Rationalization of Action in Max Weber's Sociology of Religion," *Sociological Theory* 8 (1990): 59–61.

engendered—a rationalism of world mastery that originated partly in religiously motivated ascetic practices of the self.[123] This project called for him to systematize, and elaborate on, his and Troeltsch's remarks on the social and economic ethics of the Christian church. Medieval religion's "impeding as well as conducive" influences on the rationalization of the economy, which Weber had adumbrated already in 1905,[124] could now be explored in a wider context: the rationalization of societal spheres and the development of a rationalism of world mastery in life conduct in general, rather than capitalist development alone, for "the development of the economy has to be conceived primarily as a particular aspect of the general rationalization of life," as Weber spelled out in the "Preface" to the *Outline of Social Economics* of 1914.[125] Furthermore, Weber wanted to relate the ethics of Christianity to the rationalization of conduct and society by showing not merely the impact of the former on the latter, but their mutual influence and dependence.[126] This was not merely a statement of intent. Weber's letters to Siebeck of 1913 and 1915 each contain a reference to a treatment of Christianity. Its outline may have been written before World War I; yet a separate study—if it ever existed—was not found among the manuscripts Weber left behind after his death. What remains, therefore, are references to medieval religion in Weber's other writings, the most important of which occur in the revised PE and "The Protestant Sects," which Weber worked on until shortly before his death,[127] some older parts of *Economy and Society*,[128] and passages in the lecture-based *General Economic History*.[129] These writings, particularly the revised PE, did not confine themselves

123. On the concept of "world mastery," see Schluchter, "The Paradox of Rationalization," in Roth and Schluchter, *Max Weber's Vision of History*, 45–59; idem, *Rise of Western Rationalism*, 23, 164–65; idem, *Rationalism, Religion, and Domination*, 34–35; Kalberg, "Rationalization of Action," 77–79.

124. See page 18 above.

125. Weber, "Vorwort" (preface to the *Outline of Social Economics*); reprinted in Winckelmann, *Max Webers hinterlassenes Hauptwerk*, 165. Cf. 13.

126. See Schluchter, *Rationalism, Religion, and Domination*, 44–48, 421, 425; idem, *Paradoxes of Modernity*, 110–11.

127. Max Weber, "The Protestant Sects and the Spirit of Capitalism" [1920], in *From Max Weber*, 302–22. On the composition of this essay and *The Protestant Ethic*, see Winckelmann, *Max Webers hinterlassenes Hauptwerk*, 45–49.

128. See especially the chapters "Religious Groups (the Sociology of Religion)" (399–634) and "Political and Hierocratic Domination" (1158–211), which likely represent Weber's earlier views on this topic.

129. Furthermore, Weber dealt with the theme of the bourgeois affinity for practical rational conduct in the Middle Ages (formulated in the amended research program in 1910), in conjunction with the theme of new opportunities for such conduct that followed the rise of medieval cities (formulated in the "Agrarian Conditions" in 1909), in a

to structural transformations of medieval religion and society. While the institutional structuration of conduct was important, ethical contributions and impediments to the rationalization of conduct in different medieval religious groups remained a central issue.[130]

Preliminaries to *The Christianity of the Occident*

Regarding the institutional structuration of conduct in the medieval period, Weber developed pertinent arguments in his manuscript on the Occidental city (probably early in the 1910s). This study focuses on structural opportunities for practical rational conduct, and the comparative absence of secular-ethical, magical, and religious limitations on such opportunities, in urban spaces from a comparative historical perspective. The ideal-typical medieval city was relatively unique in that impediments to, and prohibitions of, economic transactions and accumulation based upon social and religious stereotypes were comparatively weak: "In medieval Europe, especially in the central and northern European cities, ritual exclusiveness was never strong, and the sibs lost all importance as constituencies of the city. The city became a confederation of individual burghers (heads of households), and the membership of the burghers lost all practical significance for the city commune itself. . . . [T]aboo barriers like those of the Indian and Equatorial areas were absent, as were the magical totemic, ancestral and caste props of the clan organization."[131] Medieval cities organized as universalistic confraternal communes, enfranchised and bound together by an oath of allegiance (*coniuratio*), and further integrative functions were provided by guilds and other fraternal associations, which combined religious with economic purposes.[132] Cities in the central Middle

---

preliminary way in his posthumously found manuscript "The City (Non-Legitimate Domination)" (*Economy and Society*, 1212–1372).

130. While Wolfgang Schluchter (*Paradoxes of Modernity*, 325 n. 50; *Rationalism, Religion, and Domination*, 27, 488 n. 113) has convincingly refuted the views of Jeffrey C. Alexander (*The Classical Attempt at Theoretical Synthesis: Max Weber* [Berkeley and Los Angeles: University of California Press, 1983]) and Randall Collins (*Weberian Sociological Theory*, 19–44), that Weber considered ideal factors as being less important in his late sociology, he himself concludes that Weber would have emphasized institutional transformations and aspects of medieval religion. See Schluchter, *Paradoxes of Modernity*, chap. 4; idem, "Die Entstehung der bürgerlichen Lebensführung," in *Max Webers Wissenschaftslehre: Interpretation und Kritik*, ed. Gerhard Wagner and Heinz Zipprian (Frankfurt: Suhrkamp, 1994), 704. The following analysis does not support this view.

131. Weber, *Economy and Society*, 1226–65 (the quote is from 1243).

132. Ibid., 1251–58.

Ages also achieved a high degree of independence from hierocratic and secular powers, which could influence but usually not determine city politics on their own. In contrast to a predominantly political orientation of the cities in antiquity, medieval cities were economically oriented, toward a "rational, continuously organized, and in this sense specifically 'civic' (*bürgerlich*) form of acquisitive operation: systematic work for gain." Urban life provided unique opportunities for gain through peaceful trade and production.[133]

Yet in contrast to the influential theses of Werner Sombart and Lujo Brentano, the overcoming of barriers of traditionalism and the increase in chances for peaceful acquisition in urban spaces did not, for Weber, make for an emergent form of modern capitalism in the Middle Ages. The Middle Ages lacked the institutional prerequisites in legal, social, economic, and technological-scientific matters for modern capitalism to occur. Not even in the most advanced economic localities in the Middle Ages, the northern Italian cities of the Renaissance, with a more capital-friendly religious ideology than probably anywhere and anytime else in the Middle Ages, did the fecund urban soil for the nourishment of acquisitive drives result in an empowerment of the self that was both long-term oriented and extended to broader masses of the population. What was missing was an ethical temperance of acquisitive impulses, a normative-practical dimension founded upon ethical considerations of duty that extended to circles not intimately involved in rational market transactions.[134] Historically, it was foremost religions that were able to bestow—though by no means exclusively so—ethical considerations of duty upon groups and individuals.[135] With regard to the Middle Ages, Weber followed up on this argument in the revision of the PE.

An important difference between the original and the revised PE is the introduction of the concept of "disenchantment."[136] This concept is

133. Ibid., 1339–72 (the quote is from 1296; translation altered). Cf. the chapter on "Citizenship" in idem, *General Economic History*, 315–37. See also Schluchter, *Paradoxes of Modernity*, 218–25.

134. Weber, *The Protestant Ethic*, 194 n. 12, 200 n. 29. Cf. Werner Sombart, *Der Bourgeois: Zur Geistesgeschichte des modernen Wirtschaftsmenschen* (Munich: Duncker & Humblot, 1913), 135–48; Lujo Brentano, *Die Anfänge des modernen Kapitalismus* (Munich: Verlag der Akademie der Wissenschaften, 1916), 132–35. See also Schluchter, *Paradoxes of Modernity*, 68–69, 231–33; Hartmut Lehmann, "The Rise of Capitalism: Weber Versus Sombart," in *Weber's "Protestant Ethic,"* ed. Lehmann and Roth, 195–208; Guenther Roth, introduction to ibid., 16–18. On the institutional preconditions of modern capitalism, see Schluchter, *Paradoxes of Modernity*, 200–204.

135. Weber, "Author's Introduction," in *The Protestant Ethic*, 27.

136. For the view that "there is nothing to find" besides "minor clarifications" in comparing the original to the revised version of the PE, "no trace at all of any

central not only to Weber's exploration of medieval religion, but to all of his studies on the world religions.[137] Disenchantment, or the rejection of magical practices for soteriological purposes, relates to one of two main criteria Weber used as "yardsticks" in assessing the rationalizing potential of the religious sphere: "One is the degree to which the religion has divested itself of magic; the other is the degree to which it has systematically unified the relation between God and the world and therewith its own ethical relationship to the world."[138] Often the result of religious prophecy, a unified relationship between deity and the world allows for the "systematic orientation of life conduct toward one standard of value from inside," and life becomes "a whole methodically placed under a transcendental goal."[139] Magic is apt to prevent or break up such a systematic orientation of life conduct, for at least two reasons. First, following contemporary work in anthropology and religious studies, Weber viewed religion as supplication of one or several deities, whereas he characterized magic as coercion of spiritual forces. Religion, in sublimating ethical conceptions of sin and salvation, can serve to rationalize conduct, whereas magic does not.[140] Second, like Durkheim,

---

'development'" from the one to the other, see Hennis, *Max Weber*, 27, 202 n. 20; cf. idem, "Die 'Protestantische Ethik'—Ein 'Überdeterminierter' Text?" *Sociologia Internationalis* 33 (1995): 6. A short yet accurate overview of the changes in the revised version can be found in Klaus Lichtblau and Johannes Weiß, "Einleitung der Herausgeber," in Max Weber, *Die protestantische Ethik und der "Geist" des Kapitalismus*, ed. Klaus Lichtblau and Johannes Weiß (Bodenheim: Athenäum Hain Hanstein, 1993), xiv–xxiv.

137. Tenbruck, "The Problem of Thematic Unity," in *Reading Weber*, ed. Tribe, 42–84. That one should be skeptical of Tenbruck's evolutionary reading of Weber and his attempt to elevate "disenchantment" to *the* single pivotal theme in Weber's sociology overall has been shown by Tenbruck's critics. See Stephen Kalberg, "The Search for Thematic Orientations in a Fragmented Oeuvre: The Discussion of Max Weber in Recent German Sociological Literature," *Sociology* 13 (1979): 127–33; Martin Riesebrodt, "Ideen, Interessen, Rationalisierung: Kritische Anmerkungen zu F. H. Tenbrucks Interpretation des Werkes Max Webers," *Kölner Zeitschrift für Soziologie und Sozial-psychologie* 32 (1980): 111–29; Johannes Winckelmann, "Die Herkunft von Max Webers 'Entzauberungs'-Konzeption," *Kölner Zeitschrift für Soziologie und Sozialpsychologie* 32 (1980): 12–53; Schluchter, *Rise of Western Rationalism*, 4–5.

138. Weber, *The Religion of China*, 226 (emphasis removed). See also idem, *Ancient Judaism* [1917–20], ed. and trans. Hans H. Gerth and Don Martindale (Glencoe, Ill.: Free Press, 1952), 426. Weber had developed his "yardstick" early, very likely by 1913. See idem, *Die Wirtschaftsethik der Weltreligionen*, 236; cf. Schmidt-Glintzer, "Editorischer Bericht," in ibid., 36.

139. Weber, *The Religion of China*, 235 (translation altered). See also idem, *Economy and Society*, 450–51.

140. Weber, *Economy and Society*, 422–39. The same distinction between magic and religion as used by Weber appeared in J. G. Frazer, *The Golden Bough* (New York: Macmillan, [1890] 1951), 56–69. For a lucid exploration of Weber's views on the

Weber ascribed to magic a lack of a continuous, if not continual, operative cult, which impedes the transmission of sacred values to and among the congregation. Since magical acts are governed by rules of experience, they are neither arational (performed without subjective expectation of success) nor irrational (employed inconsistently); yet they lack the structuring force and persistent impact that central religious values can imbue if organized on a continuous basis. Hence, disenchantment is a necessary condition for the rationalization of conduct rooted in an orientation toward integral religious values and worldviews.[141]

For the revised PE, Weber employed the concept of disenchantment to transcend the boundaries of the original essays,[142] reflecting on orthodox medieval religiosity. "[Calvinism's] absolute abolition of ecclesiastic-*sacramental* salvation (which in Lutheranism was by no means carried out in all its consequences) was the decisive difference from Catholicism. That great religio-historical process of the *disenchantment* of the world, which had begun with the ancient Judaic prophets and, in conjunction with Hellenistic scientific thought, had repudiated all *magical* means of seeking salvation as superstition and sacrilege, here came to its conclusion."[143] Choosing Calvinism and (medieval) Catholicism as his principal cases for analysis, Weber followed Troeltsch's earlier argument that suggested selecting Catholicism over Lutheranism. Using one of the criteria for assessing the potential for rationalization, he aligned all three cases in terms of their rejection of magical means to achieve salvation.

In this way Weber addressed the problem of how to link the revised PE to his essays on the economic ethics of the world religions, which used a wider thematic framework—from religion and capitalism to religion and rationalism—and methodological framework—from an ideational analysis to one that included material factors. The introduction of

---

potential of religion and magic for rationalization, see Hartmann Tyrell, "Potenz und Depotenzierung der Religion: Religion und Rationalisierung bei Max Weber," *Saeculum* 44 (1993): 303–25.

141. Weber, *Economy and Society*, 400, 506; idem, *The Religion of China*, 226. See also idem, "Some Categories of Interpretive Sociology," trans. Edith Graber, *Sociological Quarterly* 22 (1981): 154–55; Émile Durkheim, *The Elementary Forms of the Religious Life* [1912], trans. K. Fields (New York: Free Press, 1995), 39–44; Schluchter, *Paradoxes of Modernity*, 69–73.

142. Cf. Tenbruck, "The Problem of Thematic Unity," in *Reading Weber*, ed. Tribe, 49; Schluchter, *Rise of Western Rationalism*, 139 n. 1.; Lichtblau and Weiß, "Einleitung der Herausgeber," in Weber, *Die protestantische Ethik und der "Geist" des Kapitalismus*, xxiii–xxiv.

143. Weber, *The Protestant Ethic*, 104–5 (translation altered).

disenchantment in its "absolutely fundamental importance"[144] for his religious studies circumvented the problem by providing a conceptual brace between the two. Weber further elaborated on the differences between medieval Catholicism, ascetic Protestantism, and Lutheranism in terms of their employment of magic as soteriological practice:

> The "disenchantment" of the world: the elimination of *magic* as a means to salvation, was in Catholic spirituality not carried out as consistently as in Puritan religious life. . . . To the Catholic the *sacramental grace* of his Church was available as a means to make up for his own deficiency: the priest was an enchanter, who brought about the miracle of transubstantiation and held the power of the keys. One could turn to him in contrition and repentance, he dispensed atonement, hope of grace, certainty of forgiveness, and thereby provided *relief* from that tremendous *tension* that the Calvinist was doomed to live with by an inexorable fate, admitting of no mitigation. For the Calvinist these friendly and human comforts did not exist, and he also could not hope to make up for hours of weakness and imprudence by increased good will at other times, as the Catholic, and the Lutheran as well. . . . There was no place for the Catholic, very human back-and-forth between sin, repentance, penance, absolution, new sin; a balance [of merits] for the life as a whole which could be adjusted by temporal castigations and ecclesiastical means of grace did not exist.[145]

The central argument here is the difference between medieval Catholicism and Calvinism in regard to the relations between parish clergy and believer, with important implications for the rationalization of life conduct. What Troeltsch had described as sacramentalism of the church in the later Middle Ages Weber now analyzed further in its practical consequences for lay Catholicism, going beyond his earlier tentative characterizations as well.

The role of the cleric is highlighted in two ways. First, the cleric as a priest was a relief agent for religious concerns and anxieties, presiding over a cycle of sin and atonement. Because the church, as an encompassing institution of grace and, as Troeltsch had pointed out, by virtue of the interpenetration of church and world, operated with a graded system of morals, atonement was to be achieved through

144. Ibid., 234 n. 69.
145. Ibid., 117 (translation altered).

individual good works or rituals that were aimed overall at the ethical capabilities of the average member of the church. When measured by one of the two main criteria for assessing the religious potential for rationalization—the systematization of the relationship between the deity and the world—the ensuing codification of appropriate penitential deeds and procedures in medieval handbooks of penance was indeed uniquely methodical and systematized, and successful in domesticating the masses. However, the graded system of ethics at its base reduced the potential tension between ethical standards and human abilities, and the priest, if a member of the church failed to live up to these standards, offered help as intermediary provider of salutary goods.[146]

Second, the cleric functioned as an enchanter or magician, a role partly conflicting with his primary one as a priest. This role followed from popular perception of priestly acts as manipulations of the sacred, rather than supplications to a deity. Such acts were rational in that they were often performed on the basis of rules of experience, but they lacked any consistent influence of conduct. Insofar as these acts, formally under clerical supervision, developed a life of their own and reintroduced elements of polytheism, as in the cult of saints, they engendered magical manipulations of divine favors and further diminished the potentially motivating tension between deity and believer.[147]

The character of orthodox religious ethics as achievement and assurance of salvation via institutionally provided or mediated avenues and rituals under the guidance of the priest was also influenced by structural and organizational aspects of religious life. The priest was vested with a charisma of office principally independent of his personal dignity, and in everyday life the religious role of the laity in local communities was very limited. "In medieval Western Christianity . . . the parish was essentially a passive ecclesiastical tax unit and the

146. Weber, *Economy and Society*, 465, 531–32, 561–62, 587, 598; idem, *Ancient Judaism*, 246; idem, *General Economic History*, 365–66. See also the excellent summaries in Schluchter, "The Paradox of Rationalization," in Roth and Schluchter, *Max Weber's Vision of History*, 35–37; idem, *Rise of Western Rationalism*, 167–70; idem, *Paradoxes of Modernity*, 168–71.

147. Cf. Weber, *Economy and Society*, 422. For his classification of priest and magician, see 424–27. I differ from Schluchter, *Rise of Western Rationalism*, 168, for whom Weber's characterization of a medieval cleric as a magician is erroneous. Yet a social position can come with a set of multiple and conflicting roles. Furthermore, as Weber himself (*Economy and Society*, 425, 440) pointed out, in reality the distinction between the priest and the magician was often fluid, so that the classification might vary with the particular aspect of a cleric's action under consideration.

jurisdictional district of a priest. . . . Generally, the laity completely lacked the character of a congregation."[148]

These bureaucratic aspects of orthodox religion set important limitations to external and internal religious innovation. The charisma of office is hostile to religious innovation from outside in the form of revelations entailed in charismatic prophecy. Prophecy, the "proclamation of a religious truth of salvation through personal revelation,"[149] can be a powerful ferment of religious change. A priest, however, like any functionary of the church, is not likely to look favorably upon prophetic activities that proclaim new revelations, and the novel ways of life they may engender. To the charisma of office, such religious prophecy is a dangerous challenge. For the latter undermines the officeholder's legitimacy, and the charisma of office "inevitably becomes the most uncompromising foe of all genuinely personal charisma"—to the point where the prophet "becomes suspect as a heretic or sorcerer."[150] The opposition to external religious change is exacerbated when the charisma of office as basis of authority becomes routinized and develops into long-standing traditional or bureaucratic-rational authority. *Extra ecclesiam nulla salus* not only is the motto of all hierocratic institutions, but also signifies a traditionalist stance toward prophetic creations of new ethics in the church.[151] Here Weber's thoughts once again reflect Troeltsch's thesis of a "unitary culture" in the Middle Ages.[152]

Within the boundaries of orthodoxy, the passive character of the laity provided an organizational setting that differed from the organization of ascetic Protestant sects in that it lacked a moral atmosphere conducive to the ethical rationalization of conduct. The ascetic Protestant sects derived their "penetrating efficiency of the religious regulation of life" from, as Weber specified in his earlier conceptions, their principle of

148. Weber, *Economy and Society*, 455 (translation altered).

149. Ibid., 446.

150. Ibid., 1165 (translation altered).

151. Ibid., 1167, 560, 457. The Latin phrase goes back to a letter of Saint Cyprian, a third-century bishop of Carthage, and was affirmed in the first canon of conciliar legislation in the Fourth Lateran Council of 1215. See Heinrich Denzinger, *Enchiridion Symbolorum Definitionum et Declarationum de Rebus Fidei et Morum*, ed. K. Rahner, 31st ed. (Barcelona: Herder, 1957), 200.

152. While Troeltsch more strongly than Weber emphasized the compulsory nature of this culture, neither was specific about the means of compulsion. The medieval Inquisition, which comes to mind here, was not mentioned by Troeltsch at all, while Weber discussed it only in the context of the rationalization of law (*Economy and Society*, 809, 830, 1192). See further Donald A. Nielsen, "Rationalization in Medieval Europe: The Inquisition and Sociocultural Change," *Politics, Culture, and Society* 2 (1988): 217–41.

voluntarism (only those who lived up to the standards of the sect were admitted and allowed to retain membership), their small size (members knew of and monitored one another), and their extraordinarily strict moral discipline (all spheres of life, on a permanent basis, were relevant in evaluating the moral standing of the member, and even slight transgressions could have severe consequences).[153] Thereby their lay members formed lasting social relationships with each other and were actively involved in the religious life of the congregation. This "congregational religiosity" in ascetic Protestant sects contrasted sharply with the bureaucratic nature of medieval church life. In the medieval church discipline was vested in the priestly office; such discipline worked through authoritarian means and put premiums on individual acts instead of conduct as a whole.[154] Differences in organizational settings, then, especially in the degree and kind of involvement of the respective organizations' members, contributed to the divergence in religious life between medieval orthodoxy and the ascetic Protestant sects, enabling the latter to become "the ferment for the methodical rationalization of conduct, also including economic action," while preventing the former from structuring secular conduct in accordance with religious values.[155]

Hence, in ideal-typical depiction, medieval Catholicism displayed the following features when contrasted with ascetic Protestantism: a graded system of ethical demands that was tolerant of human insufficiencies versus the absolute norms of a fierce, transcendent deity as ethical expectations; a partaking of priestly mediated sacraments and magical manipulations versus inner-worldly asceticism as means to salvation; assurance of forgiveness versus essential uncertainty as psychological states; passive bureaucratic administration of grace versus congregational religiosity as organizational structures; occasional ordering of religious and worldly behavior versus ethically systematized and methodically rationalized life conduct as behavioral patterns; and, as overall relationships to the world, a certain "naive affirmation of the world"[156] versus world mastery.[157]

153. Weber, "The Protestant Sects," in *From Max Weber*, 313 (translation altered), 316–17; cf. idem, *Economy and Society*, 1204–10. See also Stephen D. Berger, "The Sects and the Breakthrough into the Modern World: On the Centrality of the Sects in Weber's Protestant Ethic Thesis," *Sociological Quarterly* 12 (1971): 486–99.

154. Weber, "The Protestant Sects," in *From Max Weber*, 313, 315, 457 n. 24.

155. Weber, "The Social Psychology of the World Religions," in *From Max Weber*, 291 (translation altered); idem, *Economy and Society*, 455.

156. Weber, "The Social Psychology of the World Religions," in *From Max Weber*, 291.

157. Note that in contrast to his inclusion of ancient Christianity, medieval monasticism, and early modern ascetic Protestantism, Wolfgang Schluchter has never

Since neither the ethics nor the institutional settings of medieval Catholicism were apt to provide a religious contribution to rationalism for the laity, this contribution in orthodoxy came foremost from monasticism and its stress on methodical labor, which, now assessed in comparative perspective, distinguished Occidental monasticism from "almost all monastic rules anywhere in the world."[158] Despite the other-worldly orientation of monasticism, its ascetic achievements could have profound impacts on society at large (e.g., in agriculture or literary culture). But the large mass of orthodox believers was not subjected to the regimen of the monastics' ascetic life, although attempts were made to bridge the gap between monastic and lay religious life, as in the tertiary orders of the mendicants. Furthermore, Weber reiterated his earlier view that the concomitant monastic accumulation of a repository of merits and the lowering of ethical standards for the rest provided a disincentive for the laity to prove their faith in methodical ascetic conduct. He now stressed that such an incentive was also lacking in mysticism (though not necessarily in its more elite forms), which values passive over active means and contemplative over ascetic paths to salvation.[159]

Medieval heterodox sects thus remained the pivotal candidates for the harbingers of modern ascetic rationalism. "How far certain orthodox

included medieval lay orthodox religion in his otherwise exhaustive comparative schemes of the world religions. Cf. Schluchter, *Rise of Western Rationalism*, 162; idem, *Paradoxes of Modernity*, 168–71.

158. Weber, *The Protestant Ethic*, 158 (translation altered).

159. Weber, *Economy and Society*, 544–51, 1168–70; idem, *General Economic History*, 365; idem, *The Protestant Ethic*, 113–14; idem, "Religious Rejections," in *From Max Weber*, 324–26; cf. Schluchter, *Rationalism, Religion, and Domination*, 127–46. For references to the achievements of monastic rationalism in Weber's work, see Johannes Winckelmann, *Erläuterungsband zu "Wirtschaft und Gesellschaft"* (Tübingen: Mohr, 1976), 263. Wolfgang Schluchter (*Rationalism, Religion, and Domination*, 127–46) has recently pointed out that in his scheme of asceticism and contemplation (later mysticism) as the two principal paths of salvation, and of active and passive means of salvation, Weber never distinguished between these analytical levels clearly. Instead, Weber tended to conflate them onto one level on which a "culture of action" was set up against a "culture of feeling" on the basis of a postulated affinity between asceticism and activism on the one hand and contemplation (mysticism) and passivity on the other. (The otherwise excellent explication by Kalberg, "Rationalization of Action," does not allude to this important issue.) This, of course, fits well with Weber's attempts—perhaps ultimately futile—to come to grips with the "culture of feeling" in contemporary German art and social life that connoted authenticity of emotion, aestheticism, and, for some, amoralism. See Lawrence A. Scaff, *Fleeing the Iron Cage: Culture, Politics, and Modernity in the Thought of Max Weber* (Berkeley and Los Angeles: University of California Press, 1989), 19, 80–81, 124–25; Klaus Lichtblau, "The Protestant Ethic Versus the 'New Ethic,'" in *Weber's "Protestant Ethic,"* ed. Lehmann and Roth, 179–93.

and heterodox religious communities in the Middle Ages have been the forerunners of the ascetic denominations of Protestantism is not yet to be discussed here," Weber wrote in "The Protestant Sects." He also used the expression "medieval Puritan sects" (without a specific reference) in *Economy and Society*, and referred to the "spiritual ancestry" of the Protestant ethic "in the sects and in the ethics of Wyclif and Hus" in *The Protestant Ethic*.[160] Hence, did medieval puritanical sects exist that displayed lineaments of ascetic Protestantism's rationalism of world mastery and its disenchanted outlook? Were there even precursors of the "Protestant ethic"? Did these lay groups unleash an empowerment of the self that was one of the pillars of Occidental rationalism?

Conclusion

These issues were to be addressed in *The Christianity of the Occident*, the fourth and final volume of Weber's *Collected Essays in the Sociology of Religion*, but Weber died without leaving behind a manuscript, and the existing writings do not provide answers to these questions.[161] Weberian sociological scholarship has generally neglected medieval religion; where it has not, it either discusses the role of medieval religion in Weber's thought under the rubric of a "regression in the course of Western rationalism,"[162] or looks for references to institutional transformations in Weber's work.[163] I have attempted to show that Weber's ideas on medieval religion, as they developed over the last fifteen years of his life, did

160. Weber, "The Protestant Sects," in *From Max Weber*, 320 (translation altered); *Economy and Society*, 1180; *The Protestant Ethic*, 198 n. 12.

161. Based on Weber's announcement of a manuscript on medieval Christianity in a letter to his publisher, Siebeck, in 1915, Wolfgang Schluchter (*Paradoxes of Modernity*, 114–16) has surmised that such a manuscript may indeed have existed and later been published as part of, or integrated into, the section "The Great Religions and the World" in the chapter "Religious Groups (the Sociology of Religion)" in *Economy and Society*. If it did exist, it arguably covered orthodox medieval Christianity, but not heterodox groups. The section in *Economy and Society* only contains a terse ideal-typical depiction of Catholicism's relations to the economic sphere, and heterodox elements are not mentioned (Weber, *Economy and Society*, 615). The equally brief references to the Lollards and Hussites in the revised PE (197–98 n. 12) Weber could easily have taken from Troeltsch's *Social Teaching*.

162. Schroeder, *Max Weber and the Sociology of Culture*, 84.

163. Collins, "The Weberian Revolution," in *Weberian Sociological Theory*. Cf. Schluchter, *Paradoxes of Modernity*, chap. 4; idem, "Die Entstehung der bürgerlichen Lebensführung," in *Max Webers Wissenschaftslehre*, ed. Wagner and Zipprian, 704.

not show such a narrow focus in addressing medieval religion. For Weber, the central issues were how religious values and the organization of religious communities interacted to fashion ascetic practices of the self, enabling individuals and groups to influence and shape their social and cultural environment. The empowerment of the self as the basis of ascetic rationalism was a theme that ran through Weber's studies since at least a decade before his death and, with regard to the Occident, can be traced even further to the original version of the PE. It allowed the monastics to become the carrier stratum of asceticism in the West, methodically controlling their behavior, whereas orthodox medieval religion outside of monasticism lacked an ethic that put a premium on methodical conduct and was capable of permeating it with asceticism.

That Weber also was neither slave to the historical and theological scholarship of his time nor an autopoietic social scientist can be seen in the ways he used his sources and molded information from these materials into something new. It has been justly asserted that Weber, a crossover between a *Besitzbürger* and a *Bildungsbürger*, was deeply steeped in a liberal-bourgeois Protestant milieu, in part perhaps due to his Anglophile conceptions of political liberalism and a fascination with the iron Puritan industrialists in England—graduates of this "hard school of asceticism" and calculability who, in Weber's view, were so markedly different from leading contemporary German intellectual and artistic circles infatuated with *Gefühlskultur*.[164] These intellectual and cultural roots may help explain his views on orthodox Catholicism in the Middle Ages, in that he considered the potential for ascetic rationalism in lay spirituality to be low, while having considerable regard for the heroic asceticism of medieval monasticism. He was also indebted to Ernst Troeltsch, who influenced his later thought considerably.

Still, in spite of these links and reliances, Weber transcended the themes and theses of a Troeltsch, Harnack, or Ritschl. From the

---

164. See Graf, "The German Theological Sources," in *Weber's "Protestant Ethic,"* ed. Lehmann and Roth; idem, "Die 'kompetentesten' Gesprächspartner? Implizite theologische Werturteile in Max Webers 'Protestantischer Ethik,'" in *Religionssoziologie um 1900*, ed. Volkhard Krech and Hartmann Tyrell (Würzburg: Ergon-Verlag, 1995), 209–48; Guenther Roth, "Weber the Would-be Englishman: Anglophilia and Family History," in *Weber's "Protestant Ethic,"* ed. Lehmann and Roth, 83–121; Hartmut Lehmann, "Max Webers 'Protestantische Ethik' als Selbstzeugnis," in *Max Webers "Protestantische Ethik": Beiträge aus der Sicht eines Historikers* (Göttingen: Vandenhoeck & Ruprecht, 1996), 109–27. For the "hard school of asceticism" versus *Gefühlskultur*, see note 159 above and the Introduction, page 3. On the *Bildungsbürger* and *Besitzbürger* in Max Weber, see Scaff, *Fleeing the Iron Cage*, 124 n. 8; contextualized in Dirk Käsler, *Die frühe deutsche Soziologie 1909 bis 1934 und ihre Entstehungsmilieus: Eine wissenschaftssoziologische Untersuchung* (Opladen: Westdeutscher Verlag, 1984), 235–57.

beginning, Weber was intent on writing an account of his own, and the fragments he left contain the foundations for a sociology of medieval religious groups ranging from orthodox religion to fringe and heterodox sects. He provided some preliminary analyses of the relations between religion and conduct in monasticism and orthodox lay spirituality, but not in heterodox groups. The latter remained unexplored, even though, in Weber's view, they possibly qualified as precursors of Calvinist inner-worldly asceticism. This topic remains perhaps the biggest lacuna in Weber's explorations of medieval religion.

2

---<del>❧❦❧</del>---

MONASTIC ASCETICISM AND
THE SECULAR SPHERES

Monastic asceticism and its role in the development of Western rationalism have been a contentious topic in historical and sociological scholarship ever since its classical thematization by Weber and Troeltsch. The classical view, in which medieval monasticism was important for its asceticism and valorization of labor but remained other-worldly, has not gone unchallenged. An alternative has been proposed by scholars who, assessing the role of monasticism in Western history differently, have argued for a much stronger rationalizing impact of monastic asceticism. The central contention of this revisionist account is that monastic asceticism led to important rationalizations in the medieval economy and technology. The church, in the alternative view, was instrumental in bringing about technological innovations in the Middle Ages and in advancing capitalism.

In this chapter, I analyze the links between medieval monasticism and asceticism in light of newer historical and sociological scholarship, and assess the merits of both classical and revisionist accounts by probing the extent to which monasticism was linked to forms of work that served as a worldly avenue of asceticism. The analysis demonstrates that monasticism, while in theory valorizing work as ascetic practice, increasingly specialized in providing conspicuous religious services for the nobility. The performance of labor shifted to monastic affiliates of secondary status who were subjected to a lesser ascetic regimen. This monastic division of spiritual and manual labor continued in the later Middle Ages, when lay religious movements embraced asceticism and practiced it in their secular professions. Lay religious movements emerged, not as imitators of monastic forms of austerity, but as the harbingers of certain forms of inner-worldly asceticism. Central features of ascetic practices among the mendicants, it appears, were actually modeled on precedents in lay religious movements.

The Classic Account and Its Revision by Randall Collins and Lewis Mumford

Weber and Troeltsch argued, as pointed out in Chapter 1, that monastic asceticism brought forth disciplined and austere conduct and that this type of conduct was a precursor to Calvinist asceticism. In this classic view, both Calvinism and monasticism valued ascetic, methodical forms of labor, but whereas Calvinism engendered inner-worldly asceticism and contributed to the rationalization of the economy and other social spheres, monastic asceticism remained other-worldly. It was confined to the cells of the cloister and had little impact on social spheres other than religion. However, monastic asceticism was an important precursor to ascetic Protestantism in the strict regimen it imposed on the lives of the nuns and monks. Central to monasticism was an ascetic empowerment of the self, enabling the members of monastic communities to put all aspects of their lives consistently and stringently under ethical prerogatives. Confined to the cells of the cloister during the Middle Ages, this empowerment of the self centered on work as an ascetic practice. It enabled Protestant groups in early modern Europe to take advantage of new structural opportunities for methodical action and to permeate all spheres of society with methodical mastery.

Some sociological studies have followed up on Weber's and Troeltsch's remarks, which have since become the standard sociological account of the significance of monasticism in the West. Some scholars have compared the daily regime in the cloister to that of the capitalist factory, while others have studied the rigid temporal patterning of monastic life as a predecessor of modern society's highly structured time schedules.[1]

1. Hubert Treiber and Heinz Steinert, *Die Fabrikation des zuverlässigen Menschen: Über die "Wahlverwandtschaft" von Kloster- und Fabrikdisziplin* (Munich:

Randall Collins and Lewis Mumford have perhaps given the boldest assessments of the importance of monastic asceticism. Citing a strict work schedule and a predilection for advancing mechanical devices in medieval monasteries, Mumford credits medieval nuns and monks with bringing about technological advances that were "largely responsible for the fact that Western civilization caught up with, and then surpassed, the technical inventiveness of China, Korea, Persia, and India." These advances were rooted in the monasteries' ordered routines of life and technical mastery, so that, Mumford argues, "[m]ost of the habits Max Weber erroneously treated as the special property of sixteenth-century Calvinist Protestantism were in effective operation in the medieval Cistercian monastery."[2]

Collins, on the other hand, focuses less on technology than on the economic sphere. There, he finds "not only the institutional preconditions but a version of the developed characteristics of capitalism itself" in the Middle Ages. The monastic economy contributed to a kind of "church capitalism" that preceded the later forms of secular capitalism, and more generally advanced the process of societal rationalization in the Middle Ages. The basis of this societal rationalization was "'inner-worldly asceticism' in the most literal form," namely, the productivity and organizational efficacy of monastic labor.[3]

Collins and Mumford thereby argue for a revision of the classic account (see Table 1), partly turning Weber's and Troeltsch's position on its head. The classic and the revisionist account alike identify medieval monastics as the carrier stratum of asceticism in Western religious life. Both accounts agree on the austerity of monastic asceticism and the central importance of labor and methodical forms of social action for monastic rationalization, since monasticism valorized labor and methodical conduct as ascetic practice. They also concur on viewing the monks and nuns as performers of ascetic labor. But whereas the classic account holds that the overall direction of monastic asceticism was ultimately other-worldly, that is, directed at avoiding the secular spheres and trying to minimize their influence, the revision asserts that monastic asceticism was inner-worldly, that is, that it remained within the secular spheres and aimed to master them. For the classic account, the effects

Moos, 1980); Eviatar Zerubavel, "The Benedictine Ethic and the Modern Spirit of Scheduling: On Schedules and Social Organization," *Sociological Inquiry* 50 (1980): 157–69.

2. Lewis C. Mumford, *The Myth of the Machine* (New York: Harcourt Brace Jovanovich, 1967), 1:263, 272.

3. Collins, "The Weberian Revolution," in *Weberian Sociological Theory*, 47 (emphasis removed), 58, 54. A similar argument has been proposed by Hall, *Powers and Liberties*, 132.

Table 1. The Classic and the Revisionist Accounts of Asceticism in Medieval Western Society

| | Account | |
Characteristics	Classic (Weber, Troeltsch)	Revisionist (Collins, Mumford)
Carrier stratum	Monastics	Monastics
Form	Strict asceticism	Strict asceticism
Basis	Methodical labor	Methodical labor
Performers of ascetic labor	Monks and nuns	Monks and nuns
Direction	Other-worldly	Inner-worldly
Effects	Disciplined conduct	Societal rationalization
Locus	Cloister	Economy, technology

of monastic asceticism were largely limited to the sphere of conduct, in the form of methodically disciplined ways of life, whereas in the revision monastic asceticism penetrated the world and led to societal rationalization. For Weber and Troeltsch, the locus of these effects was the cloister; for Collins and Mumford, it was the economy and technology. The latter therefore paint a picture of the relations between monasticism and society that differs significantly from the classic view.

A New Account

Monastic Asceticism and the World in the Earlier Middle Ages

The historical evidence does not sustain central tenets of either the classic or the revisionist account. The classic account is wrong because it underestimates monasticism's involvement in the world, the revisionist one because it misconstrues monasticism's rationalizing impact on the social spheres. Both accounts overestimate its asceticism. The alternative account of medieval monastic asceticism and its relation to the world developed here begins with the earlier Middle Ages (c. 500–c.1100), when the basic characteristics of monasticism emphasized particularly by Weber, such as monastic discipline and the valorization of work, emerged.

Latin Christian monasticism came from the East. It had its early predecessors in colonies of hermits in the Egyptian and Palestine deserts who sought isolation from other humans in their quest to take up Christ's evangelical counsels of fasting, chastity, and the renunciation of property. With the renunciation of secular attachments, the nun or monk began a journey of continuous ascetic self-mortification with the goal of contemplative unity with God through prayer. Colonies of hermits became replaced by cenobitic (communal) monasteries organized under rules in the fourth century, and this newer type of establishment soon spread to the West. The sixth-century Rule of St. Benedict gave the various monastic establishments in Western Christianity, as Weber and Troeltsch emphasized, a normative foundation that would structure organized religious life for many centuries.[4]

The Rule of St. Benedict

Reflecting and at the same time inverting the social conditions outside the monastery, the mode of life in the cloister engendered by the Rule stressed stability, peacefulness, order, and some degree of collective self-sufficiency. At a time when western Europe was still an area of very local rule with continual political instability and declining levels of wealth, commerce, and literacy, and when many people were under continual threat of dislocation by natural or man-made calamities, the nun and monk professed to stability: they were to live their entire lives in the monastery. There they were disengaged from the acts of violence and warfare prevalent in the outside world, but only to make use of the peacefulness inside to fight a battle of a different kind: the spiritual warfare of an athlete of God. In the strict observance of the Rule lay not only the best way to personal salvation, but also the possibility of interceding, in prayer, on behalf of others.[5]

In order to fulfill these tasks best, monastic life needed order, structure, and methodicalness. The prologue to the Rule calls on monks and nuns to "establish a school for the Lord's service."[6] This school was

---

4. See George Zarnecki, *The Monastic Achievement* (New York: McGraw-Hill, 1972), 11–15; C. H. Lawrence, *Medieval Monasticism*, 2d ed. (London: Longman, 1990), 1–18; David Knowles, *Christian Monasticism* (New York: McGraw-Hill, 1969), 9–36. On female monasticism, see Susanna Elm, *Virgins of God: The Making of Asceticism in Late Antiquity* (Oxford: Oxford University Press, 1994).

5. On the social, cultural, political, and economic conditions at the time, see Georges Duby, *Rural Economy and Country Life in the Medieval West*, trans. Cynthia Postan (Columbia: University of South Carolina Press, 1968), 3–58; idem, *The Early Growth of the European Economy: Warriors and Peasants from the Seventh to the Twelfth Century*, trans. Howard B. Clarke (Ithaca: Cornell University Press, 1978); Renée Doehaerd, *The Early Middle Ages in the West: Economy and Society*, trans. W. G. Deakin (Amsterdam: North-Holland, 1978); Pierre Riché, *Ecoles et enseignement dans le Haut Moyen Âge* (Paris: Picard, 1989).

6. Timothy Fry, ed., *R[egula] B[enedicti] 1980: The Rule of St. Benedict* (Collegeville, Minn.: Liturgical Press, 1981), 165; hereafter Fry, *RB 1980*.

intended to be a training ground on which its subjects were inculcated with the virtues of obedience and discipline. Obedience meant commitment and conformity to monastic life as defined by the Rule and specified by the abbess or abbot. Abbesses and abbots had strong authority over monastic communities' secular and spiritual matters, but as elected leaders they themselves were subject to precise stipulations on conduct, militating against autocratic or imperious rule. Discipline referred to the methodical way in which nuns and monks were supposed to carry out their profession. Because "idleness is the enemy of the soul,"[7] every moment of the day was structured and filled with activities. The Rule stipulated that nuns and monks divide their time among collective prayer, *lectio*, and work. Collective prayer was the primary means by which the monastics could battle and ward off evil forces. The belief in the menacing powers of evil forces had been a prevalent feature of Christianity for some time—a legacy of the successful efforts of Christians more firmly to establish Christianity in late Roman and early medieval society by defining the ubiquitous supernatural agents, the demons, as a menacing threat, and the demons' manipulators, the sorcerers, as servants of darkness, from which only Christianity could deliver the community. To fight these evil forces, through prayer, and prevent them from bringing misfortune to the Christian community was seen as one of the most important tasks of the monastic vocation. Prayer was organized in a daily round of divine service, the *Opus Dei*. The Work of God consisted in chanting and reciting verses and psalms, starting at night and continuing throughout the day; it was the nuns' and monks' main task, around which other activities were structured.[8]

Prayer was complemented by *lectio*, the study of texts and private meditation. The monastics' literary skills soon led to the perception of the monastery as a place of learning. Even though recent historical scholarship has shown that literacy was not as closely confined to an elite of clerics, monks, and princes as previously assumed, monasteries were the foremost centers of scholarship and literary production from about the eight century until at least the eleventh century, when advances in secular and clerical schooling and the foundation of universities began to encroach on the monasteries' scholarly domain.[9]

---

7. Ibid., 249.

8. Lawrence, *Medieval Monasticism*, 32–34. See Chapter 3, pages 106–10, for the role of the portrayal of demons in the rise of Christianity and the corresponding cult of the saints during late antiquity and the earlier Middle Ages.

9. Jean Leclercq, *The Love of Learning and the Desire for God* (New York: Fordham University Press, 1961); Riché, *Ecoles et enseignement dans le Haut Moyen*

Work was a third constitutive element of the monastic profession: "When they live by the labor of their hands, as our fathers and the apostles did, then they are really monks."[10] It was also the part of the monastic profession that, according to the Rule, was most strongly oriented toward active conduct. In ancient Christianity, manual labor had been valorized by the ascetic hermits of the East, who viewed it not merely as a means of subsistence and charity, but also as a way to combat the insidious temptations of *acedia*—sloth and lethargy brought on by demons in the scalding heat of the desert. Early medieval Benedictine monastics took to manual labor in a similar vein, as a means to aid the poor and sick and to avoid falling into idleness. Labor also allowed the monastic communities to be materially self-sufficient. For if members of the monastic communities roamed outside the monastery, it was "not all good for their souls," the Rule stated, and therefore "the monastery should, if possible, be so constructed that within it all necessities, such as water, mill and garden are contained, and the various crafts are practiced."[11]

Âge; Harvey J. Graff, *The Legacies of Literacy* (Bloomington: Indiana University Press, 1991), 34–74; Robert E. Lerner, "Literacy and Learning," in *One Thousand Years: Western Europe in the Middle Ages*, ed. Richard L. DeMolen (Boston: Houghton Mifflin, 1974), 171–94; on lay literacy beyond clerical elites in Carolingian society, see Rosamond McKitterick, *The Carolingians and the Written Word* (Cambridge: Cambridge University Press, 1989).

10. Fry, *RB 1980*, 249/251.

11. Fry, *RB 1980*, 289. See also Rotraut Wisskirchen, "Das monastische Verbot der Feldarbeit und ihre rechtliche Gestaltung bei Benedikt von Nursia," *Jahrbuch für Antike und Christentum* 38 (1995): 91–96. On monastic labor in the early Middle Ages and its relation to Christian asceticism in antiquity more generally, see Antoine Guillaumont, "Le travail manuel dans le monachisme ancien: Contestation et valorisation," in *Aux origines du monachisme chrétien* (Begrolles en Mauges: Abbaye de Bellefontaine, 1979), 117–26; George Ovitt Jr., "Labor and the Foundations of Monasticism," in *The Restoration of Perfection: Labor and Technology in Medieval Culture* (New Brunswick, N.J.: Rutgers University Press, 1987), 88–106; Jacques Le Goff, "Le travail dans le systemes de valeur de l'Occident médiéval," in *Le travail au Moyen Âge*, ed. Jacqueline Hamesse and Colette Muraille-Samaran (Louvain: Institut d'Études Médiévales de l'Université Catholique de Louvain, 1990), 15; Friedrich Prinz, "Mönchtum und Arbeitsethos," in *Askese und Kultur: Vor- und Frühbenediktinisches Mönchtum an der Wiege Europas* (Munich: Beck, 1980), 68–74; E. R. Dodds, *Pagan and Christian in an Age of Anxiety* (Cambridge: Cambridge University Press, 1965), 1–36; Karl Heussi, *Der Ursprung des Mönchtums* (Tübingen: Mohr, 1936; reprint, Aalen: Scientia, 1961), 218–66; Peter Nagel, *Die Motivierung der Askese in der alten Kirche und der Ursprung des Mönchtums* (Berlin: Akademie, 1966), 98–101. For the notion of *acedia* in monastic contexts, see Siegfried Wenzel, *The Sin of Sloth: Acedia in Medieval Thought and Literature* (Chapel Hill: University of North Carolina Press, 1967), chaps. 1–2.

The combination of a thorough ordering of life with a valorization of manual labor prompted Weber's and Troeltsch's comments on the methodical character of work and the ascetic rationalization of conduct prescribed by early medieval monasticism, which made it similar to Calvinist asceticism, and has led Collins and Mumford to adduce monastic contributions to advances in the economy and technology.[12] This view is echoed in recent historical literature: "Manual labor thus becomes the link between world and asceticism; it prevents ascetic zeal from becoming petrified in world flight."[13] Studies of other world religions largely confirm Weber's view that the prescription of methodical manual labor for religious virtuosos was unique to Occidental monasticism.[14] But this, I argue, is a distorted picture of monastic asceticism and monasticism's influence on religious life and the secular spheres in the earlier Middle Ages. Just as important as the aspects of monasticism alluded to above were other aspects or developments addressed by neither the classic nor the revisionist account:[15] the direct involvement

12. In a similar vein, see Alfred Kieser, "From Asceticism to Administration of Wealth: Medieval Monasteries and the Pitfalls of Rationalization," *Organization Studies* 8 (1987): 107–23.

13. Prinz, "Mönchtum und Arbeitsethos," in *Askese und Kultur*, 71.

14. For Buddhism, see Stanley J. Tambiah, *World Conqueror and World Renouncer: A Study of Buddhism and Polity in Thailand Against a Historical Background* (Cambridge: Cambridge University Press, 1976), 362–64; for Hinduism, J. Patrick Olivelle, "Village vs. Wilderness: Ascetic Ideals and the Hindu World," in *Monastic Life in the Christian and Hindu Traditions: A Comparative Study*, ed. Austin B. Creel and Vasudha Narayanan (Lewiston, N.Y.: Edwin Mellen Press, 1990), 139; for Confucianism, Peter Weber-Schäfer, "Die konfuzianischen Literaten und die Grundwerte des Konfuzianismus," in *Max Webers Studie über Konfuzianismus und Taoismus*, ed. Wolfgang Schluchter (Frankfurt: Suhrkamp, 1983), 213–14; for Islam, C. Cahen, "Arbeit: D. Islamische Welt," in *Lexikon des Mittelalters*, vol. 1, ed. Robert-Henri Bautier (Munich: Artemis, 1980), cols. 878–79; see also Vincent L. Wimbush and Richard Valantasis, eds., *Asceticism* (Oxford: Oxford University Press, 1995). This contrasts with the positive value of manual labor even for religious virtuosos in ancient and Rabbinic Judaism (but not Judaism during the Diaspora, which was influenced by Hellenistic culture). See Arthur T. Geoghegan, *The Attitude Towards Labor in Early Christianity and Ancient Culture* (Washington, D.C.: Catholic University of America Press, 1945), 58–89.

15. Their failure derives from the fact that each account limits its strategy of cultural analysis to the level of codified forms of textual discourse, either because these texts represent the main sources for a preliminary inquiry (Weber), are purposively chosen for their programmatic contents (Troeltsch), or are reflected in a very selective historical narrative that underlies the argument (Mumford, Collins). For further discussion, see my paper "A Sociological Analysis of Ascetic Monasticism and Work in Pre-Modern Europe," presented at the annual meeting of the Society for the Scientific Study of Religion, St. Louis, Missouri, 1995.

of monasticism in lay religious life, a pervasiveness of ritualism in monastic religion, and the corresponding delegation of work to affiliates.

Interaction Between Monastics and Laity

Interaction between monastics and laity was far more common than one might assume from the small number of people taking up the monastic life (perhaps no more than half a percent of the population) and the principled enclosure and self-sufficiency of the cloister.[16] "Throughout the early Middle Ages the monastics performed a wide variety of work that brought them into contact with the laity. They ran hospices and xenodochia [guesthouses] for travellers and pilgrims, cared for the sick, distributed food to the poor at the *porta* or gate of the monastery, educated the young and advised and assisted laypeople in many other ways."[17] The most important activities that put monastics in direct contact with laity were pastoral, activities that came into practice with the development of the parish system. Until the late eighth century, a parochial system in the modern sense of the word did not yet exist. The organization of the church was largely confined to urban dioceses. Monasteries furnished bishops and priests for these dioceses and, under the leadership of Irish and Anglo-Saxon monks, were foremost involved in the conversion of people in rural areas. Due to a shortage of secular clergy, many monks performed pastoral activities such as preaching, and those of them who were ordained as priests could celebrate the mass and absolve sins—rituals considered central to the salvation of a Christian. The Carolingians successfully initiated a movement for the establishment of a church and a priest in each village and hamlet, but their efforts to remove the monks from pastoral care and replace them with an educated clergy capable of inculcating the Franks with Christian beliefs did not stem the rise in monk-priests involved in pastoral care. This tendency of monastics to perform clerical duties lasted well into the eleventh century, when the Gregorian reform movement called for members of monastic communities to renounce these secular involvements.[18]

16. See Ludo Milis, *Angelic Monks and Earthly Men: Monasticism and Its Meaning to Medieval Society* (Rochester: Boydell Press, 1992), 33, 79. Arguing for a rather negligible impact of monastics on the world, Milis tends to overlook many of the substantive aspects of monastic involvement in lay affairs mentioned in this section.

17. Giles Constable, "Monasteries, Rural Churches, and the *cura animarum* in the Early Middle Ages," *Settimane di studio del Centro italiano di studi sull'alto medioevo* 28 (1982): 353.

18. Ibid., Pierre Riché, "La pastorale populaire en Occident, VIe–XIe siècles," in *Instruction et vie religieuse dans le Haut Moyen-Âge* (London: Variorum Reprints,

Secular involvement of monastics in pastoral activities coincided with the expansion of monastic liturgy. This development became particularly evident in the Cluniac movement to revive and restore Benedictine monastic life after the decline of the Carolingians and the plundering and pillaging of monasteries by the Vikings and Saracens. The Rule prescribed about three and one-half hours of prayer and recitation of psalms, but by the time Cluny and Gorze had become major models and propagators of monastic religious life in the tenth and eleventh centuries, the number of psalms to be recited had increased from 15 to 170, and almost the whole day was spent in the choir. The increasing celebration of private and commemorative masses further added to the liturgical demands on the monks. Even daily activities such as washing, dressing, and eating became ceremonialized.[19]

The Affinity Between Monastics and Nobility

The nuns' and monks' increasing preoccupation with ritual and ceremony, which had its apex in the Cluniacs, reflects monasticism's affinity with the upper, noble strata of society, for which it provided religious and secular services in return for material endowments and protection. Corresponding to the emerging imagery of a tripartite society in the tenth and eleventh centuries, the religious services by those who prayed and interceded on behalf of other members of the Christian community were greatly expanded. These services targeted the particular spiritual needs and status expectations of those who fought and ruled—the nobility: "In its propaganda, Cluny made use of the emerging idea of a

1981), chap. 23; George W. O. Addleshaw, *The Beginnings of the Parochial System*, 3d ed. (London: Ecclesiological Society, 1982); idem, *The Development of the Parochial System from Charlemagne (768–814) to Urban II (1088–1099)*, 2d ed. (York: St. Anthony's Press, 1970); Susan Reynolds, *Kingdoms and Communities in Western Europe, 900–1300* (Oxford: Clarendon Press, 1984), 81–90.

19. Philibert Schmitz, "La liturgie de Cluny," in *Spiritualità cluniacense*, ed. Centro di studi sulla spiritualita medievale (Todi: Presso l'Accademia tudertina, 1960), 83–99; Barbara H. Rosenwein, *Rhinoceros Bound: Cluny in the Tenth Century* (Philadelphia: University of Pennsylvania Press, 1982), 84–100; Barbara H. Rosenwein and Lester K. Little, "Social Meaning in the Monastic and Mendicant Spiritualities," *Past and Present* 63 (1974): 6–15; Lawrence, *Medieval Monasticism*, 113–15; Kassius Hallinger, "The Spiritual Life of Cluny in the Early Days," in *Cluniac Monasticism in the Central Middle Ages*, ed. Noreen Hunt (Hamden, Conn.: Archon Books, 1971), 44–46. In Lester K. Little's words, in its Cluniac forms early medieval monasticism became "all-pervasively liturgical," "formulaic," and "external" ("Romanesque Christianity in Germanic Europe," *Journal of Interdisciplinary History* 23 [1993]: 460, 461), but see also the circumspect remarks by Hallinger ("The Spiritual Life of Cluny," 46).

purgatory from which lost souls could be rescued, of the belief that knights who had died in sin could still be aided by the living, and that no one was in a better position to help them than the monks, who could bury their remains close by the cloister, mention their names in the obsequies, and serve ritual dinners on the anniversary of a benefactor's death when the community gathered to share with the defunct some out-of-the-ordinary dishes. The Cluniac order made intercession its most important function. It aspired to be an instrument of resurrection, a gateway to heaven. Accordingly, within the walls of its basilicas it laid on a splendid feast. That feast, those obsequies were the secret of its success."[20]

Besides spiritual legitimation and intercession, there were other reasons for the monastics' affinity with the nobility. Many nuns and monks came from noble families; the higher ranks of the Cluniac organization were populated by men of aristocratic origins. Monasteries were an appropriate outlet for members of noble families whose social and economic position was inconsistent with their elevated status in their communities. This was particularly the case for unmarried daughters and younger sons of noble families in places such as southern Burgundy, where by the eleventh century, with the gradual emergence of patrilineage and primogeniture among upper nobles, these daughters and sons lost their claim to a share of the patrimony. The endowment of a monastery in land—which the donors often perceived as a temporary family investment rather than a permanently alienated estate—would secure their temporal and eternal welfare, and noble patronage of a monastery continued to provide privileges and means of influence on the administration of monastic life even after the Gregorian reform movement and canon law curtailed lay proprietorship of cloisters.[21] In part, this was a utilitarian *do-ut-des* transaction within an economy dominated by gift and barter, a transaction by which secular wealth and status were traded for spiritual assistance in this life and what was to

20. Georges Duby, *The Three Orders: Feudal Society Imagined,* trans. Arthur Goldhammer (Chicago: University of Chicago Press, 1980), 176. That the notion of a tripartite division of society was not merely clerical imagery has been argued by Otto G. Oexle, "Le travail au XIe siècle: Réalités et mentalités," in *Le travail au Moyen Âge,* ed. Hamesse and Muraille–Samaran, 56–60.

21. Richard W. Southern, *Western Society and the Church in the Middle Ages* (Harmondsworth, Middlesex: Penguin Books, 1970), 223–30; Lawrence, *Medieval Monasticism,* 67–74, 124–35. Changes in kin organization and inheritance are discussed, for southern Burgundy, in Georges Duby, *La société aux XIe et XIIe siècles dans la région mâconnaise* (Paris: Colin, 1953); idem, *The Chivalrous Society,* trans. Cynthia Postan (Berkeley and Los Angeles: University of California Press, 1977), 74–75, 86–87; and, for other regions, in David Herlihy, *Medieval Households* (Cambridge: Harvard University Press, 1985), 79–98.

follow thereafter; in part, however, gift transactions and transfers, as newer historical studies have shown, also served to establish, affirm, and deepen lasting social commitments and moral bonds between donors, donees, mediating agents, and their surrounding communities, thereby integrating all of these parties into a network of relations and encompassing the realms of both the sacred and the profane.[22]

The Shift of Manual Duties to Monastic Affiliates

It comes as no surprise that ritual and ceremony left the nuns and monks with little time for manual labor. Compared to the dawn of the Middle Ages, the direct involvement of the monastics in work had declined dramatically by the eleventh century, though its normative valorization never eclipsed completely and was continually upheld throughout the Middle Ages. The degree to which monastics performed menial tasks can be inferred from monastic customaries. Customaries are compilations composed for the purpose of interpreting a monastic rule and adapting it to the situation of a particular monastic community, as well as reflecting on the actual monastic practices at the time; therefore, they are a much better indicator of actual monastic practices than the monastic rules. When the late-eleventh-century monk Ulrich compiled such a customary for Cluny, he included a short chapter on manual labor. All the monks did was sometimes to bake bread in the bakery or to shell beans in the garden and remove the weeds. Even

22. For the *do-ut-des* character of monastic transactions between donors and donees, see Georg Schreiber, *Gemeinschaften des Mittelalters* (Münster: Regensberg, 1948), 99–125, 151–93, and the valid, if perhaps too strong, objections to this explanation by Constance Brittain Bouchard, *Sword, Miter, and Cloister: Nobility and the Church in Burgundy, 980–1198* (Ithaca: Cornell University Press, 1987), 229–38. See also Ilana Friedrich Silber, "Gift-Giving in the Great Traditions: The Case of Donations to Monasteries in the Medieval West," *European Journal of Sociology* 36 (1995): 209–43, and eadem, *Virtuosity, Charisma, and Social Order: A Comparative Sociological Study of Monasticism in Theravada Buddhism and Medieval Catholicism* (Cambridge: Cambridge University Press, 1995), 137–73, for valuable depictions of gift giving to monasteries in its sociocultural and -political contexts. For the moral character and extensive social relationships entailed by noble donations, see Barbara H. Rosenwein, *To Be the Neighbor of Saint Peter: The Social Meaning of Cluny's Property, 909–1049* (Ithaca: Cornell University Press, 1989); Emily Zack Tabuteau, *Transfers of Property in Eleventh-Century Norman Law* (Chapel Hill: University of North Carolina Press, 1988); Stephen D. White, *Custom, Kinship, and Gifts to Saints: The "Laudatio Parentum" in Western France, 1050–1150* (Chapel Hill: University of North Carolina Press, 1988); and, in the context of monastic establishments for women, Penelope D. Johnson, *Equal in Monastic Profession: Religious Women in Medieval France* (Chicago: University of Chicago Press, 1991), 34–60.

these activities were accompanied by a formal procession that included the chant of psalms.[23]

To increase monastic productivity, attempts were also made to automatize the labor process. The abbot of a monastery at Loches constructed a watermill, by which "he lessened the work of the monks, so that only one brother was needed for this task," though it remains controversial how much such monastic constructions contributed to the spread of this important technology.[24] But the ever-increasing demands of liturgical services on the monastics called for a different overall solution than the technical ones Lewis Mumford credits with the advance of Western society, and recent historical scholarship provides little support for Mumford's argument.[25] Cluniac monasticism found such a solution in a system of affiliated personnel composed of *familia* and *conversi*.

The monastic *familia* designates a heterogeneous group of secular people affiliated with the cloister. To this group belonged the servants who helped with the daily routines inside and around the monastery, such as mending nuns' and monks' clothes or distributing alms to the poor. It also encompassed lords or free peasant tenants who leased monastic manors for rent in cash or kind, and serfs who worked the demesne (the part of an estate retained in monastic hands and exploited directly) and its affiliated outposts. Members of the *familia* were laypeople, which distinguished them from the *conversi*. In the eleventh century, the Cluniac *conversi* were lay-monks, those who had taken the monastic vows and wore a habit but had entered the monastic life as adults, remained illiterate, and were not ordained to a clerical order.

23. Ulrich of Cluny, *Consuetudines Cluniacenses*, chap. 30, "De opere manuum," in *Patrologiae cursus completus . . . Series Latina . . .* , ed. Jacques Paul Migne (Paris: J. P. Migne, 1844–64), vol. 149, cols. 675–77. See also Étienne Delaruelle, "Le travail dans les règles monastiques occidentales du quatrième au neuvième siècle," *Journal de psychologie normale et pathologique* 41 (1948): 51–62; Jacques Dubois, "Le travail des moines au Moyen Âge," in *Le travail au Moyen Âge*, ed. Hamesse and Muraille-Samaran, 61–100; on customaries, see Kassius Hallinger, "Consuetudo: Begriff, Formen, Forschungsgeschichte, Inhalt," in *Untersuchungen zu Kloster und Stift*, ed. Max-Planck-Institut für Geschichte (Göttingen: Vandenhoeck & Ruprecht, 1980), 140–66.

24. Gregory of Tours, *Life of the Fathers*, trans. Edward James (Liverpool: Liverpool University Press, 1986), 122; Marc Bloch, "The Advent and Triumph of the Watermill," in *Land and Work in Mediaeval Europe: Selected Papers*, trans. J. E. Anderson (New York: Harper & Row, 1969), 151–52; Frances Gies and Joseph Gies, *Cathedral, Forge, and Waterwheel* (New York: HarperCollins, 1994), 48; Dietrich Lohrmann, "Travail manuel et machines hydrauliques avant l'an mil," in *Le travail au Moyen Âge*, ed. Hamesse and Muraille-Samaran, 35–48.

25. See the pertinent remarks in George Ovitt Jr., "The Cultural Context of Western Technology: Early Christian Attitudes Toward Manual Labor," *Technology and Culture* 27 (1986): 477–500, and Milis, *Angelic Monks and Earthly Men*, 27–30.

They mostly helped the monks with the liturgy. For labor and usually a donation of land, they assured for themselves a close association with a way of life that promised the greatest soteriological assurance. In the twelfth century, the *conversi* were no longer monks but laybrothers occupied in quotidian duties, including manual labor. Unlike the lay-monks, who came from all social strata, the laybrothers originated mostly in the lower tiers of society. The lay-monks and -brothers, who could easily outnumber the ordained members of the monastic community, and the people belonging to the *familia*, were therefore a human buffer between cloister and world that served to perform the menial and labor-intensive duties inside and outside a monastery. The religious stratification by status in the monastic world, derived from how close these groups came to being monks proper—in descending order: lay-monk, laybrother, and monastic *familia* (especially those who were serfs)—therefore closely mirrored the stratification by wealth and power in the outside world.[26]

Insofar as the men and women belonging to the *familia*, being monasticism's most worldly members, intermingled with their communities, they were not subject to monastic stipulations of conduct, and there is little to suggest that their way of life differed from that of the people around them. The people around them, of course, were largely the peasantry, but peasant life did not lend itself easily to the adoption of methodical and systematic conduct. Weber suggested that this was due to the volatility of conditions in nature and the exigencies of agriculture, which made steady and systematic farming very difficult and over time translated into an economic traditionalism deeply ingrained into communities of agricultural laborers.[27] Peasant life in the entire

26. The seminal writings that inform the argument in this paragraph are Kassius Hallinger, "Woher kommen die Laienbrüder?" *Analecta Sacri Ordinis Cisterciensis* 12 (1956): 1–104, and Wolfgang Teske, "Laien, Laienmönche und Laienbrüder in der Abtei Cluny," *Frühmittelalterliche Studien* 10 (1976): 248–322; 11 (1977): 288–339. On the monastic *familia*, see further Heinrich Fichtenau, *Living in the Tenth Century: Mentalities and Social Orders*, trans. Patrick J. Geary (Chicago: University of Chicago Press, 1991), 121–27. Weber (*Economy and Society*, 1168, 1171) made a brief reference to laybrothers, whose function he saw as freeing the monks for spiritual duties in the development of the Cluniacs toward a seigneurial order (but see also the critical remarks in Hallinger, "Woher kommen die Laienbrüder?" 41–42, 43–48). For the similar role of "lay functionaries" in Buddhism, see Tambiah, *World Conqueror and World Renouncer*, 363. The historical literature on the *conversi* deals exclusively with men, since very little, if anything, is known about the existence of (female) *conversae*. For the (later) Cistercians, see note 41 below.

27. Weber, "The Social Psychology of the World Religions," in *From Max Weber*, 283; *Economy and Society*, 468; *The Protestant Ethic*, 59–60.

Middle Ages was indeed entirely different from the type of disciplined conduct necessitated by industrial capitalism. "On the whole, labor time was still the time of an economy dominated by agrarian rhythms, free of haste, careless of exactitude, unconcerned with productivity." Heavy work loads in harvest periods complemented extensive periods of leisure and discontinuous work schedules at other times—a characteristic of irregular labor patterns overcome only slowly and much later with the advent of the modern factory regime.[28]

With the increasing division of labor in Cluniac monastic communities, nuns and monks could concentrate on spiritual labor. The monastics' ability to rely on intermediaries between world and cloister shielded them from active involvement in the secular spheres and, contrary to the revisionist view, negated the potential for active world mastery commended in the Rule's prescription of labor that could be rationalized under a monastic time schedule. At the time of the Cluniacs, labor in the monastic setting amounted to copying manuscripts in the *scriptoria*; work in itself was regarded as a form of penance rather than a source of virtue, in spite of an increasingly positive, though not unambiguous, reevaluation of labor in the Carolingian period and the centuries thereafter.[29] By the eleventh century, monastic conduct was dominated by liturgical obligations and more concerned with assuring salvation in the afterlife than rationalizing and mastering the secular spheres. Western monasticism also became more male-dominated. Following a period of expansion and the flowering of new monastic foundations for women in the seventh century, the proportion of houses dedicated to women declined steadily until the end of the eleventh century. The first Cluniac cloister for women was not founded until about a century and a half after the foundation of Cluny itself. The secondary status of religious women in the church, who were kept in strict lifelong enclosure and with few exceptions thus entirely separate from the world, was a

---

28. Jacques Le Goff, *Time, Work, and Culture in the Middle Ages*, trans. Arthur Goldhammer (Chicago: University of Chicago Press, 1980), 44. See also Hans-Werner Goetz, *Life in the Middle Ages: From the Seventh to the Thirteenth Centuries*, trans. Albert Wimmer (Notre Dame, Ind.: University of Notre Dame Press, 1993), 12–16, 140–59; Werner Rösener, *Peasants in the Middle Ages*, trans. Alexander Stutzer (Urbana: University of Illinois Press, 1992), 122–43; Keith Thomas, "Work and Leisure in Pre-Industrial Society," *Past and Present* 29 (1964): 50–62; E. P. Thompson, "Time, Work-Discipline, and Industrial Capitalism," *Past and Present* 38 (1967): 56–97.

29. Le Goff, *Time, Work, and Culture in the Middle Ages*, 71–86; idem, "Arbeit. V.: Mittelalter," in *Theologische Realenzyklopädie* 3 (1978): 628–31; Fichtenau, *Living in the Tenth Century*, 278; Milis, *Angelic Monks and Earthly Men*, 94. On literary production in monastic *scriptoria*, see Riché, *Ecoles et enseignement dans le Haut Moyen Âge*, 137–61; Lerner, "Literacy and Learning," in *One Thousand Years*, ed. DeMolen, 189.

mirror of the gendered vision of women's roles and social position outside the cloister at the time.[30]

A rationalizing influence of monasticism on secular conduct could be found less in the economy and general society than, as has recently been argued, in the ethics and practices of secular politics and upper culture. Here the monastic ethic contributed to the systematization of conduct among noble warriors and the emergence of a civil code of chivalry. It may have helped more generally to bring about the pacification of conflict and the stabilization of political rule. But even if this was the case, this type of rationalization of conduct was confined to the nobility, and it was not ascetic.[31]

Developments in Monasticism in the Later Middle Ages

Social change was rapid in the eleventh and twelfth centuries, and it did not leave monasticism untouched. Magyar, Muslim, and Viking incursions that disturbed economic and religious life had come to an end by

---

30. Jane Tibbetts Schulenburg, "Women's Monastic Communities, 500–1100: Patterns of Expansion and Decline," in *Sisters and Workers in the Middle Ages*, ed. Judith M. Bennett, Elizabeth A. Clark, Jean F. O'Barr, B. Anne Vilen, and Sarah Westphal-Wihl (Chicago: University of Chicago Press, 1989), 208–39; eadem, "Strict Active Enclosure and Its Effects on the Female Monastic Experience (ca. 500–1100)," in *Medieval Religious Women*, vol. 1, ed. John A. Nichols and Lillian Thomas Shank (Kalamazoo, Mich.: Cistercian Publications, 1984), 51–86; Suzanne Fonay Wemple, *Women in Frankish Society: Marriage and the Cloister, 500 to 900* (Philadelphia: University of Pennsylvania Press, 1981), 149–74; Else M. Wischermann, *Marcigny-sur-Loire: Gründungs- und Frühgeschichte des ersten Cluniacenserinnenpriorates (1055–1150)* (Munich: Fink, 1986), 149–53; Joachim Wollasch, "Frauen in der Cluniacensis ecclesia," in *Doppelklöster und andere Formen der Symbiose männlicher und weiblicher Religiosen im Mittelalter*, ed. Kaspar Elm and Michel Parisse (Berlin: Duncker & Humblot, 1992), 97–113. Cf. Johnson, *Equal in Monastic Profession*, 150–63, who argues that the enclosure of religious women was less restrictive than depicted here.

31. For the argument of monastic contributions to the pacification of nobles, see Barbara H. Rosenwein, "Reformmönchtum und der Aufstieg Clunys," in *Max Webers Sicht des okzidentalen Christentums*, ed. Wolfgang Schluchter (Frankfurt: Suhrkamp, 1988), 289–97. Weber noted, however, that warrior nobles, and feudal powers generally, do not easily respond to ethical demands of a transcendental god and become carriers of a rational religious ethic. If they do, it is often because of religious legitimation of warring, as in the Crusades (*Economy and Society*, 472–76; cf. Alexander Murray, *Reason and Society in the Middle Ages*, rev. ed. [Oxford: Clarendon Press, 1985], 350–82, who posits reasons for a *positive* affinity between noble status and religious interest). This was indeed important here, as Rosenwein acknowledges ("Reformmönchtum und der Aufstieg Clunys," 295–96). Cf. Maurice Keen, *Chivalry* (New Haven: Yale University

about 1050. The population grew fast and steadily, approximately doubling between the first millennium and the mid-thirteenth century. This population growth was made possible by relatively mild and dry weather, the expansion of arable land, improvements of the plow and plowing methods, and the widespread adoption of the three-field system.[32]

The Cistercians

Against this backdrop of external political consolidation, demographic expansion, and agricultural improvements, important changes took place in monasticism. In the twelfth century, the Cistercians were at the forefront of monastic reforms, and they superseded the Benedictines in representing religious life's "most spectacular success" at the time.[33] The Cistercians' spiritual program echoed strong religious sentiments in larger society, stressing simplicity, poverty, manual labor, and charity, to be achieved by rejecting worldly entanglements and restoring a strict, literal adherence of the Rule of St. Benedict. The appeal of this spiritual program is attested by the growth of the Cistercians, who within one hundred and fifty years expanded from the two dozen monks of Robert of Molesme's "new monastery," founded in 1098 under the charismatic Bernard of Clairvaux and other capable leaders, to an organization with perhaps over twenty thousand members by the mid-thirteenth century.[34]

Historical scholarship has long recognized the Cistercians' economic achievements. They not only opened up uncultivated frontiers, converting rural hinterlands into flourishing farmlands, but also, as newer

Press, 1984), 44–63; André Vauchez, *The Spirituality of the Medieval West: From the Eight to the Twelfth Century*, trans. Colette Friedlander (Kalamazoo, Mich.: Cistercian Publications, 1993), 69–72.

32. These changes are discussed in Duby, *The Early Growth of the European Economy*, 112–54, 186–210; Robert Fossier, *Peasant Life in the Medieval West*, trans. Juliet Vale (Oxford: Blackwell, 1988), 8–15, 94–125; Marc Bloch, *Feudal Society*, vol. 1, trans. L. A. Manyon (Chicago: Chicago University Press, 1961), 3–56; and Carlo M. Cipolla, *Before the Industrial Revolution: European Society and Economy, 1000–1700*, 3d ed. (New York: Norton, 1993), 167–74.

33. Lester K. Little, *Religious Poverty and the Profit Economy in Medieval Europe* (Ithaca: Cornell University Press, 1978), 90. However, for a caveat that the decline or crisis of Benedictine monasticism should not be overinterpreted, see John Van Engen, "The 'Crisis of Cenobitism' Reconsidered: Benedictine Monasticism in the Years 1050–1150," *Speculum* 61 (1986): 269–304.

34. Louis J. Lekai, *The Cistercians: Ideals and Reality* (Kent, Ohio: Kent State University Press, 1977), 13–14, 44.

studies have shown for France, enhanced the agricultural productivity of already developed estates. Their success in transforming the rural economy was based on a frugal religious outlook and a distinct economic organization. At the onset the Cistercians displayed simplicity and austerity, reflected in a comparatively brief and modest liturgy, plain architecture, and the absence of ornaments in their churches. Intrinsic to Cistercian austerity was an emphasis on manual work; it was regarded as a proper activity for monks and nuns, to be performed with vehemence and regularity, and as the principal means for supporting a monastic community[35]—a stark contrast to the dominant practices in Benedictine monasticism at the time.[36]

This religious attitude was complemented by the rationalized economic organization of Cistercian monastic properties, based on the grange system. A grange is an estate composed of contiguous fields and farms obtained through a combination of gifts, leases, pawns, and purchases. Organized into a single unit for agricultural production, a grange allowed a much more methodical estate management than did the previously fragmented patches of land. It was exempt from ecclesiastical tithes and other agricultural taxes, and local markets in the countryside and, if available, urban settings provided a ready outlet for its agricultural and pastoral products.[37]

---

35. For the Cistercians' economic practices and their liturgy and art, see Lekai, *The Cistercians*, 248–323. Constance Brittain Bouchard, *Holy Entrepreneurs: Cistercians, Knights, and Economic Exchange in Twelfth-Century Burgundy* (Ithaca: Cornell University Press, 1991); Constance Hoffman Berman, *Medieval Agriculture, the Southern French Countryside, and the Early Cistercians* (Washington, D.C.: American Philosophical Society, 1986); and Georges Despy, "Les richesses de la terre: Cîteaux et Prémontré devant l'économie de profit aux XIIe et XIIIe siècles," in *Problèmes d'histoire du christianisme 5*, ed. Jean Préaux (Brussels: Éditions de l'Université de Bruxelles, 1974–75), 58–80, have criticized the frontier thesis and emphasized the French Cistercians' management of previously developed lands and their strong participation in the market economy. For the Cistercian's outlook on manual labor, see Dietrich Kurze, "Die Bedeutung der Arbeit im zisterziensischen Denken," in *Die Zisterzienser: Ordensleben zwischen Ideal und Wirklichkeit* (Cologne: Rheinland Verlag, 1980), 179–202; Christopher J. Holdsworth, "The Blessings of Work: The Cistercian View," in *Sanctity and Secularity: The Church and the World*, ed. Derek Baker (Oxford: Blackwell, 1973), 59–76 (in which the author overestimates the novelty of a theoretical valorization of manual labor in Cistercian writings).

36. A classic description of these contrasts can be found in Ordericus Vitalis, *The Ecclesiastical History of Orderic Vitalis*, vol. 4, trans. Marjorie Chibnall (Oxford: Clarendon Press, 1973), 319, 321.

37. Berman, *Medieval Agriculture*, 61–93; Lekai, *The Cistercians*, 295–98; Chrysogonus Waddell, "The Cistercian Institutions and Their Early Evolution: Granges, Economy, Lay Brothers," in *L'espace cistercien*, ed. Léon Pressouyre (Paris: Comité des travaux historiques et scientifiques, 1994), 27–38.

The combination of frugal methodical production with the restriction of consumption led to the accumulation of wealth. Having few outlets for expenditure beyond charity and subsistence, the Cistercians could rein- vest their wealth in the acquisition of monastic estates, and thus further the basis of their economic success. This has led some historians and the revisionists to conceive a similarity between early modern ascetic Protestantism and high-medieval Cistercian monasticism, in that "the [P]uritans of the monastic life incurred the penalty of [P]uritanism; they became rich because they renounced the glory of riches, and powerful because they invested wisely."[38] Cistercian economic success, in this view, was an unintended consequence of a spiritual outlook that sought abnegation of the world but paradoxically produced an embarrassment of riches by turning to the world in the process. Yet there was a basic difference in the ways in which Puritan wealth and Cistercian wealth were made possible. The Puritans were inner-worldly ascetics who saw diligence in their worldly vocations as their personal obligation. The Cistercian monks and nuns, in contrast, did not pursue secular professions; instead, they emulated a quasi-Cluniac model of delegating the most worldly tasks and menial duties to an army of assiduous helpers, the *conversi*.

The *conversi*, or laybrothers, were the modal force behind the Cistercian holy enterprise. They enjoyed a religious status similar to that of the laybrothers of the Cluniac monasteries, and paralleled their status as buffer between cloister and world. Cistercian monasteries, however, employed laybrothers more efficiently and in much higher numbers than the Cluniacs. Laybrothers outnumbered Cistercian monks by as much as three to one.[39] Since the monks were to reside in the cloister, the laybrothers assumed responsibility for managing the granges. As specified in an early collection of Cistercian statutes, dated to 1134, "the work at the granges must be done by laybrothers

38. Southern, *Western Society and the Church*, 260; Little, *Religious Poverty*, 93; E. Baeck, "De economische invloed van de cisterciënzerorde," *Economische-statistische Berichten* 76 (1991): 742–44. This view is echoed by Collins, "The Weberian Revolution," in *Weberian Sociological Theory*, 53–54, and Mumford, *The Myth of the Machine*, 263–72. See, however, the prudent remarks by Ilana Friedrich Silber, "Monasticism and the 'Protestant Ethic': Asceticism, Ideology, and Wealth in the Medieval West," *British Journal of Sociology* 44 (1993): 114–15, and Waddell, "The Cistercian Institutions and Their Early Evolution."

39. Michael Toepfer, *Die Konversen der Zisterzienser* (Berlin: Dunker & Humblot, 1983), 52–55; Richard Roehl, "Plan and Reality in a Medieval Monastic Economy: The Cistercians," in *Studies in Medieval Renaissance History IX*, ed. Howard L. Adelson (Lincoln: University of Nebraska Press, 1972), 89 n. 19; Lawrence, *Medieval Monasticism*, 178–79; Lekai, *The Cistercians*, 337–38.

and hired laborers,"[40] despite the principled affirmation of manual labor by the Cistercian monks. The laybrothers also performed important secular services for Cistercian nuns, who remained anything but welcome in the order and had little direct contact with the outside world, subject to the kind of strict enclosure characteristic of earlier Cluniac establishments.[41] The laybrothers who entered the Cistercian monastic communities came from a varied social background—some peasants or artisans, others burghers or knights. Hence, they were able to draw on a considerable pool of secular expertise in managing and working the granges. Simple peasants and artisans, together with hired farmhands, took over the more menial and servile tasks, while knights from the lower nobility took up the administration of estates, and burghers served as traders of monastic products and agents of their cloisters on markets and in other economic transactions. This division of labor gave the laybrothers a comparative advantage over monastic and secular competitors. Monastic competitors relied on the input of monks proper, who, having grown up in the cloister, had less knowledge of secular affairs, while secular economic rivals had to support families and were, as peasants dependent on their lords, perhaps less committed to achieving and maintaining high levels of economic productivity or, as knights and burghers, less content with frugal living or working arrangements.[42]

40. "De conversis: Per conversos agenda sunt exercitia apud grangias et per mercenarios." Printed in Berman, *Medieval Agriculture*, 6.

41. See chapter 15 of the *Exordium parvum*, a narrative of the Cistercian beginnings, translated by Bede K. Lackner, "Early Cisterican Documents in Translation," in Lekai, *The Cistercians*, 459–60: "And while they established granges for the practice of agriculture in a number of places, they decreed that the aforementioned laybrothers, and not the monks, should manage these houses, because according to the Rule the dwelling place of monks ought to be within their cloister." In Cistercian nunneries, laysisters helped with menial tasks inside the walls of the cloister, whereas laybrothers took over the work in its outer realms. See Toepfer, *Die Konversen der Zisterzienser*, 171–79; Maren Kuhn-Rehfus, "Zisterzienserinnen in Deutschland," in *Die Zisterzienser: Ordensleben zwischen Ideal und Wirklichkeit*, 132–33, 142. The Cistercians' reluctance to admit women into the order, and the enclosed life of the Cistercian nuns, is further discussed in Sally Thompson, "The Problem of the Cistercian Nuns in the Twelfth and Early Thirteenth Centuries," in *Medieval Women*, ed. Derek Baker (Oxford: Blackwell, 1978), 227–52, and Lekai, *The Cistercians*, 347–63.

42. For the class background and recruitment of the laybrothers, see Toepfer, *Die Konversen der Zisterzienser*, 182–83; Berman, *Medieval Agriculture*, 53–60; Bouchard, *Holy Entrepreneurs*, 165, 169; Lekai, *The Cistercians*, 339–40. Their activities and comparative advantage over other monastic and secular competitors are discussed in Berman, *Medieval Agriculture*, 78–82; Toepfer, *Die Konversen der Zisterzienser*, 180–89; Roehl, "Plan and Reality," 93.

The importance of the *conversi* for the order's prosperity is further illustrated by the fact that the decline of Cistercian monasticism in the thirteenth century coincided with its diminishing success in recruiting laybrothers. *Conversi* professed to celibacy and were not admitted as children; it was therefore imperative to replenish their ranks continuously from a pool of suitable adults. Many of those recruited among the peasantry had become *conversi* when the lands they were working were acquired by the Cistercians. In the second part of the thirteenth century, Cistercian land acquisition came to a halt, and the natural supply of peasants-turned-laybrothers from newly acquired lands ceased. The peasantry in general also had perhaps fewer material incentives to join, with serfdom disappearing, markets for agricultural products expanding, and cultivation methods improving by the late twelfth century. Burghers and knights, too, found other spiritual avenues. Knights, as decreed by the General Chapter, the supreme authority of the order, were to join as monks, not *conversi*, and the burgers of the cities were better served spiritually by the urban mendicant orders. In a highly aristocratic order, the system of religious and social apartheid, in which some did most or all of the manual work yet were relegated to secondary status and kept physically separate from the monks and nuns proper, became more salient. *Conversi* riots and revolts were not at all uncommon.[43]

Hence, by the thirteenth century the "new monastery" in some ways looked like the monastery of old. The potential of ascetic rationalization of secular spheres was greatly diminished. The order's original principles of austerity and simplicity had given way to more elaborate displays of status. From the beginning, it had relied in its quest for "sanctification through labor"[44] on laybrothers as an industrious workforce and buffer between the world and the cloister. As this arrangement was breaking down, Cistercian lands that were previously cultivated by the *conversi* and laborers were, in violation of the letter and spirit of the early Cistercian reform, leased and parceled out to tenants, and Cistercian estate organization changed from direct exploitation to a *rentier* landlordship. Agrarian enterprise was no longer carried predominantly on the shoulders of a motivated, ascetic labor force, but on those of a

43. On the decline of the conversi system and the aristocratization of the order, see Lekai, *The Cistercians*, 309–10, 40–42; Berman, *Medieval Agriculture*, 57; Toepfer, *Die Konversen der Zisterzienser*, 68–72; Lawrence, *Medieval Monasticism*, 197–202. For changes in the peasantry, see Duby, *The Early Growth of the European Economy*, 181–210.

44. Kurze, "Die Bedeutung der Arbeit," in *Die Zisterzienser: Ordensleben zwischen Ideal und Wirklichkeit*, 197.

rent-paying peasantry not otherwise linked to the Cistercian religious program.[45] Furthermore, in spite of the Cistercians' innovating role in rationalizing agriculture, their innovative methods of administration and cultivation pertained to the primary sector of the economy, and hence to rural settings. More momentous social, cultural, and economic change was underway elsewhere. The spiritual issues that arose in the wake of this development came to be addressed by a radically different type of religious elite in the mendicant orders, which ascended to prominence in the thirteenth century.[46]

The Mendicants

The rise of the mendicants occurred in the context of an expanding commercial economy, the rise of the cities, a newly found individualism, and increasing levels of lay literacy. All of these factors were important in bringing about new forms of spirituality, to which the mendicants responded. During the steady and rapid expansion of industry and commerce known as the "commercial revolution" of the twelfth century a "profit economy" emerged. Goods were produced and traded for money, which as a widely available exchange medium supplanted previous modes of economic interaction such as gift exchange or barter. By 1150, money had begun to penetrate economic life thoroughly, even in the countryside. Hence, opportunities for social mobility by mastery of markets through calculation and industry increased greatly.[47]

Concomitant to economic growth and monetarization were the revitalization of cities and a new constitution of citizenship. The city that emerged in the twelfth century was more than a territorial space fortified by walls. Politically, it was pacified and independent from feudal lordship. Economically, it was a center of industrial production and had a market for exchange. Culturally, it lodged subjects whose self-concept differed from that of peasants or nobles: the burghers. Burghers were free citizens: they associated with one another through a bond of

45. See particularly Roehl, "Plan and Reality," 95–113; Wolfgang Ribbe, "Die Wirtschaftstätigkeit der Zisterzienser im Mittelalter: Agrarwirtschaft," in *Die Zisterzienser: Ordensleben zwischen Ideal und Wirklichkeit*, 203–15.

46. This point is stressed in Little, *Religious Poverty*, 96, and Raoul Manselli, "Appunti sul lavoro dai Cistercensi agli Umiliati," in *I Cistercensi e il Lazio*, ed. Istituto Nazionale d'Archeologia e Storia dell'Arte (Roma: Multigrafica, 1978), 145–47.

47. See Robert S. Lopez, *The Commercial Revolution of the Middle Ages, 950–1350* (Englewood Cliffs, N.J.: Prentice Hall, 1971); Little, *Religious Poverty*; Peter Spufford, *Money and Its Use in Medieval Europe* (Cambridge: Cambridge University Press, 1988), 109–263; Murray, *Reason and Society*, 50–58, 81–109.

mutual rights and responsibilities. They were apt to take advantage of the structural opportunities in the new markets, and increasingly organized their economic life in specialized craft and merchant guilds for the production and distribution of commodities.[48]

The notion of the citizen as political and economic subject emerged parallel to novel notions of the individual in theology and philosophy. The metaphor of the "awakening of the conscience in medieval civilization" in the twelfth century denotes a (re)discovery of the individual in a subjectivist turn in ethics, most notably in the writings of Peter Abelard, which began causally to relate moral wrongs to intentions of individuals, to develop new notions of conscience and inner self, and more deeply to reflect on the individual as a social and spiritual entity. Increasingly subjected to interpretation and contextualization, ecclesiastical and philosophical traditions lost some of their guiding role. The status of the individual as an ethical and intellectual being increased.[49]

Increasing levels of lay literacy accompanied the previous developments. The clergy lost their monopoly on literary instruction, and a significant proportion of students was no longer destined for a clerical life. Cathedral schools and collegiate church schools found their homes in towns, and urban commercial transactions, especially in the centers of northern Italy, were increasingly based on written records and demanded literate agents and scribes. In the thirteenth century, such skills were taught in universities and primary schools, clerical and lay, the latter of which began teaching reading and writing in the vernaculars. This secularization of learning signified the ascendance of practical literacy, governed by utilitarian demands and considerations, particularly those of secular business.[50]

These economic, political, intellectual, and sociocultural trends had major implications for religious life. An economically differentiated, increasingly literate, and politically conscious urban populace, which could be sharply critical of ecclesiastical shortcomings, faced novel ethical

48. See Reynolds, *Kingdoms and Communities*, 155–218; Edith Ennen, *The Medieval Town*, trans. Natalie Fryde (Amsterdam: North-Holland, 1979), 63–136; Goetz, *Life in the Middle Ages*, 201–39.

49. M.-D. Chenu, *L'éveil de la conscience dans la civilisation médiévale* (Montreal: Institut d'études médiévales, 1969); Colin Morris, *The Discovery of the Individual, 1050–1200* (New York: Harper & Row, 1972); John F. Benton, "Consciousness of Self and Perceptions of Individuality," in *Renaissance and Renewal in the Twelfth Century*, ed. Robert L. Benson and Giles Constable (Cambridge: Harvard University Press, 1982), 263–95.

50. See particularly Lerner, "Literacy and Learning," in *One Thousand Years*, ed. DeMolen, 194–227; M. T. Clanchy, *From Memory to Written Record: England, 1066–1307*, 2d ed. (Oxford: Blackwell, 1993), 328–34; Graff, *Legacies of Literacy*, 53–74.

questions and concerns that have long been associated with rapid change driven by money and markets and their impersonalizing effects on social relations,[51] and the church, both in its teachings and in its personnel, was at first ill equipped to respond. The clerical views of the three estates in society, composed of those who prayed (ecclesiastics), those who fought (nobles), and those who worked (peasants), were sorely outdated by the emergence of commercially active urban citizens. What was their proper place and function in the social hierarchy? From a religious point of view, moreover, commercial dealings constituted an ethical problem. "The merchant hardly or never is able to please God," decreed the *Concordance of Discordant Canons*, which the Bolognese monk Gratian assembled in about 1140 as the first comprehensive and systematic legal treatise in the West. The moral dangers of involvement in business were linked to ecclesiastical reservations about the potential vices of city life as such.[52] Furthermore, pastoral care of town dwellers was perhaps an even bigger problem. Modes of piety in urban settings were not addressed well by the existing parochial structure. "The diocesan and parochial structure of the Church had developed to serve the needs of a rurally based population. Its clergy, apart from an educated elite which was absorbed by the schools and the ecclesiastical bureaucracy, were largely recruited locally from the ranks of the free peasantry, and educationally most of them were only a little above the level of their rustic parishioners. The numerous churches that were to be found in many medieval towns were generally appropriated to monasteries or collegiate bodies and were too poorly endowed to attract the services of educated clerks."[53]

The Franciscan and Dominican mendicants responded to this predicament by radically breaking with received monastic traditions.

51. "Curiously enough," Georg Simmel remarked wryly, "money, although or rather because it is the most sublimated economic value, may release us from economic bondage—though only, it is true, at the price of confronting us with that relentless question of those activities whose meaning does not lie in economic success" (*The Philosophy of Money* [1902], trans. Tom Bottomore and David Frisby, 2d ed. [London: Routledge, 1990], 311). Similar views can be found, of course, in the writings of Marx, Weber, and Durkheim.

52. Emil Friedberg, ed., *Corpus Iuris Canonici* (1879; reprint, Graz: Akademische Druck- und Verlagsanstalt, 1955), Ia pars, dist. LXXXVIII, c. XI: "homo mercator vix aut numquam potest Deo placere." See also Harold J. Berman, *Law and Revolution: The Formation of the Western Legal Tradition* (Cambridge: Harvard University Press, 1983), 143–48; John T. Gilchrist, *The Church and Economic Activity in the Middle Ages* (London: Macmillan, 1969), 53–58; Aron Gurevich, "The Merchant," in *Medieval Callings*, ed. Jacques Le Goff, trans. Lydia G. Cochrane (Chicago: University of Chicago Press, 1990), 243–83; Little, *Religious Poverty*, 29–41.

53. Lawrence, *Medieval Monasticism*, 240.

The mendicants did not question the contemplative life as the ultimate form of Christian perfection, and prayer as the pivotal means to achieve it. But they were the first large-scale ascetic associations governed by ecclesiastical rules whose explicit raison d'être and purpose of training were preaching to the populace. As popular preachers admonishing the laity to repent and to seek inner conversion, they left the seclusion of the cloister for the busy streets of the city, voluntarily renouncing all forms of property, be it personal, as their monastic predecessors had done, or corporate. Instead of collective stability and withdrawal from society they chose individual mobility and participation in secular affairs.[54]

With this turn monastic spirituality opened itself to the world. The mendicants rejected the legacy of world flight in monasticism that had begun to break down in some rural French Cistercian establishments, and recentered the meaning of asceticism on notions of strict poverty and active ministry. The attraction of the mendicants was extraordinary: in the first one hundred years, they grew from a few men around Saint Francis and Saint Dominic to a total of about twenty-eight thousand Franciscans and about twelve thousand Dominicans.[55] Rapid organizational growth, however, brought about significant changes in mendicant spirituality, in which some of their early ideals were compromised or completely abandoned. This was particularly evident for the Franciscan views on manual labor, learning, and the use of money.

The first friars who joined Saint Francis shared his ideal of imitating a simple, austere life like the apostles. Much like other religious charismatics at the time, Francis denounced the vanities of the world, which in his case meant the comfortable lifestyle of a wealthy merchant's son, for the transient existence of an itinerant preacher. Money was not even to be touched, and academic studies were not encouraged. The early Franciscans were assumed to support themselves by working and begging. Toward the end of his life (c. 1226), Francis wrote in his Testament: "I worked with my hands, and continue to

54. For pertinent accounts of mendicant spirituality and their embeddedness in urban culture, see Little, *Religious Poverty*, 146–69; Southern, *Western Society and the Church*, 272–99; Lawrence, *Medieval Monasticism*, 238–73; Rosalind B. Brooke, *The Coming of the Friars* (London: Allen & Unwin, 1975).

55. Southern, *Western Society and the Church*, 285. These numbers should, of course, be taken with a grain of salt. See also William A. Hinnebusch, *The History of the Dominican Order* (Staten Island, N.Y.: Alba House, 1966), 1:331, who has estimated their number at about twenty thousand around 1300, and John Moorman, *The History of the Franciscan Order* (Oxford: Clarendon Press, 1968), 351, who arrives at a number of about twenty-five thousand Franciscans around 1340.

work like this, and urge all other friars to engage in honest work. Those who do not know how to work must learn to do so. They must not work hoping to be paid for their work but as a good example and to expel idleness."[56] These views are echoed in the *Regula bullata*, an outline of religious life devised by Francis that was approved as the definitive rule of the order by Pope Honorius III in 1223: "Let the friars to whom the Lord has given the grace to work do so faithfully and devoutly. They should work so that they expel idleness, the enemy of the soul, but do not extinguish the spirit of holy prayer and devotion."[57]

In what is clearly a tribute to the Rule of St. Benedict, the virtue of manual labor is extolled as a means to distract those who are called to do work from the temptations of slothfulness. An earlier and lengthier version, the *Regula non bullata*, written by Francis in 1221 for the sprawling Franciscan movement, the earliest extant rule of the order (the original rule of 1210, written by Francis for his fellow men around Assisi, is lost), was more specific regarding the secular calling of the brothers: "Let the brothers who know how to work practice their former trade if it is not harmful to the soul's salvation and if it is convenient to do so. For the Psalmist says, 'Thou shalt eat the labors of thy hands: blessed art thou, and it shall be well with thee' (Ps. 128:2). And the apostle Paul writes, 'If any man will not work, neither let him eat' (2 Thess. 3:10). And let each keep to the employment or trade to which he was called (see 1 Cor. 7:24)."[58]

That these admonitions to rely on artisanal and handicraft work for sustenance were actually heeded by the friars is confirmed in contemporary commentary. Francis and his early companions worked in leper houses and at lesser jobs, and it is reported that Francis sent away one of them who did not work and pray sufficiently.[59] Jacques de Vitry, one of the most astute observers of religious life at the time, commented in 1216 that in Italy people called Lesser Brothers and Lesser Sisters, well liked by the pope and the cardinals, "care not at all for temporal things, but work fervently and with vehemence to draw imperiled souls away from the vanities of the world," and that the women in particular

---

56. Halycon Backhouse, ed., *The Writings of St. Francis of Assisi* (London: Hodder & Stoughton, 1994), 59. For the following, see also the detailed analysis in Kajetan Esser, "Die Handarbeit in der Frühgeschichte des Minderbrüderordens," *Franziskanische Studien* 40 (1958): 146–66, which contains the passages from the rules and Francis's testament in Latin.

57. Backhouse, *Writings of St. Francis*, 45.

58. Ibid., 26.

59. See Esser, "Handarbeit," 163.

"live together near cities in various houses; they accept nothing, but live from the labor of their hands."[60]

Less than forty years later the Franciscans' commitment to manual labor had changed, together with their views on the futility of learnedness and absolute avoidance of money. In 1259 Saint Bonaventure, then minister general of the Friars Minor, interpreted in his *Commentary on the Rule of the Brothers Minor* the passages on work (in the Regula bullata quoted above) in a vein very different from the interpretation of the founder of the order: "The most laudable way to acquire those things necessary to the body is to keep up the labors of preaching and doctrine. . . . The labor of wisdom [i.e., study] is simply better than manual labor, even though in some cases salaried work might be necessary for the [friar] preacher. The Lord, therefore, choosing what is simply better for the preacher, did not work for money lest learned people [in the church] who did not work be criticized [for not working] or be impeded by such work from studying the word of God."[61]

In practice this meant that manual labor was abandoned. The trend toward emphasizing study rather than manual toil is attributable not solely to Bonaventure's personal predilection but also to some general changes both within and outside the order. In its beginning, the order, which proved very valuable to the papacy for its obedience to the church and its decided opposition to the various shades of heterodox religious movements, had only a rudimentary organization. It attracted people from a broad social spectrum that reflected the friars' ubiquitous religious appeal. These people had little, if any, concern for secular affairs and institutional matters and no distinction between friars who

60. R.B.C. Huygens, ed., *Lettres de Jacques de Vitry* (Leiden: Brill, 1960), 75–76: "A domno papa et cardinalibus in magna reverentia habentur, hii [Fratres Minores et Sorores Minores] autem circa temporalia nullatenus occupantur, sed ferventi desiderio et vehementi studio singulis diebus laborant ut animas que pereunt a seculi vanitatibus retrahant et eas secum ducant. . . . Mulieres vero iuxta civitates in diversis hospitiis simul commorantur; nichil accipiunt, sed *de labore manuum <suarum>* vivunt." For other accounts, see Esser, "Handarbeit," 158–65.

61. Saint Bonaventure, *Doctoris seraphici S. Bonaventurae . . . Opera Omnia*, vol. 8 (Ad Claras Aquas [Quaracchi]: Ex Typographia Collegii S. Bonaventurae, 1888), 420: "Modus autem laudabilissimus corpori necessaria acquirendi est in praedicationis et doctrinae laboribus exerceri. . . . [L]abor sapientiae simpliciter melior est corporeo labore, quamvis in casu possit labor stipendarius esse necessarius praedicanti. Dominus igitur quod simpliciter est praedicanti melius eligens, non laboravit stipendiarie, ne doctores non laborantes arguerentur, vel labore tali impedirentur a studio verbi Dei." See also the similar views expressed in idem, *The Works of Banaventure*, vol. 4, *The Defense of the Mendicants*, trans. José de Vinck (Paterson, N.J.: St. Anthony Guild Press, 1966), 265–70. On this, see also Moorman, *History of the Franciscan Order*, 142–43, 152–53.

were laity and those who were clerics was made. Over time it became evident, however, that growth in numbers and the inevitable routinization of charisma necessitated changes in the order's structure and some of its defining spiritual characteristics. The precarious existence of itinerant beggars and laborers was difficult to reconcile with the need for some institutional and economic stability. It became necessary to impose organizational structures onto the order and to regulate the avenues of admission and advancement, as well as to adopt a less unworldly stance toward money. Furthermore, a great number of priests joined the order, and heresy continued to be viewed as a primary threat. The rustic views of Francis on learning and the unresolved relation of the friars-priests to the secular clergy were at odds with the view shared by many clerics and more-learned members of the order that active ministry required a trained, professional apostolate and a clear definition of their rights and duties vis-à-vis the parish priests.

The resolution of these issues and problems is reflected in the passages quoted from Saint Bonaventure above. "Poverty began to give place to security, simplicity to learning, and humility to privilege," as one historian noted. By about the mid-thirteenth century, the Friars Minor were a highly clericalized and learned institution, steeped in university life. Earlier notions of absolute poverty gave way to the permission for corporate use, if not ownership, of property, and full control over it. The Friars Minor received ample material support by means of alms, papal indulgences for contributions toward the building of convents, estates from benefactors, and so-called Letters of Fraternity, in which donors conveyed money to third-party administrators for the privilege of being prayed for by the friars.[62]

---

62. The issues and processes treated in this and the previous paragraphs are addressed in Moorman, *Origins of the Franciscan Order*, 46–154 (the quote is from 94); Rosalind B. Brooke, *Early Franciscan Government: Elias to Bonaventure* (Cambridge: Cambridge University Press, 1959). Herbert Grundmann, *Religiöse Bewegungen im Mittelalter*, 2d ed. (Hildesheim: Olms, 1961), 164–67; Kajetan Esser, *Origins of the Franciscan Order*, trans. Aedan Daly and Irina Lynch (Chicago: Franciscan Herald Press, 1970), 32–37; and C. H. Lawrence, *The Friars: The Impact of the Early Mendicant Movement on Western Europe* (London: Longman, 1994), 34–35, explore the social origins of the early Franciscans. Later developments are discussed in John B. Freed, *The Friars and German Society in the Thirteenth Century* (Cambridge: Mediaeval Academy of America, 1977), 109–34, and Daniel R. Lesnick, *Preaching in Medieval Florence: The Social World of Franciscan and Dominican Spirituality* (Athens: University of Georgia Press, 1989), 46–49. On the issue of changing notions of Franciscan poverty, see Malcolm D. Lambert, *Franciscan Poverty* (London: S.P.C.K, 1961); and for the ways in which the imagery of Saint Francis was constructed in later hagiography and artistic depictions so as to portray his life and teachings as compatible

The other major mendicant order, the Dominicans, did not experience the same organizational dilemmas and shifts in spiritual orientation or emphasis. From the beginning it was conceived to be a priestly order devoted to preaching. The meaning and extent of poverty, while important, was not as contested as among the Franciscans, and intellectual training was considered paramount for an active apostolate. For the professional pastors and preachers who stood at the forefront of the defense of the church as inquisitors and who attended to the spiritual needs of the laity, a solid foundation in theology and the art of preaching was essential. Since the nature of the order was clerical and its orientation priestly, there was no place for work. In the daily routine, manual toil and meditative reading, two of the pillars of the Rule of St. Benedict, gave way to a brief liturgy and the occupations of preaching, studying, and teaching. In both orders, therefore, asceticism was channeled toward the methodical training of the intellect and the endurance of corporeal and social renunciations such as chastity and penury, but not toward active pursuit of worldly activities in a secular profession.[63]

The friars' principal stance toward commercial transactions was that of personal abstention, which does not mean that they were hostile to the world of markets and trade. Exegeses of their sermons addressing the new commercial classes of northern Italy's mercantile centers in the late thirteenth century have shown their moral support of mercantile transactions and other urban activities in a carefully circumscribed form. Impregnating their theological discourse with an imagery of market activities, the friars struck a precarious balance between justifying economic advancement and exhorting morally responsible and conscientious market behaviors. As they gradually became more understanding of and perhaps even sympathetic to the commercial world of enterprise and calculation, they found sophisticated ways to sidestep established hallmarks of the church's economic teachings, such as the prohibition of usury and notions of fair price, while promoting individual acquisitiveness with far fewer moral strings attached than previously considered necessary. Yet whether this amounted to an elaboration of a mercantile protocapitalist ideology, as has recently been argued, remains doubtful. Not only was this ideology still a far cry from the later, ascetic

with the direction the order had taken, see William R. Cook, "Fraternal and Lay Images of St. Francis in the Thirteenth Century," in *Popes, Teachers, and Canon Law in the Middle Ages*, ed. James R. Sweeney and Stanley Chodorow (Ithaca: Cornell University Press, 1989), 263–89.

63. See Hinnebusch, *History of the Dominican Order*, especially 46–47, 121, 147 (manual labor), 145–68 (poverty), 347–53 (liturgy).

Protestant attribution of immediate soteriological significance to personal success and diligence in economic behavior, but it also was only one part in a considerably larger repertoire of imageries available to, and used in, mendicant preaching. Given the friars' predilection for wide use of such imageries, it is not surprising to find that they employed different, less commercial imagery in other circumstances. Hence, both content and form of delivery appear to have varied widely with the context. This is evident in sermons addressed to a more diverse spectrum of audiences and social settings, which are fairly mute on economic life. Furthermore, even the emergence of a new hagiographic type, the "merchant saint," should not be taken as an unequivocal exaltation of secular means of sanctification. Frequently the sanctification of individuals was perceived to have commenced only after they cast their earthly commerce aside and graduated to the heights of the contemplative life, committing themselves to the traditional form of seeking salvation.[64]

64. "As long as the profits were used for the benefit of the poor, even the profession of the merchant did not seem to be incompatible with the search for Christian perfection. . . . But it is worth noting that, in many of these *Vitae* [Saints' Lives], when the religious experience of the saint becomes richer and more intense, his earthly work is no longer mentioned, either because he actually abandoned it or because the weight of hagiographic conventions led the biographer to remain silent about these temporal activities in order to display more prominently his hero's progress in spiritual life" (André Vauchez, *The Laity in the Middle Ages: Religious Beliefs and Devotional Practices*, trans. Margery J. Schneider [Notre Dame, Ind.: University of Notre Dame Press, 1994], 65). On this, see also Diana M. Webb, "A Saint and His Money: Perceptions of Urban Wealth in the Lives of Italian Saints," in *The Church and Wealth*, ed. W. J. Sheils and Diana Wood (Oxford: Blackwell, 1987), 61–73. The strongest argument for the friars as capitalist ideologues is made by Lesnick, *Preaching in Medieval Florence*, and, in more cautious way, by Little, *Religious Poverty*, 197–217. Cf. Rosenwein and Little, "Social Meaning in the Monastic and Mendicant Spiritualities," 20–32. These views are to be seen in the light of the pertinent remarks by D. L. D'Avray, *The Preaching of the Friars: Sermons Diffused from Paris Before 1300* (Oxford: Clarendon Press, 1985), 204–59; Jennifer Fisk Rondeau, "Lay Piety and Spirituality in the Late Middle Ages: The Confraternities of North-Central Italy, ca. 1250 to 1348" (Ph.D. diss., Cornell University, 1988), 304–8; Bernadette Paton, *Preaching Friars and the Civic Ethos: Siena, 1380–1480* (London: Centre for Medieval Studies, 1992), chap. 5; and Michel Zink, *La prédication en langue romane avant 1300* (Paris: Champion, 1976), 413–28, even though the latter focuses on premendicant preaching. For changes in moral theology with regard to economic activities, see Raymond de Roover, "The Scholastic Attitude Toward Trade and Entrepreneurship," in *Business, Banking, and Economic Thought in Late Medieval and Early Modern Europe: Selected Studies of Raymond de Roover*, ed. Julius Kirshner (Chicago: University of Chicago Press, 1974), 336–45; John W. Baldwin, *Masters, Princes, and Merchants: The Social Views of Peter the Chanter and His Circle*, 2 vols. (Princeton: Princeton University Press, 1970), 1:261–311. Since the remarks in this paragraph pertain to mendicant and, more

The previous remarks pertain to the main body, or first order, of the Franciscans and Dominicans, composed of men living under the rule approved for them by the papacy. Members of the Dominican first order were from the beginning almost exclusively clerics ordained as priests, not laity, although their ranks included a small number of laybrothers. The laybrothers' primary functions were begging, keeping the priories in running order, and tending to other everyday needs, and they received some instruction in manual skills.[65] The Franciscans, who initially comprised both laity and clerics, became predominantly clerical as well, because it soon became difficult for laity to join them. Yet for women ready to take up the religious life, or interested laity who were not willing or able to leave their families, vocations, and possessions behind, other means to take part in the mendicants' religious program were found.

Dominic established a cloister for women at Prouille in 1206, some nine years before the first religious community of the order for men was founded, as an imitation of Cathar houses of *perfectae*, with the purpose of winning over converts from them. Unlike Francis, who remained reserved toward the idea of women affiliating with his order, Dominic appears to have been open to women's wishes to join the religious life. The establishment of other monasteries for Dominican nuns followed, and their number increased to 141 convents for nuns by 1303, in spite of a quota system put in place to regulate demand. Franciscan convents, inspired by the saintly example of Clare of Assisi, proliferated as well.

---

generally, ecclesiastical views on capitalist activities in the High Middle Ages, the issue is not whether and to what extent *secular* protocapitalist ideologies existed in the Middle Ages. The debate on that issue, going back to the dispute between Weber and Sombart (see Chapter 1, pages 14–15, 47), continues, but much of this debate in the sociological literature is marred by an overly simplistic presentation of Weber's views or a failure to come to grips with the primary and secondary sources. See, e.g., Jere Cohen, "Rational Capitalism in Renaissance Italy," *American Journal of Sociology* 85 (1980): 1340–55; Luciano Pellicani, "Weber and the Myth of Calvinism," *Telos* 75 (1988): 57–85; and the responses by R. J. Holton, "Max Weber, 'Rational Capitalism,' and Renaissance Italy: A Critique of Cohen," *American Journal of Sociology* 89 (1983): 166–80; and Guy Oakes, "Farewell to *The Protestant Ethic*?" *Telos* 78 (1988–89): 81–94. For an affirmative view of the existence of a protocapitalist ideology and supportive institutional structures that is critical of both Weber and Sombart, see the magisterial study by Oscar Nuccio, *Il pensiero economico italiano, 1: Le fonti (1050–1450): L'etica laica e la formazione dello spirito economico*, 3 vols. (Sassari: Edizioni Gallizi, 1984–87). On England, see Christopher Dyer, "Were There Any Capitalists in Fifteenth-Century England?" in *Enterprise and Individuals in Fifteenth-Century England*, ed. Jennifer Kermode (Wolfeboro Falls, N.H.: Alan Sutton, 1991), 1–24, for a commentary on the existing literature and further analysis.

65. For the Dominican laybrothers, see Philip F. Mulhern, *The Early Dominican Laybrother* (Washington, D.C.: n.p., 1944), and Hinnebusch, *History of the Dominican Order*, 125, 288–90.

Yet the nuns lived a religious life quite different from that of the friars. Most important, they continued the monastic tradition of strict enclosure for women. In principle never allowed to leave the monastery (except under rare and well-specified circumstances), they were by this stipulation prevented from preaching and begging, and in the absence of a need for training in the former, no provisions were made for organized study. Certain medical and service personnel as well as royalty, higher clergy, and patrons of the cloister were on occasion allowed to enter into the enclosed part of the cloister, but other than that the nuns had little personal contact with the outside world. Theirs was a secluded life of simplicity and contemplative devotion, in some places utterly austere, in others made comfortable with the ample service of servants and lay-sisters. Removed from secular attachments, the nuns had no opportunity to minister to urban audiences and provide visible proof of religious ascetics remaining in the world. Furthermore, since the nuns were placed under the formal supervision and guidance of Dominican and Franciscan confessors and preachers, members of mendicant first orders quickly came to resent what they perceived to be services that distracted them from the primary purpose, preaching and studying. It required considerable pressure from the papacy to ensure that communities of women were properly integrated into the mendicant orders, if only in thoroughly regulated and well-defined terms. The restrictions on women's access to the apostolic life and on the ways in which they were allowed to live it had important repercussions for the ascetic life of women. "On the one hand, relatively large groups in the movement of religious women were not included in these forms of organization [the mendicant orders], but had to continue to find their own ways and remained exposed to the temptation of heresy . . . ; on the other hand, [many] religious communities of women organized under the auspices of the church found no full satisfaction for their spiritual needs in the life in orders and were thereby directed toward the 'inner journey to the self' [Weg nach innen]."[66]-Precluded from active asceticism in the world, Franciscan and Dominican nuns contributed greatly to the mystical and devotional literature in the later Middle Ages.[67]

66. Grundmann, *Religiöse Bewegungen im Mittelalter*, 312. See Susan Groag Bell, "Medieval Women Book Owners," in *Women and Power in the Middle Ages*, ed. Mary Erler and Maryanne Kowaleski (Athens: University of Georgia Press, 1988), 160, for a similar assessment.

67. Grundmann, *Religiöse Bewegungen im Mittelalter*, 208–318, remains the seminal account of this topic. See also Brenda M. Bolton, "Mulieres Sanctae," in *Sanctity and Secularity*, ed. Baker, 77–85; Kaspar Elm, "Die Stellung der Frau im Ordenswesen, Semireligiosentum und Häresie zur Zeit der heiligen Elisabeth," in *Sankt Elisabeth:*

Whereas for professed nuns the mendicants only offered a way out of this world and into the confinement of cloistered walls, they offered an opposite form of life to interested laity in their Third Orders. The Third Orders obfuscated the boundaries between the religious life and the secular life in several ways, drawing a fine line between living in the world (which was encouraged) and being of it (which, of course, was not). Third Orders of the Franciscans and Dominicans were associations of laymen or -women who remained in their own homes, continuing in their vocations and family life, but bound themselves permanently to a penitential life. The idea of living a life of penance while remaining in the world was not a new one. It went back many centuries, the institution of *conversi* in traditional monasticism being one of its derivatives, but around the beginning of the twelfth century there was a definite change in its appeal and the way it was organized. Growing significantly in number, penitents formed larger associations of laity retaining their worldly bonds. While some of these confraternal associations steered clear of any institutional ties and almost constituted a parish within a parish, others became affiliated with established clerical, monastic, or heterodox groups, or developed out of these. The Benedictines and Premonstratensians had such associations with laity, but the ultimate predecessor of the mendicant tertiaries, as members of the Third Orders were called, was the Humiliati, who populated the urban centers of northern Italy.[68] By the time the friars arrived on the scene, a diversity of confraternities of laypeople existed, some of whom eventually entered into a formal relationship with the mendicant orders, while others constituted parish confraternities or guilds, which were independent of ecclesiastical influences and put more emphasis than the Third Orders on economic and social concerns. Common to all these groups was their voluntary association for secular and religious purposes, and the constraint of their members by certain standards of

---

Fürstin, Dienerin, Heilige, ed. Philipps-Universität Marburg (Sigmaringen: Thorbecke, 1981), 11–13; Patricia Ranft, *Women and the Religious Life in Premodern Europe* (New York: St. Martin's Press, 1996), chap. 6; Hinnebusch, *History of the Dominican Order,* 96–104, 377–400; Moorman, *History of the Franciscan Order,* 32–39, 205–15, 406–16; Johnson, *Equal in Monastic Profession,* 147; Caroline Walker Bynum, *Jesus as Mother: Studies in the Spirituality of the High Middle Ages* (Berkeley and Los Angeles: University of California Press, 1982), 184–85; Vicaire, *Histoire de Saint Dominique,* 1:258–59, 2:271–72; Geneviève Brunel-Lobrichon, "Diffusion et spiritualité des premières clarisses méridionales," *Cahiers de Fanjeaux* 23 (1988): 277–78. Patricia Wittberg, *The Rise and Fall of Catholic Religious Orders: A Social Movement Perspective* (Albany: State University of New York Press, 1994), 90, gives examples of the cloistering for Catholic religious women in later periods.

68. See pages 97–98 below.

conduct. A contemporary observer vaguely described the members of these groups as "people who live in a holy and religious manner in their own homes, not because they are subject to a precise rule but because their life is simpler and more rigorous than that of other laypeople, who live in a purely worldly manner."[69]

The penitential life of the Franciscan and Dominican tertiaries was more precisely prescribed in their constitutions and statutes. Francis's charismatic personality led many penitential groups to adhere to his admonitions. These groups were regulated in a rule of 1221, the *Memoriale propositi*, extant in a revised form of 1228; penitential groups affiliated with the Order of Preachers had similar statutes. Accordingly, the life of tertiaries consisted in regular observance of religious activities such as recitation of prayers and attendance of mass, sexual continence and periodical abstinence from meat and food, display of humble public demeanor and dress, support of the church and defense against heresy through public witness to their faith, and assistance to each other and their communities. Since tertiaries, in the tradition of the religious life, refused to bear arms and to swear oaths binding them to secular authorities, they provoked conflicts with municipalities, which considered such activities essential to citizenship. The papacy and municipal communes, however, did require lists to document membership in tertiary

69. Henry of Susa, cardinal of Ostia, writing in the mid–thirteenth century in a work called *Summa aurea* (Venice: Apud haeredes Melchioris Sessae, 1570), bk. 3, 193; quoted in Vauchez, *The Laity in the Middle Ages*, 113. Cf. Lester K. Little, "Laienbruderschaften in norditalienischen Städten," in *Max Webers Sicht des okzidentalen Christentums*, ed. Schluchter, 401, who notes a puritanical tone in confraternal regulations. On confraternities and associations of penance, see Gilles G. Meersseman, *Ordo Fraternitatis: Confraternite e pietà dei laici nel medioevo*, 3 vols. (Rome: Herder, 1977). See also Lester K. Little, *Liberty, Charity, Fraternity: Lay Religious Fraternities at Bergamo in the Age of the Commune* (Northampton, Mass: Smith College, 1988), 49–97, who also deals with parish confraternities. For the development of the penitential movement and its relationship to the *conversi* and tertiaries, see also Raffaele Pazzelli, *St. Francis and the Third Order: The Franciscan and Pre-Franciscan Penitential Movement* (Chicago: Franciscan Herald Press, 1989), 1–66; Vauchez, *The Laity in the Middle Ages*, 107–27. On guilds and other confraternal associations, the difficulties in distinguishing between them, and their spiritual and secular functions, see Reynolds, *Kingdoms and Communities*, 67–78; Jeanne Deschamps, *Les confréries au Moyen Âge* (Bordeaux: Imprimerie Bière, 1958), especially 103–19, 138–57; N. J. Housley, "Politics and Heresy in Italy: Anti-Heretical Crusades, Orders, and Confraternities, 1200–1500," *Journal of Ecclesiastical History* 33 (1982): 193–208; and Gabriel Le Bras, *Études de sociologie religieuse* (Paris: Presses Universitaires de France, 1956), 2:423–62, who notes, "Du XIIIe au XVe siècle, la plupart des chrétiens sont enrôlés dans les confréries, beaucoup dans le multiples confréries, qui renforcent tous leurs liens temporels et spirituels" (433–34).

groups and related confraternities, and these provide information about such groups' social recruitment. The tertiaries appear to have recruited widely from all but the lowest social strata, with the bulk of support coming from urban tradesmen and artisanal professionals. Yet assessing to what extent normative prescriptions of tertiary life translated into day-to-day activities remains an elusive task. Ecclesiastical observers and chroniclers had much more reason to concern themselves with heterodox religious movements or groups on the fringes of orthodoxy; nor did tertiary writers detail the habits of their groups. Besides having a reputation for austerity and sincerity, the tertiaries received little notice. An exemplary study of numerous Tuscan *conversi* found in and around religious corporations in the late thirteenth and the early fourteenth centuries shows them to have come from areas in the vicinity of the religious institutions they were joining and to have been at least moderately well-off and often married and elderly. While they officially gave themselves, individually or as couples, and their property to a convent, local church, or hospital, in practice it was not uncommon that they were accommodated comfortably. They were subject only to modest rules of continence if married, and, in the words of bishop Enrico of Lucca, continued to "immerse themselves in secular business and affairs just as before," without religious burden. Their ill-defined ecclesiastical status and the continual accusations of draft dodging and tax evasion against them led religious and secular authorities to restrict access to *conversi* life, at the same time as the Third Orders of the mendicants moved toward communalization and more claustration. But before drawing similar conclusions about the life of the tertiaries, one should note that the stipulations for the *conversi* were less severe than for tertiaries, that the conversi did not have to pass through a novitiate, and that they were not as closely supervised by ecclesiastical authorities and bound into the church hierarchy.[70]

Conclusion

Weber's classic account has argued for an important role of monasticism in the development of Western rationalism. The classic account's central

70. Duane J. Osheim, "Conversion, *Conversi*, and the Christian Life in Late Medieval Tuscany," *Speculum* 58 (1983): 368–90 (the quote is from 387). On the status of the *conversi*, see also Ronald N. Swanson, *Religion and Devotion in Europe, c. 1215–c. 1515* (Cambridge: Cambridge University Press, 1995), 114–15, who remarks: "The extent to which such people were subjected to the institution's religious regime is . . .

tenet is that monastic precepts on labor and disciplined, methodical conduct imbued nuns and monks with a strong work ethic capable of transforming other, nonreligious spheres; yet in practice rationalizing effects on the world remained limited. The revision of this account in recent sociological scholarship by Randall Collins and Lewis Mumford has argued for an even stronger link between monasticism and asceticism and an inner-worldliness of monastic asceticism. The comparative historical analysis in this section comes to different conclusions with respect to the centrality of work in monastic asceticism and the relations between the cloister and the world in the Middle Ages. It shows that monasticism was not as ascetic and removed from the world as the classic account of Weber and Troeltsch has maintained, nor did it, as Collins and Mumford have argued in their revision of the classic account, turn inner-worldly and bring about significant economic and technological advancements.

In the earlier Middle Ages, until about 1100 (see Table 2), the monastics were the carrier stratum of asceticism in the West. Their asceticism and labor for God was increasingly oriented toward assurance of salvation by ritual and expiatory action for the world rather than methodical action in the world. This development had its origins in a fragmentary society susceptible to disruption and warfare, particularly in the post-Carolingian period, when the division of social and religious responsibilities tied the monastics to providing for those who were their patrons, protected them, and wanted to see their worldly status reflected in conspicuous religious services provided for them. The ever-wider disjunction between monastic prayer and work, and the functional specialization in the former, lessened the potential of monastic life for rationalizing the secular spheres, especially the economy. Though perhaps not as disengaged from the world as has recently been asserted in the historical literature,[71] at the end of the period monastic asceticism had few direct inner-worldly effects and applications, with the possible

---

generally unknown" (115). On the tertiaries, see Pazzelli, *St. Francis and the Third Order*, 100–54; Moorman, *History of the Franciscan Order*, 40–45, 216–25, 417–28, 560–68; Hinnebusch, *History of the Dominican Order*, 400–404; Gilles G. Meersseman, *Introduction to the Order of Penance in the Thirteenth Century* (Rome: n.p., 1983). For the text of the *Memoriale propositi*, see idem, *Ordo Fraternitatis*, 390–94. Social recruitment is discussed in Moorman, *History of the Franciscan Order*, 221; Little, *Liberty, Charity, Fraternity*, 73; Meersseman, *Introduction to the Order of Penance*, 288. Little (*Liberty, Charity, Fraternity*, 83–84) notes the existence of institutions analogous to Christian confraternities in contemporary Islam and Confucianism.

71. Cf. Milis, *Angelic Monks and Earthly Men*.

Table 2. A New Account of Asceticism in Medieval Western Society

	Period	
Characteristics	Earlier Middle Ages	Later Middle Ages
Carrier stratum	Monastics	Lay religious groups
Form	Moderate asceticism	Strict asceticism
Basis	Expiatory rituals	Methodical labor
Performers of ascetic labor	Conversi	Laymen and -women
Direction	Other-worldly	Inner-worldly
Effects	Pacification of nobility (?)	Penetration of secular spheres with asceticism
Locus	Cloister	World

exception of a pacifying effect on the nobility. Its overall direction remained other-worldly. Toward the end of the period, the performance of labor had almost completely shifted to dependent intermediaries, the *conversi* and *familia*. These groups, however, enjoyed only secondary status relative to the monks and nuns proper and, with increasing proximity to everyday economic and social life, were less and less subject to the original, austere rules of monastic conduct. Hence, an ascetic regimen of labor was likely confined to the *conversi*.

In the later Middle Ages (after c. 1100), the view of the monastics as the carrier stratum of Western asceticism, in spite of impressive contributions to new agricultural techniques (Cistercians) or the opening of monasticism to emerging forms of urban spirituality (Franciscans, Dominicans), is inaccurate. The Cistercians, soon after their foundation, relied on a quasi-Cluniac model of assigning manual labor to affiliated groups. The mendicants either did not, as a matter of principle, consider labor an appropriate activity for the friars and nuns (Dominicans) or, with the routinization of charisma, abandoned their founder's emphasis on combining the preaching life with manual labor (Franciscans). Women in all groups remained removed from active ministry and other inner-worldly activities that would have brought them into direct contact with the populace. In the tertiary orders, institutions for adjunct laity who retained their worldly affiliations but religiously committed to austerity and simplicity, the mendicants continued a trend in earlier medieval monasticism, to relegate ascetic labor to groups of secondary religious status.

Should the thesis of the importance of monastic asceticism for Western rationalism and the empowerment of the self in monastic precepts on labor, going back to Max Weber, therefore be abandoned? Not necessarily, if one considers Weber's argument, which after all was never fully developed, in a wider temporal and thematic context. Weber was correct in pointing to the theoretical, if not practical, valorization of methodical labor as ascetic practice in the Rule of St. Benedict, which provided the normative foundation of medieval monastic asceticism. Not unlike early Christianity, it privileged what Weber termed active asceticism, or "God-willed *activity* as a tool of God," over a religious outlook that sought its means of achieving salvation more exclusively in intellectual reflection and the acquisition of knowledge in contemplation.[72] But in early Christianity and early medieval monasticism this activity was a restrained asceticism. It was never as demanding on its practitioners as the stern encratism among the Gnostics and other groups in the West, and it fell short of the rituals of dissociation required from virtuosos in Hinduism and Buddhism, which in their harshness remained unparalleled elsewhere. Nor did the medieval West know of such figures as the Syrian stylites, or pillar saints, the most famous of whom, Saint Simeon, lived in the open on top of a pillar more than fifty feet high for some forty-seven years, communicating with the world only by way of a ladder that others could climb up and a basket that could be lowered down. In contrast, the religious landscape of the West in the early Middle Ages had what Peter Brown has called "a marked shortage of living holy men" and comparatively few "ascetic stars" seeking salvation in complete abstention and world renunciation.[73] The Rule of St. Benedict deliberately tempered ascetic requirements. The passage specifying that true monks live by the labor of their hands is immediately followed by the exhortation that "all things are to be done

72. Weber, "Religious Rejections," in *From Max Weber*, 325 (translation altered, emphasis in original). See also idem, *Economy and Society*, 630–34; Troeltsch, *The Social Teaching*, 102–10; Shmuel N. Eisenstadt, "Max Webers Sicht des frühen Christentums und die Entstehung der westlichen Zivilisation," in *Max Webers Sicht des antiken Christentums*, ed. Wolfgang Schluchter (Frankfurt: Suhrkamp, 1985), 509–24. For a measured study of labor as ascetic practice in early Christianity, see Geoghegan, *The Attitude Towards Labor in Early Christianity and Ancient Culture*.

73. Peter Brown, *Society and the Holy in Late Antiquity* (Berkeley and Los Angeles: University of California Press, 1982), 109, 185. On Gnostic encratism and orthodox asceticism in Christianity, see idem, *The Body and Society: Men, Women, and Sexual Renunciation in Early Christianity* (New York: Columbia University Press, 1988), 201–9; Gedaliahu G. Stroumsa, "Ascèse et gnose: Aux origines de la spiritualité monastique," *Revue thomiste* 81 (1981): 557–73. On the unique ascetic demands on Hindu and Buddhist virtuosos, see Weber, *The Religion of India*, 146–58, especially 148–49; idem, *Economy and Society*, 537; Ilana Friedrich Silber, "Dissent Through Holiness: The Case of the Radical Renouncer in Theravada Buddhist Countries," *Numen* 28 (1981): 164–93; Louis Dumont, "World Renunciation in Indian Religion," in *Religion, Politics, and History in India* (Paris: Mouton, 1970), 33–60. For Simeon Stylites and other pillar saints, see Bernhard Lohse, *Askese und Mönchtum in der Antike und in der alten Kirche* (Munich: Oldenburg, 1969), 213–14.

with moderation," precisely because Benedict was acutely aware of the bodily and spiritual havoc a too stringent schedule could have on the monastic community. Moreover, the tasks of the monastic vocation were carried out communally, so that all could share in the burden. In a small world with little privacy, nuns and monks thereby supervised each other throughout the day.[74]

Weber's views on the contribution of the link between monastic asceticism and work to the development of Western rationalism thus seems not inappropriate, if too narrow. The restrained, communal character of monastic conduct in its pristine Benedictine form in combination with an emphasis on manual labor as ascetic practice, rather than the latter alone, was what constituted a distinctively Western form of active asceticism. While menial work focused an ascetic regimen on mundane tasks, temperance in requirements and communality in performance allowed it to reach beyond a small circle and be carried out by larger groups of people on a consistent basis. The rationalizing potential of this combination of features, which in early medieval monasticism remained latent due to the increasing focus on expiatory rituals, manifested itself in the late eleventh and the twelfth centuries in new forms of lay piety expressing themselves in a variety of religious movements. As I argue in the next two chapters, this was of profound importance for the further history of asceticism and religious rationalization of conduct—a topic that so far remains unaddressed in sociological scholarship beyond Weber's brief references. The emergence of confraternal associations and lay religious movements on the fringes and outside of orthodoxy signified a blurring of the boundaries between the laity and the religious. To the extent that the laity now embraced notions of austerity and methodicalness formerly required only of the monastics, religiously motivated asceticism turned inner-worldly. Religiously motivated austerity and methodicalness were practiced in lay communities and applied to vocational activities. This is strikingly illustrated in Jacques de Vitry's account of the religious situation in Milan in 1216, focusing on the Humiliati, who lived largely as workers in the wool industry in the cities of Lombardy:

> I found hardly anyone in the whole city [which he previously had called "the pit of heretics" for its lasting reputation as a hotbed of heterodoxy] who would resist the heretics, except for

---

74. Fry, *RB 1980*, 251. For commentary, see 464–66; Lawrence, *Medieval Monasticism*, 31–32, 38; Knowles, *Christian Monasticism*, 34–36.

some devout men and religious women, whom the malicious and worldly people call *Patareni* [a derogatory expression for religious dissenters derived from the eleventh-century Patarene movement in Milan], but whom the Pontifex, from whom they have the authority to preach and to resist heretics, and who also has confirmed them in their religious life, calls *Humiliati; they are the ones who,* forsaking all things for Christ, gather in various places, *live from the labor of their hands,* preach the word of God often and willingly listen to it, *perfect and firm in their faith, efficacious in their works.* So much has this form of religious life multiplied in the diocese of Milan that 150 conventual congregations have sprung up, partly composed of men, partly composed of women, not including those [men and women] who remained in their own homes.[75]

Monasticism itself incorporated some of these characteristics into adjunct groups of laity, the tertiary orders of the mendicants, and thereby mirrored and continued trends in lay spirituality, but the main carriers of religious discipline and austerity were lay religious movements, often heterodox or at the fringe of orthodoxy, as was the case with the Humiliati, the Beguines, and the Waldensians (see Table 2). To various degrees in different stages of their developments, these groups held their members to asceticism, expressed in an austere lifestyle that even staunchly orthodox commentary (like Jacques de Vitry's above) would praise on occasion. The basis of this asceticism was methodical, diligent labor, rooted in a personal and literal imitation of the apostolic life.[76] It

75. Huygens, *Lettres de Jacques de Vitry,* 72–73 (emphasis in original): "Vix autem invenitur in tota civitate qui resistat hereticis, exceptis quibusdam sanctis hominibus et religiosis mulieribus, qui a maliciosis et secularibus hominibus *Patareni* nuncupantur, a summo autem pontifice, a quo habent auctoritatem predicandi et resistendi hereticis, qui etiam religionem confirmavit, *Humiliati* vocantur; *hii sunt,* qui omnia pro Christo relinquentes in locis diversis congregantur, *de labore manuum suarum vivunt,* verbum dei frequenter predicant et libenter audiunt, *in fide perfecti et stabiles, in operibus efficaces.* Adeo autem huiusmodi religio in episcopatu Mediolanensi multiplicata est, quod CL congregationes conventuales, vivorum ex una parte, mulierum ex altera, constituerunt, exceptis hiis qui in domibus propriis remanserunt." The shift from otherworldliness to inner-worldliness is also briefly noted in Nielsen, "Rationalization in Medieval Europe," 222–23, 232–33.

76. For the Beguines and their methodical asceticism focusing on labor, see Ernest W. McDonnell, *The Beguines and Beghards in Medieval Culture, with Special Emphasis on the Belgian Scene* (1954; reprint, New York: Octagon Books, 1969), chap. 6 ("The Puritan Ethic in Liége"); Southern, *Western Society and the Church,* 326–28; and Caroline Walker Bynum, "The Mysticism and Asceticism of Medieval Women: Some

often took place in the midst of urban communities, as part of everyday cultural and economic life. These movements reflected the penetration of secular spheres by asceticism. Hence, here the locus of asceticism was the world, and those who performed ascetic labor were ordinary members of lay ascetic movements in the later Middle Ages.

Comments on the Typologies of Max Weber and Ernst Troeltsch," in *Fragmentation and Redemption: Essays on Gender and the Human Body in Medieval Religion* (New York: Zone Books, 1991), 53–78. For the Humiliati, see Lorenzo Paolini, "Gli eretici e il lavoro: Fra ideologia ed esistenzialità," in *Lavorare nel Medio Evo: Rappresentazioni ed esempi dall'Italia dei secc. X–XVI, 12–15 ottobre 1980*, ed. Università degli studi di Perugia (Todi: Presso l'Accademia tudertina, 1983), 150–60, and the classic account of Luigi Zanoni, *Gli Umiliati nei loro rapporti con l'eresia, l'industria della lana ed i communi nei secoli XII e XIII* (Milan: Hoepli, 1911). For the Waldensians, see the analysis in Chapter 4.

3

---<>●<---

MAGIC, RELIGION, AND THE DEVELOPMENT OF LAY ASCETICISM

In this chapter, the focus shifts from monasticism to the orthodox laity. From a Weberian point of view, the main issue here is the role of magic. Weber posited, as might be recalled from Chapter 1, a decidedly negative relationship between magic and the methodical rationalization of conduct among its practitioners, for three reasons. First, the medieval Catholic Church did not actively encourage the imitation of monastic ascetic achievements among the laity. For laypeople, it designated a system of lowered ethical standards, and it allowed the invocation of supplementary mediators of grace (such as saints), or offered sacramental means of achieving salvation and assurance thereof (for example, through priestly rituals in the mass and relief in confession and penance).[1] Especially if the performance of priestly rituals and services was viewed by the laity as manipulation of the deity, the boundaries between magic and religion became fuzzy. Second, the existence of provisions of grace and stipulations of divine favors, mediated through priest or saint, monasticism or magic, indicates that the disenchantment of the world was not carried

---

1. It should be noted that neither Weber nor Troeltsch denied the domesticating function of penance, but for both the ensuing effect on religious life was accommodation to some basic standards, not an internally motivated ordering of behavior as a whole.

out consistently. The tapping into supernatural means to achieve salvation could substitute for proof of faith in conduct. Third, under the guidance of priests and other functionaries of a bureaucratically organized church, the orthodox laity was involved in the religious practices of communities in a largely passive way. Lacking was congregational religiosity in which members of communities were actively involved in generating, discussing, spreading, and living up to a moral discourse with religious content.

This chapter focuses on two aspects of Weber's argument. It begins with an overview of the uses of magic in early modern Europe, discussing the contribution of religion to the disenchantment of the world. Then, I analyze the role of magic as an impediment to rationalized action in the Middle Ages, and also address the alleged ubiquity of magical beliefs and practices as a substitute for ascetic action among the medieval laity. My analysis demonstrates that Weber was correct in asserting that medieval lay spirituality was deeply steeped in an amalgam of religious and magical views and practices. For laypeople, the boundaries between religion and magic were often difficult to discern. The actual increase in support for the employment, or accommodation, of protomagical objects, particularly the sacramentals, by the Catholic Church over the course of the Middle Ages led to a reliance on the performance of ritualist actions rather than asceticism as the means to salvation. But the analysis also shows that magic rituals did not supplant asceticism in all groups of laity. Important exceptions to the prevalence of magic as a soteriological means, to which Troeltsch and Weber alluded in the context of late medieval heterodoxy, arose in lay religious movements in the eleventh and twelfth centuries. The emergence of new religious prophecies, particularly ethical prophecies, the rejection of protomagical ecclesiastical rituals, and the expansion of literacy and new organizational forms to promote religious knowledge in these religious movements promoted lay rationalism. Lay rationalism expressed itself in the valorization of ascetic patterns of action. These developments preceded, and were the basis for, the advent of more stringently ascetic types of life conduct in heterodox movements.

Medieval laity

Religious Disenchantment of the World
Before and After the Reformation

The disenchantment of the world as a result of the Reformation has been a theme that for generations has interested sociologists and historians alike. Keith Thomas's magisterial work, *Religion and the Decline of Magic*, in particular has shown how tentative the boundaries were that separated religion from magic in England before the early modern period. The very terms by which magic, as manipulation of occult forces in nature, and religion, as supplication to a deity directing the course of the world, became defined and distinguished from each other, originated in early modern Protestant discourse, rising to prominence centuries later in the writings of Frazer and Weber. English Protestantism disavowed any supernatural aids to religion that could be interpreted as magic, and drew a firm line between the two. Yet not even in the religious climate of English Protestantism did the intellectual distinction between magic and religion and rejection of the former as false religion *and* inefficacious action, in both its ecclesiastical and nonecclesiastical forms, immediately translate into a reformed spirituality. In various ways magical elements kept creeping back into English Protestant religion, with cunning men and astrologers picking up the slack. Protestantism in England only gradually dispensed with such elements, aided by secular advances in rationalist philosophy, science, and technology and by new opportunities for the mastery of one's destiny, without supernatural intercession, by means of calculated engagement in the emerging capitalist economy. An ideology of self-help displaced, or at least discredited, magic as a proper means to attain important matters in human affairs.[2]

The protracted process by which magical remedies to religious and secular concerns became lastingly delegitimized in the modern period was not confined to England, to which Thomas largely confined his observations. It can also be observed on the European continent, where Protestant groups and the post-Tridentine Catholic Church cut back on what might be labeled folklorized ritual—protomagical activities that resulted from a selective mélange of what had previously been legitimate or at least tolerated acts of religious expression.[3] But in Protestant and

2. Keith Thomas, *Religion and the Decline of Magic* (New York: Charles Scribner's Sons, 1971). For criticism of Thomas's method and conclusions, see Hildred Geertz, "An Anthropology of Religion and Magic," *Journal of Interdisciplinary History* 6 (1975): 71–89; Stanley J. Tambiah, *Magic, Science, Religion, and the Scope of Rationality* (Cambridge: Cambridge University Press, 1990), 18–24.

3. On the demarcation of folklorized and magical rituals from legitimate forms of Protestant and Catholic liturgy, see Robert W. Scribner, "Ritual and Popular Belief in Catholic Germany at the Time of the Reformation," in *Popular Culture and Popular Movements in Reformation Germany* (London: Hambledon Press, 1987), 17–48; idem, "Cosmic Order and Daily Life: Sacred and Secular in Pre-Industrial German Society," in ibid., 1–16. On magical practices in post-Tridentine Catholicism, see John Bossy, "The

Catholic regions alike, the reformation of ingrained religious activities and views did not come easily. Visitation records of French dioceses in the late sixteenth century show little knowledge of religious doctrine, and German records paint a similar picture. "Refusing to let political and church powers browbeat them into abandoning age-old folk practices and folk notions, people waged passive resistance by staying away from church and ignoring its teaching."[4] Not all people in the patchwork of territories of alternating religious affiliation that made up early modern Germany remained as passive as depicted here. Considerable numbers regularly visited the other religious confession's services in adjacent territories or, if the territorial lord permitted, had clerics celebrate a mixed liturgy.[5] As late as at the end of the nineteenth century French rural priests, heeding popular demand, celebrated mass to cure animals suspected to be under a magical spell, or threw stones with a small wax cross on them into fields to protect them from natural disasters. At about the same time the Catholic Church in Bavaria reintroduced and supported previously discredited customs such as pilgrimages and more emotive forms of veneration of the Virgin Mary to stem the erosion of support from rural strata and classes of laborers; corresponding measures were undertaken for the same purposes by its Lutheran Protestant counterpart. Other parts of Europe also witnessed cases of such a resacralization and reenchantment of religious activities in both Protestant and Catholic religion until well beyond the early modern period.[6]

Counter-Reformation and the People of Catholic Europe," *Past and Present* 47 (1970): 51–70; Anthony D. Wright, *The Counter-Reformation* (New York: St. Martin's Press, 1982), 40–83; cf. Thomas, *Religion and the Decline of Magic*, 273. For Spain, see William A. Christian Jr., *Local Religion in Sixteenth-Century Spain* (Princeton: Princeton University Press, 1989). For a masterful characterization of the initial impact of the Reformation on traditional practice, see Steven Ozment, *Protestants: The Birth of a Revolution* (New York: Doubleday, 1993), 215–16.

4. Gerald Strauss, *Luther's House of Learning: Indoctrination of the Young in the German Reformation* (Baltimore: Johns Hopkins University Press, 1978), 302. For France, see the similar findings, also based largely on visitation records, by Jean Delumeau, *Catholicism Between Luther and Voltaire* (London: Burns & Oates, 1977); but see also Larissa Taylor, *Soldiers of Christ: Preaching in Late Medieval and Reformation France* (Oxford: Oxford University Press, 1992), as a corrective to the extreme claims in Delumeau's work.

5. The mingling of Catholic and Protestant spirituality in Germany is documented and discussed in Ernst Walter Zeeden, *Die Entstehung der Konfessionen* (Munich: Oldenbourg, 1965), 68–94.

6. For examples of blurred boundaries between magic and religion in France, Germany, and other regions, see Eugene Weber, *Peasants into Frenchmen: The Modernization of Rural France, 1870–1914* (Stanford: Stanford University Press, 1976),

Against the background of these considerations pertaining to the early modern and modern era, it is at first difficult, looking backward, to conceive of the Middle Ages as anything but a period in which magic and religion were inextricably linked on a popular level. The predominant view is aptly expressed in Thomas's characterization of the medieval church as "a repository of supernatural power," "a vast reservoir . . . capable of being deployed for a variety of secular purposes," "a limitless source of supernatural aid."[7] The origins of the church's propensity to rely on magic, in this perspective, lay in its concessions to pagan forms of worship in the Christianization of England and other areas of western and central Europe. The precedent of concession then translated into an enduring ecclesiastical legacy. "The claim to supernatural power was an essential element in the Anglo-Saxon Church's fight against paganism, and missionaries did not fail to stress the superiority of Christian prayers to heathen charms. The medieval Church found itself saddled with the tradition that the working of miracles was the most efficacious means of demonstrating its monopoly of the truth."[8] The English case therefore appears to be an example of a more general process of the "routinization" of ethical demands, described by Weber, in which religious elites must ensure popular support through accommodating existing mores and folkways. The more priests "aimed to regulate the behavior pattern of the laity," the more they had "to compromise with the traditional views of the laity in formulating patterns of doctrine and behavior," ultimately rendering them unable to wrench "the faith of the masses from its bondage to traditions based upon magic."[9]

This argument, as I point out in the rest of this chapter, is problematic: in some ways, it does not go far enough, while it overgeneralizes in others. It overgeneralizes by glossing over groups that rejected magic as a means of salvation and as a solution to secular problems. And it does not go far enough in that it needs to go further back in the

---

25–29, 339–56 (the priestly cures against spells and the use of wax crosses plastered on stones are described on 346); Werner K. Blessing, "Reform, Restauration, Rezession: Kirchenreligion und Volksreligiosität zwischen Aufklärung und Industrialisierung," in *Volksreligiosität in der modernen Sozialgeschichte*, ed. Wolfgang Schieder (Göttingen: Vanderhoeck & Ruprecht, 1986), 97–122; Hartmut Lehmann, ed., *Säkularisierung, Dechristianisierung, Rechristianisierung im neuzeitlichen Europa: Bilanz und Perspektiven der Forschung* (Göttingen: Vandenhoeck & Ruprecht, 1997). See also Robert W. Scribner, "The Reformation, Popular Magic, and the 'Disenchantment of the World,'" *Journal of Interdisciplinary History* 23 (1993): 475–94, on reenchantment and resacralization in Protestantism.

7. Thomas, *Religion and the Decline of Magic*, 32, 45, 77.

8. Ibid., 26.

9. Weber, *Economy and Society*, 465–66.

history of Christianity to address the linkages between Christian religion and magic.

Medieval Magic and Lay Religion

From its very conception, Christianity had to ward off allegations of magic. Jesus was reported to have worked many wonders and miracles. These acts could easily have counted as magic had it not been for his claim to divine power invoked in their performance. In the centuries that followed, pagans and Jews alike argued that Christians manipulated supernatural powers in an antisocial and harmful way. In their meetings, held secretly, Christians exorcised demons in the name of Jesus and by use of the sign of the cross. Of particularly ill reputation was the Eucharist, in which Christians, it was charged, performed cannibalistic acts in consuming the body and the blood of Christ. In light of the prevalence of such views and allegations, Christians were hardly able to argue that their miraculous wonder-working and many other of their religious practices could be distinguished from their magical counterparts by form or result. What made them different, they argued, was the authority that stood behind the act. God worked miracles, whereas magic was the work of the devil and his helpers, the demons. This line of argument continued into late antiquity. After the Roman Empire became officially Christian in the fourth century, leading ecclesiastical circles, facing attempts by members of the upper Roman class to appropriate and privatize Christian religious practices, proffered their holy men, the saints, vis-à-vis non-Christian sorcerers, as an earthly and public locus of spiritual power. Accusations of sorcery, which flared up particularly in times of political turmoil, furthered the belief in demonic forces, against whom the monastics battled in prayer and saints could be called to aid. Unlike the saints in Eastern Christianity, the western holy men usually were dead, and their shrines became sites of veneration and patronage for all strata in Christian communities. The remains of saints circulated as relics, and they signaled the presence of divine grace in worldly communities, which could be affirmed in collective rites.[10]

10. Stephen Benko, "Magic and Early Christianity," in *Pagan Rome and the Early Christians* (Bloomington: Indiana University Press, 1986), 103–39 (for charges of cannibalism, see 60, 70); Brown, *Society and the Holy in Late Antiquity*, 103–52, 166–95; idem, *Religion and Society in the Age of Saint Augustine* (London: Faber & Faber,

By the beginning of the Middle Ages the church was therefore already involved in ideological "boundary-work,"[11] by which it actively recommissioned some previously inadmissible acts in new forms for Christian ends. This practice continued and, if anything, appears to have become more prevalent during the early medieval period. Attempting to convert the Germanic and Celtic peoples, Christian missionaries faced ample competition in the form of diviners, seers, soothsayers, and other manipulators of the supernatural. These magicians offered those who sought their services the affirmation of some preternatural control over nature at a time of widespread political instability and social uncertainty, and as intercessory agents of considerable influence and authority, they were a well-established part of the culture of the pre-Christianized peoples. Instead of taking this cultural world head on, for which it had neither the personnel nor the necessary means of communication, the church contributed to the rise of magic in early medieval Europe by selectively borrowing practices from competing pagan manipulators and promoting these practices as part of the pool of interceding acts considered legitimate for Christian purposes. At the same time, the church vilified those who continued to perform such practices under different authority and without authorization from the church. Places where people showed reverence toward stones, fountains, or trees were turned into sites for oratories, chapels, and shrines. Magical springs became sources for baptismal water. Demons were held in check by countermagic that invoked angels by means of prayers, litanies, and charms. Medical and love magic were adjusted to contribute to a Christian cause. Even the drawing of lots and certain forms of astrology were cast into Christian molds. In turn, some licit religious artifacts proved to be amendable to magical forms, as Christian formulas turned into spells and the consecrated host was put to magical use. In the realignment of religious worship and magical manipulations, of course not all of these practices in the realm of the supernatural came to run together. At least officially the office of the Christian priest was painstakingly guarded against all semblance of a pagan magician's activities, and similar lines were firmly drawn between admissible and inadmissible practices bearing on the sacred. But in all cases the line

---

1972), 119–46; idem, *The Cult of the Saints: Its Rise and Function in Latin Christianity* (Chicago: University of Chicago Press, 1982); Richard Kieckhefer, *Magic in the Middle Ages* (Cambridge: Cambridge University Press, 1989), 33–42. An extreme view of Jesus' charisma as based on his miracle-working abilities is presented in Morton Smith, *Jesus the Magician* (San Francisco: Harper & Row, 1978).

11. For this concept, see Thomas F. Gieryn, "Boundary-Work and the Demarcation of Science from Non-Science," *American Sociological Review* 48 (1983): 792.

between licit and illicit practices was a fine one, especially from the viewpoint of a largely illiterate and theologically unschooled populace.[12]

As a result of the mutual adaption of pagan magic and Christian religion and the protracted process of negotiating cultural differences between the two in the early medieval period, the boundaries between orthodoxy and heterodoxy, when it came to the delineation of fidelity from superstition, were permeable. They remained permeable until the end of the Middle Ages, and definitions of how the two realms were demarcated varied over time. The notion that many aspects of life could be influenced by attempts to subordinate and to command hidden powers on the supernatural plane, whether by licit or illicit means, is an expression of what Richard Kieckhefer has called a "common tradition of medieval magic." It was an undercurrent of medieval culture sufficiently diffused and shared widely enough to transcend distinctions between elite and popular culture, learned and illiterate circles, though it was realized in more particularized systems of meaning. It signified the intersection of analytically distinguishable, but in actual life overlapping, practices and sets of corresponding beliefs in a cultural space. Using a cognitive grid that many people in medieval times might have used or at least might have recognized, the map of this cultural space might be drawn as follows:[13] The outer spatial territories were occupied by religion and science. Science was meant to deal with the normal manifest operation of forces in nature. Religion involved divine powers or actions. The large territory in between was the realm of magic, which may be said to be "the exercise of a preternatural control

---

12. "[I]t was not magic itself, nor the 'magical view of the world' shared by clergy and laymen alike, that bothered the churchmen, but merely the 'authority' which performed the rites. If it was securely in their hands, clergy did not object to magic and believed in it, just as simple peasants did" (Aron Gurevich, *Medieval Popular Culture: Problems of Belief and Perception*, trans. János A. Bak and Paul A. Hollingsworth [New York: Cambridge University Press, 1990], 103; similarly 62, 91). But see also the cautionary remarks on this position by Richard Kieckhefer, "The Specific Rationality of Medieval Magic," *American Historical Review* 99 (1994): 832–36. The magisterial account of the magical aspects of Dark Age culture is provided by Valerie I. J. Flint, *The Rise of Magic in Early Medieval Europe* (Princeton: Princeton University Press, 1991); complemented by Heinrich Fichtenau, *Living in the Tenth Century*, 303–32. See also the remarks on Flint's work by Alexander Murray, "Missionaries and Magic in Dark-Age Europe," *Past and Present* 136 (1992): 186–205, and Kieckhefer, "The Specific Rationality of Medieval Magic," 813–36. Kieckhefer, *Magic in the Middle Ages*, 43–55, provides an analysis of magic in early Germanic and Celtic cultures.

13. I owe the inspiration to use this metaphor to Mitch Berbrier. A more general and theoretical approach to mapping the "religious field" is to be found in Pierre Bourdieu, "Genesis and Structure of the Religious Field," *Comparative Social Research* 13 (1991): 1–44.

over nature by human beings, with the assistance of forces more powerful than they."[14] Within this territory, two types of magic can be distinguished: natural magic and demonic magic. Natural magic concerned itself with exploring or using hidden powers in nature amenable to human craft and thought to be emanating from celestial bodies, but not involving demonic forces. Demonic magic was labeled by ecclesiastical authorities as entailing the aid of demons and thus as having much more sinister overtones than did natural magic.[15]

How diaphanous the boundaries between science, religion, natural magic, and demonic magic were in practice is evidenced in the major forms of popular devotion and some more-mundane magico-religious activities. In the earlier Middle Ages, when relics and the cult of the saints stood at the center of popular religion, the physical remains of saints, and objects that had been in close contact with them, were seen as channels of communication with the holy and symbols of divine patronage. Relics were present on every altar in churches and monasteries. In the Carolingian period secular and ecclesiastical authorities actively supported their use in nearly all facets of life and their veneration in shrines by means of pilgrimage, and by the ninth and tenth centuries relics had become the object of a large trade. Even though, according to ecclesiastical doctrine, they were mere channels through which God let his grace flow to the community of believers if Relic supplicated by worship, the populace appears to have attributed automatic efficacy to the mere presence of relics. Relics served to protect against misfortune and signaled the presence of the divine in earthly communities. The efficacy of relics was based on the conviction that the Christian saint had "greater powers through his miracles than the demons offered by magical deceits; the effectiveness of the demons' powers was challenged, not their possibility. . . . The methods of magic and miracle could appear identical; and they could not always be distinguished by their results. The vengeance of the saints could fall as heavily on men [and women] as the results of maleficent magic."[16] In turn, when saints failed to deliver, they were subjected to monastic rites of humiliation and parallel lay practices of coercion intended to stir them into action, like the placement of thorns around relics, entreaties, the extinguishing of candles in a saint's church, abandonment, and even

14. Flint, *Rise of Magic*, 3.

15. On these distinctions, cf. Kieckhefer, *Magic in the Middle Ages*, 8–14 and the chapter on the common tradition of medieval magic; idem, "The Specific Rationality of Medieval Magic," 833.

16. Benedicta Ward, *Miracles and the Medieval Mind: Theory, Record, and Event, 1000–1215*, rev. ed. (Philadelphia: University of Pennsylvania Press, 1987), 10–11.

their physical punishment. The veneration of saints continued to be one of the most popular forms of religious devotion in the later Middle Ages.[17] Even when the employment of holy objects remained within proper limits, as defined by ecclesiastical authorities, boundaries between religion and certain forms of natural magic were easily crossed. This holds true for the later Middle Ages as well, even though many forms of magic became associated with sorcery and heresy. The locus of holiness and supernatural power began to shift from relics to the Eucharist in the eleventh and twelfth centuries. Eucharistic devotion came to signify an emotive type of piety that stressed the humanity of Christ and humankind's creation in the image and likeness of God and that manifested itself in the cult of the Virgin Mary, the multiplication of other intercessory agents, and various forms of mysticism. There was popular enthusiasm for seeing the eucharistic host at the moment of consecration, when it changed its substance, in the miracle of transubstantiation, from bread into the body of Christ. As an extension of the miraculous power of the host, it was held to work as a love charm if eaten, or to prevent bodily injury if carried along.[18]

17. Patrick J. Geary, *Furta Sacra: Thefts of Relics in the Central Middle Ages*, rev. ed. (Princeton: Princeton University Press, 1990); Jonathan Sumption, *Pilgrimage: An Image of Mediaeval Religion* (Totowa, N.J.: Rowman & Littlefield, 1975), 22–53. On the automatic efficacy of relics, see František Graus, Volk, *Herrscher und Heiliger im Reich der Merowinger* (Prague: Nakladatelsví Československé akademie vĕd, 1965), 181. For theological aspects of relics and veneration of saints, see Jaroslav J. Pelikan, *The Christian Tradition: A History of the Development of Doctrine*, vol. 2, *The Growth of Medieval Theology (600–1300)* (Chicago: University of Chicago Press, 1978), 174–84. The humiliation of saints is explored in Patrick J. Geary, *Living with the Dead in the Middle Ages* (Ithaca: Cornell University Press, 1994), 95–124. For sainthood in the later Middle Ages, see André Vauchez, *La sainteté en Occident aux dernièrs siècles du Moyen Âge d'après les procès de canonisations et les documents hagiographiques* (Paris: Boccard, 1983); Donald Weinstein and Rudolph M. Bell, *Saints and Society: The Two Worlds of Western Christendom, 1000–1700* (Chicago: University of Chicago Press, 1986).

18. For the emergence of eucharistic piety and emotive forms of spirituality, see Bynum, *Jesus as Mother*, 16, 19, 129–46; eadem, *Holy Feast and Holy Fast: The Significance of Food to Medieval Women* (Berkeley and Los Angeles: University of California Press, 1987), 48–69; Miri Rubin, *Corpus Christi: The Eucharist in Late Medieval Culture* (Cambridge: Cambridge University Press, 1991). Cf. Francis Rapp, *L'Église et la vie religieuse en Occident à la fin du Moyen Âge* (Paris: Presses Universitaires de France, 1971), 146–52; Virginia Reinburg, "Liturgy and the Laity in Late Medieval and Reformation France," *Sixteenth-Century Journal* 23 (1992): 526–47 (focusing on the associative aspects). See also Steven Ozment, *The Age of Reform, 1250–1550: An Intellectual and Religious History of Late Medieval and Reformation Europe* (New Haven: Yale University Press, 1980), 115–34, on different strands of mysticism. Uses and abuses of the host are reported and discussed in Rubin, *Corpus Christi*, 334–42; Peter Browe, "Die Eucharistie als Zaubermittel im Mittelalter," *Archiv*

While the use of sacraments for such purposes was considered abusive and could result in excommunication, there were similar practices that ecclesiastical authorities allowed or at least did not actively combat: the sacramentals. In the use of sacramentals, distinctions between religion and magic broke down further. Sacramentals are rites and objects that the church put in place for liturgical purposes, for the defense against demonic influences, and for the furtherance of spiritual and corporeal well-being. According to ecclesiastical doctrine that emerged in twelfth- and thirteenth-century scholasticism, sacramentals were, unlike the sacraments, not necessary for salvation and worked *ex opere operantis*; that is, their efficacy depended on the proper disposition of the user. Popular sacramentals included benedictions and objects blessed by a priest, making religious rituals effective in everyday life and aiding popular piety. A vivid example of the use of a benediction is the blessing of church bells, whose sound was held to dispel demons conjuring damaging weather storms. The bells' efficacy could be augmented by baptizing them, attaching a relic to them, or, as was the case as late as the eighteenth century, by having the formula "Lord, liberate us from lightnings and tempest" inscribed on them. The list of objects and benedictions used for apotropaic and therapeutic purposes is almost endless.[19]

It is this area of popular religious culture on the fringe, or slightly outside the penumbra of official liturgy that historians have increasingly recognized as a central aspect of medieval piety. The common use of sacramentals denotes a fairly unregulated area of activity where objects

für Kulturgeschichte 20 (1930): 134–54; Adolph Franz, *Die Messe im deutschen Mittelalter* (1902; reprint, Darmstadt: Wissenschaftliche Buchgesellschaft, 1960), 95–98. Edward Peters, *The Magician, the Witch, and the Law* (Philadelphia: University of Pennsylvania Press, 1978), describes the ways in which medieval invectives against magic gave way to the early modern persecution of witchcraft. The multiplication of intercessory agents is addressed in Swanson, *Religion and Devotion in Europe*, 142–72.

19. See the encyclopedic list of benedictions and sacramental objects in Adolph Franz, *Die kirchlichen Benediktionen im Mittelalter*, 2 vols. (1909; reprint, Darmstadt: Wissenschaftliche Buchgesellschaft, 1960). On early medieval weather conjurations, see Monica Blöcker, "Wetterzauber: Zu einem Glaubenskomplex des frühen Mittelalters," *Francia* 9 (1981): 117–31. On the demarcation of sacraments from sacramentals, see Franz, *Die kirchlichen Benediktionen im Mittelalter*, 1:1–42; Scribner, "Ritual and Popular Belief," in *Popular Culture and Popular Movements*; idem, "Cosmic Order and Daily Life," in ibid., 5–7; Swanson, *Religion and Devotion in Europe*, 183–85. The use of bells is evidenced in Franz, *Die kirchlichen Benediktionen*, 2:42–43; Flint, *Rise of Magic*, 189; for later periods, see Thomas, *Religion and the Decline of Magic*, 31 (sixteenth-century England), and Weber, *Peasants into Frenchmen*, 28 (eighteenth-century France).

consecrated by a priest were given over to local customs. Decisions about how and when to use them resided largely in the hands of the laity.[20] The sacramentals' continuing and perhaps increasing popularity can be related to the changing role of the parochial clergy and their relations with their parishioners. In the earlier Middle Ages, local customs and the boundaries of the parish circumscribed the activities of a parochial clergy closely tied to their congregations. "The priest was semi-literate, probably trained locally by the previous priest (who might have been his father). . . . He was probably married, despite increasing pressure from reformers—he would have needed a wife to run the household, and sons to take his place. In sum, he lived close to the earth and was akin to his parishioners in background and needs. On the other hand, his meager clerical training allowed him a special position in the community: his weak command of Christian ritual, due to poor training, illiteracy, and lack of access to books, nonetheless made him a prime resource for spiritual help with the everyday ills besetting a rural community, with which he could identify."[21] Toward the end of the first millennium the obligations of the parishioners had become defined as the payment of tithes and attendance of church services, but their role in the official liturgy remained passive.[22] The role of both clergy and laity changed significantly from the eleventh century onward. In the papal reforms the church strove to reduce lay influence in its affairs; the clergy, no longer allowed to marry, emerged as a status group clearly set apart from the congregation in its sacredness and sacerdotal functions. To the degree that the relations between clergy and laity became more formal and the parochial priest was presented as a necessary intermediary between the soul and God, the gulf between priest and parishioners widened. Furthermore, the role of a priest expanded in that he was

20. Scribner, "Cosmic Order and Daily Life," in *Popular Culture and Popular Movements*, 6; Rubin, *Corpus Christi*, 340.

21. Karen Louise Jolly, "Magic, Miracle, and Popular Practice in the Early Medieval West: Anglo-Saxon England," in *Religion, Science, and Magic in Concert and in Conflict*, ed. Jacob Neusner, Ernest S. Frerichs, and Paul V. McCracken Flesher (New York: Oxford University Press, 1989), 174–75.

22. On the parish in the earlier Middle Ages, see Patricia A. DeLeeuw, "The Changing Face of the Village Parish, I: The Parish in the Early Middle Ages," in *Pathways to Medieval Peasants*, ed. James A. Raftis (Toronto: Pontifical Institute of Mediaeval Studies, 1981), 311–22. On liturgy, see Megan McLaughlin, "The Laity and the Liturgical Community," in *Consorting with Saints: Prayer for the Dead in Early Medieval France* (Ithaca: Cornell University Press, 1994), 102–32; Kenan B. Osborne, *Ministry: Lay Ministry in the Catholic Church, Its History and Theology* (New York: Paulist Press, 1993), 303–4. On the "essentially vicarious experience" of (official) religion, see also Little, "Romanesque Christianity," 463–67.

now expected to be a skillful preacher, teacher, and counselor, and he was bound more firmly into the ecclesiastical hierarchy by higher requirements for formal training and stricter supervision and control. In all of this the laity retained a passive role in central rites of official religious life, and in fact were more dependent than before on priests as arbiters of access to salvation.[23] But many in the priesthood had hardly the knowledge, and sometimes lived too loose a lifestyle, to convey central values of their church aptly and convincingly and to provide effective ethical guidance to their flock. Clerical education in particular remained woefully inadequate throughout the later Middle Ages.[24]

23. Joseph W. Goering, "The Changing Face of the Village Parish, II: The Thirteenth Century," in *Pathways to Medieval Peasants*, ed. Raftis, 323–33; Emma Mason, "The Role of the English Parishioner, 1100–1500," *Journal of Ecclesiastical History* 27 (1976): 17–29; Christopher N. L. Brooke, "The Church of the Middle Ages, 1000–1500," in *The Layman in Christian History*, ed. Stephen C. Neill and Hans-Ruedi Weber (Philadelphia: Westminster Press, 1963), 113–15; Bynum, *Jesus as Mother*, 9–19; Yves Congar, "Clercs et laïcs au point de vue de la culture au Moyen Âge: 'Laicus' = sans lettres," in *Études d'ecclésiologie médiévale* (London: Variorum Reprints, 1983), chap. 5, 324–32; Rolf Zerfaß, *Der Streit um die Laienpredigt* (Freiburg: Herder, 1974), 178–90. Cf. Brian Stock's poignant assessment that "[a]s the immediacy of the sacrament was threatened by the implicit division of popular and learned culture, 'the conscious participation of the community' was lost. The mass gradually became a mystery which one had to 'wonder at and contemplate from afar'" (*The Implications of Literacy: Written Language and Models of Interpretation in the Eleventh and Twelfth Centuries* [Princeton: Princeton University Press, 1983], 267; citing Joseph A. Jungmann, *The Mass of the Roman Rite: Its Origin and Development (Missarum Sollemnia)* [New York: Benziger, 1951], 1:84). For a view of the laity as less passive than described here, see Reinburg, "Liturgy and the Laity in Late Medieval and Reformation France."

24. See, for France, Olga Dobiache-Rojdestvensky, *La vie paroissiale en France au XIIIe siècle d'après les actes épiscopaux* (Paris: Picard, 1911); Paul Adam, *La vie paroissiale en France au XIVe siècle* (Paris: Sirey, 1964); Jacques Toussaert, *Le sentiment religieux en Flandre à la fin du Moyen-Âge* (Paris: Librairie Plon, 1963); Jacques Chiffoleau, "La religion flamboyante (v. 1320–v. 1520)," in *Histoire de la France religieuse*, ed. François Lebrun (Paris: Seuil, 1988), 2:17–44; for England, Leonard E. Boyle, "Aspects of Clerical Education in Fourteenth-Century England," chap. 9 in *Pastoral Care, Clerical Education, and Canon Law, 1200–1400* (London: Variorum Reprints, 1981); Peter Heath, *The English Parish Clergy on the Eve of the Reformation* (London: Routledge & Kegan Paul, 1969); Gerald R. Owst, *Preaching in Medieval England* (Cambridge: Cambridge University Press, 1926), 25–47; Colin Platt, *The Parish Churches of Medieval England* (London: Secker & Warburg, 1981), 48–87; for Italy, Denys Hay, *The Church in Italy in the Fifteenth Century* (Cambridge: Cambridge University Press, 1977), 49–71; for Germany, Friedrich Wilhelm Oediger, *Über die Bildung der Geistlichen im späten Mittelalter* (Leiden: Brill, 1953), 98–120, 132–37. On the required knowledge and methods of instruction of clergy and laity, see Bernard Hamilton, *Religion in the Medieval West* (London: Arnold, 1986), 68–75, 104–11.

Sacramentals, then, as "a do-it-yourself means of access to sacred power,"[25] gave individuals and groups a certain independence from ecclesiastically mediated channels of salvation and assurance in temporal and eternal matters. Often employed in communal rites and for the benefit or protection of all community, para-liturgies centered on sacramentals and developed alongside main liturgical practices. They were a vehicle for the affirmation of communality, particularly in the later Middle Ages, when medieval society become more differentiated and many types of social action took on more individualistic forms, loosened from traditions and their embeddedness in small, local contexts.[26] Yet people employed sacramentals and other magico-religious practices not merely to generate interpersonal bonds and to affirm sociability in expressive rites. What was important to people, it appears, was also efficacy. One might surmise that people thought of many magico-religious practices as being automatically efficacious (*ex opere operato*); what mattered was whether they worked, not the principles behind their operation or what personal dispositions rendered them efficacious. Sacramentals and other popular practices of drawing on supernatural power at the crossroads of magic and religion therefore do not deserve the label of "superstition" in that they were irrational or arational. Weber's observation that the use of magic usually follows some empirical criteria of efficacy and was meant be an adequate means to a goal, either spiritual or secular, is applicable to medieval magic. Just like acts that sought to invoke divine power fully within the officially delineated boundaries of orthodox religious practice, acts considered magical entailed means-end considerations. Richard Kieckhefer has argued that the "specific rationality of medieval magic" pertained to two issues: "To conceive of magic as rational was to believe, first of all, that it could actually work (that its efficacy was shown by evidence recognized within the culture as authentic) and, secondly, that its workings were governed by principles (of theology or of physics) that could be coherently articulated."[27]

Even though one might question the generalizability of the second assertion, that is, that people knew precisely what rendered the

25. Scribner, "Cosmic Order and Daily Life," in *Popular Culture and Popular Movements*, 7.

26. Cf. Vauchez, *The Spirituality of the Medieval West*, 29, who uses the term *parallel liturgies*. Many aspects of social change mentioned here can be located in the eleventh and twelfth century; see Peter Brown, "Society and the Supernatural: A Medieval Change," in *Society and the Holy in Late Antiquity*, 302–32.

27. Kieckhefer, "The Specific Rationality of Medieval Magic," 814. See also idem, *Magic in the Middle Ages*, 75; Keith Thomas, "An Anthropology of Religion and Magic, II," *Journal of Interdisciplinary History* 6 (1975): 101; and Scribner, "Ritual and Popular

magical act efficacious, the first assertion is pertinent. Men and women in the Middle Ages manipulated the supernatural not only because they affirmed their social relations, but also because they expected favorable results from this manipulation. Analogous findings in anthropological research on pristine societies, which usually emphasize the first aspect, support this conclusion.[28] Yet while individual acts of medieval magic and religion were infused with what could be regarded as instrumentally rational calculations, much larger and more important questions remain. Were acts of magic conducive to an ethically motivated, methodical rationalization of life as a whole? Furthermore, did individual acts transcend a situational logic to constitute a systematic whole, and direct this whole toward mastery of the secular realm? These questions motivated Weber's inquiries into the economic ethics of the world religions, and for the Middle Ages his answer was decidedly negative.

On the cognitive grid developed previously to map the cultural space of people's dealings with the supernatural, an amalgam of natural magic and religion occupied the central area. It constituted a good part of popular magico-religious practices and expressed itself in a variety of para-liturgies. Whether or not they were controlled by a cleric, many such para-liturgies entailed ritualistic participation in acts that were intended to invoke benign supernatural powers, not to stipulate reflection on ethical values or to govern conduct on a lasting and methodical basis. The ringing of church bells against demonic forces, perhaps followed by a weather-and-field-blessing procession in which the eucharistic host was carried around to dispel hail, or the blessing of fields to ward off damage by caterpillars (which, in one reported case, were then excommunicated), to use but two examples, can hardly be held to have contributed to rationalization of conduct. These practices constituted a part of the increasingly large reservoir of legitimate or at least tolerated beliefs and practices available to medieval men and

---

Belief," in *Popular Culture and Popular Movements*, 39, on the intended efficacy of medieval magic. That the theological distinctions between the *ex opere operato* workings of the sacraments and *ex opere operantis* workings of the sacramentals did not extend to the laity is argued in Scribner, "Ritual and Popular Belief," in *Popular Culture and Popular Movements*, 40; Thomas, *Religion and the Decline of Magic*, 47; and Vauchez, *The Laity in the Middle Ages*, 91.

28. Bronislaw Malinowski, *Magic, Science, and Religion* (Glencoe, Ill.: Free Press, 1948). See the discussion of this and newer anthropological studies in Geertz, "An Anthropology of Religion and Magic"; Tambiah, *Magic, Science, Religion, and the Scope of Rationality*; and Hans H. Penner, "Rationality, Ritual, and Science," in *Religion, Science, and Magic*, ed. Neusner et al., 11–24.

women by which they could address soteriological concerns and ward off negative influences on earthly life by supernatural powers. While people therefore actively employed means to salvation and to other goals touching on the supernatural, these means were nonascetic and non-disciplinary. They rank among the many cultic or ritualistic salvation techniques, known to most world religions, that were not suitable for lasting self-perfection and methodical self-regimentation.[29]

Similar conclusions pertain to demonic magic. This type of magic, compared to official religion, lacked religion's wide range of social and spiritual functions, its moral code and systematic theology, and its institutional framework.[30] The marginalization of what the church considered demonic magic, in Kieckhefer's words, "encouraged a privatization of numinous and dangerous powers, a removal of the spiritual process away from the public sphere and into a relationship of independent practitioners to their clients that was guaranteed to arouse suspicion. . . . [T]he magicians were professional or semi-professional healers and diviners who worked privately, for a fee, on behalf of their clients. . . . There is no evidence that such practitioners were expected to serve as community leaders, to teach, or to set any sort of moral example for people under their charge. Not being thought of as priests, they did not really have followers for whose care they were regularly responsible."[31] This description strongly resembles Weber's ideal-typical distinction between priest and magician. Magicians differ from priests in that they do not operate permanent cults and do not have the backing of any systematized ethic or set of religious teachings but work with changing groups of people who seek their services on a temporary basis, rather than with firmly associated congregations, and are under more pressure to prove their qualifications by bringing about desired results. The application of these ideal-typical concepts to the Middle Ages warrants Weber's conclusion that because of these characteristics a magician's influence on his or her followers prevented, rather than contributed to, the rationalization of conduct.[32]

Parochial clergy, finally, as arbiters of official religion, were in a comparatively better position to bring about such a result. They were backed

29. Weber, *Economy and Society*, 529–32. For a theoretical elaboration of this point, see Schluchter, *Rationalism, Religion, and Domination*, 131–32.

30. Thomas, *Religion and the Decline of Magic*, 154, for Reformation England.

31. Kieckhefer, "The Specific Rationality of Medieval Magic," 830–31. I am aware that Kieckhefer describes the situation in the Carolingian and Ottonian eras, but I think his remarks apply to later periods as well.

32. Weber, *Economy and Society*, 424–57.

by a developed theology, a powerful organization, and a permanent net of relations with their parishioners. But a variety of factors proved detrimental to a thorough religious regulation of life: the often low levels of clerical education, the church's lowered ethical standards for the laity when compared to those for the monastics, its emphasis on priests as brokers of divine powers in the sacraments, moderate participatory requirements for laity in ecclesiastical life, and a very small measure of spiritual training for them.

By the High Middle Ages, then, the Catholic Church was well on its way to becoming a "religious achievement society" in which priests controlled a variety of pious religious works and devotional practices that were very popular but did not require systematic action.[33] Hence, it remains doubtful whether the church exerted much influence toward methodical rationalism in the secular realm. Since magic and religion were inextricably linked on a popular level, few provisions existed for, as Weber put it, "breaking down the power of magic and instituting the rationalization of conduct."[34]

---

33. Bernd Moeller, *Deutschland im Zeitalter der Reformation*, 3d ed. (Göttingen: Vandenhoeck & Ruprecht, 1988), 54; Francis Oakley, *The Western Church in the Later Middle Ages* (Ithaca: Cornell University Press, 1979), 113–30; John Bossy, *Christianity in the West, 1400–1700* (Oxford: Oxford University Press, 1985), 1–88. One might add the existence of a penitential system whose relatively lenient disciplinary function Weber (and Troeltsch) had emphasized in particular (see Chapter 1, pages 33, 50). Weber's and Troeltsch's position, which probably was informed by the predominant perspective among German Protestant theologians (see, e.g., Adolf von Harnack, *Lehrbuch der Dogmengeschichte*, cited here in its fourth edition [Tübingen: Mohr, 1910], 601–10) has come under attack from Stephen Ozment (*The Reformation in the Cities: The Appeal of Protestantism to Sixteenth-Century Germany and Switzerland* [New Haven: Yale University Press, 1975]) and Jean Delumeau (*Sin and Fear: The Emergence of a Western Guilt Culture, 13th–18th Centuries*, trans. Eric Nicholson [New York: St. Martin's Press, 1990], chap. 6), who argue that the penitential system was a semi-inquisitorial process imposing a heavy burden of guilt and *Angst* on the penitents. Other historians, however, analyzing such diverse sources as confessional manuals, sermons, and moral treatises, have come to the conclusion that confessional discipline was balanced with consolation, and that people could deal quite comfortably with the acts of penitence required from them (Thomas N. Tentler, *Sin and Confession on the Eve of the Reformation* [Princeton: Princeton University Press, 1977]; Lawrence G. Duggan, "Fear and Confession on the Eve of the Reformation," *Archiv für Reformationsgeschichte* 75 [1984]: 153–75; Taylor, *Soldiers of Christ*, 126–33; Paton, *Preaching Friars and the Civic Ethos*, 59–63, 310 n. 10). See also the further sociological discussion in Alois Hahn, "Zur Soziologie der Beichte und anderer Formen institutionalisierter Bekenntnisse: Selbstthematisierung und Zivilisationsprozess," *Kölner Zeitschrift für Soziologie und Sozialpsychologie* 34 (1982): 408–34; idem, "Sakramentale Kontrolle," in *Max Webers Sicht des okzidentalen Christentums*, ed. Schluchter, 229–53.

34. Weber, *General Economic History*, 362 (translation altered).

The Decline of Magic, Lay Asceticism, and the Rise of Religious Movements

The evidence brought into relief in the previous section supports Weber's views on the prevalence of medieval magic, its large overlap with religion in everyday life, and the impeding effects of magico-religious beliefs and practices on methodical secular conduct. But not all groups of laity thought of magical rituals as primary means to salvation. Weber noted an affinity between urban strata and ethical rationalism, which predisposed them toward a "practical rationalism in conduct."[35] Thomas made a similar point when he credited some medieval urban dwellers with a "realistic social outlook." In religious circles, he pointed out, the English Lollards in particular furthered such an outlook by relying on a spirit of "sturdy self-help" not amenable to magic. This assessment echoes that of Troeltsch, who saw the Lollards turning away from sacramental magic and toward ethically rationalized action.[36] The Lollards' break with ecclesiastical or other manipulations of the supernatural, however, was preceded by lay religious movements on the continent. These groups were critical of magic and sometimes created rationalized religious ethics and ascetic forms of conduct. This was a significant new aspect of religious rationalism in the West.

Already in the eleventh century, there was a surge of religious groups that were less enthusiastic than the general populace in their support for sacramental, para-liturgical, or outright magical numinous practices. Instead of relying on manipulations of the sacred, they sought to achieve salutary goals by giving more weight to their own behavior. The emergence of these groups can be seen partly as a reaction to ecclesiastical changes instigated by the Gregorian reform movement. Affirming papal authority against secular influence exercised through simony (the purchase of ecclesiastical office) and lay investiture (the appointment of clerics by the laity), the Gregorian reforms brought about a more clearly defined status of the clergy. The clergy were also held to higher moral and professional standards.[37] I have described above how the proliferation of

35. Weber, "The Social Psychology of the World Religions," in *From Max Weber*, 284; idem, *Economy and Society*, 479, 482–84. See also Chapter 1, pages 38, 40, 43, 45 n. 129, 47.

36. Thomas, *Religion and the Decline of Magic*, 47, 663. For Troeltsch's position, see Chapter 1, page 35.

37. A succinct statement of the goals of the Gregorian reforms is given in Karl Morrison, "The Gregorian Reform," in *Christian Spirituality: Origins to the Twelfth Century*, ed. Bernard McGinn and John Meyendorff (New York: Crossroad, 1985),

para-liturgies and sacramentals can be viewed as a reaction to this shift toward sacerdotalism, a reaction by which people circumvented ecclesiastical channels to the supernatural.[38] A different reaction can be observed in lay religious movements. As standards of clerical conduct increased, so did expectations, and shortcomings in clerical education and behavior continued to provide some of the laity with ample reason to express their religious thoughts and feelings without the guidance of an ecclesiastic.[39] Lay religious movements, trying to surpass the religious standards set for the clergy, often adopted simple but austere ways of life and valued religious asceticism as a means and a path to salvation.

The following report on one of the earliest organized lay religious groups foreshadowed some of the themes that were to arise in lay spirituality and the ways in which they were put into practice in the following centuries. It is taken from the acts of a synod at Arras, 1025, in which the bishop of Cambrai-Arras, a diocese in northeastern France, is reported to have inquired into the faith of certain heretics in his diocese that he had arraigned, asking them:

> "[W]hat is your doctrine, your discipline and your way of life, and from whom have you learned it?"—They replied that they were followers of an Italian called Gundolfo. They had learned from him the precepts of the Gospels and the apostles, and would accept no other scriptures but this, to which they would adhere in word and deed. Since it had come to the bishop's ears that they abhorred the ceremony of holy baptism, rejected the sacrament of the body and blood of Christ, denied the authority of the Church, condemned legitimate matrimony, saw no virtue in holy confession and held that nobody after the time of the apostles and martyrs ought to be venerated, he began to question them on these points. . . . [Responding to the bishop's further questions] they replied, "Nobody who is prepared to examine with care the teaching and rule which we have learned from our master will think that they contravene either the precepts of the Gospels or those of the apostles. This is its tenor:

177–92. Berman, *Law and Revolution*, 85–113; Southern, *Western Society and the Church*, 100–17; Hamilton, *Religion in the Medieval West*, 19–22; and I. S. Robinson, *The Papacy, 1073–1198: Continuity and Innovation* (Cambridge: Cambridge University Press, 1990), 209–43, place them in a wider social and ecclesiastical context.

38. See pages 111–16 above.

39. This point is strongly argued in R. I. Moore, *The Origins of European Dissent*, rev. ed. (New York: Blackwell, 1985), 78–81.

to abandon the world, to restrain the appetites of the flesh, to earn our food by the labor of our own hands, to do no injury to anyone, to extend charity to everyone of our own faith. If these rules are followed baptism is unnecessary; without them it will not lead to salvation."[40]

This passage reveals elementary characteristics of a lay religious group that can be found in many, if not all, others that followed in the next two or three centuries.[41]

First, the emergence of a group can be attributed to the activities of a charismatic leader. Even though nothing more appears to be known of this Gundolfo,[42] the leaders of other groups are described as charismatic, gathering captive crowds around them. Some of these men were merely firebrands rebelling against orthodox religion, but some were formulators of faith, like Gundolfo, capable of conveying a message of lasting impact. In Weber's categories these charismatic leaders may be called religious prophets, or proclaimers "of a religious truth of salvation through personal revelation."[43] Weber emphasized that prophecy can be a much more powerful ferment of religious change and rationalization than can the activities of a magician or the pastoral care of a priest. A prophet as the bearer of metaphysical revelations challenges the orthodox ways of religious life and attempts to establish a new set of religious conceptions. The prophet's ideas bring forth certain worldviews that, if taken up by the audience, can serve as switchmen in guiding ethical notions and ways of life in new directions.[44] As a result, prophecy creates a systematization of conduct according to ethical standards,

40. I use the translation in R. I. Moore, *The Birth of Popular Heresy* (London: Arnold, 1975), 16–17.

41. For the following I have relied on the analyses in Stock, *The Implications of Literacy*, 120–39; Moore, *The Origins of European Dissent*, 9–20; Jeffrey Burton Russell, *Dissent and Reform in the Early Middle Ages* (Berkeley and Los Angeles: University of California Press, 1965), 21–27; Heinrich Fichtenau, *Ketzer und Professoren: Häresie und Vernunftglaube im Hochmittelalter* (Munich: Beck, 1992), 22–28; and Malcolm D. Lambert, *Medieval Heresy: Popular Movements from the Gregorian Reform to the Reformation*, 2d ed. (Oxford: Blackwell, 1992), 22–25.

42. Moore, *The Origins of European Dissent*, 18.

43. Weber, *Economy and Society*, 446. Cf. Bourdieu, "Genesis and Structure of the Religious Field," 24, who calls a prophet a "petty independent entrepreneur of salvation." Sophia Menache (*The Vox Dei: Communication in the Middle Ages* [Oxford: Oxford University Press, 1990], 214) makes a brief reference to the foundation of heresy by prophets, but does not further elaborate on her use of the term.

44. Weber, "The Social Psychology of the World Religions," in *From Max Weber*, 280. This, of course, is Weber's famous switchmen metaphor.

methodically guided as a whole toward a religious goal.[45] Yet the life spans of lay groups that emerged through religious prophecy were often short, varying with the type of prophecy that gave rise to them. Weber distinguished between two types of prophecy: exemplary prophecy, where the prophet was an exemplary charismatic who demonstrated the way to salvation and demanded imitation of his acts, and ethical prophecy, where the prophet was a mere instrument for the proclamation of divine norms and demanded adherence to these norms. For the religious groups emerging up to the early twelfth century, the founding prophecy was typically exemplary, not ethical, and many of the problems that Weber associated with the routinization and depersonalization of charisma vested in an exemplary prophet manifested themselves soon and contributed to the demise of these groups.[46] Of the religious groups springing forth in the late eleventh and early twelfth centuries, those that continued to exist thereafter were generally founded by reform-minded, if idiosyncratic, eremitic preachers like Peter Damian or Robert of Arbrissel, who did not rely solely on exemplary prophecy but started communities that were eventually organized under a rule and assimilated to orthodox monastic forms of religious life.[47] From about the mid-twelfth century onward, however, religious laity responded increasingly to ethical forms of prophecy that were bolstered by the availability of religious texts. Some of these forms crystallized into stable movements with numerous and dedicated members.[48]

45. See Chapter 1, pages 48, 52.

46. Weber, *Economy and Society*, 246–54. For the distinction between ethical and exemplary prophecy and its implications, see 447–50; "The Social Psychology of the World Religions," in *From Max Weber*, 285. In the burgeoning literature on charisma and its routinization, some of most important theoretical refinements have come from Thomas F. O'Dea, "Five Dilemmas in the Institutionalization of Religion," *Social Compass* 7 (1960): 61–67; Constans Seyfarth, "Alltag und Charisma bei Max Weber," in *Alfred Schütz und die Idee des Alltags in den Sozialwissenschaften*, ed. Walter M. Sprondel and Richard Grashoff (Stuttgart: Enke, 1979), 155–77; Dirk Käsler, *Revolution und Veralltäglichung* (Munich: Nymphenburger Verlagshandlung, 1977), 161–92; and Schluchter, *Rationalism, Religion, and Domination*, 392–408.

47. Henrietta Leyser, *Hermits and the New Monasticism: A Study of Religious Communities in Western Europe, 1000–1150* (New York: St. Martin's Press, 1984), particularly chaps. 5, 9, 10; Little, *Religious Poverty*, 70–83; Lawrence, *Medieval Monasticism*, 149–59.

48. Cf. Moore's stark characterization of earlier forms of heresy and dissent as centered on charismatic yet "lonely and embattled men" without elaborate doctrine and organized following (*The Origins of European Dissent*, 83), arguing against Russell, *Dissent and Reform in the Early Middle Ages*. See also Leyser, *Hermits and the New Monasticism*, 45–49. For a discussion of exemplary prophets' ragged attire as mark of asceticism, see Gábor Klaniczay, *The Uses of Supernatural Power: The Transformation*

A second characteristic of the group investigated at Arras is the rejection of ecclesiastical practices considered indispensable for salvation in orthodoxy. Concomitant to a contemporary trend in intellectual life toward individualization of the self,[49] this entailed the replacement of such practices with personal and collective responsibility for matters of faith, expressed in simple but austere forms of life. What members of the group at Arras described as their resolution to adhere "in word and deed" to "the precepts of the Gospels and the apostles" was soon to become perhaps *the* dominant theme in Western spirituality. A common feature of the sprawling religious communities between the late eleventh and early thirteenth centuries, both within and outside of the church, that embraced new forms of religious life or advanced popular dissent was advocacy of the "apostolic life." The apostolic life, as it came to be understood, consisted in community, humility in voluntary poverty, and preaching among the laity. In communal preaching and humble life, laypersons assumed the right, and even the duty, to tell others about the Gospels and to live accordingly. The laity thereby assumed a new role as active preachers and austere practitioners of faith. In their search for a more fulfilling religious life than offered in the parishes, they turned to the model of the early Christian communities, imitating what they saw as the apostles' and early Christians' austerity and simplicity. The established tradition that Christian perfection was best achieved in the monastery came under question. Even though the group at Arras echoed the monastic aim to "abandon the world" by imitating the humility of Christ in the mortification of the flesh, they, like many other groups of laypeople, quite characteristically valued manual work as another emulation of early apostolic communities. As Weber emphasized, such unworldliness can very well go hand in hand with stringent asceticism if magical means to salvation become ethically devalued and methodical conduct acquires an instrumental quality: "Where the religious virtuoso was placed in the world as the instrument of God and cut off from all magical means to salvation, with the imperative that he prove himself through the ethical quality of his conduct within the spheres of the world—and solely through this ethical quality of his conduct—as being called upon to salvation before God . . . the world could be religiously devalued and rejected as carnal and a vessel of sin to the highest degree:

of Popular Religion in Medieval and Early-Modern Europe, trans. Susan Singerman (Oxford: Polity Press, 1990), 69–74. Erwin Iserloh, *Charisma und Institution der Kirche: Dargestellt an Franz von Assisi und der Armutsbewegung seiner Zeit* (Wiesbaden: Steiner, 1977), discusses charisma in lay religious movements at the time.

49. See Chapter 2, page 81.

it [the world] was thereby only all the more affirmed psychologically as a place of God-willed activity in one's worldly calling."[50] Correspondingly, the ascetic deeds of lay associations like the Humiliati or Beguines, who saw such instrumental value in ascetic simplicity and methodical conduct, appear to have equaled or surpassed those of established Benedictine and Cistercian monastic communities, and helped to spark the early Franciscan movement and the mendicant tertiaries.[51]

Third, notions of the apostolic life were grounded in lay knowledge of the contents of scripture. In the group arraigned at Arras, this knowledge was imparted to them by their master, Gundolfo. It appears that members of the group, even though probably not literate, nevertheless knew of biblical contents and had at least some elementary doctrinal competence.[52] This group is one of the earliest documented examples of a "textual community." Brian Stock has coined this term to refer to an association of medieval laypeople organized around a core body of texts and literate interpreters. The purpose of such an association was to listen to, discuss, and reflect upon texts, and to disseminate their contents. The heretical group at Arras was only the harbinger of a large number of lay groups organized as such communities.[53]

There is yet some larger significance to the proliferating organization of lay groups in textual communities. Somewhat neglected by Weber and Troeltsch, Reformation historians have repeatedly stressed the importance of printing and literacy in the success of the Reformation, which went beyond the provision of a technical means of expressing dissent. Printing and literacy also have important cognitive, ideological, and social implications. Communication based on written records transcends

50. Weber, "The Social Psychology of the World Religions," in *From Max Weber*, 290–91 (translation altered; emphasis removed).

51. M.-D. Chenu, *Nature, Man, and Society in the Twelfth Century: Essays on the New Theological Perspectives in the Latin West*, ed. and trans. Jerome Taylor and Lester K. Little (Chicago: University of Chicago Press, 1983), 202–69; Grundmann, *Religiöse Bewegungen im Mittelalter*, 13–50; Vauchez, *The Spirituality of the Medieval West*, 80–88; Moore, *The Origins of European Dissent*. For the Humiliati and other lay groups as carriers of asceticism and as an influence on the mendicants, see Chapter 2, pages 91, 97–98. The communitarian aspects of religious life are stressed in Bynum, *Jesus as Mother*, 82–109; Reynolds, *Kingdoms and Communities*; Klaniczay, *The Uses of Supernatural Power*, chap. 3.

52. See Stock, *The Implications of Literacy*, 127–28.

53. Ibid.; for the definition of the term *textual community*, see 238, 522. See also more recently Brian Stock, *Listening for the Text: On the Uses of the Past* (Baltimore: Johns Hopkins University Press, 1990), 23, where Stock defines textual communities as "microsocieties organized around the common understanding of a script." See also Fichtenau, *Ketzer and Professoren*, 128–30, for pertinent remarks.

the constraints of time and place inherent in oral communication; it allows for more differentiated and subtle messages. Besides allowing higher levels of cognitive complexity, written communication promotes ideological competence by facilitating the deliberation and memorization of a text, and the incremental accumulation of additional components to a message. Socially, it provides a translocal medium around which people can cluster, a communality of interests and ideas through which men and women in different places and times can associate with one another.[54]

Stock's study shows that to some extent these implications of the advance of literacy and the written word commonly associated with the early modern period already became evident in textual communities of the eleventh and twelfth centuries. Already in their earliest manifestations in the eleventh century, Stock observes, "the sacral, mystical, and miraculous accretions of older tradition were discarded in favor of a rationalistic ethic based on the principles of the New Testament. Rationality in turn was a byproduct of the literate mentality, since the various interpretations of texts were subsequently codified into a set of written rules governing conduct. These norms structured the behavior of the individual in the group and resulted in a set of interactions between the members which were designed to break down the barriers between the literate and the nonliterate."[55] In an environment of generally rising lay literacy, these communities, particularly the Waldensians, were at the forefront of groups fostering a more systematized religious discourse, a greater degree of complexity and competence in their theological arguments, and communal strength and social bonds between their members in advancing their views.[56]

The emergence in the twelfth and thirteenth centuries of lay religious groups who displayed signs of the sturdy self-help characteristic of the

54. Jack Goody and Ian Watt, "The Consequences of Literacy," in *Literacy in Traditional Societies*, ed. Jack Goody (Cambridge: Cambridge University Press, 1968), 27–68; Elizabeth Eisenstein, *The Printing Press as an Agent of Change* (Cambridge: Cambridge University Press, 1979); and Jack Goody, *The Logic of Writing and the Organization of Society* (Cambridge: Cambridge University Press, 1986), have provided the classic argument. For further reflections on these points, see David Zaret, *The Heavenly Contract: Ideology and Organization in Pre-Revolutionary Puritanism* (Chicago: University of Chicago Press, 1985), 29–34, and D. H. Green, "Orality and Reading: The State of Research in Medieval Studies," *Speculum* 65 (1990): 273.

55. Stock, *The Implications of Literacy*, 150.

56. Margaret Deanesly, *The Lollard Bible and Other Medieval Biblical Versions* (Cambridge: Cambridge University Press, 1920), 25–55; Stock, *Listening for the Text*, 24–29; Alexander Patschovsky, "The Literacy of Waldensianism from Valdes to c. 1400," in *Heresy and Literacy, 1000–1530*, ed. Peter Biller and Anne Hudson (Cambridge: Cambridge University Press, 1994), 113–23.

later Lollards can thus be explained by the coincidence of several factors. Material reasons for an ascetic empowerment of the self were the commercial revolution and the reemergence of politically autonomous cities, which went hand in hand with the ascendance of socioeconomic groups predisposed to practical rationalism and new structural opportunities and professional conduits for methodical conduct.[57] But these factors are not sufficient to explain the trend toward rationalization of conduct, at least not in religious groups. What was equally important was the generation and propagation of ethical prophecy by charismatic leaders. The content of ethical prophecy was the rejection of ritualist adherence to standard forms of religious worship, and the appeal to the austere and simple forms of life of the early apostolic communities, carried out within the confines of worldly attachments and professions. Magico-religious practices were considered a lesser means to salvation. These doctrinal foundations of ascetic action became relevant to larger numbers of people because ethical ideals were disseminated by means of networks of active congregational groups. The nuclei of these networks were textual communities and other microcongregations, the smallest organizational units for socioreligious discourse, in which belief and conduct were measured against scriptural prescriptions, insofar as such prescriptions were a salient feature of a group's belief system. "[I]t was not simply arguments and opinions that were brought to bear . . . [but an] *ethically rationalized* religious lifestyle."[58] It is therefore in these networks of textual communities and small local religious associations at the fringe of orthodoxy or outside of it that one should look for, to use Weber's words, "medieval Puritan sects" and "forerunners of the ascetic denominations of Protestantism."[59]

---

57. See Chapter 2, pages 80–81.

58. Klaniczay, *The Uses of Supernatural Power*, 36. See also R. I. Moore, "Literacy and the Making of Heresy, c. 1000–c. 1150," in *Heresy and Literacy, 1000–1530*, ed. Biller and Hudson, 20; Anne Brenon, "L'hérésies de l'an mil: Nouvelles perspectives sur les origines du catharisme," *Heresis* 24 (1995): 26–27.

59. See Chapter 1, page 55.

Part Two

ASCETICISM IN LAY RELIGIOUS MOVEMENTS IN THE MIDDLE AGES

Two Case Studies

4

OTHER- AND INNER-WORLDLY ASCETICISM IN MEDIEVAL WALDENSIANISM

There was certainly no shortage of heresies in the Middle Ages. In number and in terms of their belief systems, heresies spanned from small congregations proclaiming faith in salvation through women, as was the case for the Guglielmites, to movements organized for political insurrection, such as factions of the Hussites.[1] Except for their opposition to established religious doctrine or cult, they often had little in common; yet some heretical movements succeeded in gaining substantial support. What set the Waldensians and the Cathars apart from the rest was the extent to which they successfully spread religious dissent in the very heartlands of western Christendom: the industrial centers of northern Italy, the politically fragmented areas of southern France, the German Empire's trade routes and, at least in the case of the Waldensians, its eastern territories. Never before, and not again until the Reformation, would the Catholic Church face dissent of such

This chapter is a substantially revised and enlarged version of my article "Other- and Inner-Worldly Asceticism in Medieval Waldensianism: A Weberian Analysis," *Sociology of Religion* 56 (1995): 91–119.
   1. Stephen E. Wessley, "The Thirteenth-Century Guglielmites: Salvation Through Women," in *Medieval Women*, ed. Baker, 289–303; Howard Kaminsky, *A History of the Hussite Revolution* (Berkeley and Los Angeles: University of California Press, 1967).

magnitude that was not confined to a smaller geographical area or to the periphery of its influence. In the case of the Cathars, analyzed in Chapter 5, dissent was rooted in a belief system that had radically distinct metaphysical origins: Zoroastrian dualism. For the Waldensians, just the opposite was true: as "the most geographically widespread and the longest-lived of all medieval popular heresies, [and] most likely . . . also the largest in terms of aggregate numbers of believers,"[2] their dissent sought not a different type of religion but, on the contrary, pristine Christian forms of religious life. The Waldensians wanted to restore the early apostolic communities' austere ideals that they thought central to Christianity. Historical scholarship has considered them the harbinger of ascetic discipline among the laity.[3]

Given the Waldensians' potential for an ascetic empowerment of the self, it is surprising that they have received scant attention from sociologists. As has been pointed out in Chapter 1, Weber did not mention the Waldensians, even though detailed historical writings about this group were already available by the early twentieth century.[4] Likewise, Troeltsch described the Waldensians as the most important medieval sect but limited his treatment to just one page, largely derivative of other historical work,[5] and hardly any sociological research has been done on the Waldensians since.[6] The same, of course, cannot be said of historians. Yet in spite of the many detailed analyses of the Waldensian movement, few historians have linked their studies to Weber's work and his thematic focus on the links between religious asceticism and secular rationalism. Historical analyses of Waldensianism remain largely confined to the context of

2. Robert E. Lerner, "Waldensians," in *Dictionary of the Middle Ages*, ed. Joseph A. Strayer (New York: Charles Scribner's Sons, 1989), 12:508.

3. For a comparison of the Waldensians to other medieval religious movements, see the seminal works by Grundmann, *Religiöse Bewegungen im Mittelalter*, and Lambert, *Medieval Heresy*.

4. This has been well documented in Kurt-Victor Selge, "Die Erforschung der mittelalterlichen Waldensergeschichte," *Theologische Rundschau*, n.s., 33 (1968): 291–309.

5. See Chapter 1, page 35. The shortcomings of Troeltsch's dependence on Volpe are noted in Robert E. Lerner, "Waldenser, Lollarden und Taboriten: Zum Sektenbegriff bei Weber und Troeltsch," in *Max Webers Sicht des okzidentalen Christentums*, ed. Schluchter, 330–31.

6. There is a brief treatment of the Waldensians in Rebecca Jean Emigh, "Poverty and Polygyny as Political Protest: The Waldensians and Mormons," *Journal of Historical Sociology* 5 (1992): 462–84. I do not share the author's view of the Waldensians as a political movement.

medieval religious dissent, with few references to its secular implications or ascetic potential.[7]

Sources and Analytical Outline

The analysis in this chapter draws on evidence from the main geographical centers of Waldensianism—southern France, northern Italy, and the eastern parts of the German Empire—between its beginnings in the late twelfth century and its decline in the late fourteenth century. After this period, larger Waldensian communities survived in remote mountainous areas south of the Alps only; in the German Empire the Hussites in Bohemia superseded the Waldensians as the main representative of heterodox beliefs and practices.[8]

Evidence of Waldensian practices and beliefs derived from primary sources consists mainly of three types of documents, each with different strengths and problems. The first type of document is Waldensian writings. Among the most interesting is the *Liber antiheresis* of Durand of Huesca, likely composed around 1186/87. Written by a companion of Waldes, it is a splendid affirmation of early Waldensian religious life and an expression of their theological and social views.[9] However, as is generally the case with heretical texts in the High Middle Ages, this document focuses on the lives and thoughts of the spiritual leadership, not on the views and behavior of Waldensian supporters and followers. Furthermore, when compared to the Cathars, the other major heretical group of the High Middle Ages, the Waldensians appear to have composed fewer doctrinal expositions.[10]

---

7. Exceptions to this rule are Kurt-Victor Selge, "Max Weber, Ernst Troeltsch und die Sekten und neuen Orden im Spätmittelalter (Waldenser, Humiliaten, Franziskaner)," in *Max Webers Sicht des okzidentalen Christentums*, ed. Schluchter, 316–20, and Robert E. Lerner, "Waldenser, Lollarden und Taboriten," in ibid., 329–35. Both accounts treat the ethical foundations of Waldensianism only briefly.

8. Gabriel Audisio, *Les "vaudois": Naissance, vie et mort d'une dissidence (XIIme–XVIme siècles)* (Turin: Meynier, 1989), 65–91; Jean Gonnet and Amedeo Molnár, *Les vaudois au Moyen Âge* (Turin: Claudiana, 1974), 211–82; Lambert, *Medieval Heresy*, 284–300.

9. See the authoritative analysis in Kurt-Victor Selge, *Die ersten Waldenser*, 2 vols. (Berlin: de Gruyter, 1967), vol. 1.

10. Cf. the section "Catharist Literature of the Thirteenth and Fourteenth Century" in Walter L. Wakefield and Austin P. Evans, *Heresies of the High Middle Ages: Selected Sources, Translated and Annotated* (New York: Columbia University Press, 1969), 447–630. Nothing of this extent is available for the Waldensians.

The second type of document, reports by ecclesiastical observers, also focuses, though to a lesser degree, on the leading echelons in Waldensian groups. A significant number of ecclesiastical observers used firsthand experience with Waldensians to reveal the heretics' particular characteristics and warn others of their (alleged) depravity. Written with the intention to be effective in their warning against heresy, not all reports were slanderous defamations, and some were even reasonably accurate in pointing to specific aspects of Waldensian ethics, organization, and conduct. Accuracy was perhaps greatest during the earlier periods of the Waldensian movement, when ecclesiastics still knew little about them and had to rely heavily on the information provided in such reports. But again, ecclesiastical observers frequently focused on leaders rather than followers, and they gave more weight to the Waldensians' theological peculiarities and allegations of sociomoral deviance than to their everyday life.

The third type of document is Inquisition records, which exist from about the 1240s onward. Inquisition records are at the same time the most problematic, challenging, and revealing sources on the life and thought of medieval Waldensians. They are problematic because the probative value of statements frequently obtained under conditions of forced compliance is difficult to assess, even though torture was used less frequently and at later periods than one might surmise.[11] They are challenging because of the sheer number of depositions that have been made available by the discovery of new manuscripts, many of them available in printed and edited form, and the wealth of details they contain. They are revealing because for the Waldensians they exist in a sufficient quantity to contain a variety of references to the religious and social customs of the ordinary members of Waldensian congregations. A great many of those interrogated were willingly guided by inquisitors into making statements that conformed to certain topoi, or familiar clichés and stereotypes, of heretics, such as being unlettered or deviant. In Inquisitions, these topoi were reflected in the use of interrogatories, used to lead suspects into admitting heretical affiliation and thus confirming the allegations. The focus of such records can therefore be very selective and the statements heavily biased, if not completely without value. But some Inquisition records also contain pertinent exceptions: statements made by members of heretical groups who firmly stood up for their convictions, despite the obvious threat to their well-being by the inquisitors. The value of such exceptional statements, which provide the closest insights into the Waldensians' religious life

---

11. I address these conditions more specifically in the sections below.

and perhaps some of the best available evidence on forms of popular religiosity in Western history before the Reformation, often far better than anything that is available for heterodox spirituality or the smaller heterodox religious groups, has increasingly been recognized in historical scholarship.[12]

The following sections in this chapter deal with three distinct stages in the history of medieval Waldensianism. Each stage constitutes a separate case in the comparative historical analysis, which focuses on the following religious and social conditions (see Table 3): political situation (inquisitorial persecution), social organization, class and gender basis, religious doctrines, the doctrines' psychological-pragmatic consequences, and life conduct engendered by the interplay of these conditions. The first case is early Waldensianism, a charismatic religious movement at a time when the Inquisition did not yet exist. It found ready support in urban civic strata and allowed women to be preachers. Key elements of Waldensian religious beliefs, such as the idea of a "calling" and the notion of proof of faith in conduct, also developed early. The onset of inquisitorial persecutions and other, internal developments led to crucial changes in the ethics and organization of Waldensian groups.   # 1

The Waldensians in Italy, France, and the eastern parts of the German Empire after the 1240s and 1250s constitute the second case. # 2 Losing support in urban areas and from upper social strata, Waldensianism became a counterchurch that rejected the Catholic Church and excluded women from the ministry. Its salvation economy stressed the mediating salutary powers of the Waldensian itinerant confessors. Despite the differences between early and later Waldensianism, in both cases ascetic behavior was other-worldly oriented and confined to leadership strata. The third case is the Austrian Waldensians. In # 3 the absence of effective persecution, the Waldensians organized in egalitarian textual communities and derived support especially from artisans. While rejecting orthodoxy, Austrian Waldensianism stressed

12. On the issues raised in this paragraph, see Herbert Grundmann, "Ketzerverhöre des Spätmittelalters als quellenkritisches Problem," in *Ausgewählte Aufsätze*, vol. 1, *Religiöse Bewegungen* (Stuttgart: Hiersemann, 1976), 364–416; Jean-François Gilmont, "Sources et critiques des sources" (with debate), in *Les vaudois des origines à leur fin (XIIe–XVIe siècles)*, ed. Gabriel Audisio (Turin: Meynier, 1990), 105–17; Alexander Patschovsky, "Probleme ketzergeschichtlicher Quellenforschung," in *Mittelalterliche Textüberlieferung und ihre kritische Aufarbeitung* (Munich: Monumenta Germaniae Historica, 1978), 86–91. A wider range of sources are summarily discussed in Wakefield and Evans, *Heresies of the High Middle Ages*, 56–64. For the topos of certain heretical characteristics, particularly unlearnedness, see Peter Biller, "The Topos and Reality of the Heretic as Illiteratus," forthcoming.

Table 3. Social and Religious Conditions in Early, Later, and Austrian Waldensianism

	Political Conditions: Inquisition	Social Organization	Class and Gender Basis	Religious Doctrines	Psychological-Pragmatic Consequences	Conduct
Early Waldensianism (c. 1173–1240s)	No	Charismatic religious movement	Urban civic strata; male and female preachers	Apostolic life, biblicism, calling for preachers, not followers	Preachers: proof of faith in conduct; followers: unknown	Preachers: other-worldly asceticism; followers: similar to orthodoxy
Later Waldensianism in eastern Germany, France, and Italy (c. 1240s–1400s)	Yes	Hierarchical sect, counter-church	Middle and lower middle strata; male preachers only	Rejection of Catholic Church, calling for preachers, not followers	Preachers: mediators; followers: adoration of itinerant saintly confessors	Preachers: other-worldly asceticism; followers: similar to orthodoxy
Austrian Waldensianism (c. 1250)	Ineffective	Open, egalitarian textual communities, schools	Artisans; male and female preachers	Rejection of Catholic Church, calling for preachers and followers	Preachers and followers: proof of faith in ascetic conduct	Preachers and followers: inner-worldly asceticism

proof of faith in ascetic conduct among its members. In contrast to other Waldensian groups, the Austrian Waldensian's asceticism was inner-worldly and encompassed followers and leaders, including women, alike. The Austrian Waldensians' rationalized methodical conduct in the secular sphere represented a form of inner-worldly asceticism that in some ways—though not in others—preceded ascetic Protestantism by more than three centuries.

The Early Waldensians:
Prophetic Foundation to Persecution

The history of the Waldensian movement began around 1173 with the conversion of the Lyonese citizen Waldes from a prosperous merchant to a preacher. The Dominican preacher Stephen of Bourbon, a vigilant observer of religious life,[13] recollects the accounts of eyewitnesses present at the scene:

> He [Waldes] resolved to devote himself to evangelical perfection, just as the apostles had pursued it. After having sold all his possessions, in contempt of the world, he broadcast his money as dirt to the poor and presumptuously arrogated to himself the office of the apostles. Preaching the Gospels and those things he had learned by heart in the streets and the broad ways, he drew to himself many men and women that they might do the same, and he strengthened them in the Gospels. He also sent out persons of the basest occupations to preach in the nearby villages. And these, men and women alike, unlettered and uneducated, wandering through the villages, going into homes, and preaching in the squares and even in the churches, induced others to do likewise.[14]

13. For a succinct account of Stephen of Bourbon's activities, see Jean-Claude Schmitt, *The Holy Greyhound: Guinefort, Healer of Children Since the Thirteenth Century*, trans. Martin Thom (Cambridge: Cambridge University Press, 1983), 11–13.

14. "proposuit servare perfectionem evangelicam ut apostoli servaverent; qui, rebus suis omnibus venditis, in contemptum mundi, per lutum pauperibus pecuniam suam proiciebat, et officium apostolorum usurpavit et presumpsit, evangelia et ea que corde retinuerat per vicos et plateas predicando, multos homines et mulieres ad idem faciendum ad se convocando, firmans eis evangelia. Quos eciam per villas circum-jacentes mittebat ad predicandum, vilissimorum quorumcunque officiorum. Qui eciam, tam homines quam mulieres, idiote et illiterati, per villas discurrentes et domos

In this description Waldes fits Weber's category of prophet. The bearer of a religious revelation, Waldes became a central religious figure by challenging established ways of life and proclaiming new religious conceptions. These conceptions were capable of systematizing conduct by directing patterns of social action toward a central religious value. Waldes's activities were highly successful; the zeal of his missionary preaching and that of others expressed in this document soon led to the emergence of Waldensian groups in many places in western Europe in the late twelfth century.[15] Stephen of Bourbon was by no means the only bystander who was impressed by the charismatic appeal of the Waldensian preachers and by how quickly and adeptly they spread their message, carrying it right into the midst of civil life.[16] Waldes, together with his early companions, thereby established the doctrinal basis and spiritual foundations of Waldensianism for generations to come.

Doctrinal Foundations

The success and ethical contents of Waldensian preaching must be understood against the background of profound social change at the time. Social change was wrought by an expanding market economy, political autonomization in the cities, the aftermath of ecclesiastical changes instigated by the Gregorian reforms, and a fluidity in social relationships and established hierarchies—to name but some salient aspects. A more literate, critical, and individualistic laity, particularly in urban spaces, was at the time no longer well served by the dominant spiritual regime.[17] The Waldensians' enthusiasm for the ethical ideals of the apostolic life among the laity was a response to this phenomenon, and subsequently turned Waldensianism into one of the most pertinent expressions of popular dissent in the Middle Ages. The Waldensians advocated the way of life prescribed in the Gospels and the austere morals of the apostles—a worldview that reverberated as *the* model for Christian life in many segments of society at the time—and they framed their message in simple and succinct discourse: repent and follow the basic

---

penetrantes et in plateis predicantes et eciam in ecclesiis, ad idem alios provocabant" (Alexander Patschovsky and Kurt-Victor Selge, eds., *Quellen zur Geschichte der Waldenser* [Gütersloh: Mohn, 1973], p. 16, lines 8–17).

15. See the map in Lambert, *Medieval Heresy*, 70–71.

16. Christine Thouzellier, *Catharisme et valdéisme en Languedoc à la fin du XIIe et au début du XIIIe siècle*, 2d ed. (Louvain: Nauwelaerts, 1969), 11–129; Gonnet and Molnár, *Les vaudois au Moyen Âge*, 41–83.

17. See Chapter 2, pages 80–82.

ethical precepts of the Bible. The Waldensians derived these precepts from a literalist understanding of the Gospels and the Ten Commandments. To preach to others, to live in voluntary poverty, and not to swear, lie, kill, or slander were key tenets of the Waldensian ethics throughout the Middle Ages. Complementary to this ethic of conviction, from early on, was a stringent emphasis on practicing scriptural commandments to the letter and on combining faith with the appropriate works.[18]

The early Waldensians' sincerity in complementing faith with deeds went beyond a notion of "justification by works" characteristic of Catholic spiritual life and its ever-increasing panoply of devotional acts and para-liturgies. Early Waldensianism did not know of such practices. Durand of Huesca's *Liber antiheresis*, arguably the best source on the early Waldensians' religious perceptions, reveals a deep contempt for ecclesiastical rituals as a substitute for proper behavior. "[Waldensianism] is, so to speak, reactionary in its piety when compared to the high and late medieval tendency toward increasing the means and ways of attaining grace."[19] Works, instead, were to be understood as concrete acts in their daily lives, and thus an immediate complement to, and ultimate demonstration of, their convictions.[20] In their emphasis on a close correspondence between faith and behavior, the early Waldensians established their religious life on a spiritual premise that later became fundamental to the inner-worldly asceticism of ascetic Protestantism in the early modern period: perseverance or proof of faith in conduct. This notion implies that a person's soteriological status is indicated by the methodicalness and diligence of his or her conduct, upon which the

18. Gonnet and Molnár, *Les vaudois au Moyen Âge*, 371–400; Audisio, *Les "vaudois,"* 12–14; Giovanni Gonnet, "The Influence of the Sermon on the Mount upon the Ethics of the Waldensians of the Middle Ages," *Brethren Life and Thought* 35 (1990): 34–40; Lerner, "Waldensians," in *Dictionary of the Middle Ages*, ed. Strayer, 510–11. With regard to preaching and poverty, I follow Heinrich Boehmer, "Waldenser," in *Realencyklopädie für protestantische Theologie und Kirche*, 3d ed., ed. Albert Hauck (Leipzig: J. C. Hinrichs'sche Buchhandlung, 1908), 20:812–13; Selge, *Die ersten Waldenser*, vol. 1; and Grado G. Merlo, "Le mouvement vaudois des origines à la fin du XIIe siècle" (with debate), in *Les vaudois des origines à leur fin (XIIe–XVIe siècles)*, ed. Audisio, 15–42, who stress that voluntary poverty was a necessary means to evangelical preaching rather than the ultimate goal in early Waldensianism. For the latter interpretation, see Thouzellier, *Catharisme et valdéisme en Languedoc*, 79 n. 112, 179–80, and Malcolm D. Lambert, *Medieval Heresy: Popular Movements from Bogomil to Hus* (New York: Holmes & Meier, 1977), 353–55. On the new dignity of (voluntary) poverty and the potential spiritual opportunities for the pauper, see Michel Mollat, *The Poor in the Middle Ages: An Essay in Social History* (New Haven: Yale University Press, 1986), 102–13.

19. Selge, *Die ersten Waldenser*, 1:317.

20. Ibid., 35–38, 95–127; Selge, "Die Erforschung der mittelalterlichen Waldensergeschichte," 330–31.

notion of proof thus bestows the heaviest psychological premium possible: assurance of grace. Long before ascetic Protestantism, the early Waldensians rediscovered the idea of proof of faith in conduct and attempted to disseminate this notion among the laity.

Other doctrinal developments added to the ascetic orientation in Waldensian ethics and demarcated them further from similar contemporary religious movements. First, Waldensians' views on salvation were characterized by a dichotomous soteriology and a semi-Pelagian understanding of how salvation could be achieved. The dichotomy in their soteriology—based on soteriological rather than metaphysical dualism[21]—consisted of a strong belief in the existence of only two ways in life: the narrow path to salvation through Christ, in repentance and living according to his commands, and the broad way straight to hell.[22] In its semi-Pelagian component, an emphasis on the human capability to choose righteousness and reject evil deliberately,[23] Waldensianism stressed that it was in the here and now, in faith and in works, that every Christian could and had to choose between the two.[24] While the semi-Pelagian component in early Waldensian ethics stressed the active pursuit of sanctification, the notion of the two ways made a Waldensian's moral probity in the process of achieving salvation all the more imperative.

Second, the Waldensians legitimized their activities by reference to a divine mission. God had given them a "calling," necessitated in part by the negligence of the priesthood, in part by heretical apostasy: "When He saw the works of the prelates set upon cupidity, simony, pride, avarice, vainglory, concupiscence, concubinage, and other disgraces . . . , the Son of the Highest Father commissioned you, Waldes, choosing you for the apostolic calling, so that through you and your companions He might resist the [heretical] errors, since those put in charge [i.e., the prelates above] were not able to."[25]

21. These should be strictly distinguished. Soteriological dualism refers to a dualistic notion of the paths to salvation, whereas metaphysical dualism, represented by Cathar religion, refers to the belief in a fundamental opposition between good and evil or mind and matter. For further discussion of the nature and implications of these differences, see Chapter 5.

22. Selge, *Die ersten Waldenser*, 1:113–18.

23. Cf. Jaroslav J. Pelikan, *The Christian Tradition: A History of the Development of Doctrine*, vol. 1, *The Emergence of the Catholic Tradition (100–600)* (Chicago: University of Chicago Press, 1978), 313–18.

24. See Selge, *Die ersten Waldenser*, 1:112, 145, who argues that the Waldensians radicalized Pelagian notions that were also latent in contemporary orthodox theology. See also Thouzellier, *Catharisme et valdéisme en Languedoc*, 75.

25. "videns prelatorum opera summi patris filius cupiditati, simonie, superbie, philargie, cenodoxie, castrimargie, pellicatui, aliisque flagiciis intenta . . . te, domne

God had called upon the Waldensians as laity to restore ethical sobriety in his communities and to strive against heretical infidelity (i.e., the Cathars)—a task, as they saw it, grossly neglected by the priests. When Waldes made his *Profession of Faith* at a diocesan council at Lyon in 1180 in order to demonstrate his righteous intentions, he not only professed his belief in the Catholic Church, outside of which no one can be saved, but also affirmed the anti-Donatist position that even a sinful priest could administer the sacraments. Thus, the proper place of the Waldensians' calling was originally within the Catholic Church, as a reform movement.[26]

Third, the Waldensians' assertion of orthodoxy did not stop at embracing the traditional moral standards of the church. Their particular mission and responsibility—facing incapable priests on the one hand, heretics on the other—demanded that they hold themselves to stricter ethical standards than were required of them in their lay status by the church. The church distinguished between "commands," as espoused in the Ten Commandments, which were to reign over the mundane life, and "evangelical counsels," which applied to monks and nuns.[27] Weber described these two different systems of morals as the "ethic of the average" and the "ethic of heroes."[28] In his *Profession of Faith*, Waldes and his companions, however, affirmed the "ethic of heroes," despite their official status as laity. "Our resolve has been to follow the evangelical counsels as commands."[29] By evangelical counsels,

---

valdesi, eligens in apostolico aporismate, ut per te et tuosque comites, quod inposti non poterant, renitatur allegavit erroribus" (Selge, *Die ersten Waldenser*, vol. 2, p. 8, lines 31–37). The text includes a similar reference to the ministry God had given as divinely ordained task to Paul (*ministerium*, Acts 20.24) and now gave to the Waldensians. See Selge, *Die ersten Waldenser*, vol. 2, p. 81, line 124; p. 85, line 220; also 1:53, 315; Zerfaß, *Der Streit um die Laienpredigt*, 63.

26. The text was presented to Waldes in this form. The part on the church, outside of which no one can be saved, existed in prior formulas, but not the anti-Donatist affirmation. See Giovanni Gonnet, *Enchiridion fontium Valdensium* (Torre Pellice: Claudiana, 1958), 1:34. An annotated translation of Waldes's *Profession of Faith* is contained in Wakefield and Evans, *Heresies of the High Middle Ages*, 206–8. See also Thouzellier, *Catharisme et valdéisme en Languedoc*, 30–36; Selge, *Die ersten Waldenser*, 1:25–35.

27. E. Dublanchy, "Conseils Évangéliques," in *Dictionnaire de théologie catholique*, vol. 3, ed. A. Vacant and E. Mangenot (Paris: Letonzey et Ané, 1938), cols. 1176–82; Franz Lau, "Evangelische Räte," in *Die Religion in Geschichte und Gegenwart: Handwörterbuch für Theologie und Religionswissenschaft*, 3d ed., ed. K. Galling (Tübingen: Mohr, 1958), cols. 785–88.

28. See Chapter 1, page 21.

29. "Consilia quoque evangelica velut precepta servare proposuimus" (Gonnet, *Enchiridion fontium Valdensium*, p. 35, lines 20–21).

Waldes probably meant quite literally the familiar tasks and duties that Jesus had given to his disciples in his Sermon on the Mount and when he sent them out (Mt 5–7, 10.5–42, Mk 6.7–11, Lk 6.20–49, 9.1–5), while the ecclesiastics hoped—in vain, as it turned out—that they effectively consigned the Waldensians to the monastic way of life, that is, poverty, chastity, and obedience to the church.[30]

Taken together, the dogmatic foundations of Waldensianism made for a highly rationalized form of lay religion. An ethic of conviction based on simple and stringent evangelical ideals, the idea of a calling in spreading them, a perception of a dichotomous division of the path to salvation from the path to perdition, a semi-Pelagian activism in pursuing the one that leads to heaven, the rejection of a system of graded ethical duties, and, perhaps most important, the notion of perseverance of faith in conduct—all these, added to rejuvenated notions of apostolic life among the laity, formed a whole that was far more conducive to the development of methodical rational ways of life than was Catholicism's spiritual regime at the time.

Textual Communities

If these were the ethical notions that gave meaning to Waldensian life, it was their organization that provided them with institutional resources and gave force to their movement. The early Waldensians were "textual communities." Waldes hired a grammarian to translate the Gospels and passages from the church fathers, and a scribe to write down the translations. Waldes then learned these translations by heart and passed his newly acquired knowledge on to others, who did the same.[31] Waldes's skills in Latin, which for a former merchant must at least have been elementary, were apparently not enough to do the reading and translating himself (Stephen of Bourbon described him as *non esset multum litteratus*),[32] but other members of the early Waldensians, such as Durand of Huesca, were able to read religious works in Latin and then interpret and expound on them in the vernacular.[33] Most of the

---

30. See Gonnet and Molnár, *Les vaudois au Moyen Âge*, 396–97; Selge, *Die ersten Waldenser*, 1:47–48, 253; Zerfaß, *Der Streit um die Laienpredigt*, 16 n. 30.

31. See Patschovsky and Selge, *Quellen zur Geschichte der Waldenser*, 15–16.

32. Ibid., p. 16, line 3.

33. Durand of Huesca notes in his *Profession of Faith* of 1208 that the members of his group were almost all literate, that is, able to read and write Latin, since the group consisted for the most part of (former) clerics ("ex magna parte clerci simus et pene omnes litterati"; Gonnet, *Enchiridion fontium Valdensium*, p. 133, lines 12–13).

preachers, however, must have preached on the basis of vernacular scripture, since "Waldensianism and the work of translating the Bible into the vernacular were virtually synonymous around the year 1200."[34]

From these textual communities' inner circles of translators and interpreters of texts, the Waldensian message radiated to supporters and other interested people. The most common form of transmission of heresy in the Middle Ages was interpersonal communication: preaching by core adherents and discussion between them and outsiders (and sometimes adversaries) who could be convinced and drawn into the group. For these activities the restless itinerary of the Waldensians was apt.[35] But preaching and discussion were not the only communication channels. They also involved homes of supporters and schools. The career of a Waldensian preacher would begin as a novice in one of the houses that had been made available to the Waldensians by their supporters for the purpose of schooling in biblical texts.[36] A simple supporter could also attend these lessons, so that in one case a young and illiterate herdsman was able within a year to memorize word for word forty passages from the Bible and other religious messages during Sunday services, simply by listening to the sermons and repeating them in his mind. Others, we are told, concentrated so hard on learning the lessons by heart that they would barely miss a word.[37]

---

34. Patschovsky, "The Literacy of Waldensianism," in *Heresy and Literacy*, ed. Biller and Hudson, 116. Patschovsky's account supersedes Margaret Deanesly's classic and still valuable treatment in *The Lollard Bible and Other Medieval Biblical Versions*, 25–55, which has been corrected by Leonard E. Boyle, "Innocent III and Vernacular Versions of Scripture," in *The Bible in the Medieval World: Essays in Memory of Beryl Smalley*, ed. Katherine Walsh and Diana Wood (Oxford: Blackwell, 1985), 97–108.

35. On transmission of heresy, see Arno Borst, "La transmission de l'hérésie au Moyen Âge," in *Hérésies et sociétés dans l'Europe pré-industrielle, 11e–18e siècles*, ed. Jacques Le Goff (Paris: Mouton, 1968), 273–75; Menache, *The Vox Dei*, chap. 11. For the Waldensians, see also Zerfaß, *Der Streit um die Laienpredigt*, 59–82.

36. Selge, *Die ersten Waldenser*, 1:136 n. 24, 260–65. For other references to Waldensian schools, see Jean Duvernoy, "Albigeois et vaudois en Quercy d'après le registre des pénitences de Pierre Sellan," in *Moissac et sa région: Actes du XIXe Congrès d'études régionales tenu à Moissac, les 5 et 6 Mai 1963*, ed. Fédération des Sociétés académiques et savantes, Languedoc-Pyrénées-Gascogne (Albi: Ateliers professionels et d'apprentissage de l'Orphelinat Saint-Jean, 1964), 119 n. 61; Martin Schneider, *Europäisches Waldensertum im 13. und 14. Jahrhundert: Gemeinschaftsform–Frömmigkeit–sozialer Hintergrund* (Berlin: de Gruyter, 1981), 32 n. 8, 96 n. 6.

37. Stephen of Bourbon reports: "Vivi ego juvenem bubulcum, qui solum per annum moram fecerat in domo cujusdam heretici Valdensis, qui tam diligenti attencione et sollicita ruminacione affirmabat et retinebat que audiebat, quod infra annum illum firmaverat et retinuerat quadraginta evangelia dominicalia, exceptis festivitatibus, que omnia verbum ad verbum in lingua sua didiscerat, exceptis aliis verbis sermonum et oracionum" (Patschovsky and Selge, *Quellen zur Geschichte der Waldenser*, 48).

These examples, and the early success of Waldensian preaching in general, show that the Waldensians were very capable in setting up such discursive conventicles for the transmission of religious knowledge. They were exemplars of new levels of literacy and communicative rationality and sociability in religious communities[38] at a time when the church not only discouraged preaching by the laity but, in a number of synodal decrees for areas afflicted by heresy in the second half of the thirteenth century, forbade the laity to own any books of scripture in the vernacular or to do translations into it.[39] Furthermore, with their religion founded on texts, the Waldensians quickly moved away from their status as being an emergent religious movement guided solely by the exemplary prophecy of a Waldes or Durand of Huesca. Not only their sermons but also vernacular translations of scripture and exegetical materials were the sources of divine norms and standards against which Waldensian beliefs and conduct were measured. Ethical prophecy based on the interpretation of texts therefore supplemented exemplary prophecy from early on and furthered the impetus toward a rationalized religion.

Socioeconomic Background and Participation of Women

Waldensian support initially derived to a large extent from urban civic strata. Major lay religious groups of the late twelfth century and the first half of the thirteenth century, such as the Cathars, the Humiliati, the Waldensians, and the Beguines, had strongholds in the more commercialized and urbanized regions in Europe (Lombardy and the Low Countries) and along the waterways and trade routes connecting them (the Rhône valley, the Rhineland, and southwestern parts of the German Empire).[40] With the exception of the Low Countries, the Waldensians spread predominantly in these areas.[41] The ecological correlation between support for Waldensianism and economic development and urbanization holds up for smaller units of analysis. As Herbert Grundmann's seminal

---

38. Stock, *Listening for the Text*, 24–29. See also Patschovsky, "The Literacy of Waldensianism," in *Heresy and Literacy*, ed. Biller and Hudson, 113–23.

39. Grundmann, *Religiöse Bewegungen im Mittelalter*, 447–48; but see also Hamilton, *Religion in the Medieval West*, 60, who notes that these prohibitions were ineffective in the long run.

40. See John Hine Mundy, *Europe in the High Middle Ages, 1150–1309*, 2d ed. (New York: Longman, 1991), 81–100; N.J.G. Pounds, *An Economic History of Medieval Europe* (New York: Longman, 1974), 103–8.

41. Grundmann, *Religiöse Bewegungen im Mittelalter*, 197; Little, *Religious Poverty*, 113, 125; Lambert, *Medieval Heresy*, 70–71.

exploration of the socioeconomic background of late-twelfth- and early-thirteenth-century Waldensians has revealed, the economically destitute were not the Waldensians' prime constituency, despite Stephen of Bourbon's derogatory remark that they were "of the basest occupations."[42] Besides nobles and former ecclesiastics, burghers, rather than urban proletarians or peasants, were drawn to Waldensianism,[43] which only later, as ecclesiastical persecution grew in strength, gravitated toward lower urban strata and rustics. Even Marxist accounts now support this conclusion.[44] In this way Waldensian ethics met with a socioeconomic group that was already predisposed to a practical rationalism in conduct. The material status of burghers as autonomous political citizens and their involvement in market transactions provided a potentially fertile soil for the asceticism and methodicalness associated with Waldensian beliefs.

Women also responded to the Waldensian call for apostolic life. They bore witness to their faith while moving through town and country, preaching to the public, and instructing supporters on Waldensian beliefs.[45] Waldensianism thus offered women an active and more egalitarian role at a time when women in orthodox religion were increasingly excluded from exercising clerical authority and pastoral functions. In the twelfth century, it was still unclear whether their male orthodox counterparts would regard them as "sisters or handmaids"[46] in the established Catholic religious orders; in the thirteenth century, women took advantage of new religious opportunities for laywomen in convents and lay associations such as the Beguines only to be met with suspicion

42. See page 135 above.

43. Grundmann, *Religiöse Bewegungen im Mittelalter*, 161–65; also Selge, *Die ersten Waldenser*, 1:266–69; Lambert, *Medieval Heresy*, 69.

44. Ernst Werner and Martin Erbstösser, *Ketzer und Heilige: Das religiöse Leben im Hochmittelalter* (Vienna: Böhlau, 1987), 280, 294. Note that the analysis of Waldensianism's class basis is difficult not only because of the ambiguity of the terminology that is used to describe its adherents' social origins and professions and the scarcity of sources (Grundmann, *Religiöse Bewegungen im Mittelalter*, 161–62; see also Stock, *The Implications of Literacy*, on earlier religious movements), but also, if Weber is correct, because a charismatic upsurge tends to transcend class boundaries (*Economy and Society*, 486, 1117, 1121). On the class basis of later Waldensianism, which is less difficult to determine, see page 151 below.

45. Grado G. Merlo, *Valdesi e valdismi medievali*, vol. 2, *Identità valdesi nella storia e nella storiografia: Studi e discussioni* (Turin: Claudiana, 1991), 93–112, provides an outstanding analysis. See also Gottfried Koch, *Frauenfrage und Ketzertum im Mittelalter: Die Frauenbewegung im Rahmen des Katharismus und des Waldensertums und ihre soziale Wurzeln (12.-14. Jahrhundert)* (Berlin: Akademie, 1962), 158–62; Giovanni Gonnet, "La femme dans les mouvements paupéro-évangéliques du Bas Moyen Âge (notamment chez les Vaudois)," *Heresis* 22 (1994): 27–41.

46. Lawrence, *Medieval Monasticism*, 216.

and to be directed into semimonastic channels. By then, ecclesiastical censure was threatening wandering evangelists, especially if they were religiously active women.[47] In contrast, early Waldensianism allowed its female preachers to perform sacerdotal functions, to be ascetics, and to pursue an active ministry.[48]

The Lay Dimension

But how far did the ethics of the early Waldensians actually penetrate into lay activities? And did these ethics guide them in an inner-worldly direction? Waldes and certainly many of his followers and successors underwent a conversion in which they left everything behind that had been materially essential to them. They took on a new life that required the austere lifestyle of a wandering preacher. The Waldensians' austerity, a visible sign of their dedication and sincerity, was described by the chronicler Walter Map, who confronted a Waldensian group at the Third Lateran Council at Rome in 1179: "They have no fixed habitations. They go about two by two, barefoot, clad in woolen garments, possessing nothing, holding all things common like the apostles, nakedly following the naked Christ." Map added, perhaps sardonically, "If we admit them, we shall be driven out."[49] But this asceticism was other-worldly rather than inner-worldly; it required withdrawal from the world in favor of the celibacy and voluntary poverty associated with itineracy. Waldes professed: "We have renounced the world. . . . We are not going to accept either gold or silver or anything else of such sort from anyone beyond food and clothing for the day."[50] This is the very spirit of the early Waldensians. It is a spirit of religious virtuosos who are resolved to overcome the world. The urgency of their task—both to oppose heretics and to admonish those of their fellow Christians

47. See Bynum, *Jesus as Mother*, 250; eadem, *Holy Feast and Holy Fast*, 13–30; Grundmann, *Religiöse Bewegungen im Mittelalter*.

48. For a similar role of women in early Christian circles and their contributions to the rise of Christianity, see Rodney Stark, *The Rise of Christianity: A Sociologist Reconsiders History* (Princeton: Princeton University Press, 1996), chap. 5.

49. "Hii certa nusquam habent domicilia, bini et bini circueunt nudi pedes, laneis induti, nichil habentes, omnia sibi communia tanquam apostoli, nudi nudum Christum sequentes. . . . si admiserimus, expellemur" (Walter Map, *De nugis curialium*, ed. M. R. James, rev. C.N.L. Brooke and R.A.B. Mynors [Oxford: Clarendon Press, 1983], 126).

50. "seculo abrenunciavimus . . . nec aurum nec argentum vel aliquid tale preter victum et vestitum cotidianum a quoquam accepturi sumus" (Gonnet, *Enchiridion fontium Valdensium*, p. 35, lines 16, 19–20).

insufficiently attended to by priests—simply did not allow for continuing an ordinary vocation. "Work" for them was not engagement in manual toil, but apostolic labor, that is, preaching.[51] The Waldensians' task also was incompatible with fixed residence, at least after the initial period of schooling. This period served as a time of probation as well, after which a virtuoso took a vow and was ordained as a preacher. This was almost certainly an exclusive and irreversible procedure.[52]

There were also supporters and sympathizers who stayed within their social groups and vocations. In contrast to the ascetic lifestyle of the Waldensian preachers, their ways of life were probably far less affected by the Waldensians' ethical precepts. Certainly the preaching of a Waldensian could arouse intense religious feelings, doubts, and sincere resolutions. But did this preaching result in a lasting ethical rationalization of conduct, one in which the Waldensians' idea of proof of faith in upright behavior applied to inner-worldly conduct? Since the historical sources available for this period almost exclusively concentrate on the Waldensian preachers and their immediate and temporary audiences, this question is difficult to answer. Nevertheless, one may doubt a strong influence of Waldensian ethics on the ways of life of sympathizers and supporters, for two reasons.

First, although Waldensian soteriology was dichotomous in that it postulated only two ways, one to heaven and one to hell, at this early stage in their history the Waldensians did not see their way of living as the only one possible. Unlike their main heterodox adversaries, the Cathars, they held that their particular path to heaven was not exclusive; rather, there were many paths, principally open to all Christians.[53] To the supporters and sympathizers of the Waldensians, this must have somewhat eased their minds and decreased the necessity of seeking salvation through asceticism.

Second, and more important, the boundaries between an orthodox Catholic believer and a Waldensian sympathizer were not yet salient.

51. See Durand of Huesca's chapter "De labore" in his *Liber antiheresis* (Selge, *Die ersten Waldenser*, 2:77–89). On this, see Selge, *Die ersten Waldenser*, 1:50–64; Paolini, "Gli eretici e il lavoro," in *Lavorare nel Medio Evo*, ed. Università degli studi di Perugia, 120–34.

52. "It seems impossible that the community included supporters who would never be able to teach" (Selge, *Die ersten Waldenser*, 1:264; on probation, see 264–65). Peter Biller ("Multum Ieiunantes et se Castigantes: Medieval Waldensian Asceticism," in *Monks, Hermits, and the Ascetic Tradition*, ed. W. J. Sheils [Oxford: Blackwell, 1985], 217–18) notes that the basic selection and training procedures for Waldensian preachers did not change substantially over the next centuries.

53. Selge, *Die ersten Waldenser*, 1:114–27. On the Cathars, see Chapter 5, pages 178–79.

The church's ideological boundary work aiming at the demarcation of orthodox fidelity from Waldensian heterodoxy only slowly translated into effective ecclesiastical policy.

From the beginning, there was suspicion about the Waldensians' preaching. From the church's view, the authority to preach was given to priests, not to laity, since lay preaching was increasingly viewed as sacrilegious presumption.[54] When the Waldensians appealed to the pope at the Third Lateran Council in Rome in 1179 and asked for his authorization to preach, it was ruled that they were allowed to preach only if authorized by their local priests. Bishop and priests at the Lyon diocese were rather unsympathetic to the request of the Waldensians, who, including their female members, resumed preaching.[55] As a result of their continued opposition to ecclesiastical restrictions on lay preaching, the Waldensians were first locally excommunicated and expelled from Lyon. Then followed, in 1184, their general excommunication as schismatics, for defying church authority, by Pope Lucius III, whose decretal *Ad abolendam* put them under perpetual anathema and instituted the formal Inquisition of heresy.[56] Yet not until the 1230s (in France and Germany) and 1250s (in Italy) were severe decrees and laws against heretics fully and effectively implemented in persecutions. Until then, the Waldensians were still able to preach their views openly and with relative ease in most areas. "When at that time a listener was animated by a Waldensian sermon, it does not follow that he subsequently was to

54. See particularly Zerfaß, *Der Streit um die Laienpredigt*.

55. In technical terms, Waldensians were only allowed to give exhortations or admonitions, that is, to witness their personal faith, especially against heretics. They were not allowed to preach or to engage in theological disputations with them. Since there were female Waldensian preachers, ecclesiastics often phrased their abhorrence in misogynist discourse. Bernard of Fontcaude in particular thundered against the Waldensians' assertion that women may preach, and also commented on those that were especially prone to heretical seduction, stating that among those easily seduced was the "dumb and clamorous woman. . . . [She is] [d]umb because of her foolish mind, and clamorous because of her babbling." Men, too, were afflicted, but especially those "of feminine debility." ("Declaratur, quos maxime seducant. . . . III. . . . Seducunt et viros femineae debilitatis. . . . IV. . . . Mulier stulta et clamosa est haeretica pravitas. Stulta scilicet per fatuum intellectum; et clamosa per garrulitatem" [*Adversus Waldensium sectam liber*, in *Patrologiae cursus completus . . . Series Latina . . .* , ed. Migne, vol. 204, col. 821].)

56. R. I. Moore, *The Formation of a Persecuting Society: Power and Deviance in Western Europe, 950–1250* (Oxford: Blackwell, 1990), 6–27; Edward Peters, *Inquisition* (Berkeley and Los Angeles: University of California Press, 1989), 40–74; Lambert, *Medieval Heresy*, 63–69, 91–104. But see also Richard Kieckhefer, "The Office of Inquisition and Medieval Heresy: The Transition from Personal to Institutional Jurisdiction," *Journal of Ecclesiastical History* 46 (1995): 36–61.

'become a Waldensian,' in the sense of becoming a member in a new organization. He rather may have decided to give up swearing and lying, to hear Waldensian sermons as often as possible, and to support their preachers with alms. Otherwise this sympathizer would have remained a Catholic and continued to receive the Catholic sacraments."[57] Hence, as long as the Waldensians had not emerged into a clearly demarcated heterodox sect that demanded exclusive solidarity, and the Catholic Church did not have the legal, political, and cultural resources to define *and* enforce its criteria of membership, there remained a gray area between hierocratic administration of grace and alternative sectarian experience. In this gray area the Waldensian sympathizer could dwell, open to the ideas of the Waldensians but not ready to leave the Catholic Church openly. The religious experience of Waldensian sympathizers, who remained outside of the Waldensians' inner circles, lacked the firm dedication to Waldensian ideals that was characteristic of the preachers. The preachers' appeal to austerity may therefore not have had much impact on the everyday life of their listeners.

Waldensianism in the Fourteenth Century

External and Internal Developments

Direct evidence on ethics, organization, and behavior of lay Waldensians is available for a later period and different geographical region: the southeastern parts of the German Empire (Austria) around 1250, and its eastern territories in the fourteenth century. The diffusion of Waldensian faith in those geographical areas came in the aftermath of developments in the early thirteenth century. In 1205, shortly before the death of Waldes, the Waldensians split into two main factions, one French (*Poor of Lyons*) and one Italian (*Poor Lombards*), while north of the Alps the Waldensians made further inroads in Germany.[58] In 1218, an attempt to reconcile the two main factions at a conference of their leaders at Bergamo, Italy, failed. Three major issues split the Waldensians, as is known from a letter the *Poor Lombards* sent to a group of associated

57. Lerner, "Waldenser, Lollarden und Taboriten," 331.
58. In addition to these internal factions, parts of the Waldensians were reconciled with the church in 1208 and 1210. Those were Durand of Huesca's *Poor Catholics* and Bernard Prim's *Reconciled Poor*. See Grundmann, *Religiöse Bewegungen im Mittelalter*, 100–27; Selge, *Die ersten Waldenser*, 1:188–225; Gonnet and Molnár, *Les vaudois au Moyen Âge*, 106–21.

German Waldensians soon after the conference had broken up in disagreement.[59] First, should the Waldensian preachers devote themselves exclusively to preaching, and thereby remain itinerant and less vulnerable to distraction from their mission by entanglement in the world, or should they settle down and support themselves through manual labor? Second, should the Waldensians continue to recognize the administration of the sacraments by the Catholic clergy, even if sinful, or affirm a Donatist position and have their own ministers administer them? Third, should the Waldensian organization remain relatively decentralized and be guided by a commune that would choose two governing rectors on a yearly basis, or should the Waldensians have a more centralized and hierarchical organization with a permanent group of leaders around one central figure, chosen for life? The *Poor of Lyons* supported the former positions, the *Poor Lombards* the latter. But these two strategies to deal with the problem of routinization of charisma in an emergent religious movement remained theoretical. With the increasing number of persecutions in the 1230s, Waldensian groups no longer had a choice between alternatives. Their preachers now had to preach secretly and to travel in disguise. Women—as preachers a highly visible and easy target—became largely excluded from this circle. Men thus entirely dominated the higher levels in the hierarchy of Waldensian organizations.[60] The only exceptions to this rule were the small Waldensian "Order of Sisters"[61] and the more prominent role of women among fourteenth-century Waldensians

---

59. Patschovsky and Selge, *Quellen zur Geschichte der Waldenser*, 20–43; analysis in Selge, *Die ersten Waldenser*, 1:172–88; Gonnet and Molnár, *Les vaudois au Moyen Âge*, 90–103.

60. "The establishment of a hierarchy of office, decreasing mobility, and declining intensity of religious life led in [here: Waldensian] heterodoxy to phenomena similar to the ones that could be observed in orthodoxy. Enclosure, domestication, subordination, and limitation of the apostolic life took the place of abundant opportunities for growth and development and of a relative equality [between the sexes]" (Elm, "Die Stellung der Frau in Ordernswesen, Semireligiosentum und Häresie," in *Sankt Elisabeth*, ed. Philipps-Universität Marburg, 19; emphasis removed). On these processes, see also Audisio, *Les "vaudois,"* 31–39; Gonnet and Molnár, *Les vaudois au Moyen Âge*, 189 n. 297; Koch, *Frauenfrage und Ketzertum im Mittelalter*, 169–75; Schneider, *Europäisches Waldensertum*, 17, 45, 47, 72; Peter Segl, "Die religiöse Frauenbewegung in Südfrankreich im 12. und 13. Jahrhundert zwischen Häresie und Orthodoxie," in *Religiöse Frauenbewegung und mystische Frömmigkeit im Mittelalter*, ed. Peter Dinzelbacher and Dieter R. Bauer (Cologne: Böhlau, 1988), 99–116. Cf. Ronald N. Swanson's (*Religion and Devotion in Europe*, 303) peculiar assertion that "[i]n Waldensianism the status of women remained similar to that of orthodox nuns," for which he offers no evidence.

61. Peter Biller, "Medieval Waldensian Abhorrence of Killing pre–c. 1400," in *The Church and War*, ed. W. J. Sheils (Oxford: Basil Blackwell, 1983), 138 n. 48; idem, "Multum Ieiunantes et se Castigantes," 219–20.

dwelling in remote Piedmontese valleys, who may also have had some preachers living in stable residency.[62] Otherwise, the marginalization of Waldensian women by the Inquisition was likely similar to that of female spiritual leaders, the *perfectae*, in Catharism.[63]

It also became much more dangerous for sympathizers of the Waldensians to listen to the preachers and support them. "Believers" and "friends," as they were called, grouped more closely around the preachers, and in the face of persecution they were required to make a conscious decision about becoming a member of the Waldensians or remaining in the church. Membership in the Waldensian movement thus became an exclusive choice.[64] In the case of the French Waldensians, by 1400 membership in the *societas* ran along family lineages. The *societas* was organized similarly to an order, to which admission was granted to young applicants from Waldensian families, who underwent a lengthy instruction and probation period.[65] In Italy, the boundaries between Waldensianism and Catholicism were even more sharply drawn in that the Waldensians there understood themselves more as a counterchurch.[66] In both countries, confession to a member of the higher echelons in the highly hierarchical organization became a central aspect of Waldensian spirituality, whereby *seygnores* or *barbi* (Italy) and *maiores* or *presbiteri* (France) periodically provided ethical instruction and advice. The predominant prophecy changed back to an exemplary type.[67]

The German Waldensians

The much stronger demarcation of Waldensianism from Catholicism and concomitant changes in Waldensian religious life are best documented

---

62. Grado G. Merlo, *Eretici e inquisitori nella società piemontese* (Turin: Claudiana, 1977), 46, 49–51; Schneider, *Europäisches Waldensertum*, 85.

63. See Chapter 5, page 214.

64. Boehmer, "Waldenser," 812; Selge, *Die ersten Waldenser*, 1:306; Schneider, *Europäisches Waldensertum*, 133; Lerner, "Waldenser, Lollarden und Taboriten," 332.

65. Schneider, *Europäisches Waldensertum*, 39–55; Grado G. Merlo, *Valdesi e valdismi medievali*, vol. 1, *Itinerari e proposte di ricerca* (Turin: Claudiana, 1984), 45–86.

66. Schneider, *Europäisches Waldensertum*, 70–91; Merlo, *Eretici e inquisitori nella società piemontese*, 20–41.

67. Schneider, *Europäisches Waldensertum*, 52–54, 73, 86, 90; Merlo, *Eretici e inquisitori nella società piemontese*, 41–52; Guillaume Mollat, ed., *Bernard Gui: Manuel de l'Inquisiteur* (1926; reprint, Paris: Champion, 1980), 1:60; Giovanni Gonnet, "Natures et limites de l'épiscopat vaudois au Moyen Âge," *Communio Viatorum* 2 (1959): 311–23; Gonnet and Molnár, *Les vaudois au Moyen Âge*, 185–93.

for a third branch of Waldensianism with large numbers: the German Waldensians in the southeastern and eastern parts of the German Empire. In historical scholarship, it had long been known that in those areas Inquisitions took place periodically: under Conrad of Marburg in the 1230s, other inquisitors in the 1260s and 1310s, Gallus of Neuhaus in the 1330s, and Peter Zwicker in the late fourteenth century.[68] Yet not until 1979, when the German historian Alexander Patschovsky published the newly discovered surviving fragments of the records of Gallus of Neuhaus's activities in Bohemia between 1335 and 1353/55, did the full extent of the Waldensian heretical movement become known.[69] Patschovsky unearthed a historical event in which probably more than 4,400 examinees, or close to 5 percent of the total German population of that area, were involved in a ruthless Inquisition that lasted about twenty years. Based on conservative extrapolations of numbers compiled from the existing fragments of the original document, at least 2,600 of the examinees were Waldensians, many of whom underwent a systematic interrogation about their religious beliefs.[70] Interpreted together with some other invaluable records from surrounding areas,[71] this source provides a lively and revealing picture of Waldensian religious life in the fourteenth century.[72]

68. Richard Kieckhefer, *Repression of Heresy in Medieval Germany* (Philadelphia: University of Pennsylvania Press, 1979), 53–73; Lambert, *Medieval Heresy*, 147–60.

69. It has been called one "of the most important publications achieved by any medievalist in the twentieth century" (Robert E. Lerner, "A Case of Religious Counter-Culture: The German Waldensians," *American Scholar* 55 [1986]: 235).

70. Alexander Patschovsky, *Quellen zur Böhmischen Inquisition im 14. Jahrhundert* (Weimar: Böhlau, 1979), 11–24.

71. Besides Patschovsky (*Quellen zur Böhmischen Inquisition im 14. Jahrhundert*), the main sources on German Waldensianism in the fourteenth century are the records on the Waldensians in Brandenburg and Pomerania in 1392–94, published and discussed by Dietrich Kurze, "Zur Ketzergeschichte der Mark Brandenburg und Pommerns vornehmlich im 14. Jahrhundert," *Jahrbuch für die Geschichte Mittel– und Ostdeutschlands* 16/17 (1968): 50–94; idem, ed., *Quellen zur Ketzergeschichte Brandenburgs und Pommerns* (Berlin: de Gruyter, 1975); and Wilhelm Wattenbach, "Über die Inquisition gegen die Waldenser in Pommern und der Mark Brandenburg," in *Kleine Abhandlungen zur mittelalterlichen Geschichte* (1886; reprint, Leipzig: Zentralantiquariat der Deutschen Demokratischen Republik, 1974), 127–226. Testimonies obtained during the persecution of Waldensians in Schweidnitz (Silesia) in 1315 are published and discussed in Alexander Patschovsky, "Waldenserverfolgung in Schweidnitz 1315," *Deutsches Archiv für Erforschung des Mittelalters* 36 (1980): 137–76.

72. The circumstances under which the Bohemian Waldensians testified caution against taking these testimonies at face value. They often tried to dodge the issue when it came to reporting their heretical beliefs, and to avoid incriminating their fellow Waldensians (Patschovsky, *Quellen zur Böhmischen Inquisition im 14. Jahrhundert*, 49–55)—which is hardly surprising, given the reign of terror under Gallus of Neuhaus.

One of the most immediate consequences of the many persecutions that followed the initial onslaught in the 1230s was a change in the class structure of the Waldensian adherents. In France, Italy, and many parts of the German Empire the Waldensians became a movement of rustics and simple craftsmen and -women in rural areas. There, Waldensianism's socioeconomic basis was now limited to social strata with far less affinity to practical rationalism than the early Waldensians.[73] In Bohemia, the situation was different; the German settlers who had colonized the area were experiencing new opportunities on the basis of legal freedoms and the availability of arable land. Some of the settlers might already have been Waldensians fleeing religious persecution in Austria and other parts of the empire, but Waldensianism spread enormously among all groups, and it included not only the peasantry and craftsmen, as in Brandenburg and Pomerania,[74] but also and especially the upwardly oriented and prosperous strata.[75] The socioeconomic composition of Waldensianism reverted to its earlier basis, in social strata whose material practices and patterns of conduct lent themselves more easily than those of other strata to a rationalizing influence of certain religious conceptions.

In Pomerania and Brandenburg, the Inquisition under Zwicker proceeded differently. Persecution was relatively lenient, and comparatively mild penances for the convicted (not even prison sentences were given) encouraged others to come forward. "In general, the interrogated were not reluctant to answer all questions addressed to them promptly and without reservation" (Kurze, "Zur Ketzergeschichte der Mark Brandenburg und Pommerns," 74; see also 74–77 for the procedures involved; similarly Wattenbach, "Über die Inquisition gegen die Waldenser in Pommern und der Mark Brandenburg," in *Kleine Abhandlungen*, 158). And the questions were neutral enough not to obliterate the peculiarities of the life and teachings of the Waldensians (Kurze, "Zur Ketzergeschichte der Mark Brandenburg und Pommerns," 76). Yet in spite of these differences in the methods of eliciting testimonies, the core tenets and main features of the Bohemian and Brandenburg-Pomeranian Waldensians' spirituality thus reported are virtually identical and far too esoteric to have originated in the mind of vicious inquisitors or imaginative witnesses. This allows me to conclude that the statements in the Inquisition records do attest to the Waldensian beliefs and practices with a considerable degree of accuracy.

73. Schneider, *Europäisches Waldensertum*, 37–39, 89; Merlo, *Eretici e inquisitori nella società piemontese*, 107–11; Lambert, *Medieval Heresy*, 164; Martin Erbstösser, *Sozialreligiöse Strömungen im späten Mittelalter: Geißler, Freigeister und Waldenser im 14. Jahrhundert* (Berlin: Akademie, 1970), 119–31; Audisio, *Les "vaudois,"* 39–42.

74. Kurze, "Zur Ketzergeschichte der Mark Brandenburg und Pommerns," 88–90; Wattenbach, "Über die Inquisition gegen die Waldenser in Pommern und der Mark Brandenburg," in *Kleine Abhandlungen*, 144.

75. Patschovsky, *Quellen zur Böhmischen Inquisition im 14. Jahrhundert*, 55–71. There are similar findings for the Waldensians persecuted in Schweidnitz; idem, "Waldenserverfolgung in Schweidnitz 1315," 159–61.

Doctrinal Developments

In this atmosphere of civic self-confidence and moderate social mobility, a strong doctrinal demarcation of Waldensianism from Catholicism occurred in Bohemia, likely spurred by previous experiences of persecution. First, the Waldensians moved closer to the Donatist and anticlerical positions that had first been advanced by the *Poor Lombards*. "How can the priest who is a sinner absolve me?" and "All clergy, regular and secular alike, are heretics, except one" are among the most expressive statements made by Bohemian Waldensians in this matter, paralleling the views of the Italian Waldensians.[76] Second, the rejection of the Catholic priesthood also included a stronger renunciation of major facets of orthodox religious beliefs and practices, such as confession, veneration of saints, suffrages for the dead, and the belief in purgatory.[77] This continued a trend in Waldensian spirituality that had been visible since the early 1200s. "Gradually all provisions by the ecclesiastical institution of grace that pastorally facilitate[d] justification in works and

---

76. "Quid potest me sacerdos, qui est peccator absolvere?" (Waldensian Henzlin, in Patschovsky, *Quellen zur Böhmischen Inquisition im 14. Jahrhundert*, p. 242, lines 7–8); "quod omnes sacerdotes tam seculares quam religiosi essent heretici excepto uno" (ibid., p. 216, lines 8–9). Given the incriminatory nature of anticlerical statements, there are not many of them, but Patschovsky concludes cautiously that probably a large number of people were critical of the clergy (122). Schneider (*Europäisches Waldensertum*, 36, 72, 83, 90) provides an account of the differences between the Italian and French Waldensians regarding their views of clerical authority after the persecutions, an account that points to much more radical attitudes among the Italians. See also Lerner ("Waldensians," 510), who considers Donatism to be a pillar of Waldensian faith after 1200, and Audisio (*Les "vaudois,"* 54–55).

77. Examples: confession—"The priests of the Catholic Church cannot absolve those confessing to them" (Ministri Romane ecclesie non possunt absolvere sibi confitentes; Waldensian Heynuš Lugner, goldsmith, in Patschovsky, *Quellen zur Böhmischen Inquisition im 14. Jahrhundert*, p. 266, lines 10–11); saints—"that saints ought not to be invoked nor venerated nor the Blessed Virgin" (quod sancti non sunt invocandi nec venerandi nec beata virgo; ibid., Waldensians in Prague, p. 321, lines 14–15); deeds for the dead (*suffragia mortuorum*)—"that alms made on behalf of the dead are worth nothing" (quod elimosine facte pro mortuis nichil valerent; ibid., Waldensians in Prague, p. 321, lines 12–13). Kurze ("Zur Ketzergeschichte der Mark Brandenburg und Pommerns," 84–85) and Biller ("Les vaudois dans les territoires de langue allemande vers la fin du XIVe siècle," *Heresis* 13/14 [1989]: 220–21) point out that such views were also common among the Waldensians interrogated under Zwicker. Similarly for the Italian Waldensians, according to Merlo (*Eretici e inquisitori nella società piemontese*, 27–29, 32–37, 40); Schneider (*Europäisches Waldensertum*, 90); Audisio (*Les "vaudois,"* 52–53, 59). On purgatory, see Jacques Le Goff, *The Birth of Purgatory*, trans. Arthur Goldhammer (Chicago: University of Chicago Press, 1984), 278–80, and notes 85 and 116 below.

open[ed] additional gateways to grace [were] excluded."[78] Third, the dichotomy in Waldensian soteriology became more pronounced in that it came to be understood that few, if any, apart from the Waldensians, were on the path to paradise, while the rest were to end in hell. The early-fourteenth-century Waldensian poem *La Nobla Leyçzon* (The noble lesson) reads: "All people will go away from this world on two ways: the good will go to glory, the wicked to torture. . . . Few are those who are saved."[79] Claus Hufener, a Waldensian interrogated in Stettin in 1392, was more blunt about this point: "When he was asked whether he believed that his sect had been the true Christian faith and no one could be saved outside of it, he replied that it was true, and he therefore believed that all prelates were to be damned."[80]

If one uses Weber's major criteria to assess the level of rationalization in a religion, that is, systematic unity and coherence of its views on the relation between deity and the world, and absence of magical means of attaining and assuring salvation,[81] the doctrinal changes discussed so far point to a more rationalized belief system compared to that of the early Waldensians. With the stronger demarcation from orthodoxy, the Waldensian ethics became a more unified and forceful expression of religious dissent. At the same time, the magical means of achieving salvation prevalent in popular religion and the interceding function of the Catholic priest were removed from the Waldensian religious agenda. This deprived the Waldensians of the "salutary goods"—proxies for the state of grace[82]— available to Catholics in the sacraments and many other semimagical practices for manipulating divine favors. Since the Waldensian movement had traditionally scorned ecstatic or contemplative means of achieving

---

78. Selge, *Die ersten Waldenser*, 1:317.

79. "tuit li ome del mont per dui chamin tenren: li bon yren en gloria, li fellon en torment. . . . poc son li salva" (Éduard Montet, *La Noble Leçon* [Paris: Fischbacher, 1888], p. 26, lines 20–21 and 26, with French translation); *La Nobla Leyçzon* was written in a Waldensian dialect in the early 1400s; see Gonnet and Molnár, *Les vaudois au Moyen Âge*, 329–31. For other expressions of such a view among Italian and French Waldensians, see Mollat, *Bernard Gui: Manuel de l'Inquisiteur*, 62; Merlo, *Eretici e inquisitori nella società piemontese*, 204; Ignaz von Döllinger, *Beiträge zur Sekten-geschichte des Mittelalters*, 2 vols. (Munich: Beck, 1890), 2:307.

80. "Interrogatus, an crederit, sectam suam fuisse veram fidem christianam et nullum extra eam posse salvari, respondit, quod sic, et ideo omnes prelatos crediderit esse dampnandos" (Kurze, *Quellen zur Ketzergeschichte Brandenburgs und Pommerns*, 94, no. 16). For other references, see idem, "Zur Ketzergeschichte der Mark Branden-burg und Pommerns," 86 n. 198; Biller, "Les vaudois dans les territoires de langue allemande," 220.

81. See Chapter 1, page 48.

82. Weber, *Economy and Society*, 541.

salvation in favor of active asceticism, a more urgent notion that hell was waiting for those outside Waldensianism now furthered the pressure to proceed on the pathway to heaven through methodical and austere conduct in the belief of being an "instrument," or "tool," of God.[83]

Links Between Ethics and Behavior Among the Laity

Yet other aspects of Waldensian religious life interfered with this link between ethics and behavior, providing Waldensian lay believers with a means of attaining and assuring salvation other than methodical ascetic conduct. The single most striking feature in the testimonies of fourteenth-century German Waldensians is their belief in the exalted salutary function of the itinerant Waldensian preachers. These preachers were seen as holy men, as mediators between the profane and the sacred. In 1315, the Silesian Waldensian Sybotho, himself a Waldensian confessor who was later burned, is reported to have said "that he never cared about his parish, or about the clerics, nor did he believe that they could absolve or bind, but that they [the Waldensians] had for themselves lay confessors, to whom they confessed and who absolved them, and that the confessors came two or three times a year and preached and absolved."[84] The smith Henry of Jareschau, "when he was asked [by Bohemian inquisitors] what the aforesaid laypeople [the Waldensian itinerant preachers] had taught him, . . . replied: 'That I should not swear, and that I should be faithful, and that there are only two ways, namely to heaven and to hell, and that there is no purgatory of the souls.' When he was asked how they call themselves within their sect, he replied: 'They call themselves the known [by God] and virtuous men.'"[85] Cecilia Bukeman, a widow interrogated in 1393, said that "she considered their Waldensian confessors to be good men, more so than priests were, and that they—and not the priests—had the ability from God to forgive sins, and that the person to whom they spoke once a year

83. Weber, "The Social Psychology of the World Religions," in *From Max Weber*, 289–91.

84. "Sybotho dixit, quod numquam curavit parrochiam nec fratres nec credebat, quod possent absolvere vel ligare, sed haberent per se confessores laycos, quibus confitentur et qui eos absolvunt, et veniunt aliquociens in anno bis vel ter et predicant et absolvunt" (Patschovsky, "Waldenserverfolgung in Schweidnitz 1315," p. 163, line 4; p. 164, line 2).

85. "Interrogatus quid instruxerint eum dicti laici, respondit: 'Ut non deberem iurare, et quod essem fidelis, et quod sint tantummodo due vie, videlicet ad celum et ad infernum, et quod purgatorium animarum non sit.' Interrogatus quomodo ipsi se denominent in secta eorum, respondit: 'Ipsi appellant se notos et probos homines'" (Patschovsky, *Quellen zur Böhmischen Inquisition im 14. Jahrhundert*, p. 204, lines 5–11).

could not be damned."[86] And Beata Ruerbeke explained the source of the confessors' legitimation, saying that "two of them once a year went to paradise, and received there from God the authority to forgive sins better than the priests."[87] The final witness to be mentioned here is the Waldensian Jacob Hildebrant, who was interrogated in the same year as Cecilia Bukeman. Hildebrant's parents had been Waldensians, and over the previous twenty years he had confessed annually to a total of six Waldensian itinerant confessors. The last time he had confessed was a year ago, in his home. The penances for his wrongdoing had been fasting, fifty Paternosters on weekdays and one hundred on festive days, plus water and bread on half a dozen Fridays. "These penances he held, and he thought that he was absolved and also that these penances were beneficial to his salvation."[88]

Through these reports—and there are many more with the same message[89]—it appears that fourteenth-century Waldensianism's salvation economy was not that different from Catholicism's after all. Rather than confide in a priest, who might have been morally suspect, the Waldensian believer waited for a visit from a Waldensian itinerant confessor (all of whom were male),[90] to whom she or he could confess. Like the early Waldensian preachers, these confessors set themselves apart from their followers by ascetic detachment from society in fasting, prayer, and self-mortification.[91] They underwent strict admission and training procedures that probably made them more competent than many Catholic priests to address the spiritual needs of their audience.[92] But the salutary goods that the confessors provided were rather easily attained, and the anthropolatry shown to these exemplary prophets

86. "quod tenuerit eos (= heresiarcas) pro bonis hominibus plus presbiteris, et non prosbiteros, posse a deo dimittere peccata, et quod, cui loquerentur semel in anno, non posset dampnari" (Kurze, *Quellen zur Ketzergeschichte Brandenburgs und Pommerns*, 200, no. 16).

87. "quod semel in anno venirent ad paradisum duo ex ipsis [heresiarchis], et reciperent ibi a deo auctoritatem melius presbiteris dimittendi peccata" (ibid., 208, no. 16).

88. "hanc penetenciam tenuit et se absolutum credidit et hanc penitenciam sibi proficere ad salutem" (ibid., 112–14; the quote is from p. 113, lines 12–13).

89. See Wattenbach, "Über die Inquisition gegen die Waldenser in Pommern und der Mark Brandenburg," in *Kleine Abhandlungen*, 166–69.

90. Kurze ("Zur Ketzergeschichte der Mark Brandenburg und Pommerns," 80 n. 152). See also idem, *Quellen zur Ketzergeschichte Brandenburgs und Pommerns*, 350–51. Biller ("Les vaudois dans les territoires de langue allemande," 215) has a list of twenty Waldensian masters. Patschovsky (*Quellen zur Böhmischen Inquisition im 14. Jahrhundert*, 27) mentions a list of six male names.

91. Biller, "Multum Ieiunantes et se Castigantes," 225.

92. Patschovsky, *Quellen zur Böhmischen Inquisition im 14. Jahrhundert*, 29; Kurze, "Zur Ketzergeschichte der Mark Brandenburg und Pommerns," 81–82; Audisio,

may not have differed from the veneration of the many local saints who populated the spiritual world of late medieval Catholicism.[93] Thereby the religious function of the German Waldensian leading circles was identical to that of the spiritual leaders of the Italian and French Waldensians, so that they were no exception to the succinct evaluation Jean Gonnet and Amedeo Molnár arrived at before the publication of Gallus of Neuhaus's Inquisition records: "More and more, the itinerant preachers [became] *directeurs d'âmes*."[94] Consequently, salvation through penance was "merely a different form of the [Catholic] justification of works."[95] And while it may be true that confession was held in an atmosphere of awe toward the confessor and the penances imposed could be quite harsh,[96] is it reasonable to believe that one to three confessional meetings annually, at the most,[97] were enough to carry confessional admonitions and resolutions through the rest of the year, especially since the Waldensian leaders did not live with the believers, let alone pursue a regular vocation? It appears that the Waldensian confessors were becoming bearers of a strong "charisma of office" whose extraordinary status was proved partly by their personal ascetic acts but was otherwise vested in the acquired qualities and the effectiveness of salutary functions.[98] This salvation economy did not transcend the stereotyping of singular acts.[99]

Les "vaudois," 117–52. For a later period, see idem, *Le barbe et l'inquisiteur: Procès du barbe vaudois Pierre Griot par l'inquisiteur Jean de Roma* (Apt, 1532) (La Calade: Édisud, 1979), 38.

93. See Chapter 3, pages 109–10.

94. Gonnet and Molnár, *Les vaudois au Moyen Âge*, 194.

95. Wattenbach, "Über die Inquisition gegen die Waldenser in Pommern und der Mark Brandenburg," in *Kleine Abhandlungen*, 170. See also Audisio, *Les "vaudois,"* 53–54; Erbstösser, *Sozialreligiöse Strömungen im späten Mittelalter*, 147–53.

96. Biller, "Multum Ieiunantes et se Castigantes," 225; idem, "Les vaudois dans les territoires de langue allemande," 221; Wattenbach, "Über die Inquisition gegen die Waldenser in Pommern und der Mark Brandenburg," in *Kleine Abhandlungen*, 169; Audisio, *Les "vaudois,"* 130–31.

97. Patschovsky, *Quellen zur Böhmischen Inquisition im 14. Jahrhundert*, 27–28; idem, "Waldenserverfolgung in Schweidnitz 1315," 144; Kurze, "Zur Ketzergeschichte der Mark Brandenburg und Pommerns," 77–78; Wattenbach, "Über die Inquisition gegen die Waldenser in Pommern und der Mark Brandenburg," in *Kleine Abhandlungen*, 166. Similar numbers hold for a later period, according to Euan Cameron, *The Reformation of the Heretics: The Waldenses of the Alps, 1480–1580* (Oxford: Clarendon Press, 1984), 86–90; and Gabriel Audisio, *Les vaudois du Luberon* (Mérindol: Association d'Études Vaudoises et Historiques du Luberon, 1984), 241.

98. In Weber's terms, this is a transitional state in which, in a process of *Versachlichung*, or impersonalization, the legitimacy of charisma originally rooted in qualities of a person shifts to institutional acts or offices (*Economy and Society*, 248).

99. See ibid., 578.

Nor is there much evidence that the fourteenth-century Waldensians had schools or congregational houses in which textual communities could have established themselves and given deeper meaning to the main tenets of their religion.[100]

Therefore the organizational division of Waldensianism into a closed circle of itinerant holy men and a secondary stratum of supporters without much access to the closed circle, and the supporters' reliance on occasional confession and penitential deeds to attain salvation, were detrimental to methodical ways of life outside of the small group of austere yet world-renouncing ascetics. These Waldensians, fairly far removed from the notion of proof of faith in deeds in original Waldensianism and excluding women from the ministry, were definitely not one of the "medieval Puritan sects" that Weber was looking for. There is no need, however, to close the book on methodical and active inner-worldly asceticism among medieval Waldensians quite yet. Evidence of such asceticism exists for another, smaller group of Waldensians. These were the Austrian Waldensians of the mid-thirteenth century.

The Austrian Waldensians Around 1250

In the early 1230s the infamous German inquisitor Conrad of Marburg stirred up the masses as he proceeded zealously in the Rhine Valley to extirpate heretics. His seemingly unchecked brutality and fanaticism caused a reaction that resulted in a relative absence of persecutions in

---

100. Some Bohemian Waldensians held regular meetings in cellars and barns and at a few houses in which instruction might have taken place. With the possible exception of two houses in Prague and Jareschau, no locations permanently set up for teaching and learning are mentioned (Patschovsky, *Quellen zur Böhmischen Inquisition im 14. Jahrhundert*, 28 n. 51, with references). For the Waldensians in Pomerania and Brandenburg no regular assemblies or schools seem to have existed (Kurze, "Zur Ketzergeschichte der Mark Brandenburg und Pommerns," 77; see also Biller, "Les vaudois dans les territoires de langue allemande," 218 n. 66). Consequently, "even the leading circles were intellectually anaemic" (Patschovsky, "The Literacy of Waldensianism," in *Heresy and Literacy*, ed. Biller and Hudson, 135), and "the usual Waldensian tenets of faith . . . were known to the Brandenburg-Pomeranians in their principles, but hardly any insistent reflection upon them existed" (Kurze, *Quellen zur Ketzergeschichte Brandenburgs und Pommerns*, 6). A substantial minority among them interspersed Waldensian faith with Catholic beliefs and practices, especially in their reverence of the Virgin Mary (idem, "Zur Ketzergeschichte der Mark Brandenburg und Pommerns," 84–87; Wattenbach, "Über die Inquisition gegen die Waldenser in Pommern und der Mark Brandenburg," in *Kleine Abhandlungen*, 179–87). For the organization and

the German Empire for about thirty years,[101] during which period German Waldensianism, helped by ongoing quarrels between Emperor Frederick II and the papacy, expanded to the east and southeast. Particularly conducive to the spread of Waldensianism was the situation in the duchy of Austria, where in the 1240s political turmoil diverted the secular powers away from the combat of heresy and papal interdicts disrupted religious life in the parishes.[102] In the following decade the duke of Austria, Ottokar II Přemysl, together with the energetic bishop of the diocese of Passau, Otto of Lonsdorf, who had found many a parish in a state of religious dilapidation during visitation, initiated the persecution of heresy.[103] Some of the experiences gathered during the ensuing Inquisition there were written down around 1260/66 by an anonymous Dominican friar. The *Passau Anonymous*, as this source came to be called, is a unique document on Waldensian ethics and the state of the Catholic clergy.[104]

activities of a leading stratum of Waldensian supporters just below the confessors, see Martin Erbstösser, "Strukturen der Waldenser in Deutschland im 14. Jahrhundert," in *Mentalität und Gesellschaft im Mittelalter: Gedenkschrift für Ernst Werner*, ed. Sabine Tanz (Frankfurt: Lang, 1993), 95–106.

101. Alexander Patschovsky, "Zur Ketzerverfolgung Konrads von Marburg," *Deutsches Archiv für Erforschung des Mittelalters* 37 (1981): 641–93; more generally, see Kieckhefer, *Repression of Heresy in Medieval Germany*, 14–18; Peter Segl, *Ketzer in Österreich: Untersuchungen über Häresie und Inquisition im Herzogtum Österreich im 13. und beginnenden 14. Jahrhundert* (Paderborn: Schöningh, 1984), 42–61; Lambert, *Medieval Heresy*, 148–49; Dietrich Kurze, "Anfänge der Inquisition in Deutschland," in *Die Anfänge der Inquisition im Mittelalter*, ed. Peter Segl (Vienna: Böhlau, 1993), 131–93.

102. Segl, *Ketzer in Österreich*, 61–135.

103. Ibid., 153–65; Josef Breinbauer, *Otto von Lonsdorf: Bischof von Passau, 1254–1265* (Cologne: Böhlau, 1992), 285–87, 339–49.

104. See Alexander Patschovsky, *Der Passauer Anonymus: Ein Sammelwerk über Ketzer, Juden, Antichrist aus der Mitte des 13. Jahrhunderts* (Stuttgart: Hiersemann, 1968), v, 4 n. 7; idem, "Wie wird man Ketzer? Der Beitrag der Volkskunde zur Entstehung von Häresien," in *Volksreligion im hohen und späten Mittelalter*, ed. Peter Dinzelbacher and Dieter R. Bauer (Paderborn: Schöningh, 1990), 149–50. The relevant parts on the Waldensians are published in Patschovsky and Selge, *Quellen zur Geschichte der Waldenser*, 70–103 (partly translated in Edward Peters, ed., *Heresy and Authority in Medieval Europe: Documents in Translation* [Philadelphia: University of Pennsylvania Press, 1980], 150–63); Margaret Nickson, "The 'Pseudo-Reinerius' Treatise, the Final Stage of a Thirteenth Century Work on Heresy from the Diocese of Passau," *Archives d'histoire doctrinale et littéraire du Moyen Âge* 34 (1967): 294–303; and Wilhelm Preger, "Beiträge zur Geschichte der Waldesier im Mittelalter," *Abhandlungen der königlich bayerischen Akademie der Wissenschaften, 3. Klasse* 13/1 (1875): 242–45. Two other sources provide valuable additional information on Waldensians living in adjacent regions, although they are less perceptive and discriminating than the *Passau Anonymous*. These are the *Treatise on the Inquisition of Heretic* (printed in idem, "Der Tractat des David von Augsburg über die Waldesier,"

The *Passau Anonymous* openly describes clerical negligence and abuse. In its zeal for spreading the Catholic faith, the clergy fares poorly in comparison to their heterodox counterparts. "One ought to be ashamed of the negligence of the teachers of the faithful [i.e., Catholic priests], who do not show as much eagerness for the truth of the Catholic faith as the perfidious Waldensians show for the error of infidelity."[105] As the friar reports, not without embarrassment, such negligence consisted in the clergy's using vinegar instead of wine in the Eucharist,[106] storing eucharistic bread in their chambers or gardens,[107] offering a host full of worms,[108] celebrating the Mass a second time while tipsy from drinking the ablution left from the previous celebration, or celebrating the Mass in an undershirt after gambling the whole previous night in a tavern.[109] Confessors heard ten confessions simultaneously, and contents of confessions became public.[110] Some pastoral practices had severe consequences. One woman, after having an abortion or a miscarriage, was sent to the bishop, thus exposing her to the public, and was killed by her suspicious husband upon return.[111]

Abhandlungen der königlich bayerischen Akademie der Wissenschaften, Historische Klasse 14/2 [1878]: 183–235), formerly attributed to the Franciscan David of Augsburg and composed between 1256 and 1272, which deals with the situation of the Waldensians in the Bavarian part of the diocese of Passau (see ibid., 193–94; Schneider, *Europäisches Waldensertum*, 142–45; Antoine Dondaine, "Le manuel de l'inquisiteur (1230–1330)," *Archivum Fratrum Praedicatorum* 17 [1947]: 104–5), and the sermons against heretics by the famous Franciscan preacher Berthold of Regensburg (printed in Anton E. Schönbach, *Studien zur Geschichte der altdeutschen Predigt, III: Das Wirken Bertholds von Regensburg gegen die Ketzer* [1904; reprint, Hildesheim: Olms, 1968], 2–82), who encountered Waldensians during his missions in southeastern parts of the German Empire in the mid-thirteenth century (see Schönbach, *Das Wirken Bertholds von Regensburg gegen die Ketzer*, 85–86).

105. "Erubescat negligencia fidelium doctorum, qui non sic zealant catholice fidei veritatem, sicut perfidi Leoniste zelant infidelitatis errorem" (Patschovsky and Selge, *Quellen zur Geschichte der Waldenser*, p. 71, lines 3–5).

106. "alii conficiunt cum aceto" (ibid., p. 83, line 4).

107. "eucharistiam servant in cameris et in ortis" (ibid., p. 84, line 1).

108. As witnessed by members of a religious order: "eucharistia vermibus scaturivit iuxta Zwetel; testes monachi ibidem" (ibid., p. 84, lines 3–4).

109. "quidam post ablucionem sumptam iterum celebrant" (ibid., p. 83, lines 3–4); the second incident was observed by the heretical leader Goth: "dyaconus tota nocte ludens in thaberna, mane in camisia celebravit teste Goth heresiarcha" (ibid., p. 84, lines 2–3).

110. "confessio decem simul auditur" (ibid., p. 86, lines 19–20); "quidam confessiones produnt indirecte" (ibid., p. 87, lines 11–12). A translator was used in confession by Slavic members of the parish: "confessio fit per interpretem" (ibid., p. 87, line 1).

111. "uxor occulte procurans aborsum vel simile mittitur ad episcopum; et sic suspecta marito occiditur" (ibid., p. 87, lines 13–14).

Other women were forced to fast shortly before delivery, which led to miscarriages.[112] Some priests did not bury children without extorting burial fees.[113]

Religious guidance by priests like these was obviously not conducive to ethical rationalization of life conduct in their parishes. Even though there certainly were other priests in the diocese who cared for their flock diligently, clerical mishandling of religious matters, as the Dominican frankly concedes, was ubiquitous and serious enough to discredit the Catholic Church in general and provide the Waldensians with occasions to "blaspheme against the Roman church and clergy, in which [blasphemy] a great number of laypeople easily believe."[114] On the basis of

---

112. "que partui est vicina cogitur ad carrinam; et sic laborans aborsum facit" (ibid., p. 89, lines 5–6).

113. "quia [sacerdotes] ab omnibus aliquid exigitur, eciam ab infantibus" (ibid., p. 100, lines 22–23). See also the catalogue of ecclesiastical problems contributing to heresy in Preger, "Beiträge zur Geschichte der Waldesier im Mittelalter," 242–45; similar views are reported for the Waldensians in Bavaria by Pseudo-David, in Preger, "Der Tractat des David von Augsburg über die Waldesier," p. 214, line 17; p. 215, line 4; p. 219, lines 16–18. See also Segl, *Ketzer in Österreich*, 247–70; Patschovsky, "Wie wird man Ketzer?" in *Volksreligion im hohen und späten Mittelalter*, ed. Dinzelbacher.

114. "hec Leonistarum . . . solummodo Romanam ecclesiam blasphemant et clerum, cui multitudo laicorum facilis est ad credendum" (Patschovsky and Selge, *Quellen zur Geschichte der Waldenser*, p. 73, lines 10–14). It was not unusual for an ecclesiastical observer to comment on the less-than-perfect conditions in many parishes in this period. For example, Alan of Lille reported (c. 1200): "The prelates of our time seat themselves upon a throne before they are instructed beneath the birch: they don the robes of a Master before they undertake the hard work of a student. They choose to be eminent, not to be useful; the reward of honor, not the burden of hard work. To such a prelate it can be said: 'Physician, heal yourself'. . . Some hide in a handkerchief the talent of divine wisdom which has been committed to them–that is, those who, out of idleness, do not wish to preach. Some hide it in a dung-heap—that is, those who in their deeds contradict their own words; others hide in the mud—those who hide their word out of envy (*The Art of Preaching*, trans. Gillian R. Evans [Kalamazoo, Mich.: Cistercian Publications, 1981], 145). Stephen of Bourbon complained (c. 1250) about the "negligence of Catholics . . . many of whom are so careless about this negligence and their salvation that they scarcely know their *Pater noster* or *Credo*, or teach them to their kin" (negligenciam catholicorum . . . quorum plures sunt ita negligentes circa suam et suorum salutem, ut vix suum *Pater noster* aut *Credo* sciant vel famulis suis doceant; in Albert Lecoy de la Marche, ed., *Anecdotes historiques, légendes et apologues, tirés du recueil inédit d'Étienne de Bourbon, dominicain du XIIIe siècle* [Paris: Renouard, 1877], 309). For clerical criticism in the fourteenth century, see František Graus, "The Church and Its Critics in Time of Crises," in *Anticlericalism in Late Medieval and Early Modern Europe*, ed. Peter A. Dykema and Heiko A. Oberman (Leiden: Brill, 1993), 65–81. The specificity and frankness of the friar's account is nevertheless unique. Animosity between the Dominican (as a member of the regular clergy) and the secular clergy, which was not uncommon at the time (see Lawrence, *Medieval Monasticism*, 261–63;

apparently close personal contact with the Waldensians,[115] he then outlines the doctrinal contents of this "blasphemy" and the organization of the Waldensian communities. Many Waldensian views appear as direct and detailed quotations in the record.

Doctrinally, the Austrian Waldensian upheld early Waldensianism's religious legacy of proof of faith in ascetic conduct, but also adopted some of the tenets that later characterized Waldensianism in Bohemia and eastern Germany. They held the familiar notion of the two ways, combined with a strong rejection of the Catholic Church as the church of the wicked and the whore of the Apocalypse.[116] The Austrian Waldensians saw the Catholic clergy as being "blind and leaders of the blind," either rejecting them completely or at least taking a Donatist stance toward them.[117]

Zerfaß, *Der Streit um die Laienpredigt*, 313–59), might have come into play here, but cannot explain away the existence of such abuse (similar views are expressed by Patschovsky, "Wie wird man Ketzer?" in *Volksreligion im hohen und späten Mittelalter*, ed. Peter Dinzelbacher, 150).

115. See Patschovsky, *Der Passauer Anonymus*, 78–89, 117, 151–53.

116. "purgatorium negant dicentes tantum duas vias, unam electorum ad celum et dampnatorum ad infernum" (Patschovsky and Selge, *Quellen zur Geschichte der Waldenser*, p. 101, lines 13–14; see also Nickson, "The 'Pseudo-Reinerius' Treatise," p. 302, lines 18–19); "quod ecclesia Romana non sit ecclesia Iesu Christi, sed ecclesia malignancium et meretrix in Apocalypsi [17.3]" (Patschovsky and Selge, *Quellen zur Geschichte der Waldenser*, p. 77, lines 16–18). See also Preger, "Der Tractat des David von Augsburg über die Waldesier," p. 206, lines 28–29; p. 208, lines 15–18; Schönbach, *Das Wirken Bertholds von Regensburg gegen die Ketzer*, p. 5, line 10; p. 27, lines 6–8.

117. "[doctores Romanae ecclesiae] ceci sunt et duces cecorum" (Patschovsky and Selge, *Quellen zur Geschichte der Waldenser*, p. 76, line 16). Some Waldensians held that priests were not a priori inept to absolve, since they advanced the Donatist position "that a priest bound in mortal sin can absolve no one" (quod sacerdos in mortali peccato ligatus nullum possit absolvere; p. 86, lines 9–10; for a similar statement, see Nickson, "The 'Pseudo-Reinerius' Treatise," p. 298, lines 1–2). Others held a more antisacerdotalist position, "calling prelates scribes and religious pharisees," and "damned all clergy because of their idleness, saying that they ought to work with the hand as the apostles did" (vocantes prelatos scribas et religiosos phariseos [Patschovsky and Selge, *Quellen zur Geschichte der Waldenser*, p. 79, lines 22–23]; et omnem clerum dampnant propter ocium dicentes eos debere manibus operari sicut apostoli fecerunt [Nickson, "The 'Pseudo-Reinerius' Treatise," p. 297, lines 8–9]). That the Waldensians were doctrinally not an entirely homogeneous group is also obvious in their stance toward marriage. One Waldensian was proud of the chaste life he and his fellow men lived with their wives; others thought that married partners sinned mortally if they slept with each other without hope for offspring; still others thought that married people could not be saved. Some, however, thought that even priests should be married, for marriage dissuades from fornication (Patschovsky and Selge, *Quellen zur Geschichte der Waldenser*, p. 76, lines 1–2; p. 88, lines 2–3, 9–10; p. 90, lines 13–14). Segl (*Ketzer in Österreich*, 216–33) further addresses differences between the *Pauperes de Lugdano* and *Runkarii* strands in Austrian Waldensianism.

They also entirely rejected the many religious practices by which Catholics could alleviate soteriological doubts, such as the salutary employment of benedictions, pilgrimages, indulgences, fasts, deeds for the dead, or veneration of saints. The Waldensians deemed nothing of that sort proper as a means of salvation. There was no diaphanous boundary between religion and magic; in fact, both were so sharply delineated that the Austrian Waldensians displayed what might be considered one of the most disenchanted views of the secular and sacred realms before the ascent of ascetic Protestantism.[118] Two decisive differences, however, distinguished the Austrian Waldensians from later Waldensian groups.

First, the Austrian Waldensians did not replace the Catholic means of achieving salvation with the dispensation of grace by their own itinerant saintly preachers. There is no evidence for the existence of such holy men or the predominance of either exemplary prophecy or authority based on a "charisma of office." Regarding penance, any "good lay person" (*bonus laycus*) had the authority to absolve.[119] In the manner of the apostles, the forgiveness of sin was a simple procedure: one put a hand on the person confessing and conferred the Holy Spirit.[120] Similarly, "a good layperson, even a woman, if [she or] he knows the words, can procure the Eucharist," of which they partook daily.[121] A "good layperson" was thereby simply a member of the Waldensians who lived according to the Waldensians' tenets of faith. No one was greater than the others in their community, and all were called upon to preach and teach—including female members of the congregation.[122] This is not to deny that some kind of hierarchy among the Waldensians

118. See the detailed list of orthodox religious practices abhorred by the Waldensians in Preger, "Beiträge zur Geschichte der Waldesier im Mittelalter," 245; Patschovsky and Selge, *Quellen zur Geschichte der Waldenser*, 85–103; Nickson, "The 'Pseudo-Reinerius' Treatise," 299–302. See also Preger, "Der Tractat des David von Augsburg über die Waldesier," p. 206, line 29; p. 207, line 5; p. 224, lines 5–6; Schönbach, *Das Wirken Bertholds von Regensburg gegen die Ketzer*, p. 5, lines 6–10; p. 26, line 22; p. 27, line 4; p. 47, lines 33–37.

119. "De sacramento penitencie dicunt, quod sacerdos in mortali peccato ligatus nullum possit absolvere, sed pocius bonus laycus. . . . Item dicunt, quod bonus laycus potestatem habeat absolvendi. . . . Item dicunt, quod bonus laycus potestatem habeat absolvendi" (Patschovsky and Selge, *Quellen zur Geschichte der Waldenser*, p. 86, lines 9–10, 15–18).

120. "quod ipsi per manus impositionem peccata dimittant et dent spiritum sanctum" (Nickson, "The 'Pseudo-Reinerius' Treatise," p. 298, lines 15–16).

121. "dicunt, quod bonus laycus, eciam mulier, si sciat verba, possit conficere" (Patschovsky and Selge, *Quellen zur Geschichte der Waldenser*, p. 82, lines 6–7); "ipsi cottidie communicant" (Nickson, "The 'Pseudo-Reinerius' Treatise," p. 298, line 6).

122. "quod nemo sit maior altero in ecclesia" (Nickson, "The 'Pseudo-Reinerius' Treatise," p. 296, lines 23–24); "dicunt, quod omnis homo, eciam femine, debeant

existed,[123] but the saintlike life of an itinerant ascetic preacher was
neither necessary (given the political and ecclesiastical conditions before
the Inquisition in the 1260s) nor compatible with Austrian Waldensian
tenets of faith committing each of them to work. Consequently, the
Catholic priests' avoidance of labor was scandalous to these Waldensians, and they adamantly insisted on the apostolic roots of manual
work for all members.[124]

Second, the Austrian Waldensians could practice their faith openly in
their own congregations and schools:

> All, men and women, greater and lesser, at night and day do not
> cease to learn and to teach; the menial laborer works at day,
> learns or teaches at night. Therefore they pray too little,
> because of their zeal. Moreover, they teach and learn without
> books. They teach even in leper houses. For an introduction,
> they teach to avoid the seven deadly sins and three [others],
> namely, lying, slandering, and swearing. These they prove with
> many [scriptural] authorities, and they call them the Ten
> Commandments. A student of seven days seeks out another
> person whom he teaches, just as a curtain draws another one.
> He who excuses himself because he is unable to learn is told:
> learn one word each day, and after one year you will know
> three hundred, and you will progress this way. . . . I have seen
> and heard an unlettered rustic who recited the Book of Job

predicare" (Patschovsky and Selge, *Quellen zur Geschichte der Waldenser*, p. 80, line 6;
see also Nickson, "The 'Pseudo-Reinerius' Treatise," p. 299, line 14).

123. During the Inquisition in Krems in 1315, a Waldensian named Newmaister
confessed that he had been a Waldensian "bishop" (a title very likely chosen by the
inquisitors) and teacher for the last fifty years ("qui autem in Wienna crematus est
nomine Newmaister fassus est se quinquaginta annis eorum fuisse Episcopum et
magistrum." Nickson, "The 'Pseudo-Reinerius' Treatise," p. 307, lines 19–21). The
Passau Anonymous reports the residence of such a "bishop" in Anzbach, but in two other
instances uses the expression "heresiarch" for a Waldensian leader and mentions
perfecti only once ("item in Enzinsbach et ibi scole et episcopus." Ibid., p. 294, line 17).
See also ibid., p. 303, lines 5–6; Patschovsky and Selge, *Quellen zur Geschichte der
Waldenser*, p. 72, line 9; p. 84, line 3. The Bavarian Waldensians, in contrast, appear to
have had a much more hierarchical organization. See Preger, "Der Tractat des David
von Augsburg über die Waldesier," p. 209, line 24; p. 210, line 12.

124. "nos vero manibus operamur," "dicunt non operantes clericos peccare"
(Patschovsky and Selge, *Quellen zur Geschichte der Waldenser*, p. 76, line 10; p. 79, line
23); "item omnem clerum dampnant propter otium, dicentes eos debere manibus operari
sicut apostoli fecerunt" (Nickson, "The 'Pseudo-Reinerius' Treatise," p. 297, lines 8–9).
See also note 117 above and the brief remarks in Paolini, "Gli eretici e il lavoro," in
Lavorare nel Medio Evo, ed. Università degli studi di Perugia, 140–42.

word for word, and many others who knew the New Testament perfectly.[125]

This friar's description is instructive. Apparently the moral climate in the Waldensian communities was strict and the web of relations among the community members tightly knit. This distinguished them from their predecessors in early Waldensianism, who were only loosely associated with a circle of itinerant preachers. Unlike later Waldensians, moreover, members of Austrian Waldensian communities were not merely passive recipients of moral advice and absolution offered in confession by exemplary prophets. Instead, the political and ecclesiastical circumstances at the time allowed them to organize in textual communities, where they were actively involved in teaching the young,[126] learning, and advising each other in spiritual matters. They met in smaller study groups and in schools. These institutions were crucial for the transmission of ethical prophecy.[127] Of the forty parishes (and two additional places) in which the Inquisition found heretics, twelve had schools. The parish of Kematen alone (Kematen itself had fewer than two thousand inhabitants), the *Passau Anonymous* reports, had ten of them.[128] This indicates that some schools were likely houses in which congregations regularly met, but perhaps also instructional centers where congregational meetings, liturgical practices, charitable activities

125. "omnes: viri et femine, parvi et magni, nocte et die non cessant discere et docere; operarius in die laborans, nocte discit vel docet. Ideo parum orant propter studium. Docent eciam et discunt sine libris. Docent eciam in domibus leprosorum. Item pro introduccionibus docent vitare septem mortalia peccata et tria, scilicet mendacium, detraccionem et iuramentum. Hec multis auctoritatibus confirmant, et hec vocant decem precepta. Item discipulus septem dierum alium querit quem doceat, ut cortina cortinam trahat. Qui excusat se, quod not possit discere, dicunt ei: Disce cottidie unum verbum, et post annum scies trecenta, et sic proficies. . . . Vidi et audivi rusticum ydiotam, qui Iob recitavit de verbo ad verbum, et plures alios, qui totum novum testamentum sciverunt prefecte" (Patschovsky and Selge, *Quellen zur Geschichte der Waldenser*, p. 70, lines 4–12; p. 71, lines 7–9).

126. See Pseudo-David of Augsburg (in Preger, "Der Tractat des David von Augsburg über die Waldesier," p. 213, lines 3–4): "They teach little girls the words of the Gospels and the Epistles, so that from their childhood they accustom themselves to embracing error" (Puellas parvulas docent verba ewangelii et epistolas, ut a puericia consuescant errorem amplecti).

127. Cf. Menache, *The Vox Dei*, chap. 11, who pays too little attention to institutional aspects of the transmission of heresy.

128. "computate sunt in dyocesi XL ecclesie, que heresi infecte fuerunt. Et in sola parrochia Comnath decem scole hereticorum" (Patschovsky and Selge, *Quellen zur Geschichte der Waldenser*, p. 73, lines 1–2). See also Nickson, "The 'Pseudo-Reinerius' Treatise," p. 294, lines 8–9.

(such as the care of people afflicted with pestilence), and the education of Waldensian believers and leaders took place. Compared to Waldensianism in other periods, the social organization of the Austrian Waldensians most closely resembled Weber's ideal type of a sect. Its characteristics were strict discipline, upheld through mutual control, membership status based upon appropriate personal conduct, and strong involvement of all members in congregational activities.[129]

Given the Austrian Waldensians' pragmatic stress on the simplicity, transparency, and parsimony of moral rules—as they put it: "The multiplication of precepts induces a multiplication of transgressions"[130]— the network of schools and congregations was ideal for transforming these rules into practice. Still, the Waldensians' zest for learning was not sufficient to feed their congregations, and laboring in the secular realm and pursuing their regular vocations in order to make a living remained important. After all, the social milieu of the Waldensians consisted of a varied yet often humble people. Mentioned are unlettered laypeople, such as the aforementioned rustic with a liking for Job, a menial laborer, other modest ones able to memorize only one word a day, teachers or learned ones (in their faith) who were also weavers and shoemakers, a leader who was a glover, but also some who were better off or familiar enough with the jewelry trade to attempt the proselytization of nobles and lords.[131] While these allusions to social status do not allow for a more detailed analysis, they seem to indicate that, as in early and fourteenth-century Bohemian Waldensianism, middle social strata composed the bulk of Waldensian support, though here it was more strongly linked to the lower middle ranks of craftsmen and artisans and came to a lesser degree from those with more elite urban backgrounds.

In a section entitled "How the Heretics Are to Be Recognized," the friar addresses how the Waldensians put their beliefs to work:

> The heretics are recognized by their morals and their words. In moral behavior they are composed and modest: They do not take

129. On schools as congregational centers, see Segl, *Ketzer in Österreich*, 193–95; Schneider, *Europäisches Waldensertum*, 122–25. There is a the reference to "scole leprosorum" in Neuhofen (in Nickson, "The 'Pseudo-Reinerius' Treatise," p. 295, line 17). See also note 125 above, where it is reported that the Waldensians taught "in domibus leprosorum."

130. "multiplicacio preceptorum multiplicacionem transgressionum inducit" (Patschovsky and Selge, *Quellen zur Geschichte der Waldenser*, p. 78, line 12).

131. Ibid., p. 70, line 4; p. 72, line 10; p. 74, lines 6–7; p. 75, line 11; and page 163 above. See also Segl, *Ketzer in Österreich*, 342–44; Schneider, *Europäisches Waldensertum*, 113–17.

pride in their clothes, which are neither fancy nor very abject. They do not engage in (larger) trade business because of the lies and oaths and fraud, which ought to be avoided, but rather they live only by the work of their hands as craftsmen. Even their teachers are weavers and shoemakers. They do not accumulate riches, but are content with necessities. The Waldensians are also very chaste. They are moderate in food and drink. They do not go to taverns or to dances or to other vanities. They subdue their anger. They always work or learn or teach, and thus they pray too little. . . . They are also recognized by their precise and modest way of speaking: they avoid slander and scurrility and meaningless speech, lies and oaths, nor do they say "truly" or "certainly" or use similar expressions, because they think of them as oaths.[132]

For an inquisitor, this is an unusual account. It was certainly common among inquisitors to refer to a deceptive outward appearance of holiness among heretics as a distinctive sign of inward perdition,[133] but this case seems different. For the Dominican appears to be convinced that the Waldensian efforts are genuine and sincere; his point here is that all their zeal for working and learning makes them only more stubborn in their error and distracts them from the proper means of seeking salvation (hence the allegation that they have no time for prayer, the most important religious practice).[134] This follows an earlier statement in which the inquisitor claims that the Waldensians' efforts are ultimately futile altogether, since they are based on their rustic and faulty interpretation of scripture, which they learn "without books."[135]

132. "Quomodo heretici cognoscantur. Cognoscuntur heretici per mores et verba. Sunt enim in moribus compositi et modesti: Superbiam in vestibus non habent, quia nec preciosis nec multum abiectis utuntur. Negociaciones non habent propter mendacia et iuramenta et fraudes vitandas, sed tantum vivunt de labore manuum ut opifices; doctores eciam ipsorum sunt textores et sutores. Divicias non multiplicant, sed necessariis sunt contenti. Casti eciam sunt maxime Leoniste. Temperati sunt in cibo et potu. Ad tabernas non eunt nec ad choreas nec ad alias vanitates. Ab ira se cohibent. Semper eciam vel operantur vel discunt vel docent, et ideo parum orant. . . . Cognoscuntur eciam in verbis precisis et modestis: Cavent eciam a detraccione et a scurilitate et verborum levitate et a mendacio et a iuramento, nec dicunt 'vere' vel 'certe' et similia, quia hec reputant iuramenta" (Patschovsky and Selge, *Quellen zur Geschichte der Waldenser*, p. 74, lines 1–11, 14–16).

133. Herbert Grundmann, "Der Typus des Ketzers in mittelalterlicher Anschauung," in *Ausgewählte Aufsätze*, vol. 1, *Religiöse Bewegungen*, 313–27.

134. See also the quote on page 163 above.

135. "Et quia sunt layci ydiote, false et corrupte scripturam exponunt" (referring then to several mistakes in their translation of scripture; Patschovsky and Selge,

The inquisitor's strategy therefore is to discredit the spiritual foundations of Waldensianism, not their behavior per se, which he finds anything but objectionable. Pseudo-David of Augsburg makes a similar argument and comparable, albeit brief, observations about their secular conduct.[136]

If these observations reflect actual conditions and patterns of behavior at the time with some degree of accuracy—a view that recent historical scholarship tends to corroborate[137]—then the Austrian Waldensians' work ethic thus revealed is indeed deeply ascetic. It was consistent with the dogmatic foundations of their belief system and fairly simple. The Waldensians were to avoid excess and to work honestly and diligently in their vocations, preferably manual work, while refraining from the temptations and turpitude associated with large-scale trade business.[138] In these labors, the original Waldensian concept of proving faith in works found an inner-worldly outlet and application. The resulting rationalization of conduct, in its methodical character and ascetic approach, preceded inner-worldly asceticism in ascetic Protestantism by more than three hundred years.

<hr>

Quellen zur Geschichte der Waldenser, p. 71, lines 9–14). On their learning without books, see page 163 above. As Grundmann ("Der Typus des Ketzers in mittelalterlicher Anschauung," in *Ausgewählte Aufsätze*, vol. 1, *Religiöse Bewegungen*, 322–23) points out, inquisitors often attempted to disprove heretics' claims to saintliness by reference to their (alleged) sexual misconduct and clandestinity. Such references are almost entirely absent in the *Passau Anonymous*.

136. Preger, "Der Tractat des David von Augsburg über die Waldesier," p. 212, lines 1–16; p. 213, lines 20–24; p. 216, line 25; p. 217, line 1.

137. Schneider, *Europäisches Waldensertum*, 116 n. 21; Segl, *Ketzer in Österreich*, 197. See also Lambert, *Medieval Heresy*, 151–52.

138. *Negotiationes* (the Latin word used here) is a general term that could refer to a wide range of trade and commerce (see Charles Du Cange, *Glossarium Mediae et Infimae Latinitatis* . . . , 10 vols. [Niort: Favre, 1883–87], s.v. *negotiatio, negotium*). It is known that in orthodoxy the term took on a negative connotation when referring to long-distance trade by prosperous merchants, especially in luxury items, involving financial loans, speculation, and the potential for rapid and large profits, which from a religious point of view was regarded with much suspicion (see Jacques Le Goff, *Marchands et banquiers du Moyen Âge* [Paris: Presses Universitaires de France, 1956], 6, 11–19, 70–74; Paton, *Preaching Friars and the Civic Ethos*, 165–77). I am inclined to see in the Waldensians' use of the term a reference to the extensive long-distance trade on the main waterways Danube, Enns, and Traun that was often carried on by itinerant and well-to-do traders (Ferdinand Tremel, *Wirtschafts- und Sozialgeschichte Österreichs* [Vienna: Deuticke, 1969], 90–91, 96, map 1 in the appendix; see also Herbert Knittler, "Städtewesen, Handel und Gewerbe," in *Österreich im Hochmittelalter (907 bis 1246)*, ed. Kommission für die Geschichte Österreichs der Österreichischen Akademie der Wissenschaften [Vienna: Österreichische Akademie der Wissenschaften, 1991], 473–95; Siegfried Haider, *Geschichte Oberösterreichs* [Munich: Oldenbourg, 1987], 135–36).

The historical opportunity for a lay ascetic group, and for women in particular, to display such behavior and to practice a type of faith that closely addressed their social and spiritual needs did not last long, however. By the early fourteenth century, heretics were sentenced to the stake in Steyr, Krems, St. Pölten, Vienna, and Himberg.[139] Many Austrian and other Waldensians paid dearly for their convictions.

Conclusion

Using mainly primary sources, this chapter, through a comparative historical analysis of different stages in medieval Waldensianism, has explored the interplay of religion and its cultural, socioeconomic, and political environments, of historical constraints and contingencies, of religious doctrine and social organization. The outcome of the interplay of these factors was patterns of ascetic conduct that were rationalized on a religious basis. The analysis reveals that the assertion in some of the historical literature that the history of medieval Waldensianism can be divided into two major phases has to be qualified.[140] It also indicates the datedness of Troeltsch's view associating medieval heterodox groups with abstention from, or antagonism to, the world, which is still repeated in recent writing.[141] The Waldensians' "social teachings" were important, but they were neither static nor the sole determinant of Waldensian behavior. Their teachings were part of a larger theme, the apostolic life, which resonated among many social strata and groups in society in the twelfth and thirteenth centuries. Waldes, in contrast to Saint Francis, gave priority to preaching over accommodation to church authority, but the specific meaning of the apostolic life for the Waldensians, and the ways in which they could practice it and give it institutional stability, varied with social and political conditions.

139. Segl, *Ketzer in Österreich*, 271–341. That this did not end the sporadic appearance of Waldensians and other heretical groups in Austria is shown in Werner Maleczek, "Die Ketzerverfolgung im Österreichischen Hoch- und Spätmittelalter," in *Wellen der Verfolgung in der österreichischen Geschichte*, ed. Erich Zöllner (Vienna: Österreichischer Bundesverlag, 1986), 18–39.

140. For this assertion, see Lerner, "Waldenser, Lollarden und Taboriten," 331–32; for a similar earlier view, see Boehmer, "Waldenser," especially 818.

141. See, e.g., Dietrich Kurze ("Häresie und Minderheit im Mittelalter," *Historische Zeitschrift* 229 [1979]: 557): "Especially the most numerous and lasting medieval heresies (Cathars, Waldensians, Beguines/Beghards), because of their negation of the world and their attitudes and hopes concerning the hereafter or individual salvation, have impeded rather than furthered inner-worldly social change."

Before Waldes's death in the early 1200s and perhaps even up to the onset of the persecutions in the 1230s, the Waldensians were a charismatic movement. Relying on a rationalized divinity that stressed active proof of faith in ascetic deeds, itinerant religious virtuosos gathered followers by preaching and personally displaying austerity in religious and social life. The virtuosos' asceticism was world renouncing and other-worldly oriented, and there is no evidence that firmly committed congregations of believers applied Waldensian tenets to their everyday activities and professions. Subsequent repression drove the Waldensians underground and contributed to the increasingly sectarian character of the French and Italian Waldensians. The exceptional combination of secular turmoil and clerical negligence in Austria, and the colonizing eastern expansion of the German Empire, created spaces in which the German Waldensians were able to set up congregations. Though fourteenth-century Bohemian, Silesian, Pomeranian, and Brandenburgian Waldensians rejected the semimagical aspects of contemporary Catholicism, a parallel development arose within Waldensianism in the form of itinerant saintly confessors and exemplary prophets, who mediated between the sacred and the profane. One must remain skeptical whether the salutary goods readily available through these confessors—assurance of grace through periodic fulfillment of penitential recommendations—were conducive to the rationalization of life conduct. The late medieval Waldensians fell back to a two-tiered system of ethical demands analogous to the one in Catholicism for monastics and laity. While asceticism in early and later Waldensianism extended largely to Waldensian itinerant preachers, the case of the Austrian Waldensians was different. Among the Austrian Waldensians asceticism not only extended to the lay congregations of Waldensians, but was also inner-worldly oriented. For them, the world was a task and had to be mastered through diligent, methodical conduct. In the secular realm the key Waldensian concept of proving faith in works and ascetic deeds found an inner-worldly outlet and application. This outlook had its organizational basis in ethical prophecy transmitted in egalitarian textual communities, which sprawled over the Austrian landscape mostly south of the Danube.

Given the appearance of inner-worldly asceticism in this smaller but popular lay religious movement, it is tempting to raise the more speculative question whether the Austrian Waldensians displayed lineaments of a "Protestant ethic" and perhaps also of a modern capitalist ethos of the sort Weber found in Puritanism. Addressing the latter issue first, one should note that it would be improper to infer the *absence* of a capitalist ethos from the lack of large-scale capitalist enterprise in medieval Austria's predominantly feudal-agrarian economy. A capitalist economy can exist without capitalist spirit, and in turn, as Weber noted in a somewhat elusive statement defending himself against Rachfahl, there might have been cases in which "the spirit of capitalism existed without a capitalist economy."[142] A capitalist ethos may exist even if the economic system provides little or no opportunity to implement this ethos. Likewise, the Austrian Waldensians' avoidance of involvement in larger trade business because of the "lies and oaths and fraud, which ought to be avoided," did not necessarily preclude their becoming thrifty small merchants, peddlers, and artisans. Consider the frugal Nehemiah Wallington, an early-seventeenth-century Puritan turner in London, who wrote in his diary that all too often capitalist enterprise depended on "lying, deceit, oppression, bribery, usury, false weights, false measures, . . . like iniquity."[143] Yet in Puritanism such a sober view of the temptations of successful entrepreneurship similar to that of the Austrian Waldensians went hand in hand with the promulgation of diligent work and acquisitive proprietorship in the market place.[144]

A more pertinent difference between the forms of inner-worldly asceticism engendered by Austrian Waldensianism and Puritanism lies in the particular focus of the latter on economic activities. Although Weber inferred, rather than documented, the psychological mechanisms involved in Puritanism, and paid little attention to the fact that the notion of sanctification of life in worldly vocations and acquisitive activities evolved only gradually into a central means of assuring grace and alleviating salvation anxiety, the part of Weber's argument that addresses the religious significance of the methodical pursuit of a secular calling has received support from more recent scholarship.[145]

142. Weber, "Antikritisches zum 'Geist' des Kapitalismus," in *Die protestantische Ethik, II*, ed. Winckelmann, 192.

143. Paul S. Seaver, *Wallington's World: A Puritan Artisan in Seventeenth-Century London* (Stanford: Stanford University Press, 1985), 129–30.

144. Richard B. Schlatter, *The Social Ideas of Religious Leaders, 1660–1688* (London: Oxford University Press, 1940), 187–25; Richard L. Greaves, *Society and Religion in Elizabethan England* (Minneapolis: University of Minnesota Press, 1981), 377–95, 616–22.

145. Robert S. Michaelsen, "Changes in the Puritan Concept of Calling or Vocation," *New England Quarterly* 26 (1953): 315–36; Christopher Hill, *Society and Puritanism in Pre-Revolutionary England*, 2d ed. (New York: Schocken, 1967), 124–44; R. T. Kendall, *Calvin and English Calvinism to 1649* (Oxford: Oxford University Press, 1979), 197–208; Greaves, *Society and Religion in Elizabethan England*, 8, 14; Charles Lloyd Cohen, *God's Caress: The Psychology of Puritan Religious Experience* (New York: Oxford University Press, 1986), 111–33; John Morgan, *Godly Learning: Puritan Attitudes*

While the Puritans embraced the notion of a "calling" that exalted the godly life specifically in economic activities, Austrian Waldensians did not accord secular economic activities such a pivotal status for spiritual assurance. The absence of the notion of a "calling" in this particular sense may indirectly reflect the vast difference in economic resources between early modern England and thirteenth-century Austria. In *Communities of Discourse*, Robert Wuthnow has pointed out the importance of economic resources for the spread of cultural and political movements in the Reformation, the Enlightenment, and European socialism. Wuthnow demonstrates that these resources not only influenced some of the movements' ideologies, but also enabled them to transform their environments.[146] More concretely, in English covenant theology, as David Zaret has argued, Puritan clerics adapted economic precedents and practices, such as acquisitive activities in markets based on contractarian notions of exchange, ownership, and accumulation, and incorporated in their sermons the imagery of market rationality. This enabled the ministers to retain popular support from an audience already active in markets and thereby familiar with this imagery without prejudice to their role as members of a state church. At the same time, this development instilled in the lay supporters of Puritanism exactly those qualities that Weber ascribed to the modern calling: diligence, systematic self-monitoring, abhorrence of idleness and ostentation, and a sense of individualistic proprietorship in the worldly spheres. Yet Puritan leaders did not predicate their views upon notions derived from ideational sources, as Weber assumed. Rather, they may have modeled central aspects of their practical social and economic ethics in part on already existing market conditions and precedents.[147] However, while this points to an important omission in Weber's account, the basis for this argument is still somewhat slim. It rests on the analysis of a singular case—Puritanism.

Towards Reason, Learning, and Education (Cambridge: Cambridge University Press, 1988), 23–40.

146. Robert Wuthnow, *Communities of Discourse: Ideology and Social Structure in the Reformation, the Enlightenment, and European Socialism* (Cambridge: Harvard University Press, 1989).

147. Zaret, *The Heavenly Contract.* The use of economic maxims and marketplace vocabulary in Christian discourse is, of course, much older than Puritanism; it was used extensively in the sermons of the friars (Little, *Religious Poverty*, 200, and particularly the work of David Lesnick; see Chapter 2, note 64) and can be traced back to the parables of Jesus. See Martin Wenglinsky, "The Economic Meaning of the Parables" (paper presented at the annual meeting of the Association for the Sociology of Religion, Washington, D.C., 1995).

This chapter's analysis of the medieval Waldensians provides strong, if indirect, support for Zaret's modification of the Weber thesis. It also supports his and Wuthnow's more general argument that material resources are important for the generation of new ideologies leading to social change. In spite of many similarities between Puritan and Waldensian ethics, leaders of the Austrian Waldensians had few material-economic precedents for their ethics, and not many resources to spread them. Neither the general economic development nor the vocations of the Waldensians provided a blueprint or model for the creation of theological precepts that could redirect the ethical impera- tives in the Waldensian belief system into the channels of capitalist acquisition, and center their calling on market activities.[148] Thirteenth- century southeast Germany, after all, was still a society with often little, if any, surplus above subsistence level, whereas sixteenth- and seventeenth-century England ventured into a commercialized market economy that provided many more avenues to bring together heterodox religion and capitalist acquisition.[149] While the Waldensians had a general notion of a calling in the sense of proof of faith in ascetic behavior, they lacked the Puritans' stress on proof in *economic* activities. In their somewhat pristine esteem for manual labor, the Waldensians

---

148. See Weber, *The Protestant Ethic*, 79–81, for the argument that modern notions of the calling as an ethical valorization of methodical professional conduct did not exist before the Reformation. Weber expanded this section greatly in the revision, mainly as a response to Lujo Brentano, who had disputed this claim (*Die Anfänge des modernen Kapitalismus*, 136–42). Weber's use of sources has been criticized for its sloppiness in Tatsuro Hanyu, "Max Webers Quellenbehandlung in der *Protestantischen Ethik:* Der Begriff 'Calling,'" *Zeitschrift für Soziologie* 22 (1993): 65–75; idem, "Max Webers Quellenbehandlung in der *Protestantischen Ethik:* Der 'Berufs'-Begriff," *European Journal of Sociology* 35 (1994): 72–103. For the ensuing debate regarding the validity of Weber's argument, a debate that proceeded along confessional lines, see Nikolaus Paulus, "Die Wertung der weltlichen Berufe im Mittelalter," *Historisches Jahrbuch* 32 (1911): 725–55; idem, "Zur Geschichte des Worts Beruf," ibid., 45 (1925): 308–16; Karl Holl, "Die Geschichte des Worts Beruf," in *Gesammelte Aufsätze zur Kirchengeschichte*, vol. 3, *Der Westen* (Tübingen: Mohr, 1928), 189–219. A defense of Weber's position has recently been offered by Goldman, *Max Weber and Thomas Mann*, 35–49, and Annette Disselkamp, *L'éthique protestante de Max Weber* (Paris: Presses Universitaires de France, 1994), 169–90. See also Hartmut Lehmann, "Max Webers Lutherinter- pretation," *Berliner Journal für Soziologie* 5 (1995): 349–58.

149. "Business [in England] in the seventeenth century was often equated with heresy and irreligion. Traders were suspect because they had both the opportunity and the means to challenge dogma and credulity; they were mobile, self–employed, literate, individualist, competitive and less wedded to the communal traditions of an agrarian society." Richard Grassby, *The Business Community of Seventeenth-Century England* (Cambridge: Cambridge University Press, 1995), 271.

remained a religious group steeped in premodern traditionalism. This appears to be a strong indication of just how significant the availability of such material precedents was for the "Protestant ethic" *in statu nascendi*. One might hope that further comparative studies of early modern religious and nonreligious groups involved in nascent capitalist activities will shed more light on this important issue.[150]

150. Note that this position on the importance of material factors does not "refute" Weber's argument. Nor was Weber unaware of the economic discourse used in Puritanism: "commercial similes . . . are thoroughly characteristic of Puritanism" (Weber, *The Protestant Ethic*, 238 n. 102). Yet the PE was not the place to address the "processes of mutual adaptation and [mutual] relationships" (277 n. 84; translation altered) between economics and religion that he explicitly acknowledged and dealt with in his *Collected Essays in the Sociology of Religion*.

5

DUALISM AND ASCETICISM IN CATHARISM

The Religious Ethics of Catharism

Dogmatic Foundations

Basic to Cathar theology and religious philosophy was a metaphysical dualism whose roots went back several millennia to the prophet Zoroaster in Persia. Dualism spread from there to the east and west, and in the areas of Europe, the Near East, and Northern Africa, it was adopted by religious groups such as the Gnostics, the Manichees, and the Paulicians during antiquity and the early Middle Ages. Through Bogomil missionaries from Bulgaria, where it was revived in the tenth century by the preaching of a priest by that name, dualism reached parts of central and western Europe.[1] In Cologne in 1143–44 the

A shortened part of this chapter, on Cathar organization, has been published as "Weavers into Heretics? The Social Organization of Early-Thirteenth-Century Catharism in Comparative Perspective," *Social Science History* 21 (1997): 111–37.

    1. On the history of dualism in philosophical thought and the major religions in general, see Simone Pètrement, *Le dualisme dans l'histoire de la philosophie et des religions: Introduction à l'étude du dualisme platonicien, du gnosticisme et du manichéisme* (Paris: Gallimard, 1946); for ancient and medieval Christianity in specific, see

Premonstratensian prior Eberwin of Steinfeld wrote a letter to Bernard of Clairvaux about his encounters with a new heretical group. This was the first time in the West that a distinctly Cathar group of heretics, organized as a sectarian association, was publicly exposed and their views were made known.[2] Some twenty years later the abbot Eckbert of Schönau invoked the name Cathars (from the Greek *katharos*, or "pure") in his sermons against members of the group, and thereafter the name stuck to them in the orthodox literature. In the interval Catharism had spread north of the Rhine to the Low Countries, northern and southern France, northern Italy, and (though very briefly) to England.[3]

Catharism knew of two types of dualism: mitigated (or relative) dualism and absolute (or radical) dualism. The early Cathars appear to have been adherents of a mitigated dualism prevalent among the Bogomils, but after a series of events in 1167 radical dualism became the dominant strand in Catharism. That year Nicetas, the bishop of a radical-dualist Bogomil congregation in Constantinople, visited Lombardy and convinced one of the first Italian converts to Catharism, the Cathar leader Mark, to adopt a radical-dualist stance with other members of the Cathar church there. Together, Nicetas and Mark then converted the Cathar leaders of northern and southern France to radical dualism at a council at Saint-Félix-de-Caraman, as is known from what is believed to be a copy of an account of the council.[4] With its adoption of radical dualism, less than a decade before the emergence of the first

Raoul Manselli, *L'eresia del male*, 2d ed. (Naples: Morano, 1980); Steven Runciman, *The Medieval Manichee: A Study of the Christian Dualist Heresy* (1947; reprint, Cambridge: Cambridge University Press, 1960); Hans Söderberg, *La religion des cathares: Étude sur le gnosticisme de la basse antiquité et du Moyen Âge* (1949; reprint, New York: AMS Press, 1978); Milan Loos, *Dualist Heresy in the Middle Ages* (Prague: Academia, 1974).

2. Eberwin of Steinfeld, "Epistola ad S. Bernardum," in *Patrologiae cursus completus . . . Series Latina . . .* , ed. Migne, vol. 182, cols. 676–80; translated in Wakefield and Evans, *Heresies of the High Middle Ages*, 127–32. On this, see Manselli, *L'eresia del male*, 179–85; Moore, *The Origins of European Dissent*, 168–72.

3. Eckbert of Schönau, "Sermones tredecim contra haereticos," in *Patrologiae cursus completus . . . Series Latina . . .* , ed. Migne, vol. 195, cols. 11–102; partly translated in Moore, *The Birth of Popular Heresy*, 89–94. The text has been edited, with a commentary, by Robert Joyce Harrison, "Eckbert of Schönau's 'Sermones Contra Kataros'" (Ph.D. diss., Ohio State University, 1990), vol. 1. The spread of early Catharism is comprehensively treated in Jean Duvernoy, *Le catharisme*, vol. 2, *L'histoire des cathares* (Paris: Privat, 1986), pt. 2, chaps. 1–8; more briefly in Arno Borst, *Die Katharer* (Stuttgart: Hiersemann, 1953), 81–98; Moore, *The Origins of European Dissent*, 175–82, 185–86, 197–240; Lambert, *Medieval Heresy*, 55–61.

4. See Bernard Hamilton, "The Cathar Council of S. Félix Reconsidered," *Archivum Fratrum Praedicatorum* 48 (1978): 23–53; Franjo Šanjek, "Le rassemblement hérétique de Saint-Félix-de-Caraman (1167) et les églises cathares au XIIe siècle," *Revue d'histoire*

Waldensians, the majority of the Cathars adhered to a religion that not only differed from orthodox Christianity in regard to its ecclesiological structure, but also became entirely incompatible with it and other Christian heterodox groups in its theological premises.[5]

Absolute dualism is founded on the notion of two coeternal principles, irreducible to each other, and their corresponding deities. The one is the principle of light, represented by the good god, who created all spiritual, immaterial things. The other is the principle of darkness, represented by the evil god, who created all temporal, material things. The human soul partakes of the former realm, the human body of the latter. In Cathar mythology, the Fall designates the event in which souls fell from the good, spiritual realm, leaving a good part of them, the spirit, behind. Fallen souls are trapped in bodies, human and animal, in the realm of evil. This realm is the material world, in which souls migrate from one body, after its death, to the next (metempsychosis). Salvation consists in a soul's liberation from material entrapment and its reunion with the spirit in the realm of the good principle. Mitigated dualism differs from this radical form of dualism in that it is monistic; that is, only one God, the creator of all things, is believed to exist, and the representative of evil, Satan, is believed to have been created by God. In mitigated dualism, good will eventually prevail over evil.[6]

Dualism is one of the most rational theodicies in the major world religions, Weber noted.[7] Particularly in the form of the radical-dualist

---

écclésiastique 67 (1972): 767–99, with Latin text 772–79; translated in Brooke, *The Coming of the Friars*, 153–55.

5. See Arno Borst, "Die dualistische Häresie im Mittelalter," in *Barbaren, Ketzer und Artisten: Welten des Mittelalters* (Munich: Piper, 1990), 215–27. On the comparatively moderate elements of dualism in Christianity's core tenets, see Pètrement, *Le dualisme dans l'histoire*, 13–15. Cf. Weber, "Religious Rejections," in *From Max Weber*, 358–59.

6. On absolute and relative dualism in Catharism, see René Nelli, *Les cathares ou l'éternel combat* (Paris: Grasset, 1972), 96–106; Jean Duvernoy, *Le catharisme*, vol. 1, *La religion des cathares* (Paris: Privat, 1986), pt. 1, chap. 2, and chaps. 3 and 5 for Cathar cosmology and eschatology.

7. Weber, *Economy and Society*, 523–26; see also idem, "The Social Psychology and the World Religions," in *From Max Weber*, 275. Cf. the editor's reference in idem, *Die Wirtschaftsethik der Weltreligionen*, ed. Schmidt-Glitzer, 95 n. 15; idem, "Religious Rejections," in *From Max Weber*, 358–59. Weber noted an influence of Zoroastrianism on late Judaism ("Religious Rejections," 359) and intended to include in his *Collected Essays in the Sociology of Religion* "a short depiction of the . . . Zoroastrian religious ethics" (see Chapter 1, page 42). In his systematic treatise on religion in *Economy and Society* (505, 524), he referred to Gnosticism and Manichaeism, but not Catharism, as dualist belief systems. Troeltsch's references to the Cathars are as brief as his references to the Waldensians (see Chapter 1, page 35).

notions adopted by the majority of the Cathars after 1167, it is a pertinent answer to the problem of the existence of evil, injustice, and misfortune in the face of a powerful deity. Dualism solves the problem by reference to a principle opposing the good: pain and suffering are attributed to the powers of the devil. In its logical-dogmatic under-pinnings, dualism is an expression of utmost negation of the world as the sphere of evil. Since the whole course of *Heilsgeschichte* is explicable in terms of a battle between good and evil, dualism is a logically consistent and theoretically coherent system of meaning.[8] This system of meaning renders a systematically ordered worldview, which acts as a switchman directing patterns of action in certain directions. The means and paths to the highest religious goal, salvation, are clearly laid out. In the words of Arno Borst, author of a still authoritative account of Catharism, "the basic tension in the Christian faith between turning from the world and turning to it" is resolved in terms of the first alternative: "The religious dualist sides decidedly with the pure spirit and the other-worldly good, fleeing from the world and seeking deliverance himself from it, because [she or] he does not believe that it could be redeemed."[9] In its premises, Catharism is a prime case of what Troeltsch mistakenly generalized to all medieval heterodox groups, namely, a religious movement that derived its motivation from abstention from, or antagonism to, the world.[10]

    In Cathar soteriology, the path to salvation was abhorrence of material things and of the secular sphere in general. In this regard the differences between radical and mitigated dualism in Catharism were of secondary importance. This is also true for Catharism's salutary means. The sole technique to achieve salvation was to undergo a spiritual

    8. In a manner similar to Weber's, this has been cogently argued by Moore, *The Origins of European Dissent*, chap. 6.
    9. Borst, "Die dualistische Häresie im Mittelalter," in *Barbaren, Ketzer und Artisten*, 202, 200. This issue is further explored in idem, *Die Katharer*, 122, 142, 175, 177, 179, 221, 227. A view sharply critical of general characterizations of Cathar religion can be found in Gerhard Rottenwöhrer, *Der Katharismus*, vol. 4, *Glaube und Theologie der Katharer* (Bad Honnef: Bock & Herchen, 1993), who details the finer theological tenets of various Cathar groups. While Rottenwöhrer skillfully documents considerable differences between these groups, his argument is more pertinent to accounts that take Catharism as their sole reference (Borst, Duvernoy) and that focus on issues of belief. It is less appropriate for comparative studies of heretical groups that go beyond Catharism and studies that look at the relations between Cathar beliefs and other aspects of Cathar religion, such as organization or conduct. These latter studies, like this study, call primarily for an analysis of common Cathar tenets and of the foundations of Cathar religious views, not of differences among them. More subtle theological points, whose existence must not be denied, necessarily have to be neglected.
    10. See Chapter 1, page 35.

baptism, the central Cathar sacrament of consolation, the *consolamentum*, upon which the soul would no longer be trapped in its earthly
prison but would return to the spirit in the good realm after death. Since
the world is the realm of evil, consoled persons would have to remain
pure for the rest of their earthly existence. This meant not be tainted by
certain types of contact with the world or by practices that could
adversely affect the salutary status of other souls, and led to a rigid
stereotyping of action, mainly through taboo-norms. The most severe
taboo-norms were those prohibiting sexual intercourse (which originated
in carnal, hence evil, desires and could result in the creation of new
bodies subject to the devil), marriage (for the same reasons), the eating
of animal products (the result of carnal procreation and also a potential
or actual host of a soul), and, referring to scripture as the Waldensians
did, lying, swearing, or killing. Positively prescribed, on the other hand,
were three fasts of forty days each per year and an elaborate rhythm of
prayers.[11] After an adherent of Cathar faith became a perfect in the
consolamentum, the rite of passage to purity, the imperative to maintain
this soteriological trajectory was strengthened by the stipulation that
the person not deviate from this path and prevent the return of the soul
to heaven. Ermengaud of Béziers, a former Waldensian and companion
of Durand of Huesca who was knowledgeable about Cathar doctrines
and morals, wrote a lengthy section on their central sacrament in his
treatise *Against the Heretics*, which he composed in the first decade of
the thirteenth century:

> They believe, moreover, that if the person who administers the
> *consolamentum* has fallen into any of the sins that they call
> *criminal* [i.e., the equivalent of a mortal sin in orthodoxy], like
> eating meat, or an egg, or cheese, or killing a bird or any animal
> apart from small creeping ones, or into even those that the
> Roman church calls criminal, like murder, adultery, fornication,
> impurity, robbery, false testimony, perjury, rapine, the *consola-
> mentum* [that the person administers] is of no avail to those who
> receive it. For they say that the person who has thus fallen does
> not have the Holy Spirit, and because the person does not have
> it, they believe that [she or] he can not give it to others. They

11. Duvernoy, *Le catharisme*, vol. 1, pt. 2, chap. 2; Michel Roquebert, *Cathar
Religion* (Portet-sur-Garonne: Éditions Loubatières, 1988), 11; Borst, *Die Katharer*,
180–88. On the *consolamentum*, see Borst, *Die Katharer*, 193–97; exhaustively docu-
mented in Gerhard Rottenwöhrer, *Der Katharismus*, vol. 2, *Der Kult, die religiöse
Praxis, die Kritik an Kult und Sakramenten der Katholischen Kirche* (Bad Honnef: Bock
& Herchen, 1982), bk. 1, 145–341.

indeed believe it is necessary for this person to receive the *consolamentum* from another [Cathar], if [she or] he desires to be saved, and that it is proper that this be done, as is said, by all, men and women alike, who have fallen.[12]

A perfect must have found it difficult to adhere to the various prohibitions. The path to salvation was narrow. The prohibitions covered a wide spectrum of social activities, some usually performed in public, others in private, but none of them removed from the scrutiny of bystanders, supporters, and the associates of the perfect. Adherence was sanctioned by the threat of losing the state of grace. According to Ermengaud of Béziers, not only had the perfect to be reconsoled, but also any *consolamentum* performed since the transgression that prompted the fall from grace was invalid. In his history of the Albigensian Crusade, Peter of Vaux-de-Cernay, a young Cistercian monk, wrote a few years later about even more dire consequences of this act: "They [the Cathars] affirmed that if any one of the perfected commit mortal sin . . . , all those consoled by him lose the Holy Spirit and must be reconsoled, and they even say that those already saved fall from heaven because of the sin of the one who consoled them."[13]

Transgression by mortal sin retroactively invalidated previous consolations administered by the perpetrator and thereby gravely endangered the salutary prospects of the consoled. This, of course, gave the consoled a strong incentive to monitor the conduct of the perfects closely.[14]

12. "Credunt etiam hoc, quod si ille, qui facit illud 'consolamentum,' in aliquo peccatorum, quàe ipsi 'criminalia' vocant, lapsus fuerit: sicut est comedere carnem, aut ovum, vel caseum, vel interficere avem, vel aliquod animal, praeter repentia; vel etiam illa peccata, quae Ecclesia Romana 'criminalia' nominat, veluti homicidium, adulterium, fornicationem, immunditiam, furtum, falsum testimonium, perjurium, rapinam, 'consolamentum' illius recipientibus nihil prodest. Dicunt enim eum talem si lapsum, Spiritum sanctum non habere; et quod non habet credunt non posse alicui dare. Imo eumdem credunt iterum oportere illud 'consolamentum' recipere ab alio, si salvari desiderat, et hoc universaliter de omnibus, tam viris, quam mulieribus lapsis ita oportet fieri, ut dictum est" (Ermengaud of Béziers, *Contra Haereticos, in Patrologiae cursus completus . . . Series Latina . . .* , ed. Migne, vol. 204, cols. 1262–63). See further Thouzellier, *Catharisme et valdéisme en Languedoc*, 278–79.

13. "[D]icebant, quod si quis de perfectis peccaret mortaliter . . . , omnes consolati ab illo amittebant Spiritum Sanctum et oportebat eos iterum reconsolari; et etiam jam salvati pro peccato consolatoris cadebant de celo" (Petrus Sarnensis, *Petri Vallium Sarnaii monachi Hystoria albigensis*, ed. Pascal Guébin and Ernest Lyon, 3 vols. [Paris: Champion, 1926–39], vol. 1, no. 17; I use the translation of Wakefield and Evans, *Heresies of the High Middle Ages*, 240).

14. Rainerius Sacconi, a Dominican friar and inquisitor and former heresiarch, described the psychological consequences of this doctrine in his *Summa on the Cathars*

Patterns of Conduct Among the Cathar Perfects

The seriousness of Cathar morals was often doubted in orthodox commentary. Ecclesiastical observers generally had a vested interest in portraying Cathar heretics in the worst light possible and used any occasion to slander them. When several heretical groups were found, the Cathars, and not the Waldensians or other groups, were usually the focus of ecclesiastical interest. Among the most pernicious portrayals were those that claimed the Cathars were wont to give in to the temptation of licentiousness and practiced unfettered intercourse between unmarried persons. Peter of Vaux-de-Cernay, for the Languedocian Cathars, and the Italian inquisitor Anselm of Alessandria, for the Italian Cathars, both refer to the claim that Cathars do not think that one can sin from the waist down.[15] A document from about 1300 listing heretical errors of the Cathars includes their alleged tenet that "simple fornication is no sin."[16] Related to this charge was the inference that Cathar believers could transgress freely before admission to the group of perfects, since consolation conferred forgiveness of sin. Peter of Vaux-de-Cernay gives an illustrative account of this: "Those who were called believers were absorbed in usuries, robberies, murders, sins of the flesh, perjuries, and all sorts of perversities. They felt, in truth, more secure and unbridled in their sinning because they believed that they would be

---

and the Poor of Lyon in a section entitled "A Notable Uncertainty Among Them": "All Cathars labor under very great doubt and danger of soul. To specify, if their prelate, especially their bishop, may secretly have committed some mortal sin—and many such persons have been found among them in the past—all those upon whom he has imposed his hand have been misled and perish if they die in that state" (*Notabilis dubietas inter eos*. Proinde omnes Cathari laborant in maximo dubio et periculo anime. Verbi gratia si prelatus eorum, et maxime episcopus, occulte commiserit aliquod mortale peccatum, quales etiam multi olim reperti sunt inter eos, omnes illi quibus ipse manum suam imposuit, sunt decepti et pereunt, si in eo statu decedunt" (François Šanjek, "Raynerius Sacconi, O.P., *Summa de Catharis*," *Archivum Fratrum Praedicatorum* 44 [1974]: 49; I use the translation in Wakefield and Evans, *Heresies of the High Middle Ages*, 336). See also the report formerly attributed to the Franciscan James Capelli and the report of the Dominican Anselm of Alessandria, in Wakefield and Evans, *Heresies of the High Middle Ages*, 303, 367. On the retroactive invalidation of the *consolamentum*, see also Moore, *The Origins of European Dissent*, 221–22; Raoul Manselli, "Églises et théologies cathares," *Cahiers de Fanjeaux* 3 (1968): 159–60.

15. See Wakefield and Evans, *Heresies of the High Middle Ages*, 170, 240. Rainerius Sacconi makes a similar claim for Cathar believers; ibid., 332.

16. "Dicunt quod simplex fornicatio non est peccatum aliquod" (Claude de Vic and Joseph Vaissete, *Histoire générale de Languedoc* [Toulouse: Privat, 1879], vol. 8, col. 984). See also Wakefield and Evans, *Heresies of the High Middle Ages*, 233, 239, 333, for related allegations in other documents.

saved, without restitution of ill-gotten gains, without confession and penance, so long as they were able in the last throes of death to repeat the Lord's Prayer and receive the imposition of hands from their officials."[17]

The Cathar practice of deathbed heredication that the last sentence refers to has received a lot of attention in the historical literature. From Inquisition records of the late thirteenth and early fourteenth centuries it appears that by then deathbed heredication was the predominant form of becoming a Cathar perfect for hardened believers who clung to a heresy in vast decline at the time. In Emmanuel Le Roy Ladurie's study of Montaillou, eleven people of that hamlet and seven outside of it received consolations on their deathbeds,[18] and more references can be found in documents of the Inquisitions in Languedoc in the late thirteenth and early fourteenth centuries.[19] Related to this are reports of deathbed heredication occurring in conjunction with the *endura*, a practice in which the heredicated, in order to make sure that no relapse could spoil the coming eternal bliss, starved themselves to death following the administration of the sacrament. "Since many of them [the

---

17. "qui dicebantur credentes hereticorum dediti erant usuris, rapinis, homicidii et carnis illecebris, perjuriis et perversitatibus universis: isti quidem ideo securius et effrenatius peccabant, quia credebant sine restitutione ablatorum, sine confessione et penitentia, se esse salvandos, dummodo in supremo mortis articulo 'Pater noster' dicere et manuum impositionem a magistris suis recipere potuissent" (Petrus Sarnensis, *Petri Vallium Sarnaii monachi Hystoria albigensis*, ed. Guébin and Lyon, vol. 1, no. 13; I use the translation in Wakefield and Evans, *Heresies of the High Middle Ages*, 239).

18. Emmanuel Le Roy Ladurie, *Montaillou: The Promised Land of Error*, trans. Barbara Bray (New York: Vintage Books, 1979), 218–20. Cf. Matthias Benad, *Domus und Religion in Montaillou: Katholische Kirche und Katharismus im Überlebenskampf der Familie des Pfarrers Petrus Clerici am Anfang des 14. Jahrhunderts* (Tübingen: Mohr, 1990), 4, 113–14, 318, who considers deathbed heredication to have been fairly typical and views it as expressing a lack of ethical convictions in the Cathar believers.

19. Ample testimony about deathbed heredication can be found in the records of an Inquisition at Carcassonne, Toulouse, and Albi between 1283 and 1289, printed in Alphonse J. Mahul, *Cartulaire et archives des commune de l'ancien diocèse et de l'arrondissement administratif de Carcassonne*, vol. 5 (Paris: Didron, 1867), 630–45. Additional references can be found in records of the Inquisitions in the county of Foix in 1300–1309 and at Albi in 1299–1300. See Annette Pales-Gobilliard, *L'Inquisiteur Geoffroy d'Ablis et les cathares du comté de Foix* (1308–1309) (Paris: Éditions du Centre national de la recherche scientifique, 1984), 67, and s.v. *hérétication* in the general index; Georgene W. Davis, *The Inquisition at Albi, 1299–1300: Text of Register and Analysis* (New York: Columbia University Press, 1948), 43. For further commentary, see Anne Brenon, *Les femmes cathares* (Paris: Perrin, 1992), 299; Koch, *Frauenfrage und Ketzertum im Mittelalter*, 71, 87; John Hine Mundy, *The Repression of Catharism at Toulouse: The Royal Diploma of 1279* (Toronto: Pontifical Institute of Mediaeval Studies, 1985), 9.

Cathar believers] when ill have sometimes asked those who nursed them not to put any food or drink into their mouths if the invalids could not at least say the Lord's Prayer, it is quite evident that many of them thus commit suicide," wrote the converted heresiarch Rainerius Sacconi.[20] Believers who wanted to ensure their reconsolation on the deathbed, even if too sick or otherwise incapacitated to relate their wish to a perfect and repeat the obligatory prayer, could enter into a pact with the perfect called *covenensa*, in which the latter agreed to console the person by imposition of hands alone.[21] But neither the *endura* nor the *covenensa* appeared on a large scale before the mid-thirteenth century, after massive inquisitorial persecutions, and they did not apply to those who lived in the state of perfection during their lifetimes.[22]

To gauge the moral sincerity and strictness of the perfects, a better analytical strategy than the exclusive use of polemical testimonials of inquisitors and others is to augment those testimonials with references to their conduct in sources that appear to balance common biases with astute observations. A small number of such references exist; each requires careful interpretation. One such reference was made in the *Treatise Against Heretics*, written perhaps as early as 1220 and formerly attributed to James Capelli, a Franciscan friar in Milan. In the orthodox literature, the treatise contains one of the most stunning defenses of Cathar morals against public accusations and rumors:[23]

---

20. "Siquidem ex eis multi in suis infirmitatibus dixerunt aliquando eis, qui ministrabant eis, quod ipsi non ponerent aliquid cibi uel potus in os eorum, si illi infirmi non possent dicere 'pater noster' ad minus, under uerisimile est multi ex eis occiderunt seipsos hoc modo" (Šanjek, "Raynerius Sacconi, O.P.," 47; I use the translation of Wakefield and Evans, *Heresies of the High Middle Ages*, 334).

21. See Wakefield and Evans, *Heresies of the High Middle Ages*, 382, 756 n. 5.

22. This view is shared by the vast majority of historians, whether or not they view the endura as a historical myth; see Yves Dossat, "Les cathares d'après les documents de l'Inquisition," *Cahiers de Fanjeaux* 3 (1968): 83–87; Eugène Dupré Theseider, "Le catharisme languedocien et l'Italie," ibid., 313; Manselli, "Églises et théologies cathares," 160–62; Duvernoy, *Le catharisme*, 1:164–70; Borst, *Die Katharer*, 197 n. 22; Walter L. Wakefield, *Heresy, Crusade, and Inquisition in Southern France, 1100–1250* (Berkeley and Los Angeles: University of California Press, 1974), 40–42; Moore, *The Origins of European Dissent*, 224; Lambert, *Medieval Heresy*, 139; Brenon, *Les femmes cathares*, 327–32; eadem, *Le vrai visage du catharisme*, rev. ed. (Portet-sur-Garonne: Éditions Loubatières, 1990), 84–85.

23. On this work, see Walter L. Wakefield, "The Treatise Against Heretics of James Capelli: A Study of Medieval Writing and Preaching Against Catharan Heresy" (Ph.D. diss., Columbia University, 1951), crediting it with "an unusual temperateness of expression when the author is describing the lives and religious ritual of heretics. . . . Such scruples are not common in doctrinal argument and may persuade one to regard the author as knowledgeable and fair, and his description of heresy as reliable" (8). See

[T]hey administer this imposition of hands [in the rite of consolation] to believers in their sect who are ill, out of which has stemmed the popular rumor that they kill them by strangulation, so that they may be martyrs or confessors. From personal knowledge we affirm this to be untrue and we urge that no one believe that they commit so shameful an act. For we know that they suppose their behavior to be virtuous and they do many things that are in the nature of good works; in frequent prayer, in vigils, in sparsity of food and clothing, and—let me acknowledge the truth—in austerity of abstinence they surpass all other religious.[24]

In making his argument, Pseudo-Capelli follows a strategy similar to that in the *Passau Anonymous* for describing the Austrian Waldensians about two decades later.[25] Both do not question so much the actual austerity and sincerity of the heretics' way of life as their underlying motives and false interpretation of scripture leading to a false appearance of holiness and vainglory in regard to their behavior. Equating them with cunning serpents, Pseudo-Capelli sees them spreading false doctrine under their veil of good works. "They flavor them [their pernicious traditions] . . . with a certain seasoning of simulated virtue so that the underlying poison is less perceptible through the pleasing sweetness of the honey. They put on a certain show of piety but . . . they have not the virtue of sanctity."[26] Nevertheless, when he illustrates this view with reference to the Cathars' disregard for matrimony, he combines his scorn for the evilness of their religion with attention to correcting false, superficial perceptions of their behavior:

[T]hese most stupid of people, seeking the purity of virginity and chastity, say that all carnal coition is shameful, base, and

also Mariano D'Alatri, "La polemica antieretica di Fra Giacomo de' Capelli," in *L'inquisizione francescana nell'Italia centrale nel secolo XIII* (Rome: Istituto Storico dei Frati Minori Cappuccini, 1954), 25–36. For a discussion of recent scholarship on the authorship of the treatise and its date, see Pilar Jimenez-Sanchez, "Des études récentes sur les sources hérétiques et anti-hérétiques en Italie," *Heresis* 24 (1995): 103.

24. As translated in Wakefield and Evans, *Heresies of the High Middle Ages*, 303–4. I was unable to consult the edition of the manuscript in Dino Bazzocchi, *L'eresia catara: Appendice: Disputationes nonnullae adversos haereticos: Codice inedito Malatestiano del secolo XIII* (Bologna, 1920).

25. See Chapter 4, page 166.

26. Wakefield and Evans, *Heresies of the High Middle Ages*, 306. Cf. the list of insulting characterizations of the heretics by Pseudo-Capelli in D'Alatri, "La polemica antieretica di Fra Giacomo de' Capelli," in *L'inquisizione francescana*, 32.

odious, and thus damnable. Although spiritually they are prostituted and they pollute the word of God, they are, however, most chaste of body. For men and women observing the vow and way of life of this sect are in no way soiled by the corruption of debauchery. . . . Actually, the rumor of the fornication which is said to prevail among them is most false. . . . They are wrongfully wounded in popular rumor by many malicious charges of blasphemy from those who say that they commit many shameful and horrid acts of which they are innocent. . . . They are all bound by their superstitious and false religion, as we said [in a previous passage], to the vow of continence.[27]

A corroborative hint in regard to Cathar continence can be gleaned from Rainerius Sacconi. Repeating the claim that Cathar believers fornicate freely even among their own families, he adds that many of them "often grieve when they recall that they did not indulge their passions more frequently in the days when they had not yet professed the heresy of the Cathars."[28] Actually, if unwittingly, Rainerius Sacconi adds to the credibility of the views expressed in the *Treatise Against Heretics*.

A different source of Cathar behavior, the chronicle of William Pelhisson, a Dominican friar at Toulouse, written in the 1240s, gives a narrative of the events mainly in and around Toulouse between 1229 and 1238. In 1233 Pope Gregory IX authorized the establishment of the Inquisition in Languedoc and commissioned the Dominicans, to be assisted by the bishops, to combat heresy. The first inquisitors in Toulouse were Pons of Saint Gilles, Peter Seila, and William Arnold, who started their proceedings in 1234 with a public sermon, combined with a call for confessions and an appeal to come forward. During a period of grace, a voluntary disclosure of information was encouraged by lenient treatment for the admission of guilt. After listening to witnesses and recording accusations, Pelhisson reports, the inquisitors summoned one of their main suspects of Cathar heresy, a man named Peter Textor. Speaking out in public at his summoning, Textor chose a memorable line of defense, which Pelhisson gives as a quotation: "Gentlemen, listen to me! I am not a heretic, because I have a wife and sleep with her, and I have sons, and I eat meat, and I lie and swear, and I am a faithful

27. Wakefield and Evans, *Heresies of the High Middle Ages*, 305–6.

28. "sepe dolent dum recolunt quod non adimpleuerunt sepius libidinem suam tempore quo nondum fuerant professi heresim Catharorum" (Šanjek, "Raynerius Sacconi, O.P.," 45; I use the translation of Wakefield and Evans, *Heresies of the High Middle Ages*, 332).

Christian. Therefore do not let them [his accusers] say these things about me, for I truly believe in God."[29]

Textor's appeal to the public was based on the argument that his lifestyle, ordinary or "faithful" as it was, in that it reflected his giving in to various temptations of the flesh, was incompatible to that of a Cathar perfect. Cathars, he argued implicitly, do not have spouses, practice continence, abstain from eating certain foods, and take their word seriously. His statement thus corroborates virtually every aspect of conduct for Languedocian Catharism that Pseudo-Capelli described for contemporary Italian Cathars. John Textor, a defendant nonpareil, did not make his case well enough, however. He was put in prison and later burned—a punishment for apostasy usually confined to dead heretics— after confessing his adherence to Catharism.[30]

By the time the Dominicans conducted their first major inquiry into heresy in Languedoc, their order had been approved by the papacy for only about twenty years. The activities of Dominic and others in the decade preceding papal approval in 1216 and the very orientation of Dominican spirituality were significantly influenced by their encounters with the Cathars. Reports of these encounters provide further documentation of Cathar austerity. Dominic first came into contact with Catharism when, accompanying his bishop, Diego of Osma, on a trip to Denmark, he found out that an innkeeper of a hostel they stayed at in Toulouse was a Cathar supporter. Dominic argued with his host the whole night and, as the Dominican historiographer Jordan of Saxony reports, eventually won him back to orthodox faith.[31] Jordan of Saxony

---

29. "Domini, audite me. Ego non sum haereticus, quia uxorem habeo et cum ipsa jaceo; et filios habeo, et carnes comedo, et mentior et juro, et fidelis sum Christianus. Ideo non sustineatis ista mihi dici, quia Deum bene credo" (Célestin Douais, "Chronique de Guilhem Pelhisso," in *Les sources de l'histoire de l'Inquisition dans le Midi de la France, aux XIIIe et XIVe siècles* [Paris: Librairie de Victor Palmé, 1881], 93). The early development of the Inquisition in Languedoc is described in Yves Dossat, *Les crises de l'Inquisition toulousaine au XIII siècle (1233–1273)* (Bordeaux: Imprimerie Bière, 1959), 118–43; Wakefield, *Heresy, Crusade, and Inquisition in Southern France*, 146–49; Lothar Kolmer, *Ad Capiendas Vulpes: Die Ketzerbekämpfung in Südfrankreich in der ersten Hälfte des 13. Jahrhunderts und die Ausbildung des Inquisitionsverfahrens* (Bonn: Rohrscheid, 1982), 127–45.

30. See Douais, "Chronique de Guilhem Pelhisso," in *Les sources de l'histoire de l'Inquisition*, 93–95. On punishment of dead heretics at the time, see Kolmer, *Ad Capiendas Vulpes*, 129, who estimates the number of heretics that were burned alive at "hardly more than 20 persons."

31. Jordan of Saxony, *On the Beginnings of the Order of the Preachers*, ed. and trans. Simon Tugwell (Chicago: Parable, 1982), chap. 2, no. 15. For the events described here and in the following, see Marie-Humbert Vicaire's eminent analysis in his *Histoire de Saint Dominique*, vol. 1, chaps. 4 and 6. See also Hinnebusch, *History of the*

also chronicles the return of Dominic and the bishop of Osma to this area three years later, when they met at Montpellier with three Cistercians. The Cistercians had been sent to Languedoc as papal legates to preach against heresy, but their mission had little success and was ridiculed by the Cathars. The reason for Cathar ridicule was not only that the lower clergy did not appear to be up to the task but that the Cistercians themselves would not travel without the usual entourage and pomp—conditions the Cathars were quick to adduce in order to underscore their own sanctity.[32] Upon hearing the Cistercians' admission of failure, Diego proposed a new method of winning this spiritual battle:

> No, brethren, I do not think that you are setting about things in the right way. In my opinion you will never be able to bring these people back to the faith just by talking to them, because they are much more inclined to be swayed by example. Look how the heretics urge their ways on the simple people by displaying an outward show of holiness, by feigning an example of evangelical austerity and asceticism. . . . Use a nail to drive out a nail. Chase off their feigned holiness with true religious life. The imposing appearance of the false apostles can only be shown up for what it is by manifest humility.[33]

What Diego suggested here was the imitation of Cathar austerity, based on orthodox faith. This suggestion would have been meaningless if the perfects had not indeed displayed such a frugal way of life. The preachers' horses and other goods were sent back, together with other provisions for them, and from there on Diego and Dominic traveled with few amenities. Within a decade preaching in poverty and humility

---

Dominican Order, 20–32; Griffe, *Le Languedoc cathare de 1190 à 1210*, 249–72; Thouzellier, *Catharisme et valdéisme en Languedoc*, 249–55.

32. See Petrus Sarnensis, *Petri Vallium Sarnaii monachi Hystoria albigensis*, ed. Guébin and Lyon, vol. 1, nos. 20–21; also Guillaume de Puylaurens, *Chronique (Chronica magistri Guillelmi de Podio Laurentii)*, ed. Jean Duvernoy (Paris: Éditions du Centre national de la recherche scientifique, 1976), no. 8.

33. "'Non sic,' ait, 'fratres, non sic vobis arbitror procedendum. Impossibile mihi videtur, homines istos solis ad fidem reduci verbis, qui potius innituntur exemplis. En heretici, dum speciem preferunt pietatis, dum evangelice parsimonie et austeritatis mentiuntur exempla, persuadent simplicibus vias suas. . . . Clavum clavo retundite, fictam sanctitatem vera religione fugate, quia fastus pseudoapostolorum evidenti vult humilitate convinci'" (Heribert C. Scheeben, "Libellus de principiis ordinis Praedicatorum auctore Iordano de Saxonia," *Monumenta Ordinis Praedicatorum Historica* 16 [1935], no. 20; I use the translation in Jordan of Saxony, *On the Beginnings of the Order of the Preachers*, chap. 3, no. 20).

became the official program of the mendicants, thus illustrating how religious asceticism in fringe and heterodox religious movements, as argued in Chapter 2, spilled over into orthodox spirituality. Furthermore, pious women were to be included in the reformed orthodox spirituality as well. Late in the same year Dominic founded Prouille, in the words of Jordan of Saxony, "to receive certain noble women whose parents had been forced by poverty to entrust them to the heretics to be educated and brought up."[34] Thus, in the events of both Montpellier and Prouille, religious asceticism was gleaned from the Cathar example. Since traditional forms of religious austerity were found lacking or deficient, and this lack or deficiency provided opportunities for the Cathars to establish themselves as the true successors of apostolic life and poverty, orthodox monasticism, the spearhead of Catholic spirituality, found it advantageous to emulate forms of heterodox religious practices. Some evidence for such emulation can also be found in the case of Saint Francis and the Italian Cathars.[35]

Finally, an altogether different yet equally relevant source of information about the religious demeanor of the perfects is Inquisition records. A great variety of these contain references to Cathar perfects. Raymunda Gondaubou said during the Inquisition at Toulouse in 1245–46 under Jean de Saint-Pierre and Bernard de Caux that "she believed the aforementioned heretics [the Cathar perfects] to be good men and to have good faith, and that she could be saved through them."[36] But this statement appears verbatim in the testimony of the preceding and the following witnesses and likely reflects the inquisitors' use of an interrogatory that suggested these statements to the witnesses.[37] As was the case for

34. "Ad susceptionem autem quarundam feminarum nobilium, quas parentes earum ratione pauperitatis erudiendas et nutriendas tradebant hereticis, quoddam instituit monasterium . . . nomem loci eiusdem Prulianum" (Scheeben, "Libellus de principiis ordinis Praedicatorum auctore Iordano de Saxonia," no. 27; I use the translation in Jordan of Saxony, On the Beginnings of the Order of the Preachers, chap. 3, no. 27).

35. See Kajetan Esser, "Franziskus von Assisi und die Katharer seiner Zeit," Archivum Franciscanum Historicum 51 (1958): 225–64. The wider context of apostolic "inspiration" of the mendicants is addressed in Marie-Humbert Vicaire, "La prédication nouvelle des Prêcheurs méridionaux au XIIIe siècle," in Dominique et ses prêcheurs, 2d ed. (Fribourg: Éditions Universitaires, 1977), 105–7; idem, "Le modèle évangélique des apôtres à l'origine de l'ordre de saint Dominique," Heresis 13/14 (1989): 331–37.

36. "Predictos hereticos credidit esse bonos homines et habere bonam fidem, et posse salvari per ipsos" (MS 609, Bibliothèque Municipale, Toulouse, fol. 5r; for more on this manuscript, see note 79 below).

37. Jean de Saint-Pierre and Bernard de Caux probably used an interrogatory similar, if not identical, to the one contained in the manual for inquisitors that is now

Waldensians persecuted in the Inquisition, many of those suspected to harbor sympathy for the Cathars tried to deflect attention away from themselves. One way of doing this was to report statements allegedly made by other Cathar supporters, some of which pointed out the sanctity of the perfects. When in 1256 Guillelmus Furnerii confessed his former involvement in Catharism to inquisitors, he implicated a certain Arnaldus de Lugano de Salbiera, who "much commended the [Cathar] heretics to the witness, saying that the heretics were *good and wise men*."[38] Guillelmus's mother was led by the perfects' appearance of holiness to instruct him to revere them and to believe "that a human being could be better saved in the heretics' faith than in the faith of the Christian church."[39] Some decades later, when asked about his contacts with Cathar perfects as part of an Inquisition at Albi in 1299–1300, Petrus Rigaudi implicated Guillermus de Mauriano, a major suspect in this Inquisition, who told him that the Cathar perfects "were good men and followed the rules of the apostles and lived in great sanctity and abstinence, and that they had the power to absolve the [Cathar] believers."[40] Similarly, during Geoffroy d'Ablis's Inquisition in the county of Foix in 1308–9, Guillelma Garsendi de Ax reported that Raymunda de Rodesio, the sister of two Cathar perfects, had attempted to lure her into becoming a Cathar believer by asking her "whether she wanted to know the way by which she could be saved and go to paradise." Raymunda then mentioned the "good men," telling her that they "followed the way of God and of the apostles and had good faith . . . , and that the heretics

---

being attributed to their colleagues Pierre Durand and Guillaume Raymond (Kolmer, *Ad Capiendas Vulpes*, 198–203). That manual has been published in Ad. Tardif, "Document pour l'histoire du *processus per inquisitionem* et de l'*inquisitio heretice pravitatis*," *Nouvelle revue historique du droit français et étranger* 7 (1883): 669–78, of which an English translation and annotation can be found in Wakefield, *Heresy, Crusade, and Inquisition in Southern France*, 250–58; for the formula for the interrogatory, see 252.

38. "dixit quod Arnaldus de Lugano de Salbiera commendavit ipsi testi multum hereticos dicens quod heretici erant *boni homines et sapientes*" (M. Belhomme, "Documents inédits sur l'hérésie des albigeois," *Mémoires de la Société archéologique du Midi de la France* 6 [1852]: 145).

39. "dicens quod aladaycis mater sua primo monuit ipsum testum pluries ut diligeret bonos homines scilicet hereticos et quod melius poterat homo salvari in fide hereticorum quam in fide ecclesie Xristiane" (ibid., 144–45). The inquisitors were Jean de Saint-Pierre and Rainaud de Chartres; for additional information, see Gerhard Rottenwöhrer, *Der Katharismus*, vol. 1, *Quellen zum Katharismus* (Bad Honnef: Bock & Herchen, 1982), bk. 1, 125.

40. "de quibus [Guillermus Desiderii and Raymundus del Boc, two Cathar perfects] dixit ipsi testi dictus Guillermus de Mauriano quod erant boni homines et erant de regula apostolorum et erant magne sanctitatis et mage astinencie et poterant absolvere credentes" (Davis, *The Inquisition at Albi, 1299–1300*, 245).

had the power to save souls and that they said they were the church of God and underwent great fasts and did not lie."[41] Such a claim to sanctity by the Cathar perfects themselves occurred also, in a testimony contained in a register of Renous de Plassac and Pons de Parnac from the Inquisition at Toulouse in 1273–79, stating that "the heretics began to commend themselves on their abstinence and the purity of life [they led] and the scandal of [their] persecution, which they endured on account of God."[42]

When viewed in isolation, none of the statements reported above would make for sufficient evidence of the severity of Cathar austerity. This may even be true for statements from any given type of source, since the validity of statements from any one of the inquisitors' systematic *summae*, reports by ecclesiastical observers, chronicles, and Inquisition records used here is difficult to gauge if the source is analyzed by itself. Yet the comprehensive exploration of all of these together appears to provide adequate and consistent documentation for a congruence of Cathar ethics and behavior. The severity and frugality of earthly life intimated in Cathar ethics were reflected in actual patterns of conduct.[43] The fact that prominent, if infrequent, cases existed in which leading Cathar figures were compromised by the discovery of conduct unbecoming of a perfect does not invalidate this argument. A salient occurrence of such conduct was the mishap of Garattus, a candidate for bishop of the Italian Cathars when two witnesses found him with a woman. Yet his infidelity was a scandal

41. "dixit sibi ipsi Ramunda [de Rodesio, sister of the Cathar perfects Pierre and Guillaume Autier] si volebat scire viam per quam posset salvari et ire in paradisum, que respondit quod libenter faceret et diceret per quod posset salvare animam suam. Tunc dicta Ramunda fecit sibi mentionem de bonis hominibus . . . dicens ei quod ipsi tenebant viam Die et apostolorum et habebant bonam fidem . . . et quod ipsi heretici habebant potestatem salvandi animas et dicebant quod ipsi erant ecclesia Dei et faciebant magnas abstinencias et non menciebantur" (Pales-Gobilliard, *L'Inquisiteur Geoffroy d'Ablis et les cathares du comté de Foix (1308–1309)*, 180). Very similar references to the Cathars can be found in the testimony of Jacobus Garsendis; see ibid., 364.

42. "Haeretici coeperunt commendare se ipsos super abstinentia sua et puritate vitae et scandalo persecutionis, quam patiebantur propter Deum" (Döllinger, *Beiträge zur Sektengeschichte des Mittelalters*, 2:37). The reference to the source is obtained from Jean Duvernoy, "Une source familière de l'heresiologie médiévale: Le tome II des 'Beiträge' de Döllinger," *Revue de l'histoire des religions* 183 (1973): 166.

43. Cf. the rather wooden characterization of a Cathar perfect as a "tense, rather literal-minded perfectionist with a strong determination, . . . perhaps a tendency to organic disgust," by Malcolm D. Lambert, "The Motives of the Cathars: Some Reflections," in *Religious Motivation: Biographical and Sociological Problems for the Church Historian*, ed. Derek Baker (Oxford: Blackwell, 1978), 54. A more nuanced characterization by the same author can be found in idem, *Medieval Heresy*, 108–9.

considered so severe that a majority of Italian Cathars thought him to be permanently disqualified from this position, and the scandal contributed to a continued state of factionalism among the Italian Cathars.[44]

Type and Direction of Cathar Asceticism

Distinctive elements of asceticism in Catharism can perhaps be best delineated when these elements are directly contrasted with those in monasticism and Waldensianism. Early in the thirteenth century the mendicants and the Waldensians shared an emphasis on apostolic preaching, carried out by mobile preachers who castigated their bodies and lived in voluntary poverty. In orthodoxy, mobility and preaching expressed a reformed spirit of monasticism, which shed its commitment to stability and seclusion from the world. Reformed monasticism's ascetic practices, however, were not altogether new but rather a continuation of the tradition of religious disciplining of body and mind that went back to the early Christian desert hermits and the Rule of St. Benedict. Human passions and natural appetites could stand in the way of the purification of the mind; the flesh was thus an object of perpetual mortification. This gave monastic asceticism its rigor and a strong teleological orientation. Within the boundaries of orthodoxy, monastic asceticism, which retained an overall other-worldly direction in spite of a turning-to-the-world in the mendicants, rendered the most assured and expedient—in Weber's words, "heroic"—if not exclusive, means to salvation.

The Waldensians were less motivated than the monastics by lofty theological reasoning and more by their literalist interpretation of passages of the New Testament, which exhorted them to communal apostolic life. Their focus on preaching necessitated the abandonment of worldly goods, and scripturally based prohibitions augmented their asceticism, which, with the exception of the Austrian Waldensians, remained other-worldly. Works and faith were complementary aspects of Waldensian spirituality, and as in monasticism, ascetic achievements reflected a way of life that sought continuous perfection and wrought methodical discipline. Waldensianism's initial tenets, too, were non-exclusive with regard to other means and paths to salvation.

---

44. This episode is recorded in an early-thirteenth-century treatise of uncertain origins, *De heresi catharorum*, which has been published in Antoine Dondaine, "La hiérarchie cathare en Italie, I: Le 'De heresi Catharorum in Lombardia,'" *Archivum Fratrum Praedicatorum* 19 (1949): 306–12, and translated into English and annotated in Wakefield and Evans, *Heresies of the High Middle Ages*, 159–67. Further implications of this event are discussed in Borst, *Die Katharer*, 100–101.

Cathar asceticism was the most austere and demanding of all three. The Cathar conception of the earthly existence as realm of evil, their prohibitions against taking part in it, and the gloomy implications of failure were part of a worldview entirely different from those of orthodoxy and other heterodox religious groups. The asceticism Catharism engendered was not that of perpetual refinement and perfection but radical abstention; its direction, principled withdrawal. One might indeed question whether the term *asceticism* is appropriate here. Using a narrower definition than Troeltsch's, whose usage included suppression of sensuality and cultivation of virtue, Weber referred to "rationalized" asceticism as systematic techniques and practices, not haphazard flight from the world and mere cultivation of sensual elements.[45] He perhaps did so in deference to the etymological roots of asceticism, denoting "exercise" or "training."[46] Training and exercise, however, are precisely what were *not* demanded from a Cathar perfect once that person had undergone the *consolamentum*. What was demanded was the cultivation of a habitus of strictest abstinence, in the absence of exercises and training that would in any way reflect a methodical rationalization of involvement in the evil world. In his comparison of asceticism in early Christianity and austerity among the Gnostics, who espoused a dualistic worldview similar to the Cathars', Gedaliahu Strousma, a scholar of comparative religion, has suggested the term *encratism* instead of *asceticism* for the religious practices of the latter.[47] Encratism refers to the repression of sensual impulses, sexual continence, and abstinence from certain foods and drink, and in the early Christian church was practiced mainly by the Encratites, a fairly small dualist sect.[48] As Strousma argues, there were important differences between Christian asceticism and the encratism practiced by dualist groups:

> The asceticism of the [Greek] philosophers, like that of the Christians, is essentially an ethical process, the moral preparation for a spiritual goal. . . . In contrast to asceticism, encratism has its goal in itself. Salvation in Gnosticism is found in the very escape, the refusal of contact with the world, the break of an illicit and impure bond [to the world]. Whereas the ascetic aims, in a continuous effort, to reach a certain state [i.e., the state of

45. See Chapter 1, pages 20, 40.
46. See the Introduction, page 2.
47. Stroumsa, "Ascèse et gnose."
48. H. Chadwick, "Enkrateia," in *Reallexikon für Antike und Christentum*, vol. 5, ed. Theodor Klauser (Stuttgart: Hiersemann, 1962), cols. 343–66. See also Brown, *The Body and Society*, 92–93.

grace], the Gnostic proceeds from the recognition that that state is given to him by nature; his goal is to free himself [by freeing himself from worldly attachments], that of the Christian ascetic to fulfill himself [in striving for perfection].[49]

Even though one might not want to follow Strousma in setting up the difference between asceticism and encratism as absolute,[50] his suggestion, to specify the dualist habitus of austerity as encratic, is valuable. The "encratic" asceticism of the Cathar perfects centered on rigorous bodily austerity and abstention, and it was irreconcilable with a methodical rationalization of earthly existence, such as the highly rationalized time economy of the monastic or the notion of existence in the world as a "task," held by certain Waldensian groups. The gulf between disavowal of the material world and active shaping and mastery of this world was insuperable. In this other-worldliness of their religious worldview, the Cathars went beyond the medieval monks and nuns and other heterodox groups.[51]

Yet Cathar encratic asceticism entailed neither world flight nor indifference toward the secular sphere. By the late twelfth and early thirteenth centuries, Catharism was well entrenched in society and culture in many areas, particularly northern Italy and southern France. In Languedoc, it took a crusade, a royal war, and almost a century of papal Inquisition to exterminate the once influential counterchurch. In order to assess the actual engagement of Cathar perfects in worldly affairs, it is not enough to infer Cathar secular involvement from its ethics[52] or to attribute an "asocial" character to religious dualism that a priori negates the possibility of such involvement.[53] What seems necessary is an approach that takes account of the interplay of ethics and organizational factors and is more microsociologically oriented. Clearly, the ways in which Cathars engaged in the world were not independent of the resistance or support they and their followers received from secular and ecclesiastical powers. It has been correctly noted that Catharism's major areas of dissemination were those in which political power was fractured and ecclesiastic authorities were either lax in their

---

49. Stroumsa, "Ascèse et gnose," 563. See also some pertinent remarks in Moore, *The Origins of European Dissent*, 219–20, whose characterization of Catholic abstinence as a spiritual end in itself, I think, is misleading, however. The discussion of this issue in Brenon, *Le vrai visage du catharisme*, 89–91, remains vague.

50. Cf. Chadwick, "Enkrateia," who sees encratism as a specific form of asceticism.

51. Cf. Moore, *The Origins of European Dissent*, 220.

52. Borst, *Die Katharer*, does not always refrain from pursuing this strategy.

53. Runciman, *The Medieval Manichee*, 17 (in the context of Manichaeism).

guidance or received little support from the secular branches of government.[54] But Cathar secular activities also hinged on the bonds between perfects and their communities on the local level. The nature and extent of these bonds must not be overlooked as an important factor in the relations between Cathar religion and other social spheres, and also in the tenacity of Catharism in Languedoc and northern Italy.

Since the most immediate link between perfects and other members of these communities was the Cathar believers and supporters, the organizational dimension is also pertinent to a consideration of the extent to which Cathar believers were constrained by the same norms of austerity as the perfects, an issue that historical scholarship has struggled with recurrently. John Hine Mundy represents the view of many historians of Catharism in arguing that "this divergent cult rested rather lightly on the social and moral conscience of its believers," and adds, "How different from Catholicism's police and the austere 'apostolic' morality of the Waldensians!"[55] Licentiousness, indeed, theoretically had no adverse consequences if practiced before the *consolamentum*, since the spiritual baptism atoned for any prior sins.[56] Yet as in Weber's now famous argument regarding the Calvinists, actual behavior is not

54. Moore, *The Origins of European Dissent*, 234–38, 281–82; Lambert, *Medieval Heresy*, 78–85; Fichtenau, *Ketzer und Professoren*, 110, 118. For southern France, this issue is explored more closely in Wakefield, *Heresy, Crusade, and Inquisition in Southern France*, especially chap. 3; Élie Griffe, *Les débuts de l'aventure cathare en Languedoc (1140–1190)* (Paris: Letouzey et Ané, 1969), chap. 1. For northern Italy, see Manselli, *L'eresia del male*, 308–27; Brian S. Pullan, *A History of Early Renaissance Italy: From the Mid–Thirteenth to the Mid–Fifteenth Century* (London: Lane, 1973), chaps. 1–4; John Kenneth Hyde, *Society and Politics in Medieval Italy: The Evolution of the Civil Life, 1000–1350* (New York: Macmillan, 1973), chaps. 4–5.

55. John Hine Mundy, *Men and Women at Toulouse in the Age of the Cathars* (Toronto: Pontifical Institute of Mediaeval Studies, 1990), 3. Similar statements can be found in M. Jean Guiraud, *Cartulaire de Notre-Dame de Prouille* (Paris: Picard, 1907), 1:cxiv; idem, *Histoire de l'Inquisition au Moyen Âge*, 2 vols. (Paris: Picard, 1935–38), 1:174–75; Dossat, "Les cathares d'après les documents de l'Inquisition," 100, 102; Jean Duvernoy, "Les albigeois dans vie sociale et économique de leur temps," *Annales de l'Institut d'études occitanes: Actes du colloque de Toulouse, années 1962–63* (1964): 64–65; Fichtenau, *Ketzer und Professoren*, 307 n. 113; Wakefield, *Heresy, Crusade, and Inquisition in Southern France*, 41; Bernard Hamilton, *The Medieval Inquisition* (New York: Holmes & Meier, 1981), 26, 61. For a correction of this view, see Borst, *Die Katharer*, 179; Loos, *Dualist Heresy in the Middle Ages*, 255–57; Carol Lansing, "Epilogue," in Joseph R. Strayer, *The Albigensian Crusades* (1971; reprint, Ann Arbor: University of Michigan Press, 1992), 211; Moore, *The Origins of European Dissent*, 223–24; Michel Roquebert, *L'épopée cathare: 1198–1212: L'invasion* (Toulouse: Privat, 1970), 108–9; Griffe, *Le Languedoc cathare de 1190 à 1210*, 56.

56. See Koch, *Frauenfrage und Ketzertum im Mittelalter*, 107, 113–21; Duvernoy, *Le catharisme*, 1:259; Borst, *Die Katharer*, 102.

necessarily consistent with the logical consequences of a belief system. Moral discipline that derived from the institutional framing of interaction between leaders and followers, I have argued in the preceding chapter, was of great importance in Waldensian heresy. This result strongly suggests the possibility that in Catharism, too, organizational factors modified the relations between ethics and behavior. The analysis of the organizational and social contexts in which Cathar beliefs were disseminated and practiced, finally, may provide answers to more general but equally pertinent questions: How did a person become affiliated with this heretical group, and how was the affiliation sustained over time? What social processes and mechanisms were involved that forged bonds among heretics strong enough, in some cases, for them to choose death rather than return to the bosom of the church?

In the next section, I address these questions and the related issues raised in the previous paragraphs by discussing, first, the merits of historical scholarship's two major competing accounts of what attracted people to medieval heresies. These accounts have marked the extremes in the spectrum of historical explanations in recent decades.[57] The first is a materialist account elucidated by Marxist historians; the other focuses on ideal factors, as proposed by the eminent historian Herbert Grundmann. I then develop an alternative account centered on the organizational contexts of Catharism. The major case of analysis is Languedocian Catharism as it reached its apogee in the early 1200s. The inquiry is based on an extensive document detailing the statements of witnesses in an Inquisition around Toulouse in 1245–46, and on earlier Inquisition records. The analysis is further developed by comparing these Cathars with other heretical groups. These groups are the Italian Cathars in Bologna toward the end of the thirteenth century and the Cathars in southern France at the beginning of the fourteenth century. Specifically, I hope to demonstrate that (1) affiliation with Catharism in early-thirteenth-century Languedoc was the outcome of a process in which Cathar leaders took people from surrounding communities into their homes or houses at an impressionable age and taught them both the skills of an artisan and the basic tenets of their faith; (2) the Languedocian Cathars in this period, like the Austrian Waldensians around 1250, relied on a dense network of supportive establishments that created a moral milieu conducive to the spread and tenacity of heresy; and (3) the less the interactions between Cathar leaders and followers were structured by permanent congregational

---

57. See the still valuable contribution by Jeffrey Burton Russell, "Interpretations of the Origins of Medieval Heresy," *Mediaeval Studies* 25 (1963): 26–53.

settings, the more transient were the boundaries between heterodoxy and orthodoxy with regard to membership and ideology.

The Social Organization of Thirteenth-Century Catharism in Comparative Perspective

Two Historical Accounts

The Marxist historians Ernst Werner, Martin Erbstösser, and Gottfried Koch have become the leading proponents of a materialist explanation of medieval heresies, and of Catharism in particular.[58] Advancing a classical Marxist argument, they explain the attractiveness of Cathar heresy in terms of the consequences of profound demographic, economic, and social change in western Europe around the twelfth century. A rapid increase in population, migration to the cities, and the commercialization and mone-tarization of the economy, particularly in urban areas, led to considerable flux in the social composition and stratification of medieval communities in town and countryside. At the bottom of the social hierarchy, these changes coincided with the proliferation of an urban underclass of indigent poor and the emergence of a proletarian class of market-dependent small artisans and craftsmen.[59] Since they were powerless to change the economic base of feudal society, the only way for them to express their economic and social grievances was through protest on the superstructural level. Religious heresy became the vehicle of this protest, while the dominant Catholic Church sided with the ruling classes and provided the legitimating ideology for the feudal mode of production. It was these poor and aggrieved classes who, according to the Marxist historians, made up the majority of Cathar support.[60]

Following a long tradition in the historical literature, Koch further identifies textile weavers in particular as having a strong affiliation

---

58. Koch, *Frauenfrage und Ketzertum im Mittelalter*; Martin Erbstösser, *Heretics in the Middle Ages*, trans. Janet Fraser (Leipzig: Edition Leipzig, 1984); Werner and Erbstösser, *Ketzer und Heilige*.

59. See Mollat, *The Poor in the Middle Ages*, 59–69; Mundy, *Europe in the High Middle Ages, 1150–1309*, 98–99, 175.

60. Koch, *Frauenfrage und Ketzertum im Mittelalter*, 13–30; Erbstösser, *Heretics in the Middle Ages*, 62, 92, 94; Werner and Erbstösser, *Ketzer und Heilige*, 334–35. Cf. the classical roots of this argument in Karl Marx and Friedrich Engels, *On Religion* (New York: Schocken, 1964), 83, 98–103, 264–65, 299–300, 317–18. See also Karl Kautsky, *Die Vorläufer des neueren Sozialismus* (Stuttgart: Dietz, 1895), 117–239.

to Catharism.[61] The textile industry developed into one of the most commercialized and protocapitalist industries in the Middle Ages, with weavers and fullers gradually becoming bound to wealthy cloth merchants.[62] Textile workers, Koch and his colleagues argue, consequently chose to become Cathars—"weavers into heretics"—to protest on an ideological plane their material exploitation and suppression.[63]

Other medievalists have been skeptical of the view of Catharism as a vehicle for social and economic grievances. They point out that at any given time and under any kind of economic and social condition, the majority of the population was undoubtedly orthodox. Based on numbers given by Rainerius Sacconi, a one-time Cathar perfect, it has been estimated that the total number of Cathar supporters around the mid-thirteenth century could hardly have exceeded a hundred thousand, and that the Cathar perfects, their virtuoso leaders, numbered below ten thousand.[64] Even if Catharism was one of the largest heresies in medieval Western Christianity, these figures still seem small when compared to the population of France and Italy (where Catharism was strongest), which may have totaled about twenty-five million around 1300.[65] A detailed analysis of Catharism in Béziers, a city known as a hot spot of heresy, revealed that in the early thirteenth century no more than about

61. The notorious association of weavers with Catharism can be traced to an observation made by Eckbert of Schönau (1163–67): "In France they are called weavers for their practice of weaving" (Gallia, *Texerant*, ab usu texendi appellat; in *Patrologiae cursus completus . . . Series Latina . . .* , ed. Migne, vol. 193, col. 13). On this, see further Harrison, "Eckbert of Schönau's 'Sermones Contra Kataros,'" 1:8; Austin P. Evans, "Social Aspects of Medieval Heresy," in *Persecution and Liberty: Essays in Honor of George Lincoln Burr* (New York: Century, 1931), 110; Duvernoy, *Le catharisme*, 1:307–8; Moore, *The Origins of European Dissent*, 174.

62. Jean Gimpel, *The Medieval Machine: The Industrial Revolution in the Middle Ages* (New York: Penguin Books, 1977), 99–105. One of the best-documented cases is that of Toulouse, a center of textile manufacturing in Languedoc and a hotbed of Catharism. Toulouse's earliest *Statutes on Clothmaking* (1227) shows that the artisans were already highly dependent on those providing them with raw materials and trading in the final products. See Mary Ambrose Mulholland, "Statutes on Clothmaking: Toulouse, 1227," in *Essays in Medieval Life and Thought Presented in Honor of Austin Patterson Evans*, ed. John Hine Mundy, Richard W. Emery, and Benjamin N. Nelson (New York: Columbia University Press, 1955), 167–80; John Hine Mundy, *Liberty and Political Power in Toulouse, 1050–1230* (New York: Columbia University Press, 1954), 79.

63. Koch, *Frauenfrage und Ketzertum*, 18–20; Werner and Erbstösser, *Ketzer und Heilige*, 335, 350–51.

64. Borst, *Die Katharer*, 205, 208. For Rainerius Sacconi's numbers, see Wakefield and Evans, *Heresies of the High Middle Ages*, 337.

65. Cipolla, *Before the Industrial Revolution*, 4; Fossier, *Peasant Life in the Medieval West*, 12; J. C. Russell, "Bevölkerung. B. Nord-, Mittel-, West- und Südeuropa," in *Lexikon des Mittelalters*, vol. 2, ed. Robert-Henri Bautier (Munich: Artemis, 1983), col. 14.

10 percent of the city's population was involved in Catharism,[66] and similarly modest figures have been found for other localities in southern France and northern Italy.[67] Certainly, Catharism was ever present in town and countryside in these parts of the Mediterranean world at this time, but its adherents were vastly outnumbered by those who sided with the Catholic Church, even among those who had every reason to be socially and economically discontented due to increasing social differentiation, population pressure, and frequent recurrence of famines, diseases, and other misfortunes.[68]

The strongest support for Catharism in fact did not come from the most aggrieved social strata. Not until the Inquisition had relegated Catharism to remote and mountainous valleys in the Pyrenees and the Piedmont did the majority of Cathar supporters originate in the poor and unlettered peasantry. As did the emergent Waldensian movement, the other major religious heresy at the time, the twelfth-century Cathars attracted men and women from heterogeneous social backgrounds; no class, group, or profession can be singled out. Disillusioned clerics, nobles, patricians, the bourgeois upper and middle strata, artisans, traders, simple craftsmen, the lower social strata—all were represented in early Catharism.[69] When the charisma of the Cathar leadership was routinized and the social structure of the Cathar church turned more hierarchical in the process of its *Verkirchlichung*, Catharism did not gravitate toward proletarian strata. On the contrary, Catharism became a "religion of the middle classes."[70] Even after the Albigensian Crusade it

66. Jean-Louis Biget, "L'extinction du catharisme urbain: Les points chauds de la répression," *Cahiers de Fanjeaux* 20 (1985): 318–19.

67. Jean Duvernoy, "Le catharisme en Languedoc au début du XIVe siècle," *Cahiers de Fanjeaux* 20 (1985): 31, 51; Marie-Humbert Vicaire, "L'action de l'enseignement et de la prédication des mendiants vis-à-vis des cathares," ibid., 281; Marcel Becamel, "Le catharisme dans le diocèse d'Albi," *Cahiers de Fanjeaux* 3 (1968): 237–52; Richard Abels and Ellen Harrison, "The Participation of Women in Languedocian Catharism," *Mediaeval Studies* 41 (1979): 225; Monique Bourin-Derruau, *Villages médiévaux en Bas-Languedoc: Genèse d'une sociabilité (Xe–XIVe siècle)*, 2 vols. (Paris: L'Harmattan, 1987), 2:117–19; Brenon, *Le vrai visage du catharisme*, 183–86; Roquebert, *L'épopée cathare: 1198–1212: L'invasion*, 101–2; Wakefield, *Heresy, Crusade, and Inquisition in Southern France*, 68–71; Manselli, *L'eresia del male*, 303–8.

68. Wilhelm Abel, *Massenarmut und Hungerkrisen im vorindustriellen Europa* (Hamburg: Parey, 1974); Mollat, *The Poor in the Middle Ages*, 59–69.

69. Grundmann, *Religiöse Bewegungen im Mittelalter*, 161–63, 524. See also Borst, *Die Katharer*, 104; idem, "La transmission de l'hérésie au Moyen Âge," in *Hérésies et sociétés dans l'Europe pré-industrielle*, ed. Le Goff, 275; Little, *Religious Poverty*, 144; Thouzellier, *Catharisme et valdéisme en Languedoc*, 425.

70. Borst, *Die Katharer*, 125. For the process of *Verkirchlichung*, see 120–42; also Lambert, *Medieval Heresy*, 125–46.

retained a strong affiliation to the lower nobility in the countryside and to artisans, patricians, and other burghers in the towns of early-thirteenth-century Languedoc.[71] In northern Italy, where the papal Inquisition undermined Cathar strongholds only after the mid-thirteenth century, the Cathars had a similar or even broader appeal and were strongly backed by nobles in the *contado* and by urban patricians, merchants, traders, and artisans in the towns. The unusually extensive records for the Inquisition in Bologna in 1291–1310, probably the best-documented inquiry into Catharism in northern Italy, allow for a more precise analysis. Here, many of the Cathar adherents were artisans and small merchants working on or trading animal skins and leather products. However, these were typically not petty traders or menial workers of salaried status. While acknowledging the socioeconomic reasons for dissatisfaction, the noted Italian scholar Eugenio Dupré Theseider summarized his analysis of the class basis of Bolognese Catharism in a wry comment: "[I]t is the employer who is a heretic, not the workman."[72]

The empirical evidence is therefore squarely at odds with a materialist approach that tries to explain affiliation with Catharism as a religious form of protest against class subordination and exploitation. Modifications of this class-interest model specify other groups' political or material interests seemingly better served by the support of Catharism than orthodoxy. To name two, it has been argued that anticlericalism, in conjunction with conflict over tithes, and the Cathars' indifference to usury account for Catharism's penetration into

71. See Mundy, *The Repression of Catharism at Toulouse*, 54–61; idem, *Liberty and Political Power in Toulouse*, 1050–1230, 78–79; Duvernoy, "Le catharisme en Languedoc," 34–38; Jean-Louis Biget, "Un procès d'Inquisition à Albi en 1300," *Cahiers de Fanjeaux* 6 (1971): 293–304; idem, "L'extinction du catharisme urbain," 319–24; Wakefield, *Heresy, Crusade, and Inquisition in Southern France*, 71–77; Roquebert, *L'épopée cathare: 1198–1212: L'invasion*, 101–3; idem, *L'épopée cathare: Mourir à Montségur* (Toulouse: Privat, 1990), 173.

72. Eugene Dupré Theseider, *Mondo cittadino e movimenti ereticali nel Medio Evo* (Bologna: Pàtron, 1978), 253. For Bologna, see 278–82; Lorenzo Paolini, *L'eresia a Bologna fra XIII e XIV secolo*, vol. 1, *L'eresia catara alla fine del duecento* (Rome: Istituto storico italiano per il Medio Evo, 1975), 157–67. The Bolognese Inquisition records have been edited and published in Lorenzo Paolini and Raniero Orioli, *Acta S. Officii Bononie ab anno 1291 usque ad annum 1310*, 3 vols. (Rome: Istituto storico italiano per il Medio Evo, 1982–84). For an overview of the class basis of Italian Catharism in general, see Dupré Theseider, *Mondo cittadino e movimenti ereticali*, 245–59, 281 n. 49; C. Violante, "Hérésies urbaines et hérésies rurales en Italie du 11e au 13e siècle," in *Hérésies et sociétés dans l'Europe pré-industrielle*, ed. Le Goff, 185–87; Manselli, *L'eresia del male*, 325–27; Moore, *The Origins of European Dissent*, 238–39.

the lower nobility and the merchant class. However, these modifications also appear inadequate or insufficient to explain the historical data.[73]

If not primarily material interests, then what was it that drew people to Catharism? In his groundbreaking work, Herbert Grundmann has proposed a view diametrically opposed to the Marxist one. For him, it was first and foremost the ideals of the *vita apostolica* in its different heterodox articulations, rather than feelings of alienation, that resonated among the populace of Western Christianity. Driven by religious impulse and enthusiasm, people turned to Catharism because Cathar perfects offered them a convincing demonstration of the apostolic life by living in poverty, practicing asceticism, and preaching the Gospels. The Cathars' goals and motives, like those in other heresies at the time, were ethical, not economic: "The confrontation between heresy and church in the Middle Ages [was] a

73. Élie Griffe (*Les débuts de l'aventure cathare en Languedoc (1140–1190)*, 172–208; *Le Languedoc cathare de 1190 à 1210*, 23–26) has argued that support for Catharism in Languedoc was rooted in anticlericalism fostered by an inadequately trained and supervised clergy and that it crystallized in a conflict between church and laity, particularly the lower nobility, over the payment and appropriation of tithes (for a similar argument, see Koch, *Frauenfrage und Ketzertum*, 26–28; Werner and Erbstösser, *Ketzer und Heilige*, 331–33). Yet while the state of the clergy apparently left much to be desired, there is little reason to believe that the southern French clergy was any more incapable or corrupt than the clergy in other regions. See Yves Dossat, "Le clergé méridional à la veille de la Croisade Albigeoise," *Revue historique et littéraire du Languedoc* 1 (1944): 263–78; Guy Devailly, "L'encadrement paroissial: Rigueur et insuffisance," *Cahiers de Fanjeaux* 11 (1976): 387–417. Nor did anticlericalism prevail throughout Languedoc (see Bourin-Derruau, *Villages médiévaux en Bas-Languedoc*, 1:289–300), and for one of Catharism's main centers, Toulouse, there is no evidence of a conflict over tithes (Mundy, *The Repression of Catharism at Toulouse*, 56).

The view that the lack of prohibitions against usury and making money made Catharism more attractive to bankers and merchants has been voiced by Koch (*Frauenfrage und Ketzertum*, 23), Werner and Erbstösser (*Ketzer und Heilige*, 340), and Evans ("Social Aspects of Medieval Heresy," in *Persecution and Liberty*, 113, 116). However, although usury and the ownership of goods were indeed not ethically problematic for Catharism (Georg Schmitz-Valckenberg, *Grundlehren katharischer Sekten des 13. Jahrhunderts* [Munich: Schöningh, 1971], 298–99; Borst, *Die Katharer*, 125–26, 188–89), Mundy finds no indication that usurers were particularly drawn to Catharism in Toulouse. Why, he argues, should a usurer run an additional risk by revealing himself as a heretic (Mundy, *The Repression of Catharism at Toulouse*, 58; idem, *Liberty and Political Power in Toulouse*, 79; see also Andrew Roach, "The Cathar Economy," *Reading Medieval Studies* 12 [1986]: 62)? Koch, and Werner and Erbstösser, also underestimate both the increasing ability of the Catholic Church to find a compromise in these matters and the laity's ingenuity in trying to circumvent ecclesiastical prohibitions. See Mundy, *Europe in the High Middle Ages*, 123–30; Gilchrist, *The Church and Economic Activity in the Middle Ages*.

struggle over the true understanding and realization of, as well as proper adherence to, Christianity."[74]

In this view, the prevalence of Catharism and other heresies in regions of advanced socioeconomic development derives from the fact that commercialized urban settings showed the strongest contrast between new wealth and ecclesiastical ostentation, on the one hand, and the ideal of apostolic poverty and a simple life modeled on early Christian communities, on the other. Hence, people disturbed by this contrast flocked to heterodox ascetic men and women exemplifying this ideal.[75] Regarding the frequent association of Cathars with weaving, Grundmann turns the Marxist explanation on its head: Cathars became weavers, he postulates, and not the other way around. Rather than turn exploitation into dissent, Cathar perfects saw weaving, sometimes practiced by journeymen, as an occupation well suited to the itinerant propagation of their faith, and to concealment if necessary. Cathars thereby became weavers for pragmatic reasons. It was their profession of choice[76]—"heretics into weavers."

The strength of Grundmann's argument rests in his strategy of construing people's ideal interests and convictions as central to the analysis of Catharism instead of treating them as epiphenomenal. Warning against "sociological prejudgments," by which he means socioeconomic reductionism, Grundmann explains a *religious* movement primarily in *religious* terms.[77] This perspective has become the dominant view in the historiography of Catharism.[78] With regard to the association between Catharism and weaving, however, Grundmann's reversal of the Marxist account is not entirely convincing for all periods in Cathar history. That weaving accommodated the demands on a Cathar can hardly be doubted for early Catharism, when the fervor of the preachers and vast areas ready for proselytization called for a profession that was urban-based and frequently itinerant. In late Catharism, becoming a weaver was an equally sensible choice because Cathars had to hide from

74. Grundmann, *Religiöse Bewegungen im Mittelalter*, especially 13–38, 493–97, 503–19; idem, *Ketzergeschichte des Mittelalters*, 3d ed. (Göttingen: Vandenhoeck & Ruprecht, 1970), 26 (the quote is from 2).

75. Grundmann, *Religiöse Bewegungen im Mittelalter*, 197–98, 524; idem, *Ketzergeschichte des Mittelalters*, 27.

76. Grundmann, *Religiöse Bewegungen im Mittelalter*, 29–34, 521–22.

77. Ibid., 503.

78. See, e.g., Dupré Theseider, *Mondo cittadino e movimenti ereticali*, 228, 234, 308; Grado G. Merlo, *Eretici ed eresie medievali* (Bologna: Mulino, 1989), 44–45; Borst, "Die dualistische Häresie im Mittelalter," in *Barbaren, Ketzer und Artisten*, 214; Lambert, *Medieval Heresy*, xiv; Moore, *The Origins of European Dissent*, 264; Thouzellier, *Catharisme et valdéisme en Languedoc*, 425.

inquisitorial persecution. As argued in Chapter 4, parallel developments can be observed in early and late Waldensianism, where similar demands for itineracy were placed upon the Waldensian leaders. For the period between the late twelfth and early thirteenth centuries in Languedoc, and for the mid-thirteenth century in northern Italy, however, the notion of a heretic-turned-weaver is less plausible in light of the fact that Catharism was well established and that Cathars hardly needed to hide. In many places in southern France before the Albigensian Crusade, and in northern Italy for some time longer, Cathar perfects could quite openly seek to make converts, and their believers, supporters, and other interested persons were equally free to hear their sermons and seek their advice. Why should Cathar perfects and supporters become weavers or choose any particular artisanal profession under these circumstances? Furthermore, is it plausible to assume that religious interests alone led Cathar supporters and converts to maintain their affiliation to this heresy over time, without regard to the ways in which Catharism was organized and its members associated with one another?

Addressing the issues raised by these questions, I revise both idealist and materialist views in the following analysis. It is not adequate, *pace* Grundmann and the Marxist historians, to describe the affiliation of certain artisanal professions with Catharism in terms of heretics-into-weavers or weavers-into-heretics accounts. Instead, evidence derived from Inquisition records in Languedoc points to the significance of organizational features for Catharism's success in attracting adherents. Central to the organization of southern French Catharism was a network of Cathar perfects' houses, where perfects took in people from surrounding communities at an impressionable age and taught them both artisanal skills and the basic tenets of their faith. These houses were crucial in securing the adherence of supporters and followers to Catharism; as the "houses of heretics," as they were called in the Inquisition records, disappeared in Languedoc, the boundaries between Catholicism and Catharism collapsed in daily life. This argument, as I show subsequently, also applies to Catharism in northern Italy.

A New Account

The Inquisition at Toulouse Under Bernard de Caux and Jean de Saint-Pierre

In the years 1245–46 the inquisitors Bernard de Caux and Jean de Saint-Pierre conducted a sweeping inquest into the state of faith in the diocese of Toulouse. All males over fourteen years of age and all females over twelve from close to a hundred villages and hamlets around Toulouse were summoned to appear at this city and be questioned about their beliefs and encounters with Cathars. About one-fifth of the registers compiled in the investigation were copied into MS 609 of the Bibliothèque Municipale, Toulouse, containing the depositions of slightly more than 5,600 persons. A major source for the analysis of Catharism in the first half of the thirteenth century, this manuscript reflects one of the most intensive inquisitions in that century.[79]

Most of the testimonies reveal little about the beliefs of Cathar supporters. While physical force was apparently never, or almost never, used, occasional incarceration between testimonies, the intimidating experience of having to answer to an inquisitorial tribunal, and the anticipation of relatively lenient penances in exchange for the acknowledgment of moderate guilt provided enough incentive to evade the inquisitors' questions and confess little about involvement in Catharism.[80] Some of the interrogated admitted to having been believers and even perfects, but they usually said that this had happened decades ago, often when they were still young, and that they had reconverted to orthodox faith a long time ago. The following statement of Guirauda Vitalis is typical: "[The witness said that] she was a Cathar perfect for three years, when she was a girl. And it was thirty years ago and more that she gave up her beliefs and left the sect of the heretics." Many

79. On MS 609 and the Inquisition conducted under Bernard de Caux and Jean de Saint-Pierre, see Dossat, *Les crises de l'Inquisition toulousaine au XIII siècle*, 56–86, 154–57, 226–65; also Kolmer, *Ad Capiendas Vulpes*, 181–89; Wakefield, *Heresy, Crusade, and Inquisition in Southern France*, 173–88; idem, "Heretics and Inquisitors: The Case of Auriac and Cambiac," *Journal of Medieval History* 12 (1986): 225–26; Abels and Harrison, "The Participation of Women in Languedocian Catharism," 220–23; Lambert, *Medieval Heresy*, 135–38. Sentences of this Inquisition are contained in MS lat. 9992 of the Bibliothèque Nationale, Paris, which has been published in Célestin Douais, *Documents pour servir à l'histoire de l'Inquisition dans le Languedoc*, 2 vols. (Paris: Renouard, 1900), 2:1–89, but MS 609, with the exception of fragments and a small part printed in Bruno Dusan, "Confessiones anni 1245–46 ou Les interrogatoires de l'Inquisition dans le Lauraguais en 1245–46," *Revue archéologique du Midi de la France* 2 (1868): 1–12, has remained unpublished. I would like to thank Dr. Michael Stoller of Butler Library, Columbia University, for making available to me a photostatic reproduction of MS 609 and an almost complete and partly annotated transcription, prepared by the late Austin P. Evans and his students. I am also greatly indebted to Professor John Hine Mundy and to Professor Walter L. Wakefield for their constructive comments and helpful suggestions in writing this chapter.

80. Dossat, *Les crises de l'Inquisition toulousaine au XIII siècle*, 211–13; Kolmer, *Ad Capiendas Vulpes*, 209; Wakefield, *Heresy, Crusade, and Inquisition in Southern France*, 179.

statements were stereotypical responses to a questioning technique usually guided by an interrogatory.[81] A few witnesses, however, were more open about their involvement in Catharism. Particularly informative are statements made by those participating in Cathar religious life who supplied details about their former or current convictions, despite the potentially incriminating nature of these statements. Of particular value here are references to the organizational structure of Catharism around Toulouse.

Cathar perfects were a common presence in the villages and hamlets around Toulouse. It has long been known in the historical literature that the Cathar "houses of heretics," the organizational centers of Catharism, formed a dense network in many regions of Languedoc.[82] Around Toulouse, at least six houses reportedly existed in Saint-Martin-la-Lande, ten in Montesquieu, and two in Issel,[83] but more important than the sheer physical presence of the houses was the combination of various kinds of activities that went on inside and around them. These activities—religious, social, and economic—have received little attention in previous studies.

The two outstanding characteristics of these houses or homes were their openness and dual purpose of religious and craft instruction. Open to people from the local communities, the Cathar houses differed markedly from the accommodations for the virtuosos of Catholic religion, the members of the religious orders, even though the physical and communicative barriers between regular clergy and laity were greatly diminished with the advent of the mendicants. Even urban mendicant convents, however, were never as open to the public as the Cathar houses and homes of the perfects, particularly not the convents of nuns, who came to live in strict enclosure. In comparison, the Cathar houses appear to have been tightly woven into the fabric of the local communities. Supporters and other people, perhaps merely curious,

81. MS 609, fol. 253r: "dixit quod ipsa testis fuit heretica induta per tres annos, quando erat parvula. Et sunt xxx. anni et amplius quod dimisit credulitatem et sectam hereticorum." For similar statements, see, e.g., fols. 20v, 22v, 92v, 133v, 143v, 173r, 198r, 252r. On the use of an interrogatory, see Kolmer, *Ad Capiendas Vulpes*, 182–85, and note 37 above.

82. Guiraud, *Cartulaire de Notre-Dame de Prouille*, 1:cvi–cxiii, cclxxiii–cclxxv; idem, *Histoire de l'Inquisition au Moyen Âge*, 1:355; Evans, "Social Aspects of Medieval Heresy," in *Persecution and Liberty*, 111; Borst, *Die Katharer*, 195 n. 26, 248; Duvernoy, "Les albigeois dans vie sociale et économique de leur temps," 68; idem, *Le catharisme*, 1:198–99, 253; Griffe, *Le Languedoc cathare de 1190 à 1210*, 189–90; Roquebert, *L'épopée cathare: Mourir à Montségur*, 112–13.

83. MS 609, fols. 30r (Montesquieu), 103r, 103v (Saint-Martin-la-Lande), 128r (Issel).

would gather quite informally in the perfects' homes and eat with them or listen to their sermons.[84]

The public character of these houses was greatly augmented by the economic transactions taking place in them. Some of the houses were workshops, where artisans employed by Cathar perfects worked for wages.[85] Weavers, however, are hardly mentioned;[86] almost all references are to artisans working with leather under the supervision of Cathar perfects, to whom the Cathar tenets of faith commended the virtues of manual labor. Arnold Picoc described his encounter with Catharism in the following terms: "In Montesquieu he saw Pons of Grazac and Arnold Cabosz, heretics, in the house of the former. And, since they were cobblers, they had there a workshop and worked there publicly. And all men and women of the village went and bought [from them] there publicly . . . And, since he was a cobbler himself, he joined them for the purpose of cobbling and working."[87] Cathar perfects also appear to have dealt in leather products, as traders of animal fur and skins, so that a fair number of people from the surrounding communities regularly came to their houses to sell, buy, or exchange products.[88]

---

84. MS 609, fols. 18r, 30r, 139v, 147r, 155r, 229v. See also Roquebert, *L'épopée cathare: 1198–1212: L'invasion*, 112–14; Brenon, *Les femmes cathares*, 122–36; Griffe, *Le Languedoc cathare de 1190 à 1210*, 55, 133, 162–63. At least with regard to establishments for women, as Abels and Harrison ("The Participation of Women in Languedocian Catharism," 228–31) have convincingly argued, these individual houses, with typically two perfects in residency, should be distinguished from Cathar convents proper, which could be larger and were enclosed. On the enclosure of the female orthodox religious in the later Middle Ages, see Chapter 2, pages 78 n. 41, 90.

85. See the testimony of Willelmus Boneti (MS 609, fol. 183v): "dixit quod vidit hereticos stantes publice apud mirapiscem, cum quibus ipse testis stetit per vices circa tres sentimanas, et suebat sutulares eorum pro mercede."

86. The only reference to weaving I have found is a statement by Arnaldus Gairaudi, who said that Cathar perfects taught him to weave (MS 609, fol. 180r). There is also a brief reference to two female Cathar perfects who were spinning when a witness observed them (fol. 5v). An early reference to Cathar activities in weavers' shops is found in Eckbert of Schönau's "Sermones contra Kataros": "Predicauerunt non in angulis, non in cellariis, aut textrinis" (see Harrison, "Eckbert of Schönau's 'Sermones Contra Kataros,'" vol. 1, p. 26, lines 27–28).

87. MS 609, fol. 103r: "Arnaldus Picoc . . . dixit quod apud Montem Esquivum in domo Poncii de Grazac vidit Poncium de Grazac et Arnaldum Cabosz hereticos. Et, quia erant sabatarii, tenebant ibi operatorium et operabantur ibi publice. Et omnes homines et femine de vila veniebant et emebant ita publice. . . . Et, quia dictus testis erat sabaterius, conducebat se cum dictis hereticis ad suendum et ad operandum." On the commitment of Cathars to manual labor, see Duvernoy, "Les albigeois dans vie sociale et économique de leur temps," 66–67; idem, *Le catharisme*, 1:196–201; Roach, "The Cathar Economy," 60.

88. MS 609, fols. 99r, 103v, 150v, 155v.

Yet the social and economic interaction in the Cathar houses went beyond these dealings. Master artisans who owned independent shops, Cathar leaders recruited people from their communities either as apprentices to be taught in their craft or as journeymen who had gained some skills already. The employment of journeymen (if they were not day laborers) was usually measured in months, whereas apprentices were trained for several years. The word *discipuli*, commonly used for the latter, denoted a bond to the master that could approximate that of a father-child relationship.[89] Even though the term was not used in these Inquisition records, the relations between Cathar perfects and their apprentices and salaried journeymen appear to have been similarly close and long-term. Bernard of Villeneuve reported that he stayed for one year with two Cathar perfects in their house in Laurac. They taught him to cobble, and he saw many people come to the heretics' shop.[90] Another witness testified that he remained for two years in the house of a Cathar furrier, who took him in to teach him his craft.[91] Apparently, Cathar perfects were not content merely to teach craft skills; professional and religious instruction went hand in hand. Arnold d'En Terren reported he "stayed for a year with Peter Columba, heretic, who taught him to cobble. And the aforementioned heretics [Columba and his *socius*] taught him and other apprentices (*scolares*) to adore [a ritual of showing reverence to the perfects], and they [he and the other students] adored them."[92]

Similar statements were made by other witnesses—all of whom, it should be remembered, were actual or potential suspects in an Inquisition and usually had an incentive to underreport their encounters with Catharism and to make them appear more casual and infrequent than they actually were. One witness reported that when he was a boy, he

89. See André Gouron, *La réglementation des métiers en Languedoc au Moyen Âge* (Paris: Minard, 1958), 243–78; Steven A. Epstein, *Wage Labor and Guilds in Medieval Europe* (Chapel Hill: University of North Carolina Press, 1991), 65–68, 103–24; Philippe Wolff and Frédéric Mauro, *Histoire générale du travail*, vol. 2, *L'age de l'artisanat (Ve–XVIIIe siècles)* (Paris: Nouvelle Librairie, 1960), 125.

90. MS 609, fol. 77r: "Bernardus de Villanova . . . dixit quod vidit bernardum de mazerolas et socium suum, hereticos, apud laurag in domibus ipsorum hereticorum et stetit cum dictis hereticis per annum et docebant eum suere et vidit plures homines venientes ad operatorium dictorum hereticorum."

91. MS 609, fol. 150v: "Bernardus de podio cauo testis juratus dixit quod in domo petri Columba heretici pillicerij fuit per biennium conductus ab heretico eodem heretico causa discendi officij de pelliparia."

92. MS 609, fol. 153v: "Arnaldus d'En Terren . . . dixit quod ipse stetit cum Petro Columba, heretico, per annum; qui docebat ipsum testem ad suendum. Et dicti heretici docebant ipsum testem et alios scolares adorare, et adoraverunt eos."

cobbled in a shop of heretics, listened to their sermons, and adored them.[93] Peter Gari revealed that he worked in a shop run by heretics in Fanjeaux, and "he cobbled with them, and earned now and again what he could, and so did many other young men of that town"; during this period they were surely exposed to Cathar proselytization.[94] And Peter Rogerii of Les Cassès told of his brother Pons, who went to Toulouse to learn the craft of a furrier and subsequently became a heretic.[95] The Cathars were audacious enough to seek to make converts of young boys taught letters by the Catholic clergy; one of these, at the age of seven, they lured with the promise to "teach him and turn him into a good clerk" if he joined them. This story, as told by his brother, was confirmed by the boy.[96] If, as in this case, the apprentices were under the legal age, their parents' approval was necessary, and given the salience of the Cathar houses of perfects, the parents surely must have known about the religious aspects of their offspring's training.

The Cathars appear to have used vehicles for the transmission of religious knowledge to novices and interested outsiders similar to those of the Waldensians. The centers of vernacular literacy of northern Italy at the time were peppered with Cathar schools that functioned as centers of scholastic learning and teaching and as repositories of Cathar theological treatises and biblical texts, and there is some evidence that such schools, perhaps smaller in number, also existed in Languedoc.[97] Beyond these institutional settings, Cathar perfects employed religious texts whenever they administered the *consolamentum* (in this case, a copy of the Gospels), but also in missionary activities, as when preaching

93. MS 609, fol. 157r: "P. de Garmassia . . . dixit quod vidit hereticos publice manentes in castro de Fano Jovis. Et tunc, cum esset puer, suebat in operatoriis eorum; et audivit predicationem eorum, et adoravit eos."

94. MS 609, fol. 159v: "Petrus Gari . . . dixit quod vidit apud Fanum Jovis hereticos publice existentes. Et ipse testis operabatur in operatoriis quorumdam hereticorum; et suebat cum eis, et lucrabatur quandoque hoc quod poterat ipse testis, et plures alii juvenes de villa similiter."

95. MS 609, fol. 226v: "Petrus Rogerii dels Cassers . . . dixit quod habuit quendam fratrem qui dicebatur Poncius Rogerii. Et ipse dictus Poncius Rogerii intravit Tholosam ad addiscendum artem pellicerie. Et ibi fecit se hereticum."

96. MS 609, fol. 29r: "heretici predicaverunt dictum P., fratrem ipsius testis, quod se redderet eis, et docerent eum et facerent bonum clericum." For the boy's testimony, see fol. 42r. A splendid description of this incident is given by John Hine Mundy, "Village, Town, and City in the Region of Toulouse," in *Pathways to Medieval Peasants*, ed. Raftis, 156.

97. Lorenzo Paolini, "Italian Catharism and Written Culture," in *Heresy and Literacy*, ed. Biller and Hudson, 96–97; Peter Biller, "The Cathars of Languedoc and Written Materials," in ibid., 74, 80 n. 115.

to a general public, in religious disputations, and in expounding the meanings of sacred texts to their followers and believers. Hence, as far as the *formal* structuring of religious functions goes, there is little to suggest that Cathar textual communities differed fundamentally from Waldensian ones in this period.[98]

Living with and learning from the perfects was not always easy. During a probation period both perfects and novice found out whether the novice could live up to the strenuous demands placed on a Cathar virtuoso. In the hamlets around Toulouse, some young novices apparently failed during the probation period because of age-related immaturity. Dulcia Fabri reported that she stayed with two female perfects in Laurac first for about a year, then for another two years as a probation period, but she did not become a perfect, because, owing to her young age, she could not perform the religious duties of the heretics.[99] Raymunda Jotglar also faced problems becoming a perfect: the heretics "did not want to heredi-cate her until she was well instructed in the morals of the heretics and did three fasts [of forty days] first." For these reasons, the heretics would not even let her lead them to Montségur, the Cathar fortress.[100]

98. Biller, "The Cathars of Languedoc and Written Materials," in *Heresy and Literacy*, ed. Biller and Hudson, is the eminent analysis of Cathar literacy in Languedoc. See also Jean Duvernoy, "Le livre des hérétiques," *Cahiers de Fanjeaux* 31 (1996): 315–31. The use of the Bible is further documented in Christine Thouzellier, "La Bible des cathares languedociens et son usage dans la controverse au début du XIIIe siècle," *Cahiers de Fanjeaux* 3 (1968): 42–57; eadem, "L'emploi de la Bible par les cathares (XIIIe s.)," in *The Bible and Medieval Culture*, ed. W. Lourdaux and D. Verhelst (Leuven: Leuven University Press, 1979), 141–56. In MS 609, illustrative references to the use of Cathar texts, in addition to those mentioned in Biller's comprehensive account, are contained in fols. 114r (two perfects who opened a book, evidently scripture, and set about preaching) and 232v (two scribes, presumably employed to ascertain authenticity, reading from such a book to an audience, and Cathar perfects expounding the meaning of the passages read).

99. MS 609, fol. 184v: "Dulcia . . . fabri . . . dixit quod ipsa testis stetit apud lauracum cum brunissenda et sociis suis, hereticabus, per unum annum vel circa; et ibi pluries adoravit hereticas et audivit predicationes eorum; et stetit in probatione cum dictis h(er)eticabus per duos annos, et non fuit hereticata quia non potuerat facere propter Iuventutem illa que heretici faciunt vel percipiunt observari." On probation and novitiate in Catharism, see Duvernoy, Le catharisme, 1:146; Schmitz-Valckenberg, *Grundlehren katharischer Sekten*, 231; Borst, *Die Katharer*, 179, 194.

100. MS 609, fol. 41r: "Ramunda Jocglar . . . dixit quod . . . dicti heretici noluerunt ipsam testem hereticare donec bene esset instructa secundum mores hereticorum et fecisset primo tres quadragenas. Item, dixit quod, ipsa testis stetisset apud Lauracum in domibus supradictis per mensem vel circa. dicte heretice recesserunt inde et tenuerunt viam suam versus Montem Securum. Et noluerunt ipsam testem secum ducere, quia ipsa testis non erat bene instructa nec bene firma in secta hereticorum; et ideo dimiserunt ipsam testem ibi."

Other Inquisitions in Languedoc

Corroborating evidence of the importance of houses of Cathar heretics and the organizational framework of heresy for shaping patterns of behavior among the perfects and guiding their interaction with believers comes from records of other Inquisitions in Languedoc during the 1240s. These records are part of the Collection Doat, Bibliothèque Nationale, Paris, a large collection of manuscript copies made in the seventeenth century under the orders of the French secretary of finance Jean Baptiste Colbert. The collection includes faithful transcriptions of Inquisition records no longer extant.[101] Of particular relevance are records from Inquisitions of the 1240s contained in volumes 21–24. The contents of these volumes are somewhat heterogeneous, since they contain documents produced at various stages of an Inquisition. Of lesser value are registers containing sentences and penances enjoined. Produced at the concluding stage of an Inquisition, they usually give only a stereotypical and summary account of a person's involvement in heresy.[102] More revealing are documents based on transcriptions of protocols produced during the often repeated interrogation of suspects. Attending scribes and notaries would jot down the testimony during such an interrogation, likely in a simultaneous translation of Occitan into Latin, and at a later period carefully transcribe their protocols into organized ledgers containing statements that the same or other witnesses could subsequently be confronted with. In those instances alterations in the transcribed protocols could be made and new ones added, culminating in a final copy of the transcription onto a parchment register.[103] The most extensive copy of such a register in the Doat is Register FFF, once

101. Lothar Kolmer, "Colbert und die Entstehung der Collection Doat," *Francia* 7 (1979): 463–89.

102. See Collection Doat, vol. 21, fols. 143v–184v (sentences given by William Arnaud and Stephen of Saint-Thibéry, 1235–41); fols. 185r–312v (penances enjoined by Peter Seila, 1241–42); fols. 313r–323v (sentences given by Ferrier and William Raimond, 1244). On the quality of the documents, see Kolmer, *Ad Capiendas Vulpes*, 154–55, 158–59 (Seila); 166–67 (Arnaud).

103. See, e.g., Collection Doat, vol. 24, fol. 255v: "testis iuratus addidit confessioni suae, dicens quod . . ." On procedural aspects of the Inquisition and the methods of compiling evidence, see Dossat, *Les crises de l'Inquisition toulousaine au XIII siècle*, 58; Kolmer, *Ad Capiendas Vulpes*, 203–7; Jacques Paul, "La procédure inquisitoriale à Carcassonne au milieu du XIIIe siècle," *Cahiers de Fanjeaux* 29 (1996): 361–96; Hamilton, *The Medieval Inquisition*, chaps. 4 and 5; Le Roy Ladurie, *Montaillou*, xvii. The role of scribes and notaries present during the inquisition of Bernard de Caux and Jean de Saint-Pierre at Toulouse is minutely analyzed in Walter L. Wakefield, "Inquisitors' Assistants: Witness[es] to Confessions in Manuscript 609," *Heresis* 20 (1993): 57–65.

contained in the archives of the Inquisition at Carcassonne, produced under the inquisitors Ferrier, Guillaume Raymond, Pons Gary, and Pierre Durand in 1243–44.[104] This register, together with other materials from volumes 21–24 of the Collection Doat,[105] is the source of the following analysis. This analysis confirms the argument made in the previous section. In turn, insights gained from the analysis of MS 609 will help in the interpretation of Cathar practices in the Doat material that has remained controversial in the historical literature.

The most significant reference in the material, both in terms of the attention received by historians and its relevance for my argument, is the deposition of Guillaume de Elves. In 1244, Guillaume de Elves, also known as Guillaume Donadieu, of Mazerac (Tarn-et-Garonne), testified to events that had taken place about twenty years before:

> He said that he saw at Najac . . . the heretics [Cathar perfects] Pierre de Caussada and Grimaldus Donadieu, the brother of this witness, and Pierre de Campo in the house that the aforementioned heretics had there publicly, and then the witness ate there from what the heretics gave him. After the meal the witness left and went his own way. . . . He said that afterward he saw the heretics [again] at Cordes, where they came into his home, and resided in public, and had a workshop in the craft of weavers, and that he saw once in the workshop of these heretics Guillaume de Virac, a knight from Cordes, staying with them. . . . He added that in that workshop also were Sicardus de Figueriis, [who was] a heretic [perfect] and was staying with the heretics, and Talafer, of Saint-Marcel, and Pierre de Gironda, of Mazerac, who [Talafer and Pierre] were learning to weave with these heretics.[106]

104. On this register, see Dossat, *Les crises de l'Inquisition toulousaine au XIII siècle*, 44. The activities of the inquisitors are described in ibid., 153–54, and in Kolmer, *Ad Capiendas Vulpes*, 169–79.

105. A valuable overview of the relevant materials contained in the Collection Doat is given in Duvernoy, *Le catharisme*, vol. 2, app. 3. The same scholar has recently published the contents of another register that was once contained in the archives of the Inquisition at Carcassonne and that became part of the *Doat*, register HHH. See Jean Duvernoy, "Registre de Bernard de Caux, Pamiers, 1246–1247," *Bulletin de la Société ariégoise des sciences, lettres et arts (Foix)* 45 (1990): 5–108.

106. "Anno Domini 1244 . . . Guillelmus de Elves, qui proprio nomine dicitur Guillelmus Donadieu, de Maserac . . . dixit se vidisse apud Najacum, in diocesi Ruthenensi, Petrum de Caussada, et Grimaldum Donadeu, fratrem ipsius testis, et Petrum de Campo, hereticos, in domo quam tenebant ibi publice prefati heretici, et tunc ipse testis comedit ibidem de his que ipsi heretici dederunt eidem testi et post comestionem ipse

This statement, often read without the additional information provided in other sources, has caused considerable confusion among historians; once interpreted in light of similar references in MS 609 of the Bibliothèque Municipale, Toulouse, the picture becomes much clearer. The Cathar workshop was not, as the historian of Cordes, Charles Portal, once stated, somehow set up in the home of Guillaume de Elves, or, as Austin Evans thought (in an erroneous reading of Portal), merely a "weaving establishment which happened to be owned by heretics," without craft instruction.[107] Borst, too, misrepresents the conditions in Cordes by writing that the workshops were "owned by artisans supportive of the Cathars, allowing them to work there"—which he readily generalizes to other locations as well.[108] Guillaume de Elves instead alluded to a workshop operated by Cathar perfects and frequented by other Cathars, where some Cathar supporters pursued their vocational education. One might surmise that vocational education was not the only type of instruction that took place there, but that it was also used for dogmatic learning.[109] In these major aspects, the situation depicted here is entirely consistent with evidence derived from MS 609. In a minor aspect, it differs from the majority of references to Cathar workshops there. Here, the perfects are reported to have exercised the craft of weaving instead of cobbling, which is hardly surprising in light of the fact that Cordes was a center of linen weaving. Austorga de Rosenguas mentions her neighbors in Toulouse, two female perfects who spun her wool for recompense.[110] In the house of a Cathar supporter a

---

testis discessit inde et abiit viam suam, de tempore quod sunt 20 anni. Item, dixit se vidisse eosdem hereticos postmodum apud Cordubam ubi intraverunt domicilium suum et steterunt publice e tenuerunt operatorium artii textorie, et vidit semel in operatorio ipsorum hereticorum Guillelmum de Virac, militem de Cordua, stantem cum ipsis hereticis. . . . Adiecit etiam quod tunc erant in ipso operatorio Sicardus de Figueriis, qui erat hereticus et morabatur cum hereticis, et Talafer, de Sancto Marcello, et Petrus de Gironda, de Mazerac, qui addiscebant ibidem ad texendum cum ipsis hereticis" (Collection Doat, vol. 23, fols. 209r–210r). Guillaume Donadieu's statement is printed and annotated in Henri Blaquière and Yves Dossat, "Les cathares au jour le jour: Confessions inédites des cathares quercynois," *Cahiers de Fanjeaux* 3 (1968): 290–98 (for which pages Yves Dossat is responsible).

107. Charles Portal, *Histoire de la ville de Cordes en Albigeois (1222–1799)*, 3d ed. (Toulouse: Privat, 1984), 18; Evans, "Social Aspects of Medieval Heresy," in *Persecution and Liberty*, 111.

108. Borst, *Die Katharer*, 105 n. 26.

109. Charles Schmidt, *Histoire et doctrine de la secte des cathares ou albigeois* (Paris: Cherbuliez, 1849), 1:289. See also Koch, *Frauenfrage und Ketzertum im Mittelalter*, 18 n. 26.

110. Collection Doat, vol. 24, fol. 1v: "Austorga uxor Petri de Rosenguas . . . dixit, quod cum esset apud Tholosam tempore guerrae vidit ibi asalmurs et alaiciam de

certain Berbegueira den Lobenx had two Cathars weave a piece of cloth for her. The same witness also said that on a different occasion she paid her debt to some other Cathar perfects whom she owed for some hides.[111] Presumably activities such as those mentioned in these testimonies led the former Waldensian Durand of Huesca in his polemical *Book Against the Manichees*, written around the same time, to convey his distaste for the Cathars' economic activities and alleged success. As he and his companions had seen and heard in southern France, the Cathars became known for owning "pastures, vineyards, and their own homes, shops, cattle, donkeys, mules, and horses, gold and silver and many other material possessions of this world; they worked day and night and were very big businessmen with the purpose of making worldly money." "By working and doing business liberally," Durand also stated, "as they did while they were in the world as seculars, they [the Cathar perfects] acquire riches."[112]

Several testimonies contained in the Inquisition records of the Collection Doat also confirm the impression from testimonies contained in MS 609 that instruction in heretical beliefs and practices could begin very early in life and be demanding. Bernardus Oth of Niort, a member of a powerful family in Languedoc, testified that his grandmother Blanche and his aunt Mabilia were *perfectae* living openly in their house with other Cathars in Laurac, and that (around 1200) in his childhood he was reared with his grandmother for four or five years.[113] Bernardus

---

cuguro haereticas manentes apud Tholosam, et erant vicinae ipsius testis, et dicta testis faciebat dictis haereticabus lanam suam filare et dedit alteri illarum sex denarios, et alteri unam quarteriam de frumento."

111. Collection Doat, vol. 24, fols. 136v–137r: "vidit dicta testis . . . ipsum bernardum Engilbertum, et socium eius haereticos, et persolvit dicta testis quinque solidos praedictis haereticis quos debebat[ur] sibi de pellibus. . . . Item dixit se vidisse duos textores haereticos in domo den Barra apud Podium laurentium qui texerunt eidem testi unam telam." Other testimonies in the Collection Doat containing references to weaving are presented in Duvernoy, "Les albigeois dans vie sociale et économique de leur temps," 67–68.

112. "vidimus et audivimus in quibusdam partibus Gothie et Aquitanie provinciarum et fere omnibus incolis diocesum in quibus manebant innotuit quod ipsi habebant agros, vineas et domos proprias, ergasteria, boves, asinos, mules et runcinos, aurum et argentum et multas alias possessiones terrenas huius mundi, et diebus ac noctibus laborabant et maximi negociatores erant pro terrena pecunia acquirenda." "[L]ibenter operando et negociando adquirunt divicias sicut faciebant dum erant in seculo seculares" (Christine Thouzellier, *Une somme anti-cathare: Le "Liber contra Manicheos" de Durand de Huesca* [Louvain: Spicilegium sacrum Lovaniense, 1964], 119–21, 109).

113. Collection Doat, vol. 24, fol. 83v: "Bernardus Oth Dominus de Aniorto . . . dixit quod Blancha Mater aymerci de Monte regali avia ipsius testis et mabilia filia eius

did not go on to become a perfect himself; he married and had a son about a decade thereafter. He later remained a militant defender of the Cathars, as did most of his brothers, and barely missed being burned at the stake for this affiliation. One of these brothers, Uzalger, became abbot of a Benedictine monastery, which may show, as Walter Wakefield has aptly noted, that "[i]t was not unusual in Languedoc for a family to produce both avowed heretics and faithful clerics in the same generation."[114]

Such ripples in a family are not evident in the kin group of Arnauda de Lamota, a better-known figure mentioned in the Inquisition records. Arnauda grew up in Montauban (Tarn-et-Garonne) in a household predisposed to heresy. Her likely father, Bernard de Lamota, was a Cathar perfect, and her mother, Austorga, and the wife of her uncle were also favorably disposed toward the Cathars. Early in Arnauda's life, when Bernard de Lamota together with the Cathar deacon of Villemur (Tarn) came to Austorga's house to preach, Austorga handed her daughters, Arnauda and Peirona, over to the heretics. Arnauda and her sister were led to the house of a *perfecta*, Poncia, and her *socia* in Villemur. There they learned the mores of the perfects, including the strenuous ritual of fasting three times a year for forty days each. Both received the *consolamentum* later, a ritual during which they gave the characteristic promise not to eat meat and certain other foods, and to abstain from lying, taking an oath, and intercourse. When asked about their ensuing endeavors, Arnauda replied that she and her sister returned to the house of the Poncia for a year or so, "eating, praying, fasting, blessing bread, performing the *apparellamentum* [the public confession of sins among perfects], adoring the heretics, and doing all the other things that the male and female heretics were used to doing." Arnauda's career to this point was quite typical in that she was ingrained with Cathar religious customs early and followed them devotedly for

---

fuerunt haereticae indutae et tenebant domum suam publice cum aliis haereticis apud Lauracum et ibi ipse testis fuit adductus in pueritia sua, et nutritus cum dicta Blanca haeretica per quattuor annos vel per quinque."

114. On the Niort family, see Walter Wakefield's masterful account in "The Family of Niort in the Albigensian Crusade and Before the Inquisition," *Names* 18 (1970): 97–117, 286–303 (the quote is from 114). Additional information on the Niorts can be found in Kolmer, *Ad Capiendas Vulpes*, 82–107. Given Wakefield's earlier statement, I was a bit surprised that in his generous comment on a previous version of this chapter he referred to maternal influence and intermarriage as greatly significant factors in the appeal of Catharism (written communication, November 1995). My account does not negate, I think, the role of the family in the transmission of heresy, but some evidence points to a far stronger role of the familial factors in later Catharism. See pages 218 and 221.

some time.[115] In this context it should be noted that, even though some *perfectae*, as seen above, practiced a craft, all references in the Inquisition records to the teaching of artisanal skills by Cathar perfects are to men teaching and being taught. None of the records refers to female Cathar novices reporting vocational training or Cathar *perfectae* giving such training. Since women of that period could find employment opportunities in handicraft professions, if in subordinate positions,[116] one might think that, as Abels and Harrison have argued, the Cathars indeed envisioned a more domestic life for their female perfects.[117] Instruction of female Cathar novices centered on religious matters, perhaps exclusively so. Moreover, even before inquisitors had such domestic groups destroyed, misogynist conceptions propagated by some male Cathars may have further limited the range of activities allowed to female perfects.[118]

Taken together, the evidence presented here sheds new light on how people were recruited into Catharism and why this heterodox lay movement became so large and tenacious in Languedoc. It is plausible that in the early years of Languedocian Catharism—that is, in the second half of the twelfth century—Cathar perfects found it opportune to pursue their religious calling in professions that allowed them to be itinerant and contributed to their material support (heretics-into-weavers). For the region around Toulouse, a large number may have chosen to become cobblers and furriers, perhaps also weavers. As the

115. "et ibi in dicto domo steterunt ipsa testis et dicta Peiroa soror ipsius testis tenendo sectam haereticam per unum annum vel circa, comendendo, orando, jeiunando, panem benedicendo de mensae in mensem, apparellando, haereticos adorando et omnia alia faciendo, quae haeretici et haereticae facere consueverunt, de tempore sunt triginta quinque anni et plus" (Collection Doat, vol. 23, fols. 5r–5v). Arnauda de Lamota's testimony comprises fols. 2v–49v (printed and annotated in part in Koch, *Frauenfrage und Ketzertum im Mittelalter*, 186–200); cf. MS 609, fols. 201v–203v. Her life and that of other Cathar supporters and *perfectae* has been analyzed in Brenon, *Les femmes cathares*, 13–19 and passim. See also Griffe, *Le Languedoc cathare de 1190 à 1210*, 68, 86–87; Roquebert, *L'épopée cathare: 1198–1212: L'invasion*, 241–43. On the *apparellamentum*, see Borst, *Die Katharer*, 199–200; Duvernoy, *Le catharisme*, 1:203–8; Rottenwöhrer, *Der Katharismus*, vol. 2, bk. 1, 383–440.

116. Epstein, *Wage Labor and Guilds in Medieval Europe*, 115, 118, 122–23; Mundy, *Men and Women at Toulouse in the Age of the Cathars*, 24–25; David Herlihy, *Opera Muliebria: Women and Work in Medieval Europe* (Philadelphia: Temple University Press, 1990), 91–97.

117. Abels and Harrison, "The Participation of Women in Languedocian Catharism," 230–33.

118. Ibid.; Peter Biller, "The Common Woman in the Western Church in the Thirteenth and Early Fourteenth Centuries," in *Women in the Church*, ed. W. J. Sheils and Diana Wood (Oxford: Blackwell, 1990), 127–57, presents an interesting comparison between Catharism and Waldensianism.

perfects convincingly demonstrated the apostolic life in austerity and preaching, other artisans in the leather and wool industry exposed to their way of life and teachings were drawn to Catharism. Material factors for the disproportionate engagement of early Cathars (weavers-into-heretics) in these and related professions, while probably not those adduced by Marxist historians, should at the same time not be dismissed. Some in these professions may have joined because of a Weberian affinity between lineaments of a practical rationalism in artisanal professions—steady daily labor, the conception of duty and reward—and rational strands in Cathar religion, namely, its consistent and intelligible dualist theodicy, which may have predisposed them toward this heterodox lay religion.[119] But the early thirteenth century differed significantly from the previous period in the organization of the Cathar religion and therefore warrants a different approach than those proposed by Grundmann and the Marxist historians. Previously itinerant Cathar perfects took up stable residence and set up a network of shops through which to spread their faith. As the organization of Catharism, with its increasing social and cultural influence, consolidated in a widespread network of houses of heretics in the late twelfth and early thirteenth centuries, a new method for recruiting future Cathar perfects and followers gained in importance. Young people from surrounding communities, taken in as apprentices by Cathar perfects, went through what could be called, in more modern terms, a dual-apprenticeship program. Initially neither heretics nor weavers, they were instructed in religious matters as future perfects and taught the skills of an artisan. Journeymen, too, were employed and exposed to Cathar religion. This craft education, it appears, was given exclusively to males, since there is no known reference to women being trained by *perfectae* in artisanal professions. Instruction by the perfects, especially in religious matters, appears to have been rigorous, and the double socialization of persons at an impressionable age into both Cathars and leather workers established a twofold bond between the virtuosos of Cathar religion and their apprentices. The Cathars could also establish ties to the families, friends, and peers of the youths and journeymen, and thereby further strengthen their influence in the villages and hamlets in southern France. Living as they did a public life in their houses, the perfects must

---

119. "For people propelled by religious and ethical impulse to ponder the nature of the world, the Catholic teachings about the world were infinitely harder to access and less intelligible that those of the Manichees [i.e., Cathars]" (Grundmann, *Religiöse Bewegungen im Mittelalter*, 26–27). For a similar judgment regarding the absolute dualist strand in Catharism, see Anne Brenon, "Les cathares: Bons chrétiens et hérétiques," *Heresis* 13–14 (1989): 136–40.

themselves have been under close scrutiny and permanent monitoring by their sympathizers, supporters, and other members of the local communities. These organizational characteristics of early-thirteenth-century Catharism, as evidenced in MS 609, made for a moral milieu that was highly conducive to the penetration of Cathar religion into social life and culture, and help explain the tenacity of this lay movement in southern France.

Early-Thirteenth-Century Cathar Organization in Comparative Perspective

In the previous section I argued that the tenacity of Catharism, like that of Waldensianism, can be explained by reference to a network of supportive establishments. The argument would be greatly strengthened if it could be shown that the deterioration or absence of organizational support was closely linked to the decline of other heretical groups and movements. For this purpose, I compare Cathar organization in early-thirteenth-century Languedoc to the organization of other Cathar groups at different times and locations: (1) the Bolognese Cathars later in the century; and (2) late Catharism in southern France in the early fourteenth century. The analysis demonstrates that the less these groups relied on a network of religious establishments to provide daily opportunities for instruction and other forms of religious and social interaction, the less they were able to maintain the adherence of their supporters and to demarcate themselves from the Catholic Church.[120]

Italian Catharism in Bologna at the End of the Thirteenth Century

For the Italian Cathars, a late but informative source is the extensive Inquisition records for Bologna. In northern Italy, one of Europe's most industrialized and urbanized areas and a Cathar stronghold until Catharism was subdued by a series of Inquisitions in the major cities

---

120. I shall not address Catharism in the German Empire. Even though Cathars in Western Christendom were first positively identified in Germany, it does not seem that Germany was a major area of Cathar proselytization. By the time Conrad of Marburg presided over large persecutions of heretics in the 1230s, as Alexander Patschovsky has noted (on the basis of the slim documentary evidence that is available), "the Cathar sect was in the process of disappearing" ("Zur Ketzerverfolgung Konrads von Marburg," 665). For further analysis, see Rottenwöhrer, *Der Katharismus*, vol. 4, bk. 3, 179–220, who arrives at the same conclusion.

after the 1250s, the association between heresy and the textile industry was less pronounced than in Languedoc.[121] The Bolognese records reveal a prevalence, similar to that in the area around Toulouse half a century earlier, of artisans and peddlers involved in the leather industry among Cathar followers and supporters.

These artisans and peddlers were geographically concentrated in a "zone of heresy" around the *capella di san Martino* in the northeastern suburbs of Bologna. Not merely an artifact of selective inquisitorial attention to the area, this nucleus of Bolognese Cathar heresy was located between the older and newer city walls along some canals that provided water for the tanners and dyers. Bologna was similar to other northern Italian cities in that enormous demographic growth and commercialization in the twelfth century brought many people from the surrounding *contado* to the cities. These new dwellers could only find a place outside the city center, demarcated by older walls that were eventually replaced by newer ones encircling the newly populated areas. Northern Italian suburbs soon became noted for heresy; it was also here that the mendicant friars and nuns founded their convents, not only because the inner city areas were crowded and parish priests did not always welcome their potential competitors, but also because the mendicants knew all too well that the battle with the heretics for the souls of the populace was to take place in this very region.[122]

The geographically concentrated zone of heresy in Bologna's periphery contained a network of believers' homes and shops where they practiced their trades. One of the Inquisition's main witnesses, Ognibene di Volta

121. Manselli, *L'eresia del male*, 326. On the Inquisition in Italy, see Mariano D'Alatri, *Eretici e inquisitori in Italia: Studi e documenti*, 2 vols. (Rome: Collegio San Lorenzo da Brindisi, 1986–87), 1:127–38; Peter D. Diehl, "Overcoming Reluctance to Prosecute Heresy in Thirteenth-Century Italy," in *Christendom and Its Discontents: Exclusion, Persecution, and Rebellion, 1000–1500*, ed. Scott L. Waugh and Peter D. Diehl (Cambridge: Cambridge University Press, 1996), 47–66. Carol Lansing, *Power and Purity: Cathar Heresy in Medieval Italy* (New York: Oxford University Press, 1997), appeared too late to be included in the analysis.

122. Lorenzo Paolini, "Domus e zona degli eretici: L'esempio di Bologna nel XIII secolo," *Rivista di storia della Chiesa in Italia* 35 (1981): 371–87; idem, *L'eresia a Bologna fra XIII e XIV secolo*, 1:157–67; Dupré Theseider, *Mondo cittadino e movimenti ereticali nel Medio Evo*, 245–51; Violante, "Hérésies urbaines et hérésies rurales en Italie du 11e au 13e siècle," in *Hérésies et sociétés dans l'Europe pré-industrielle*, ed. Le Goff, 184. On social change in Italian cities and the location of mendicant convents, see Violante, "Hérésies," 172–75; Enrico Guidoni, "Città e ordini mendicanti: Il ruolo dei conventi nella crescita e nella progettazione urbana del XIII e XIV secolo," *Quaderni Medievali* 4 (1977): 69–106; Alexander Murray, "Piety and Impiety in Thirteenth-Century Italy," in *Popular Belief and Practice*, ed. G. J. Cuming and Derek Baker (Cambridge: Blackwell, 1972), 85; Hyde, *Society and Politics in Medieval Italy*, 78–82.

Mantovana, who denounced almost three dozen Cathar perfects and about the same number of believers, reported that one of Bolognese Catharism's leading figures resided in the homes of two brother believers "for the purpose of making leather pouches." However, in Ognibene's memory this had happened about forty or more years earlier, that is, around or before 1250.[123] Cathar support seems to have steadily weakened thereafter, to the point where the spiritual leaders of Catharism were no longer able to dwell in stable residency in this area, where they had once lived and labored together with their followers, and became itinerant. There is also little evidence of ethical instruction among the Cathar believers in the late thirteenth century; the transmission of Catharism became confined to family lineages. Consequently, many aspects of Cathar spirituality became interwoven with Catholic elements. Catharism thereby lost its élan and distinctive character.[124]

Hence, although a dense heretical zone with a network of homes and workshops of leather workers constituted a favorable environment for the establishment of lasting social ties within Catharism and for its delineation from orthodoxy, the casual contacts between believers and their spiritual leaders without the benefit of instructional centers, and the confinement of proselytization mostly to family members, led to the decline of Cathar religious life and to its mingling with orthodox spirituality. The Inquisition of 1291–1310, hastening as it did the organizational breakdown of Bolognese Catharism, appears to have only served as the last nail in its coffin. By the late thirteenth and early fourteenth centuries, Catharism had all but disappeared from urban northern Italy.[125]

The End of French Catharism

In the last comparative case, French Catharism of the late thirteenth and early fourteenth centuries, the social and ideological boundaries between orthodoxy and heterodoxy had broken down almost completely, as evidenced by one of the best sources on religious and social life for the

---

123. "dicit quod bene sunt .XL. anni et ultra quod . . . habuit noticiam cuiusdam Guilielmi de Funi de Bononia . . . pluries fecit ei reverentiam, presente domino Bererio et Guillelmo de Ansandris, in quorum domibus dictus hereticus stabat ad laborandum bursas" (Paolini and Orioli, *Acta S. Officii Bononie ab anno 1291 usque ad annum 1310*, 1:3–4). See further Paolini, *L'eresia a Bologna fra XIII e XIV secolo*, 1:88–95.

124. Paolini, *L'eresia a Bologna fra XIII e XIV secolo*, 95, 160, 168–72; idem, "Domus e zona degli eretici," 38–83; Dupré Theseider, *Mondo cittadino e movimenti ereticali nel Medio Evo*, 282–83.

125. Raoul Manselli, "La fin du catharisme en Italie," *Cahiers de Fanjeaux* 20 (1985): 101–18; Lambert, *Medieval Heresy*, 144–46.

Middle Ages, the Inquisition records of Jacques Fournier. Between 1318 and 1325, Fournier, at the time bishop of the diocese of Pamiers on the French side of the Pyrenees and later Pope Benedict XII, conducted a thorough investigation of heresy in his diocese. Reeling from the blows of the Inquisition and internal disorganization, Catharism had been revitalized in the region by the missionary activities of the brothers Pierre and Guillaume Autier and Pierre's son Jacques. Dedicated itinerant perfects, they had rekindled interest in Catharism in Fournier's diocese, but the brothers were apprehended and burned at the stake in the early 1310s. Jacques, who was captured in 1305 but managed to escape, was reapprehended later and probably perished in a dungeon. Many of the witnesses in the Inquisition recollected their encounters not only with the Autiers, but also with other representatives of Cathar faith and, in the case of witnesses favoring orthodoxy, with those of Catholic religion. This is particularly true for witnesses from the village of Montaillou, whose religious and social life has been subjected to abundant scrutiny.[126]

The picture of Catharism and Catholicism that emerges in these testimonies has puzzled historians ever since the publication of the Fournier register. It is a picture in which orthodox and heterodox elements are often meshed inextricably and combined in imaginative new forms, an "amalgam of residual paganism, half-understood Christian dogmas, and strains of contemporary heretical doctrines."[127] Often, as Le Roy Ladurie noted, the "frontier between believers in Catharism and believers in the orthodox Roman dogma was vague and easily crossed in both directions."[128] But should the poor definition and shifting of the boundaries between heresy and fidelity to the church really be interpreted as "remnant[s] of a pre-Gregorian world," as evidence that

126. The Fournier register, which represents the surviving volume of at least two original volumes of depositions, has been published as Jacques Fournier, *Le registre d'Inquisition de Jacques Fournier, évêque de Pamiers (1318–1325)*, 3 vols., ed. Jean Duvernoy (Toulouse: Privat, 1965), with idem, *Corrections* (Toulouse: Privat, 1972). On Montaillou, see Le Roy Ladurie, *Montaillou*, whose views have been corrected by Leonard E. Boyle, "Montaillou Revisited: Mentalité et Methodology," in *Pathways to Medieval Peasants*, ed. Raftis, 119–40, and Benad, *Domus und Religion in Montaillou*. See also Jacques Paul, "Jacques Fournier inquisiteur," *Cahiers de Fanjeaux* 26 (1991): 39–67. Other published records of Inquisitions in southern France from around that time are, for the county of Foix, 1308–9, Pales-Gobilliard, *L'Inquisiteur Geoffroy d'Ablis et les cathares du comté de Foix (1308–1309)*; for Albi, 1299–1300, Davis, *The Inquisition at Albi*; for Carcassonne, 1301–5, Döllinger, *Beiträge zur Sektengeschichte des Mittelalters*, 2:30–32.

127. Peters, *Heresy and Authority in Medieval Europe*, 251.

128. Le Roy Ladurie, *Montaillou*, 324.

enlightened religious thought and discourse on both sides of the debate had simply passed by the remote villages and hamlets in the diocese of Toulouse, as has been argued by Malcolm Lambert, the author of the best comparative work on medieval heresy?[129]

In light of the comparative evidence provided here, a better explanation of this situation is the missing organizational structure on both orthodox and heterodox sides that prevented Catholic and Cathar believers alike from establishing lasting ties to their religion. A telling case is Montaillou, whose population was guided by Pierre Clergue, the parish priest. There were no mendicants in the area around Montaillou, and the visiting Cathar perfects came infrequently and, while respected, interacted with the villagers only for short periods.[130] Thus Pierre Clergue's spiritual authority was uncontested, and he made particular use of it. Though an ordained priest, Pierre was a Cathar believer who supported the perfects and shared some of their views. This double affiliation did not prevent him from following his own agenda, which was more carnal than spiritual. Beatrix de Ecclesia was a young widow twenty years of age when she went to confession during Lent in 1300. Her confessor, Pierre, however, had other things in mind, as she later told the inquisitors: "[As she was about to confess,] the priest, when she bent her knees in front of him, suddenly embraced her, saying that there was no woman in the world that he loved like her, upon which she, flabbergasted, left the scene."[131]

Pierre, who also told Beatrix that he became a priest because of the income that the position brought him, then successfully persuaded her to be his mistress, even after she married another man. She once more became a widow and remarried, this time to a member of the lower clergy of another parish in a civil marriage, while Pierre went on having affairs with both married and unmarried women from his parish. At the same time, although still supporting the Cathars, he began releasing information about them to the Inquisition at Carcassonne. As the tide turned against Catharism, Pierre Clergue tried to save himself by

129. Lambert, *Medieval Heresy*, 141. Cf. Gabriel de Llobet, "Variété des croyances populaires au comté de Foix au début du XIVe siècle d'après les enquêtes de Jacques Fournier," *Cahiers de Fanjeaux* 11 (1976): 109–26.

130. During their visits the perfects stayed for short periods in the houses of supporters. See Hans Christoph Stoodt, "Der Ketzerhospiz in Arques," in *Unterwegs für die Volkskirche: Festschrift für Dieter Stoodt zum 60. Geburtstag*, ed. Wilhelm Ludwig Federlin and Edmund Weber (Frankfurt: Lang, 1987), 574–89.

131. Fournier, *Le registre d'Inquisition de Jacques Fournier*, 1:224: "rector statim quando flexit genua ante ipsum, osculatus fuit ipsam, dicens quod non erat mulier in mundo quam tantum diligeret sicut ipsam, et ipsa, ut dixit, stupefacta recessit."

exposing ever more Cathar believers to the inquisitors, but in the end he, too, was arrested and died in a prison cell in 1324. By then, the history of Catharism in southern France had about drawn to a close.[132]

Given the religious and ecclesiastical conditions in Montaillou described here, it is not surprising to see just how much elements of Cathar and Catholic faith became intertwined and took on new forms in popular religion. But rather than attribute this situation to a pre-Gregorian mind-set, it is far more plausible to adduce the absence of an organizational network in both Catholicism and Catharism that could have supported adherents and believers in establishing and maintaining their religious affiliations on a more profound level than was often found in Montaillou and other places. Many Catholics and Cathar believers alike may have had sincere religious interests; yet neither the religious activities of a Pierre Clergue nor those of distant Cathar perfects visiting infrequently made for a moral milieu capable of deepening their commitment and establishing clear boundaries between orthodoxy and heterodoxy. Adherence to Catharism or Catholicism at this time was determined more by family affiliation than by religious conviction or informed choice.[133] Among all the cases considered in this chapter, the moral milieu produced by late Catharism in southern France was clearly the least conducive to the spread and tenacity of heresy.

Conclusion

The basic tone of Cathar asceticism was set by its ethics. Cathar ethics rejected involvement in the world and prescribed a moral discipline that was motivated by continuous abstention from it. Cathar asceticism, as a result, was encratic; it entailed a type of other-worldliness unlike the one found in contemporary orthodox monasticism and Waldensianism. While the latter groups were affected considerably by notions of apostolic poverty that treated the world as a task of religious significance, the

132. For meticulous documentation, see Benad, *Domus und Religion in Montaillou*, passim. On the end of Catharism in southern France, see Duvernoy, *Le catharisme*, 1:315–33; idem, "Le catharisme en Languedoc au début du XIVe siècle."

133. On the role of the family in the transmission of Cathar heresy, see Le Roy Ladurie, *Montaillou*, 24–52; Michel Roquebert, "Le catharisme comme tradition dans la 'Familia' languedocienne," *Cahiers de Fanjeaux* 20 (1985): 221–42; also Pales-Gobilliard, *L'Inquisiteur Geoffroy d'Ablis et les cathares du comté de Foix (1308–1309)*, 59. See also Lansing, "Epilogue," in Strayer, *The Albigensian Crusades*, 222–23, who argues against overemphasizing this factor.

opposite was the case in Catharism. The world was the exclusive realm of evil, and the Cathars took a principled stance against involvement in it.

That such Cathar ethics strictly governed conduct among their leading stratum, the perfects, has sometimes been doubted, but the variety of documents analyzed here demonstrate that it was indeed the case. Inquisitors' systematic *summae*, reports by ecclesiastical observers, chronicles, and, perhaps most important, Inquisition records show that Catharism was so attractive in part because the perfects lived distinctive lifestyles and did so convincingly. Even though in the later stages of Catharism the number of deviations from this rule increased markedly, a particularly stern form of religious asceticism remained Catharism's most salient feature. The characterization of Arno Borst, hardly one to be accused of depicting Catharism too positively, remains pertinent: "With very few exceptions the vast majority of the 'perfects' led, up into the fourteenth century, an exemplary life and did not waver from the strict morals of the first Bogomils."[134] Testimonies from Inquisition records also show that strict Cathar morals were not confined to the perfects, but applied to a lesser extent also to the perfects' trainees and close adherents.

Yet references to the stringency of Cathar ethics and its dogmatic coherence alone do not answer the question how the Cathars related their views to their social environment and maintained the support of their following. Focusing on their social organization, the analysis in this chapter, unlike that in existing historical accounts, postulates that differences in the forms of communal life, congregational activities, interaction between leaders and followers, and methods of instruction account for variation in the Cathars' ability to attract followers and maintain their support at various stages of their history. I have attempted not only to show that this was the case, but also to identify the ways Cathars organized themselves vis-à-vis orthodox religious groups, and the social mechanisms their leaders and followers used to establish lasting ties between one another. Institutional factors *in addition to, and in interaction with*, ethical ones were crucial to the rise and decline of a religious group that leveled one of the most significant and successful challenges at the dominant Catholic Church in the Middle Ages. At its center was an organizational network of supportive establishments in which Cathar artisans participated in economic life and educated people both religiously and vocationally. The establishments allowed the Cathar leaders to extend their mission to the larger

134. Borst, *Die Katharer*, 178.

community; this institutional framework was crucial for the transmission of heresy and the strength of Catharism.

An emphasis on organizational factors certainly does not warrant
neglecting religious ethics in the explanation of the rise and decline of
religious dissent. Catharism became as strong as it did because it
offered a coherent ethical worldview as an alternative to orthodoxy, and
its downfall, as Borst has forcefully argued, may indeed have been
precipitated by a decline in morals and dogmatic coherence.[135] Recent
sociological and historical scholarship has similarly emphasized the
distinctiveness and rigor of religious ethics as primary reasons for the
expansion and continued success of conservative religious movements
and churches in the United States' competitive religious economy over
the last two centuries.[136] One might argue that the religious scene in
some parts of Europe in the decades before the onset of the Inquisition
was also characterized by a fairly open market for ethical ideas and
worldviews. As demonstrated by the emergence of the Humiliati,
Cathars, Waldensians, Beguines, and lay orthodox fraternities from the
mid–twelfth to the early thirteenth centuries, different groups and
movements could compete for shares in the religious economy with
relatively few impediments. Nevertheless, this study raises the issue
whether the existence of distinctive and rigorous ethics is sufficient to
explain why and how people are lastingly attracted to certain religious
groups. For the period under study, it appears that institutional factors,
rather than value-related characteristics alone, were crucial to the rise
and decline of heterodoxy. What made Catharism and Waldensianism
strong were not merely "strict" ethics that gave them salience in a
religious marketplace, but also the networks of support and dense
normative milieus emulated in the houses and shops of the Cathar
perfects; in the absence of these, close interaction between perfects and
followers proved impossible, and Catharism declined rapidly. Similarly,
the Waldensians, while always guided by an austere code of conduct,
were strongest when able to establish textual communities in schools
and community houses, in which their heretical views were transmitted

---

135. Ibid., passim.
136. Laurence R. Iannaccone, "Why Strict Churches Are Strong," *American Journal
of Sociology* 99 (1994): 1180–211; R. Laurence Moore, *Selling God: American Religion
in the Marketplace of Culture* (Oxford: Oxford University Press, 1994); Roger Finke and
Rodney Stark, *The Churching of America, 1776–1990: Winners and Losers in Our
Religious Economy* (New Brunswick, N.J.: Rutgers University Press, 1992). For an
application of this perspective to organizations of religious virtuosos, see Roger Finke,
"An Orderly Return to Tradition: Explaining the Recruitment of Members into Catholic
Religious Orders," *Journal for the Scientific Study of Religion* 36 (1997): 218–30.

and from which they could rally against what they perceived as deviations from the true apostolic life prescribed in the Gospels.[137]

The difference between the two religious groups, other than incompatible belief systems, appears to lie in their respective pedagogical focuses. Whereas the Cathars' instruction had a double dimension, religious and vocational, the Waldensian instruction for which there is evidence, even in Austria, involved no vocational training or other forms of interaction in workshops. Even though there were artisans, like weavers, shoemakers, or glovers, among the Waldensian leaders, some of whom likely had their own shops and trained apprentices, heretical socialization of converts and youths in Austrian Waldensianism likely took a different avenue from that taken in Languedocian Catharism around the same time. The former focused perhaps more on religious than vocational instruction, the latter on both.[138] Nevertheless, tenacity of heresy was in both cases as strongly linked to organizational strength as to ethical coherence and strictness.

137. Further implications of my research for rational-choice models of religious growth are discussed in my paper "The 'Kelley Thesis' and Historical Sociology: Organizational Strictness in Groups of Religious Dissenters" (presented at the annual meeting of the Association for the Sociology of Religion, Toronto, 1997).

138. It is of course possible that the Dominican friar who composed the *Passau Anonymous* simply did not pay attention to vocational instruction, but neither did Pseudo-David or Berthold of Regensburg.

CONCLUSION

"[Max Weber was] a demonic, restless person, who was capable of affecting others through the strength of his personality, but to whom it was denied to leave behind a life's work that could last. . . . His time is over, his is a dead science."[1] One of Weber's critics rendered this judgment soon after the death of the *Mythos von Heidelberg*. The decades that have passed since then have shown it to be false; Weber ascended to prominence beyond Germany and beyond the academic confines of sociology. It is perhaps ironic that the man who set out to inquire about the distinctiveness of Western cultural phenomena that had universal and world-historical significance ultimately became one such distinctive phenomenon himself. Without question, Weber became an icon in the twentieth-century intellectual and cultural landscape partly because of the debates and controversies that followed in the wake of his essays in the sociology of religion, whether or not one considers these essays or his writings in "The Economy and the Societal Orders and Powers" (published as *Economy and Society*) as the core of his life's work.

Weber's sociology of religion, rather than gather dust as a dead science, spurred very diverse lines of research. Perhaps the most visible line of research relates to his "Protestant ethic" theme. If and how religion contributed to the emergence of modern capitalism in the West, but not in other areas of the world, is a question that has motivated the work of generations of social scientists, and in all likelihood will continue to do so in the future. In their attempts to find an answer, most social scientists have sought to assess the merits of the "Weber-thesis" by sharply focusing on a short temporal period (often the early modern era) and on one or very few cases (often Calvinist or comparable other religious groups). While these endeavors at times have resulted in admirable scholarship shedding new light on an old topic,[2] it is

---

1. Othmar Spann (1923), quoted in Guenther Roth, "Marianne Weber and Her Circle," in Marianne Weber, *Max Weber*, xv.

2. See, e.g., Gordon Marshall, *In Search of the Spirit of Capitalism: An Essay on Max Weber's Protestant Ethic Thesis* (London: Hutchinson, 1982); Zaret, *The Heavenly Contract*.

important to recognize that such specialized analyses do not exhaust the possibilities for research that opened up with Weber's pioneering studies in religion. His larger theme in those studies, the relations between religion and rationalism, remains less prominent in current scholarship. Only a small number of sociologists have attempted to transcend the "Protestant ethic" theme by looking at the interconnections between religious change and societal rationalizations not limited to the economy. Encompassing longer periods and more cases, these studies have usually concerned themselves with extensions of Weber's existing studies and dealt with modern Christianity (largely Protestantism), Confucianism and Buddhism, Hinduism and Taoism, and ancient Judaism. Still smaller, three-quarters of a century after Weber's death, is the number of studies thematizing the relations between religion and rationalization for those religions and groups not included in Weber's studies: Islam, Judaism after its exilic phase, ancient and medieval Christianity, and modern Catholicism.[3] The Weberian legacy of analyzing the ways in which religions "rationalize life from fundamentally different ultimate points of view and toward very different directions"[4] remains an incomplete project.

This book was written to contribute to the Weberian theme of rationalism with regard to Western medieval religion. Since medieval religion in the West is part of the history of Christianity, the analysis has focused on the type of rationalism that Weber considered one of Christianity's central features: *ascetic* rationalism. Perhaps rooted in his own familial history and the tormenting experience of a debilitating neurological disorder, Weber first studied early modern Protestantism and later the world religions in search of a regime of signification capable of methodically ordering life. His ideal type of ascetic rationalism remained a reflection of the ethically driven autonomous inner person he thought he had found in the Puritan petty merchant and shop proprietor.[5]

---

3. A notable attempt to fill some of the biggest gaps in the literature has been made in a series of books under Wolfgang Schluchter's editorship. See *Max Webers Studie über das antike Judentum* (Frankfurt: Suhrkamp, 1981); *Max Webers Studie über Konfuzianismus und Taoismus; Max Webers Studie über Hinduismus und Buddhismus* (Frankfurt: Suhrkamp, 1984); *Max Webers Sicht des antiken Christentums; Max Webers Sicht des Islams* (Frankfurt: Suhrkamp, 1987); and *Max Webers Sicht des okzidentalen Christentums*.

4. Weber, *The Protestant Ethic*, 78 (translation altered).

5. For an evaluation of Weber's views against the background of the economic propensities of dissenting groups in the late Middle Ages and early modern period, see my "On the Ideological Roots of Capitalism: Puritans, Waldensians, and Cathars as Entrepreneurs and Shop Proprietors" (paper presented at the annual meeting of the Society for the Scientific Study of Religion, Nashville, Tenn., 1996).

The ascetic-rational type of life conduct served as the sometimes explicit, sometimes implicit model in Weber's altogether tentative and fragmented inquiries into the varieties of religiously guided social action and conduct—ascetic or not—in prior Western religious history. Sketched out in Chapter 1, his inquiries into medieval Christianity concerned three distinctive topics: other-worldly asceticism in monasticism, magic as an impediment to rationalization in orthodox lay spirituality, and possible precursors of inner-worldly asceticism in lay heterodoxy. Weber's initial focus was on the medieval monastics, expressed in his well-known argument that the monastics furthered methodical austerity while dedicated to overcoming the world. This argument was clearly a response to views expressed by leading liberal Protestant theologians like Adolf von Harnack. As Weber then moved toward a more general conceptualization of the relations between religion and rationalism, his interest in monasticism did not wane, but he also explored lay religion to a greater extent than before. With regard to the orthodox laity, he used the revision of the *Protestant Ethic* to elaborate on the implications of popular magical practices for the process of disenchantment, and thereby linked this study to his thematically and methodologically more encompassing studies on the economic ethics of the world religions. Medieval religion encrusted with magic in its sacramental practices now ranked among other major religions and eras of spirituality in which preternatural beliefs and practices stood in the way of the rationalization of conduct. Weber may have developed this theme partly to follow up on Troeltsch's theses on the centrality of the sacraments in orthodox religion. He was also influenced by Troeltsch's somewhat perfunctory treatment of the types and directions of asceticism among lay religious movements on the fringes of orthodoxy and in heterodoxy. The theme of rationalism and religion in heterodox ascetic groups would very likely have been one of the cornerstones of Weber's sociology of medieval religion, as part of the projected work *The Christianity of the Occident*.[6]

The analysis of monastic religion, asceticism, and rationalization in Chapter 2 suggests a modification of some of Weber's arguments. These arguments are still the dominant sociological account of this topic, and more recently have been given a new twist in some revisionist writings, notably those by Randall Collins and Lewis Mumford. My analysis shows that other-worldly asceticism in early medieval monasticism, as

6. Future research might shed further light on the contents of this project and Troeltsch's influence on Weber. This refers particularly to forthcoming editions of Weber's letters and scholarly writings as part of the *Max Weber Gesamtausgabe*, and to the edition of Troeltsch's correspondence as part of the *Troeltsch-Studien*.

Weber and Troeltsch argued, did have a strong normative basis in the sixth-century Rule of St. Benedict. Yet it also demonstrates that the other-worldliness and ascetic component of monastic religion greatly diminished over the next centuries. This was reflected in the monastics' involvement in pastoral and liturgical activities, their ties to the nobility, which bound them to ritualized exchange relationships, and a division of monastic labor in which monks and nuns specialized in contemplative activities while *conversi* took over most, if not all, of the manual work. Monastic communities pursued a *via media* between asceticism and contemplation, and between overcoming the world and adapting to it. In the twelfth century the Cistercians rediscovered methodical work and organizational practices in agriculture. In the thirteenth century monasticism further opened itself to the world in the mendicants' abandonment of stability and their turn to individual and corporate austerity and to participation in urban life.

Yet by the late twelfth and early thirteenth centuries the ascetic momentum had already shifted to lay religious groups. For some time, lay religious groups became the spearhead of asceticism in the West, and its direction was inner-worldly. Soon to be emulated in groups of tertiaries affiliated with the mendicants, lay ascetic movements put a halo around the methodical and austere pursuit of simple craft vocations. What had originally been confined to the cells of the monastery had moved beyond the cloistered walls and into the midst of urban centers. One might be tempted to see in this the discovery of inner-worldly asceticism in religious groups in the West, even though these groups were small in number and were concentrated in handicraft artisanal professions. For them, these artisanal professions provided the proving ground of ascetic action.[7] This, I think, provides an alternative to the themes pursued by much of the conventional sociological and historical scholarship, which remains focused on orthodox virtuosos as carriers of ascetic spirituality.

In religious stratification, virtuosos can be contrasted to the masses, the laity, to whom stringent standards of austerity and methodical discipline generally did not apply. Rather, the laity had a variety of

---

7. Note that I refer specifically to inner-worldly *asceticism* practiced by members of *religious* groups. Inner-worldly asceticism engendered by religious views, while methodical, should not be equated with methodical economic acquisition and mastery of markets, since these views may very well direct asceticism to secular spheres other than the economy. Furthermore, this book does not address Sombart's question, whether before the Reformation methodical economic conduct existed that was motivated by a secular rational business ethic, particularly among the urban Italian bourgeoisie in the later Middle Ages. For references to literature that addresses this issue, see Chapter 2, page 88 n. 64.

manipulations of the supernatural at its disposal for both secular and religious ends. The analysis of the historical development of these practices in Chapter 3 not only addressed the theme of magico-religious impediments to rationalism, but also showed why these practices were an important aspect of daily life. From leading ecclesiastics to ordinary parish priests, functionaries of the church co-opted prevalent proto-magical practices while condemning the same or similar rituals when practiced under appeal to alternative authorities. The church also allowed the practice of para-liturgies, which gave individuals and groups some independence from ecclesiastical channels of salvation. The distinction between magic and religion remained fuzzy; in practice the boundaries between manipulation of preternatural powers and worship of the divinity were easily crossed.

There is ample evidence of the continuation of such officially sanctioned practices far into the modern period in Protestant and Catholic territories. This calls into question the viability of Weber's argument that emphasizes the religious roots of disenchantment. For Weber, this intellectual rationalization was started mainly by the Reformation and the religiously rationalized worldviews of ascetic Protestantism. Yet since popular religion in Catholic and even most Protestant areas came to promulgate the continuation of older magico-religious practices, such a view seems problematic. One might, as recent historical scholarship has done, look to secular developments in thought and changes in material conditions, rather than religion, as instigators of a modern worldview.[8]

Furthermore, even though my study of popular lay religious practices in the Middle Ages supports and strengthens the Weberian position of an antithetical relationship between magic and rationalization of action, it also has found important exceptions to lay reliance on magic centuries before the advent of ascetic Protestantism or distinctly modern intellectual traditions of thought. Troeltsch noted the disavowal of magical means of salvation among the Waldensians, Lollards, and Hussites, but such views already existed in earlier religious groups, not all of which were heterodox. Disenchantment informed by religious perspectives can be traced back to the emergence of lay religious movements around the twelfth century. While not all of these groups displayed antisacerdotalism or harbored antiecclesiastical sentiments, they commonly devalued the manipulation of divine powers in their religious practice. Skeptical sentiments about the efficacy of ecclesiastical rituals went hand in hand with the valorization of scriptural knowledge and the emulation of the

---

8. Cf. Thomas, *Religion and the Decline of Magic*, chap. 22; Scribner, "The Reformation, Popular Magic, and the 'Disenchantment of the World.'"

"apostolic life." Their styles of edification favored methodical life, for which they assumed collective responsibility, over magic and ritualism. For these groups the world was no longer an enchanted preserve that ultimately proved inhospitable to rational religious ethics and methodical life conduct. Moreover, as I should stress again, it was the same circles of medieval lay groups who began to affirm religious values of austerity in inner-worldly asceticism and, concomitantly, to value methodical action over magico-religious manipulations of the supernatural for secular and soteriological ends.

Heterodox religious movements stood at the center of this development, as was shown in case studies of Waldensianism and Catharism in Chapters 4 and 5. The histories of both heresies bear witness to profound transformations in these lay movements. These transformations reflected both external and internal developments and were significant enough to require that I treat each group not as one case but as several cases. For both movements the watershed in their history appears to have been the effective implementation of the Inquisition between the 1230s and the 1250s—but it was not the single decisive one. Before that, the Waldensians, originally a reform movement within the Catholic Church, had provided a widely appealing solution to the spiritual predicaments associated with the emerging profit economy and other, sociocultural change. Their solution was to embrace a type of asceticism that had strong other-worldly features, exemplified by a group of charismatic prophets dedicated to preaching and poverty, and modeled on their perception of apostolic life in early Christian communities. In their itinerant religious virtuosity, Waldensian leaders likely retained only a loose affiliation with supporters and sympathizers. The existence of an ingrained organizational framework beyond local textual communities is not evident in the initial period, and whatever strong impulse toward ascetic rationalism these Waldensian leaders may have exuded, it remains difficult to determine how much of this impulse their followers channeled into their mundane lives and occupational activities. The lack of institutional means by which a highly rationalized, ascetic ethic could permeate and lastingly guide patterns of social action among Waldensian followers was in the process of being overcome by the emergence of a formal Waldensian hierarchy that coincided with doctrinal differentiation from the Catholic Church when the Inquisition set in and quickly relegated the Waldensians to an underground movement. Moreover, inquisitorial repression truncated the development of more stable congregational patterns.

The Cathars suffered a similar fate, while the Inquisition also brought about a relative abundance of records detailing their views and manners.

These records show that they, too, cannot be treated as a singular case but require a comparative approach based on multiple cases. A highly rational theodicy, Cathar religion promulgated what I have characterized as "encratic" asceticism. The ethical imperative of world avoidance, or world flight, that followed logically from its theological-philosophical premises was mediated, however, by the fact that Cathar perfects fully participated in the daily life of local communities by running shops for instruction in crafts and their religion. Since neither Waldensian leaders nor, of course, orthodox clerics were known to have managed such or similar establishments, this put the Cathar leaders in the unique position of being able to communicate their message to their local audiences and guide them accordingly. The significance of these institutional mechanisms for transmitting heresy has not yet been fully recognized by historians.

The later histories of Waldensianism and Catharism are fairly similar. Their respective leaders' failure to get their followers to commit to ascetic lifestyles reflected the lack of organizational strength and infrequent (and evanescent) interaction between leaders and supporters. Waldensian and Cathar leaders were forced into a transient existence. The more they were removed from the everyday life of other members, and the less these members could draw on their example, either because the leaders were unavailable or lived in an unconvincing manner, the fuzzier were the boundaries between orthodox and heterodox beliefs and practices. The one heterodox group clearly demarcated from orthodoxy, and hence an exception to the demise of heresy, was the Austrian Waldensians, who had a more egalitarian structure and practiced innerworldly asceticism. Even though, as I have argued, the parallels between Austrian Waldensianism and early modern ascetic Protestantism with regard to their economic outlook and material context should not be overstated, the Austrian Waldensians are an example of a medieval religious movement that espoused ascetic rationalism in secular settings.

The variability in the linkages between ideology, organization, and conduct, particularly evident in Waldensianism over a fairly short span of time, not only has been understated in historical research, but also implies that any research venturing to take on the full scope of Weber's grand project, *The Christianity of the Occident*, will be fraught with difficulties. For if Weber in his studies on the economic ethics of the major religions worked on too high a level of aggregation and hence portrayed these religions as too monolithic,[9] then the same problem

9. This has been pointed out in Schluchter, *Paradoxes of Modernity*, 303–4 n. 1; see also 111. In part, the problem can be attributed to the types of sources Weber used.

would arise even more sharply in a contemporary study that attempted to provide a comprehensive analysis of religion and rationalism in the Middle Ages. Such a study would be in danger of overlooking the possibility of great variation in ideology, organization, and patterns of conduct in the larger and more tenacious groups, especially if it were not based on the analysis of primary sources.

This problem is not limited to studies of the Middle Ages. It is present, I think, in current American comparative historical sociology. Over the last decade or two, sociology has moved away from what Charles Tilly has called "individualizing" or "variation-finding" strategies of research. Instead of attempting to identify the uniqueness of a case or to establish a basic principle of variation among several cases, the majority of historical studies in sociology have pursued a "universalizing" research strategy. Studies governed by this strategy tend to minimize the investigation of peculiarities of each case or the investigation of systematic differences between several cases in favor of finding a general rule or causal regularities in a phenomenon.[10] The universalizing strategy promises to provide a generalized account of historical processes and may establish systematic causal inferences, but its drawbacks are an often exclusive reliance on secondary sources of data and a neglect of interpretative analysis. Though historical sociology that pursues a generalizing strategy may indeed be more prone, as Theda Skocpol has commented, to ask the "why?" than the "what happened?" question,[11] it seems to me that the "what happened?" question has to be answered first. Answers to the latter question should not be left to historians entirely. If, furthermore, the "what happened?" question remains for the most part unanswered, comparative historical sociologists have a strong justification to turn to interpretative research strategies. For sociologists, the hazard in this inquiry, "to disappear forever into the primary evidence about each case,"[12] presently appears very small; on the contrary, some of the best recent work in the field has been done by

He relied largely on translations of central doctrinal texts and writings of European observers.

10. Charles Tilly, *Big Structures, Large Processes, Huge Comparisons* (New York: Sage, 1984), chap. 4. See also Theda Skocpol, "Emerging Agendas and Recurrent Strategies in Historical Sociology," in *Vision and Method in Historical Sociology*, ed. Theda Skocpol (Cambridge: Cambridge University Press, 1984), 356–91. For a view critical of this argument, see Stephen Kalberg, *Max Weber's Comparative-Historical Sociology* (Chicago: University of Chicago Press, 1994), especially 3–15.

11. Theda Skocpol, "Emerging Agendas and Recurrent Strategies," in *Vision and Method*, ed. Skocpol, 375.

12. Ibid., 383.

sociologists intimately familiar with archival work and with records that have not sufficiently been explored by historians. Significantly, these studies are examples of fine comparative historical sociology *because* they have resisted the temptation of generalizing and overextending their argument to cases and events to which it may or may not apply, and have thus avoided exposing their whole exploration to discredit by historians familiar with the details of those other cases.[13] At the same time, they have taken advantage of a set of methodological devices more readily available to sociologists than to historians, namely, a repertoire of conceptual tools.[14]

Many of these considerations are pertinent to future sociological studies on pre-Reformation religion. Given the large number of potential cases that are a reflection of the religious pluralism especially in the High Middle Ages, comparative historical-sociological studies should focus on one group or a small number of groups that bear some relevance to a concern of theoretical or conceptual significance. Future research should, for example, continue to look into ascetic patterns of actions among the Waldensians and other groups embracing similar notions of the apostolic life, although it remains difficult to gauge just how much pertinent information about actual religious and secular practices in ascetic groups such as the Humiliati and the Beguines can be brought into relief in the absence of extensive and detailed inquisitorial records. In any case, comparative historical sociologists may find it rewarding to focus perhaps less exclusively on early modern Protestant groups in looking for the historical beginnings of distinctive features of religious rationalization commonly thought to have had their roots in the Protestant Reformation.

13. See, e.g., the studies on nineteenth-century activism in France by Mark Traugott, *Armies of the Poor: Determinants of Working-Class Participation in the Parisian Insurrection of June 1848* (Princeton: Princeton University Press, 1985), and Roger V. Gould, *Insurgent Identities: Class, Community, and Protest in Paris from 1848 to the Commune* (Chicago: University of Chicago Press, 1995). The danger mentioned here is by no means small; the situation is not helped by some sociologists' strategy to ignore historians' criticism.

14. I have dealt with this issue briefly in "Studying Medieval Culture and Society from a Sociological Perspective," *Comparative and Historical Sociology* 7, no. 4 (1995).

BIBLIOGRAPHY

Abel, Wilhelm. *Massenarmut und Hungerkrisen im vorindustriellen Europa.* Hamburg: Parey, 1974.

Abels, Richard, and Ellen Harrison. "The Participation of Women in Languedocian Catharism." *Mediaeval Studies* 41 (1979): 215–51.

Abu-Lughod, Janet. *Before European Hegemony: The World System, A.D. 1250–1350.* New York: Oxford University Press, 1989.

Adam, Paul. *La vie paroissiale en France au XIVe siècle.* Paris: Sirey, 1964.

Addleshaw, George W. O. *The Beginnings of the Parochial System.* 3d ed. London: Ecclesiological Society, 1982.

———. *The Development of the Parochial System from Charlemagne (768–814) to Urban II (1088–1099).* 2d ed. York: St. Anthony's Press, 1970.

Adelson, Howard L., ed. *Studies in Medieval Renaissance History IX.* Lincoln: University of Nebraska Press, 1972.

Alan of Lille. *The Art of Preaching.* Translated by Gillian R. Evans. Kalamazoo, Mich.: Cistercian Publications, 1981.

Alexander, Jeffrey. *The Classical Attempt at Theoretical Synthesis: Max Weber.* Berkeley and Los Angeles: University of California Press, 1983.

———. *Structure and Meaning: Rethinking Classical Theory.* New York: Columbia University Press, 1989.

Audisio, Gabriel. *Le barbe et l'inquisiteur: Procès du barbe vaudois Pierre Griot par l'inquisiteur Jean de Roma (Apt, 1532).* La Calade: Édisud, 1979.

———. *Les vaudois du Luberon.* Mérindol: Association d'Études Vaudoises et Historiques du Luberon, 1984.

———. *Les "vaudois": Naissance, vie et mort d'une dissidence (XIIme–XVIme siècles).* Turin: Meynier, 1989.

———, ed. *Les vaudois des origines à leur fin (XIIe–XVIe siècles).* Turin: Meynier, 1990.

Backhouse, Halycon, ed. *The Writings of St. Francis of Assisi.* London: Hodder & Stoughton, 1994.

Baeck, E. "De economische invloed van de cisterciënzerorde." *Economische-statistische Berichten* 76 (1991): 740–44.

Baier, Horst, M. Rainer Lepsius, Wolfgang J. Mommsen, Wolfgang Schluchter, and Johannes Winckelmann, eds. *Prospekt der Max Weber Gesam-tausgabe.* Tübingen: Mohr, 1981.

Baker, Derek, ed. *Medieval Women.* Oxford: Blackwell, 1978.

———. *Religious Motivation: Biographical and Sociological Problems for the Church Historian.* Oxford: Blackwell, 1978.

————. *Sanctity and Secularity: The Church and the World*. Oxford: Blackwell, 1973.

Baldwin, John W. *Masters, Princes, and Merchants: The Social Views of Peter the Chanter and His Circle*. 2 vols. Princeton: Princeton University Press, 1970.

Bazzocchi, Dino. *L'eresia catara: Appendice: Disputationes nonnullae adversos haereticos: Codice inedito Malatestiano del secolo XIII*. Bologna, 1920.

Becamel, Marcel. "Le catharisme dans le diocèse d'Albi." *Cahiers de Fanjeaux* 3 (1968): 237–52.

Belhomme, M. "Documents inédits sur l'hérésie des albigeois." *Mémoires de la Société archéologique du Midi de la France* 6 (1852): 101–46.

Bellah, Robert N. "Religious Evolution." *American Sociological Review* 29 (1964): 358–74.

Benad, Matthias. *Domus und Religion in Montaillou: Katholische Kirche und Katharismus im Überlebenskampf der Familie des Pfarrers Petrus Clerici am Anfang des 14. Jahrhunderts*. Tübingen: Mohr, 1990.

Benko, Stephen. *Pagan Rome and the Early Christians*. Bloomington: Indiana University Press, 1986.

Bennett, Judith M., Elizabeth A. Clark, Jean F. O'Barr, B. Anne Vilen, and Sarah Westphal-Wihl, eds. *Sisters and Workers in the Middle Ages*. Chicago: University of Chicago Press, 1989.

Benson, Robert L., and Giles Constable, eds. *Renaissance and Renewal in the Twelfth Century*. Cambridge: Harvard University Press, 1982.

Berger, Stephen D. "The Sects and the Breakthrough into the Modern World: On the Centrality of the Sects in Weber's Protestant Ethic Thesis." *Sociological Quarterly* 12 (1971): 486–99.

Berman, Constance Hoffman. *Medieval Agriculture, the Southern French Countryside, and the Early Cistercians*. Washington, D.C.: American Philosophical Society, 1986.

Berman, Harold J. *Law and Revolution: The Formation of the Western Legal Tradition*. Cambridge: Harvard University Press, 1983.

Biget, Jean-Louis. "L'extinction du catharisme urbain: Les points chauds de la répression." *Cahiers de Fanjeaux* 20 (1985): 305–40.

————. "Un procès d'Inquisition à Albi en 1300." *Cahiers de Fanjeaux* 6 (1971): 273–341.

Biller, Peter. "Les vaudois dans les territoires de langue allemande vers la fin du XIVe siècle." *Heresis* 13/14 (1989): 199–228.

————. "The Topos and Reality of the Heretic as Illiteratus." Forthcoming.

Biller, Peter, and Anne Hudson, eds. *Heresy and Literacy, 1000–1530*. Cambridge: Cambridge University Press, 1994.

Blaquière, Henri, and Yves Dossat. "Les cathares au jour le jour: Confessions inédites des cathares quercynois." *Cahiers de Fanjeaux* 3 (1968): 259–98.

Blaut, James M. *The Colonizer's Model of the World: Geographical Diffusionism and Eurocentric History*. New York: Guilford Press, 1993.

Bloch, Marc. *Feudal Society*. Vol. 1. Translated by L. A. Manyon. Chicago: Chicago University Press, 1961.

———. *Land and Work in Mediaeval Europe: Selected Papers by Marc Bloch.* Translated by J. E. Anderson. New York: Harper & Row, 1969.

Blöcker, Monica. "Wetterzauber: Zu einem Glaubenskomplex des frühen Mittelalters." *Francia* 9 (1981):117–31.

Boehmer, Heinrich. "Waldenser." In *Realencyklopädie für protestantische Theologie und Kirche,* 3d ed., edited by Albert Hauck, 20:799–840. Leipzig: J. C. Hinrichs'sche Buchhandlung, 1908.

Bonaventure, Saint. *Doctoris seraphici S. Bonaventurae . . . Opera Omnia.* Vol. 8. Ad Claras Aquas (Quaracchi): Ex Typographia Collegii S. Bonaventurae, 1888.

———. *The Works of Banaventure.* Vol. 4, *The Defense of the Mendicants.* Translated by José de Vinck. Paterson, N.J.: St. Anthony Guild Press, 1966.

Borst, Arno. *Barbaren, Ketzer und Artisten: Welten des Mittelalters.* Munich: Piper, 1990.

———. *Die Katharer.* Stuttgart: Hiersemann, 1953.

Bossy, John. *Christianity in the West, 1400–1700.* Oxford: Oxford University Press, 1985.

———. "The Counter-Reformation and the People of Catholic Europe." *Past and Present* 47 (1970): 51–70.

Bouchard, Constance Brittain. *Holy Entrepreneurs: Cistercians, Knights, and Economic Exchange in Twelfth-Century Burgundy.* Ithaca: Cornell University Press, 1991.

———. *Sword, Miter, and Cloister: Nobility and the Church in Burgundy, 980–1198.* Ithaca: Cornell University Press, 1987.

Bourdieu, Pierre. "Genesis and Structure of the Religious Field." *Comparative Social Research* 13 (1991): 1–44.

Bourin-Derruau, Monique. *Villages médiévaux en Bas-Languedoc: Genèse d'une sociabilité (Xe–XIVe siècle).* 2 vols. Paris: L'Harmattan, 1987.

Boyle, Leonard E. *Pastoral Care, Clerical Education, and Canon Law, 1200–1400.* London: Variorum Reprints, 1981.

Breinbauer, Josef. *Otto von Lonsdorf: Bischof von Passau, 1254–1265.* Cologne: Böhlau, 1992.

Brenon, Anne. "Les cathares: Bons chrétiens et hérétiques." *Heresis* 13/14 (1989): 115–55.

———. *Les femmes cathares.* Paris: Perrin, 1992.

———. *Le vrai visage du catharisme.* Rev. ed. Portet-sur-Garonne: Éditions Loubatières, 1990.

———. "L'hérésies de l'an mil: Nouvelles perspectives sur les origines du catharisme." *Heresis* 24 (1995): 21–36.

Brentano, Lujo. *Die Anfänge des modernen Kapitalismus.* Munich: Verlag der Akademie der Wissenschaften, 1916.

Brooke, Rosalind B. *The Coming of the Friars.* London: Allen & Unwin, 1975.

———. *Early Franciscan Government: Elias to Bonaventure.* Cambridge: Cambridge University Press, 1959.

Browe, Peter. "Die Eucharistie als Zaubermittel im Mittelalter." *Archiv für Kulturgeschichte* 20 (1930): 134–54.

Brown, Peter. *The Body and Society: Men, Women, and Sexual Renunciation in Early Christianity.* New York: Columbia University Press, 1988.

———. *The Cult of the Saints: Its Rise and Function in Latin Christianity.* Chicago: University of Chicago Press, 1982.

———. *Religion and Society in the Age of Saint Augustine.* London: Faber & Faber, 1972.

———. *Society and the Holy in Late Antiquity.* Berkeley and Los Angeles: University of California Press, 1982.

Brunel-Lobrichon, Geneviève. "Diffusion et spiritualité des premières clarisses méridionales." *Cahiers de Fanjeaux* 23 (1988): 261–80.

Burger, Thomas. *Max Weber's Theory of Concept Formation: History, Laws, and Ideal Types.* 2d, enlarged ed. Durham, N.C.: Duke University Press, 1987.

Bynum, Caroline Walker. *Fragmentation and Redemption: Essays on Gender and the Human Body in Medieval Religion.* New York: Zone Books, 1991.

———. *Holy Feast and Holy Fast: The Significance of Food to Medieval Women.* Berkeley and Los Angeles: University of California Press, 1987.

———. *Jesus as Mother: Studies in the Spirituality of the High Middle Ages.* Berkeley and Los Angeles: University of California Press, 1982.

Cahen, C. "Arbeit: D. Islamische Welt." In *Lexikon des Mittelalters,* vol. 1, edited by Robert-Henri Bautier, cols. 878–83. Munich: Artemis, 1980.

Cameron, Euan. *The Reformation of the Heretics: The Waldenses of the Alps, 1480–1580.* Oxford: Clarendon Press, 1984.

Centro di studi sulla spiritualita medievale, ed. *Spiritualità cluniacense.* Todi: Presso l'Accademia tudertina, 1960.

Chadwick, H. "Enkrateia." In *Reallexikon für Antike und Christentum,* vol. 5, edited by Theodor Klauser, cols. 343–66. Stuttgart: Hiersemann, 1962.

Chenu, M.-D. *L'éveil de la conscience dans la civilisation médiévale.* Montreal: Institut d'études médiévales, 1969.

———. *Nature, Man, and Society in the Twelfth Century: Essays on the New Theological Perspectives in the Latin West.* Edited and translated by Jerome Taylor and Lester K. Little. Chicago: University of Chicago Press, 1983.

Chirot, Daniel. "The Rise of the West." *American Sociological Review* 50 (1985): 181–95.

Christian, William A., Jr. *Local Religion in Sixteenth-Century Spain.* Princeton: Princeton University Press, 1989.

Cipolla, Carlo M. *Before the Industrial Revolution: European Society and Economy, 1000–1700.* 3d ed. New York: Norton, 1993.

Clanchy, M. T. *From Memory to Written Record: England, 1066–1307.* 2d ed. Oxford: Blackwell, 1993.

Cohen, Charles Lloyd. *God's Caress: The Psychology of Puritan Religious Experience.* New York: Oxford University Press, 1986.

Cohen, Jere. "Rational Capitalism in Renaissance Italy." *American Journal of Sociology* 85 (1980): 1340–55.

Collins, Randall. *Weberian Sociological Theory.* Cambridge: Cambridge University Press, 1986.

Congar, Yves. *Études d'ecclésiologie médiévale*. London: Variorum Reprints, 1983.

Constable, Giles. "Monasteries, Rural Churches, and the *cura animarum* in the Early Middle Ages." *Settimane di studio del Centro italiano di studi sull'alto medioevo* 28 (1982): 349–89.

Creel, Austin B., and Vasudha Narayanan, eds. *Monastic Life in the Christian and Hindu Traditions: A Comparative Study*. Lewiston, N.Y.: Edwin Mellen Press, 1990.

Cuming, G. J., and Derek Baker, eds. *Popular Belief and Practice*. Cambridge: Blackwell, 1972.

D'Alatri, Mariano. *Eretici e inquisitori in Italia: Studi e documenti*. 2 vols. Rome: Collegio San Lorenzo da Brindisi, 1986–87.

———. *L'inquisizione francescana nell'Italia centrale nel secolo XIII*. Rome: Istituto Storico dei Frati Minori Cappuccini, 1954.

Davis, Georgene W. *The Inquisition at Albi, 1299–1300: Text of Register and Analysis*. New York: Columbia University Press, 1948.

D'Avray, D. L. *The Preaching of the Friars: Sermons Diffused from Paris Before 1300*. Oxford: Clarendon Press, 1985.

Deansely, Margaret. *The Lollard Bible and Other Medieval Biblical Versions*. Cambridge: Cambridge University Press, 1920.

Delaruelle, Étienne. "Le travail dans les règles monastiques occidentales du quatrième au neuvième siècle." *Journal de psychologie normale et pathologique* 41 (1948): 51–62.

de Llobet, Gabriel. "Variété des croyances populaires au comté de Foix au début du XIVe siècle d'après les enquêtes de Jacques Fournier." *Cahiers de Fanjeaux* 11 (1976): 109–26.

Delumeau, Jean. *Catholicism Between Luther and Voltaire*. London: Burns & Oates, 1977.

———. *Sin and Fear: The Emergence of a Western Guilt Culture, 13th–18th Centuries*. Translated by Eric Nicholson. New York: St. Martin's Press, 1990.

DeMolen, Richard L., ed. *One Thousand Years: Western Europe in the Middle Ages*. Boston: Houghton Mifflin, 1974.

Denzinger, Heinrich. *Enchiridion Symbolorum Definitionum et Declarationum de Rebus Fidei et Morum*. Edited by K. Rahner. 31st ed. Barcelona: Herder, 1957.

de Roover, Raymond. *Business, Banking, and Economic Thought in Late Medieval and Early Modern Europe: Selected Studies of Raymond de Roover*. Edited by Julius Kirshner. Chicago: University of Chicago Press, 1974.

Deschamps, Jeanne. *Les confréries au Moyen Âge*. Bordeaux: Imprimerie Bière, 1958.

Deutsche Gesellschaft für Soziologie. *Verhandlungen des Ersten Deutschen Soziologentages*. Tübingen: Mohr, 1911.

Devailly, Guy. "L'encadrement paroissial: Rigueur et insuffisance." *Cahiers de Fanjeaux* 11 (1976): 387–417.

de Vic, Claude, and Joseph Vaissete. *Histoire générale de Languedoc*. Vol. 8. Toulouse: Privat, 1879.

Die Zisterzienser: Ordensleben zwischen Ideal und Wirklichkeit. Cologne: Rheinland Verlag, 1980.

Dinzelbacher, Peter, and Dieter R. Bauer, eds. *Religiöse Frauenbewegung und mystische Frömmigkeit im Mittelalter*. Cologne: Böhlau, 1988.

———. *Volksreligion im hohen und späten Mittelalter*. Paderborn: Schöningh, 1990.

Disselkamp, Annette. *L'éthique protestante de Max Weber*. Paris: Presses Universitaires de France, 1994.

Dobiache-Rojdestvensky, Olga. *La vie paroissiale en France au XIIIe siècle d'après les actes épiscopaux*. Paris: Picard, 1911.

Dodds, E. R. *Pagan and Christian in an Age of Anxiety*. Cambridge: Cambridge University Press, 1965.

Doehaerd, Renée. *The Early Middle Ages in the West: Economy and Society*. Translated by W. G. Deakin. Amsterdam: North-Holland, 1978.

Döllinger, Ignaz von. *Beiträge zur Sektengeschichte des Mittelalters*. 2 vols. Munich: Beck, 1890.

Dondaine, Antoine. "La hiérarchie cathare en Italie, I: Le 'De heresi Catharorum in Lombardia.'" *Archivum Fratrum Praedicatorum* 19 (1949): 282–312.

———. "Le manuel de l'inquisiteur (1230–1330)." *Archivum Fratrum Praedicatorum* 17 (1947): 85–194.

Dossat, Yves. "Le clergé méridional à la veille de la Croisade Albigeoise." *Revue historique et littéraire du Languedoc* 1 (1944): 263–78.

———. "Les cathares d'après les documents de l'Inquisition." *Cahiers de Fanjeaux* 3 (1968): 71–104.

———. *Les crises de l'Inquisition toulousaine au XIII siècle (1233–1273)*. Bordeaux: Imprimerie Bière, 1959.

Douais, Célestin. *Documents pour servir à l'histoire de l'Inquisition dans le Languedoc*. 2 vols. Paris: Renouard, 1900.

———. *Les sources de l'histoire de l'Inquisition dans le Midi de la France, aux XIIIe et XIVe siècles*. Paris: Librairie de Victor Palmé, 1881.

Drescher, Hans-Georg. *Ernst Troeltsch: His Life and Work*. Translated by J. Bowden. Minneapolis: Fortress Press, 1993.

Dublanchy, E. "Conseils Évangéliques." In *Dictionnaire de théologie catholique*, vol. 3, edited by A. Vacant and E. Mangenot, cols. 1176–82. Paris: Letonzey et Ané, 1938.

Duby, Georges. *The Chivalrous Society*. Translated by Cynthia Postan. Berkeley and Los Angeles: University of California Press, 1977.

———. *The Early Growth of the European Economy: Warriors and Peasants from the Seventh to the Twelfth Century*. Translated by Howard B. Clarke. Ithaca: Cornell University Press, 1979.

———. *La société aux XIe et XIIe siècles dans la région mâconnaise*. Paris: Colin, 1953.

———. *Rural Economy and Country Life in the Medieval West*. Translated by Cynthia Postan. Columbia: University of South Carolina Press, 1968.

———. *The Three Orders: Feudal Society Imagined.* Translated by Arthur Goldhammer. Chicago: University of Chicago Press, 1980.

Du Cange, Charles. *Glossarium Mediae et Infimae Latinitatis.* . . . 10 vols. Niort: Favre, 1883–87.

Duggan, Lawrence G. "Fear and Confession on the Eve of the Reformation." *Archiv für Reformationsgeschichte* 75 (1984): 153–75.

Dumont, Louis. *Religion, Politics, and History in India.* Paris: Mouton, 1970.

Dupré Theseider, Eugène. "Le catharisme languedocien et l'Italie." *Cahiers de Fanjeaux* 3 (1968): 299–316.

———. *Mondo cittadino e movimenti ereticali nel Medio Evo.* Bologna: Pàtron, 1978.

Durkheim, Émile. *The Elementary Forms of the Religious Life.* [1912]. Translated by K. Fields. New York: Free Press, 1995.

Dusan, Bruno. "Confessiones anni 1245–46 ou Les interrogatoires de l'Inquisition dans le Lauraguais en 1245–46." *Revue archéologique du Midi de la France* 2 (1868): 1–12.

Duvernoy, Jean. "Albigeois et vaudois en Quercy d'après le registre des pénitences de Pierre Sellan." In *Moissac et sa région: Actes du XIXe Congrès d'études régionales tenu à Moissac, les 5 et 6 Mai 1963,* edited by Fédération des Sociétés académiques et savantes, Languedoc-Pyrénées-Gascogne, 110–21. Albi: Ateliers professionels et d'apprentissage de l'Orphelinat Saint-Jean, 1964.

———. *Le catharisme.* 2 vols. Paris: Privat, 1986.

———. "Le catharisme en Languedoc au début du XIVe siècle." *Cahiers de Fanjeaux* 20 (1985): 27–56.

———. "Le livre des hérétiques." *Cahiers de Fanjeaux* 31 (1996): 315–31.

———. "Les albigeois dans vie sociale et économique de leur temps." *Annales de l'Institut d'études occitanes: Actes du colloque de Toulouse, années 1962–63* (1964): 64–72.

———. "Registre de Bernard de Caux, Pamiers, 1246–1247." *Bulletin de la Société ariégoise des sciences, lettres et arts (Foix)* 45 (1990): 5–108.

———. "Une source familière de l'heresiologie médiévale: Le tome II des 'Beiträge' de Döllinger." *Revue de l'histoire des religions* 183 (1973): 161–77.

Dykema, Peter A., and Heiko A. Oberman, eds. *Anticlericalism in Late Medieval and Early Modern Europe.* Leiden: Brill, 1993.

Eisenstein, Elizabeth. *The Printing Press as an Agent of Change.* Cambridge: Cambridge University Press, 1979.

Elm, Kaspar, and Michel Parisse, eds. *Doppelklöster und andere Formen der Symbiose männlicher und weiblicher Religiosen im Mittelalter.* Berlin: Duncker & Humblot, 1992.

Elm, Susanna. *Virgins of God: The Making of Asceticism in Late Antiquity.* Oxford: Oxford University Press, 1994.

Emigh, Rebecca Jean. "Poverty and Polygyny as Political Protest: The Waldensians and Mormons." *Journal of Historical Sociology* 5 (1992): 462–84.

Ennen, Edith. *The Medieval Town.* Translated by Natalie Fryde. Amsterdam: North-Holland, 1979.

Epstein, Steven A. *Wage Labor and Guilds in Medieval Europe*. Chapel Hill: University of North Carolina Press, 1991.

Erbstösser, Martin. *Heretics in the Middle Ages*. Translated by Janet Fraser. Leipzig: Edition Leipzig, 1984.

———. *Sozialreligiöse Strömungen im späten Mittelalter: Geißler, Freigeister und Waldenser im 14. Jahrhundert*. Berlin: Akademie, 1970.

Erler, Mary, and Maryanne Kowaleski, eds. *Women and Power in the Middle Ages*. Athens: University of Georgia Press, 1988.

Esser, Kajetan. "Die Handarbeit in der Frühgeschichte des Minderbrüderordens." *Franziskanische Studien* 40 (1958): 146–66.

———. "Franziskus von Assisi und die Katharer seiner Zeit." *Archivum Franciscanum Historicum* 51 (1958): 225–64.

———. *Origins of the Franciscan Order*. Translated by Aedan Daly and Irina Lynch. Chicago: Franciscan Herald Press, 1970.

Federlin, Wilhelm Ludwig, and Edmund Weber, eds. *Unterwegs für die Volkskirche: Festschrift für Dieter Stoodt zum 60. Geburtstag*. Frankfurt: Lang, 1987.

Fichtenau, Heinrich. *Ketzer und Professoren: Häresie und Vernunftglaube im Hochmittelalter*. Munich: Beck, 1992.

———. *Living in the Tenth Century: Mentalities and Social Orders*. Translated by Patrick J. Geary. Chicago: University of Chicago Press, 1991.

Finke, Roger. "An Orderly Return to Tradition: Explaining the Recruitment of Members into Catholic Religious Orders." *Journal for the Scientific Study of Religion* 36 (1997): 218–30.

Finke, Roger, and Rodney Stark. *The Churching of America, 1776–1990: Winners and Losers in Our Religious Economy*. New Brunswick, N.J.: Rutgers University Press, 1992.

Flint, Valerie I. J. *The Rise of Magic in Early Medieval Europe*. Princeton: Princeton University Press, 1991.

Fossier, Robert. *Peasant Life in the Medieval West*. Translated by Juliet Vale. Oxford: Blackwell, 1988.

Fournier, Jacques. *Corrections*. Toulouse: Privat, 1972.

———. *Le registre d'Inquisition de Jacques Fournier, évêque de Pamiers (1318–1325)*. Edited by Jean Duvernoy. 3 vols. Toulouse: Privat, 1965.

Franz, Adolph. *Die kirchlichen Benediktionen im Mittelalter*. 2 vols. 1909. Reprint, Darmstadt: Wissenschaftliche Buchgesellschaft, 1960.

———. *Die Messe im deutschen Mittelalter*. 1902. Reprint, Darmstadt: Wissenschaftliche Buchgesellschaft, 1960.

Frazer, J. G. *The Golden Bough*. [1890]. New York: Macmillan, 1951.

Freed, John B. *The Friars and German Society in the Thirteenth Century*. Cambridge: Mediaeval Academy of America, 1977.

Friedberg, Emil, ed. *Corpus Iuris Canonici*. [1879]. Reprint, Graz: Akademische Druck- und Verlagsanstalt, 1955.

Fry, Timothy, ed. *R[egula] B[enedicti] 1980: The Rule of St. Benedict*. Collegeville, Minn.: Liturgical Press, 1981.

Geary, Patrick J. *Furta Sacra: Thefts of Relics in the Central Middle Ages*. Rev. ed. Princeton: Princeton University Press, 1990.

————. *Living with the Dead in the Middle Ages*. Ithaca: Cornell University Press, 1994.

Geertz, Hildred. "An Anthropology of Religion and Magic." *Journal of Interdisciplinary History* 6 (1975): 71–89.

Geoghegan, Arthur T. *The Attitude Towards Labor in Early Christianity and Ancient Culture*. Washington, D.C.: Catholic University of America Press, 1945.

Gieryn, Thomas F. "Boundary-Work and the Demarcation of Science from Non-Science." *American Sociological Review* 48 (1983): 781–95.

Gies, Frances, and Joseph Gies. *Cathedral, Forge, and Waterwheel*. New York: HarperCollins, 1994.

Gilchrist, John T. *The Church and Economic Activity in the Middle Ages*. London: Macmillan, 1969.

Gimpel, Jean. *The Medieval Machine: The Industrial Revolution in the Middle Ages*. New York: Penguin Books, 1977.

Goetz, Hans-Werner. *Life in the Middle Ages: From the Seventh to the Thirteenth Centuries*. Translated by Albert Wimmer. Notre Dame, Ind.: University of Notre Dame Press, 1993.

Goldman, Harvey S. *Max Weber and Thomas Mann: Calling and the Shaping of the Self*. Berkeley and Los Angeles: University of California Press, 1988.

————. *Politics, Death, and the Devil: Self and Power in Max Weber and Thomas Mann*. Berkeley and Los Angeles: University of California Press, 1992.

Gonnet, Giovanni. *Enchiridion Fontium Valdensium*. Vol. 1. Torre Pellice: Claudiana, 1958.

————. "The Influence of the Sermon on the Mount upon the Ethics of the Waldensians of the Middle Ages." *Brethren Life and Thought* 35 (1990): 34–40.

————. "La femme dans les mouvements paupéro–évangéliques du Bas Moyen Âge (notamment chez les Vaudois)." *Heresis* 22 (1994): 27–41.

————. "Natures et limites de l'episcopat vaudois au Moyen Âge." *Communio Viatorum* 2 (1959): 311–23.

Gonnet, Jean, and Amedeo Molnár. *Les Vaudois au Moyen Âge*. Turin: Claudiana, 1974.

Goody, Jack. *The Logic of Writing and the Organization of Society*. Cambridge: Cambridge University Press, 1986.

————, ed. *Literacy in Traditional Societies*. Cambridge: Cambridge University Press, 1968.

Gould, Roger V. *Insurgent Identities: Class, Community, and Protest in Paris from 1848 to the Commune*. Chicago: University of Chicago Press, 1995.

Gouron, André. *La réglementation des métiers en Languedoc au Moyen Âge*. Paris: Minard, 1958.

Graf, Friedrich Wilhelm. "Max Weber und die protestantische Theologie seiner Zeit." *Zeitschrift für Religions- und Geistesgeschichte* 39 (1987): 122–47.

Graf, Friedrich Wilhelm, and Trutz Rendtorff, eds. *Troeltsch-Studien*. Vol. 6, *Ernst Troeltschs Soziallehren: Studien zu ihrer Interpretation*. Gütersloh: Mohn, 1993.

Graff, Harvey J. *The Legacies of Literacy*. Bloomington: Indiana University Press, 1991.

Grassby, Richard. *The Business Community of Seventeenth-Century England*. Cambridge: Cambridge University Press, 1995.

Graus, František. *Volk, Herrscher und Heiliger im Reich der Merowinger*. Prague: Nakladatelsví Československé akademie věd, 1965.

Greaves, Richard L. *Society and Religion in Elizabethan England*. Minneapolis: University of Minnesota Press, 1981.

Gregory of Tours. *Life of the Fathers*. Translated by Edward James. Liverpool: Liverpool University Press, 1986.

Green, D. H. "Orality and Reading: The State of Research in Medieval Studies." *Speculum* 65 (1990): 267–80.

Griffe, Élie. *Le Languedoc cathare de 1190 à 1210*. Paris: Letouzey et Ané, 1971.

———. *Les débuts de l'aventure cathare en Languedoc (1140–1190)*. Paris: Letouzey et Ané, 1969.

Grundmann, Herbert. *Ausgewählte Aufsätze*. Vol. 1, *Religiöse Bewegungen*. Stuttgart: Hiersemann, 1976.

———. *Ketzergeschichte des Mittelalters*. 3d ed. Göttingen: Vandenhoeck & Ruprecht, 1970.

———. *Religiöse Bewegungen im Mittelalter*. 2d ed. Hildesheim: Olms, 1961.

Guidoni, Enrico. "Città e ordini mendicanti: Il ruolo dei conventi nella crescita e nella progettazione urbana del XIII e XIV secolo." *Quaderni Medievali* 4 (1977): 69–106.

Guillaume de Puylaurens. *Chronique (Chronica magistri Guillelmi de Podio Laurentii)*. Edited by Jean Duvernoy. Paris: Éditions du Centre national de la recherche scientifique, 1976.

Guillaumont, Antoine. *Aux origines du monachisme chrétien*. Begrolles en Mauges: Abbaye de Bellefontaine, 1979.

Guiraud, M. Jean. *Cartulaire de Notre-Dame de Prouille*. Vol. 1. Paris: Picard, 1907.

———. *Histoire de l'Inquisition au Moyen Âge*. 2 vols. Paris: Picard, 1935–38.

Gurevich, Aron. *Medieval Popular Culture: Problems of Belief and Perception*. Translated by János A. Bak and Paul A. Hollingsworth. New York: Cambridge University Press, 1990.

Hahn, Alois. "Zur Soziologie der Beichte und anderer Formen institutionalisierter Bekenntnisse: Selbstthematisierung und Zivilisationsprozess." *Kölner Zeitschrift für Soziologie und Sozialpsychologie* 34 (1982): 408–34.

Haider, Siegfried. *Geschichte Oberösterreichs*. Munich: Oldenbourg, 1987.

Hall, John A. *Powers and Liberties: The Causes and Consequences of the Rise of the West*. Berkeley and Los Angeles: University of California Press, 1986.

Hallinger, Kassius. "Woher kommen die Laienbrüder?" *Analecta Sacri Ordinis Cisterciensis* 12 (1956): 1–104.

Hamesse, Jacqueline, and Colette Muraille-Samaran, eds. *Le travail au Moyen Âge*. Louvain: Institut d'Études Médiévales de l'Université Catholique de Louvain, 1990.

Hamilton, Bernard. "The Cathar Council of S. Félix Reconsidered." *Archivum Fratrum Praedicatorum* 48 (1978): 23–53.

———. *The Medieval Inquisition*. New York: Holmes & Meier, 1981.

———. *Religion in the Medieval West*. London: Arnold, 1986.

Hammerstein, Notker, ed. *Deutsche Geschichtswissenschaft um 1900*. Stuttgart: Steiner, 1988.

Hanyu, Tatsuro. "Max Webers Quellenbehandlung in der *Protestantischen Ethik*: Der Begriff 'Calling.'" *Zeitschrift für Soziologie* 22 (1993): 65–75.

———. "Max Webers Quellenbehandlung in der *Protestantischen Ethik*: Der 'Berufs'-Begriff." *European Journal of Sociology* 35 (1994): 72–103.

Harnack, Adolf von. *Das Mönchtum: Seine Ideale und seine Geschichte*. 4th ed. Giessen: Ricker'sche Buchhandlung, 1895.

———. *Lehrbuch der Dogmengeschichte*. 3 vols. 3d ed. Tübingen: Mohr, 1894–97.

Harrison, Robert Joyce. "Eckbert of Schönau's 'Sermones contra Kataros.'" Ph.D. diss., Ohio State University, 1990.

Hay, Denys. *The Church in Italy in the Fifteenth Century*. Cambridge: Cambridge University Press, 1977.

Heath, Peter. *The English Parish Clergy on the Eve of the Reformation*. London: Routledge & Kegan Paul, 1969.

Hennis, Wilhelm. "Die 'Protestantische Ethik': Ein 'Überdeterminierter' Text?" *Sociologia Internationalis* 33 (1995): 1–17.

———. *Max Weber: Essays in Reconstruction*. Translated by K. Tribe. London: Allen & Unwin, 1988.

———. *Max Webers Wissenschaft vom Menschen: Neue Studien zur Biographie des Werks*. Tübingen: Mohr, 1996.

Henrich, Dieter. *Die Einheit der Wissenschaftslehre Max Webers*. Tübingen: Mohr, 1952.

Herlihy, David. *Medieval Households*. Cambridge: Harvard University Press, 1985.

———. *Opera Muliebria: Women and Work in Medieval Europe*. Philadelphia: Temple University Press, 1990.

Heussi, Karl. *Der Ursprung des Mönchtums*. Tübingen: Mohr, 1936. Reprint, Aalen: Scientia, 1961.

Hill, Christopher. *Society and Puritanism in Pre-Revolutionary England*. 2d ed. New York: Schocken, 1967.

Hinneberg, Paul, ed. *Die Kultur der Gegenwart*. Berlin: Teubner, 1906.

Hinnebusch, William A. *The History of the Dominican Order*. Vol. 1. Staten Island, N.Y.: Alba House, 1966.

Holl, Karl. *Gesammelte Aufsätze zur Kirchengeschichte*. Vol. 3, *Der Westen*. Tübingen: Mohr, 1928.

Holton, R. J. "Max Weber, 'Rational Capitalism,' and Renaissance Italy: A Critique of Cohen." *American Journal of Sociology* 89 (1983): 166–80.

Housley, N. J. "Politics and Heresy in Italy: Anti-Heretical Crusades, Orders, and Confraternities, 1200–1500." *Journal of Ecclesiastical History* 33 (1982): 193–208.

Hunt, Noreen, ed. *Cluniac Monasticism in the Central Middle Ages*. Hamden, Conn.: Archon Books, 1971.

Huygens, R.B.C., ed. *Lettres de Jacques de Vitry*. Leiden: Brill, 1960.

Hyde, John Kenneth. *Society and Politics in Medieval Italy: The Evolution of the Civil Life, 1000–1350*. New York: Macmillan, 1973.

Iannaccone, Laurence R. "Why Strict Churches Are Strong." *American Journal of Sociology* 99 (1994): 1180–211.

Iserloh, Erwin. *Charisma und Institution der Kirche: Dargestellt an Franz von Assissi und der Armutsbewegung seiner Zeit*. Wiesbaden: Steiner, 1977.

Istituto Nazionale d'Archeologia e Storia dell'Arte, ed. *I Cistercensi e il Lazio*. Roma: Multigrafica, 1978.

Jimenez-Sanchez, Pilar. "Des études récentes sur les sources hérétiques et anti-hérétiques en Italie." *Heresis* 24 (1995): 101–5.

Johnson, Penelope D. *Equal in Monastic Profession: Religious Women in Medieval France*. Chicago: University of Chicago Press, 1991.

Jones, Eric L. *The European Miracle: Environments, Economies, and Geopolitics in the History of Europe and Asia*. 2d ed. Cambridge: Cambridge University Press, 1987.

Jordan of Saxony. *On the Beginnings of the Order of the Preachers*. Edited and translated by Simon Tugwell. Chicago: Parable, 1982.

Jungmann, Joseph A. *The Mass of the Roman Rite: Its Origin and Development (Missarum Sollemnia)*. Vol. 1. New York: Benziger, 1951.

Kaelber, Lutz F. "The 'Kelley Thesis' and Historical Sociology: Organizational Strictness in Groups of Religious Dissenters." Paper presented at the annual meeting of the Association for the Sociology of Religion, Toronto, 1997.

———. "On the Ideological Roots of Capitalism: Puritans, Waldensians, and Cathars as Entrepreneurs and Shop Proprietors." Paper presented at the annual meeting of the Society for the Scientific Study of Religion, Nashville, Tenn., 1996.

———. "Other- and Inner-Worldly Asceticism in Medieval Waldensianism: A Weberian Analysis." *Sociology of Religion* 56 (1995): 91–119.

———. "A Sociological Analysis of Ascetic Monasticism and Work in Pre-Modern Europe." Paper presented at the annual meeting of the Society for the Scientific Study of Religion, St. Louis, Mo., 1995.

———. "Studying Medieval Culture and Society from a Sociological Perspective." *Comparative and Historical Sociology* 7, no. 4 (1995).

———. "Weavers into Heretics? The Social Organization of Early-Thirteenth-Century Catharism in Comparative Perspective." *Social Science History* 21 (1997): 111–37.

———. "Weber's Lacuna: Medieval Religion and the Roots of Rationalization." *Journal of the History of Ideas* 57 (1996): 465–85.

Kalberg, Stephen. "The Rationalization of Action in Max Weber's Sociology of Religion." *Sociological Theory* 8 (1990): 58–84.

———. "The Search for Thematic Orientations in a Fragmented Oeuvre: The Discussion of Max Weber in Recent German Sociological Literature." *Sociology* 13 (1979): 127–33.

———. *Max Weber's Comparative-Historical Sociology.* Chicago: University of Chicago Press, 1994.

Kaminsky, Howard. *A History of the Hussite Revolution.* Berkeley and Los Angeles: University of California Press, 1967.

Käsler, Dirk. *Die frühe deutsche Soziologie 1909 bis 1934 und ihre Entstehungsmilieus: Eine wissenschaftssoziologische Untersuchung.* Opladen: Westdeutscher Verlag, 1984.

———. *Max Weber: An Introduction to His Life and Work.* Translated by P. Hurd. Cambridge: Polity Press, 1988.

———. *Revolution und Veralltäglichung.* Munich: Nymphenburger Verlagshandlung, 1977.

Kautsky, Karl. *Die Vorläufer des neueren Sozialismus.* Stuttgart: Dietz, 1895.

Keen, Maurice. *Chivalry.* New Haven: Yale University Press, 1984.

Kendall, R. T. *Calvin and English Calvinism to 1649.* Oxford: Oxford University Press, 1979.

Kermode, Jennifer, ed. *Enterprise and Individuals in Fifteenth-Century England.* Wolfeboro Falls, N.H.: Alan Sutton, 1991.

Kieckhefer, Richard. *Magic in the Middle Ages.* Cambridge: Cambridge University Press, 1989.

———. "The Office of Inquisition and Medieval Heresy: The Transition from Personal to Institutional Jurisdiction." *Journal of Ecclesiastical History* 46 (1995): 36–61.

———. *Repression of Heresy in Medieval Germany.* Philadelphia: University of Pennsylvania Press, 1979.

———. "The Specific Rationality of Medieval Magic." *American Historical Review* 99 (1994): 813–36.

Kieser, Alfred. "From Asceticism to Administration of Wealth: Medieval Monasteries and the Pitfalls of Rationalization." *Organization Studies* 8 (1987): 107–23.

Kippenberg, Hans Gerhard. "Max Weber im Kreise von Religionswissenschaftlern." *Zeitschrift für Religions- und Geistesgeschichte* 45 (1993): 348–66.

Kippenberg, Hans Gerhard, and Brigitte Luchesi, eds. *Religionswissenschaft und Kulturkritik.* Marburg: Diagonal, 1991.

Klaniczay, Gábor. *The Uses of Supernatural Power: The Transformation of Popular Religion in Medieval and Early-Modern Europe.* Translated by Susan Singerman. Oxford: Polity Press, 1990.

Knowles, David. *Christian Monasticism.* New York: McGraw-Hill, 1969.

Koch, Gottfried. *Frauenfrage und Ketzertum im Mittelalter: Die Frauenbewegung im Rahmen des Katharismus und des Waldensertums und ihre soziale Wurzeln (12.–14. Jahrhundert).* Berlin: Akademie, 1962.

Kolmer, Lothar. *Ad Capiendas Vulpes: Die Ketzerbekämpfung in Südfrankreich in der ersten Hälfte des 13. Jahrhunderts und die Ausbildung des Inquisitionsverfahrens.* Bonn: Rohrscheid, 1982.

———. "Colbert und die Entstehung der Collection Doat." *Francia* 7 (1979): 463–89.

Kommission für die Geschichte Österreichs der Österreichischen Akademie der Wissenschaften, ed. *Österreich im Hochmittelalter (907 bis 1246).* Vienna: Österreichische Akademie der Wissenschaften, 1991.

Krech, Volkhard, and Hartmann Tyrell, eds. *Religionssoziologie um 1900.* Würzburg: Ergon-Verlag, 1995.

Küenzlen, Gottfried. *Die Religionssoziologie Max Webers: Eine Darstellung ihrer Entwicklung.* Berlin: Duncker & Humblot, 1980.

Kurtz, Lester R. *The Politics of Heresy.* Berkeley and Los Angeles: University of California Press, 1986.

Kurze, Dietrich. "Häresie und Minderheit im Mittelalter." *Historische Zeitschrift* 229 (1979): 529–73.

———. *Quellen zur Ketzergeschichte Brandenburgs und Pommerns.* Berlin: de Gruyter, 1975.

———. "Zur Ketzergeschichte der Mark Brandenburg und Pommerns vornehmlich im 14. Jahrhundert." *Jahrbuch für die Geschichte Mittel- und Ostdeutschlands* 16/17 (1968): 50–94.

Lambert, Malcolm D. *Franciscan Poverty.* London: S.P.C.K, 1961.

———. *Medieval Heresy: Popular Movements from Bogomil to Hus.* New York: Holmes & Meier, 1977.

———. *Medieval Heresy: Popular Movements from the Gregorian Reform to the Reformation.* 2d ed. Oxford: Blackwell, 1992.

Lansing, Carol. *Power and Purity: Cathar Heresy in Medieval Italy.* New York: Oxford University Press, 1997.

Lash, Scott, and Sam Whimster, eds. *Max Weber, Rationality, and Modernity.* London: Allen & Unwin, 1987.

Lau, Franz. "Evangelische Räte." In *Die Religion in Geschichte und Gegenwart: Handwörterbuch für Theologie und Religionswissenschaft*, 3d ed., edited by K. Galling, cols. 785–88. Tübingen: Mohr, 1958.

Lawrence, C. H. *The Friars: The Impact of the Early Mendicant Movement on Western Europe.* London: Longman, 1994.

———. *Medieval Monasticism.* 2d ed. London: Longman, 1990.

Le Bras, Gabriel. *Études de sociologie religieuse.* Vol. 2. Paris: Presses Universitaires de France, 1956.

Lebrun, François, ed. *Histoire de la France religieuse.* Vol. 2. Paris: Seuil, 1988.

Leclercq, Jean. *The Love of Learning and the Desire for God.* New York: Fordham University Press, 1961.

Lecoy de la Marche, Albert, ed. *Anecdotes historiques, légendes et apologues, tirés du recueil inédit d'Étienne de Bourbon, dominicain du XIIIe siècle.* Paris: Renouard, 1877.

Le Goff, Jacques. "Arbeit. V.: Mittelalter." *Theologische Realenzyklopädie* 3 (1978): 626–35.

————. *The Birth of Purgatory*. Translated by Arthur Goldhammer. Chicago: University of Chicago Press, 1984.

————. *Marchands et banquiers du Moyen Âge*. Paris: Presses Universitaires de France, 1956.

————. *Time, Work, and Culture in the Middle Ages*. Translated by Arthur Goldhammer. Chicago: University of Chicago Press, 1980.

————, ed. *Hérésies et sociétés dans l'Europe pré-industrielle, 11e–18e siècles*. Paris: Mouton, 1968.

————. *Medieval Callings*. Translated by Lydia G. Cochrane. Chicago: University of Chicago Press, 1990.

Lehmann, Hartmut. "Max Webers Lutherinterpretation." *Berliner Journal für Soziologie* 5 (1995): 349–58.

————. *Max Webers "Protestantische Ethik": Beiträge aus der Sicht eines Historikers*. Göttingen: Vandenhoeck & Ruprecht, 1996.

————, ed. *Säkularisierung, Dechristianisierung, Rechristianisierung im neuzeitlichen Europa: Bilanz und Perspektiven der Forschung*. Göttingen: Vandenhoeck & Ruprecht, 1997.

Lehmann, Hartmut, and Guenther Roth, eds. *Weber's "Protestant Ethic": Origins, Evidence, Contexts*. Cambridge: Cambridge University Press, 1993.

Leipoldt, Johannes. *Griechische Philosophie und frühchristliche Askese*. Berlin: Akademie, 1961.

Lekai, Louis J. *The Cistercians: Ideals and Reality*. Kent, Ohio: Kent State University Press, 1977.

Lenger, Friedrich. *Werner Sombart, 1863–1941: Eine Biographie*. Munich: Beck, 1994.

Lerner, Robert E. "A Case of Religious Counter-Culture: The German Waldensians." *American Scholar* 55 (1986): 234–47.

————. "Waldensians." In *Dictionary of the Middle Ages*, edited by Joseph A. Strayer, 12:508–13. New York: Charles Scribner's Sons, 1989.

Le Roy Ladurie, Emmanuel. *Montaillou: The Promised Land of Error*. Translated by Barbara Bray. New York: Vintage Books, 1979.

Lesnick, Daniel R. *Preaching in Medieval Florence: The Social World of Franciscan and Dominican Spirituality*. Athens: University of Georgia Press, 1989.

Leyser, Henrietta. *Hermits and the New Monasticism: A Study of Religious Communities in Western Europe, 1000–1150*. New York: St. Martin's Press, 1984.

Liebersohn, Harry. *Fate and Utopia in German Sociology, 1870–1923*. Cambridge: MIT Press, 1988.

Little, Lester K. *Liberty, Charity, Fraternity: Lay Religious Fraternities at Bergamo in the Age of the Commune*. Northampton, Mass.: Smith College, 1988.

————. *Religious Poverty and the Profit Economy in Medieval Europe*. Ithaca: Cornell University Press, 1978.

————. "Romanesque Christianity in Germanic Europe." *Journal of Interdisciplinary History* 23 (1993): 453–74.

Lohse, Bernard. *Askese und Mönchtum in der Antike und in der alten Kirche.* Munich: Oldenburg, 1969.

Loos, Milan. *Dualist Heresy in the Middle Ages.* Prague: Academia, 1974.

Lopez, Robert S. *The Commercial Revolution of the Middle Ages, 950–1350.* Englewood Cliffs, N.J.: Prentice Hall, 1971.

Lourdaux, W., and D. Verhelst, eds. *The Bible and Medieval Culture.* Leuven: Leuven University Press, 1979.

Löwy, Michael. "Weber Against Marx? The Polemic with Historical Materialism in the *Protestant Ethic.*" *Science and Society* 53 (1989): 71–83.

Mahul, Alphonse. *Cartulaire et archives des commune de l'ancien diocèse et de l'arrondissement administratif de Carcassonne.* Vol. 5. Paris: Didron, 1867.

Malinowski, Bronislaw. *Magic, Science, and Religion.* Glencoe, Ill.: Free Press, 1948.

Manselli, Raoul. "Églises et théologies cathares." *Cahiers de Fanjeaux* 3 (1968): 129–76.

———. "La fin du catharisme en Italie." *Cahiers de Fanjeaux* 20 (1985): 101–18.

———. *L'eresia del male.* 2d ed. Naples: Morano, 1980.

Map, Walter. *De nugis curialium.* Edited by M. R. James. Revised by C.N.L. Brooke and R.A.B. Mynors. Oxford: Clarendon Press, 1983.

Marshall, Gordan. *In Search of the Spirit of Capitalism: An Essay on Max Weber's Protestant Ethic Thesis.* London: Hutchinson, 1982.

Marx, Karl, and Friedrich Engels. *On Religion.* New York: Schocken, 1964.

Mason, Emma. "The Role of the English Parishioner, 1100–1500." *Journal of Ecclesiastical History* 27 (1976): 17–29.

Max-Planck-Institut für Geschichte, ed. *Untersuchungen zu Kloster und Stift.* Göttingen: Vandenhoeck & Ruprecht, 1980.

McDonnell, Ernest W. *The Beguines and Beghards in Medieval Culture, with Special Emphasis on the Belgian Scene.* 1954. Reprint, New York: Octagon Books, 1969.

McGinn, Bernard, and John Meyendorff, eds. *Christian Spirituality: Origins to the Twelfth Century.* New York: Crossroad, 1985.

McKitterick, Rosamond. *The Carolingians and the Written Word.* Cambridge: Cambridge University Press, 1989.

McLaughlin, Megan. *Consorting with Saints: Prayer for the Dead in Early Medieval France.* Ithaca: Cornell University Press, 1994.

Meersseman, Gilles G. *Introduction to the Order of Penance in the Thirteenth Century.* Rome: n.p., 1983.

———. *Ordo Fraternitatis: Confraternite e pietà dei laici nel medioevo.* 3 vols. Rome: Herder, 1977.

Menache, Sophia. *The Vox Dei: Communication in the Middle Ages.* Oxford: Oxford University Press, 1990.

Merlo, Grado G. *Eretici ed eresie medievali.* Bologna: Mulino, 1989.

———. *Eretici e inquisitori nella società piemontese.* Turin: Claudiana, 1977.

———. *Valdesi e valdismi medievali.* Vol. 1, *Itinerari e proposte di ricerca.* Turin: Claudiana, 1984.

————. *Valdesi e valdismi medievali*. Vol. 2, *Identità valdesi nella storia e nella storiografia: Studi e discussioni*. Turin: Claudiana, 1991.

Merz, Peter-Ulrich. *Max Weber und Heinrich Rickert: Die erkenntniskritischen Grundlagen der verstehenden Soziologie*. Würzburg: Königshausen & Neumann, 1990.

Michaelsen, Robert S. "Changes in the Puritan Concept of Calling or Vocation." *New England Quarterly* 26 (1953): 315–36.

Migne, Jacques Paul, ed. *Patrologiae cursus completus . . . Series Latina*. . . . Paris: J. P. Migne, 1844–64.

Milis, Ludo. *Angelic Monks and Earthly Men: Monasticism and Its Meaning to Medieval Society*. Rochester: Boydell Press, 1992.

Mittelalterliche Textüberlieferung und ihre kritische Aufarbeitung. Munich: Monumenta Germaniae Historica, 1978.

Moeller, Bernd. *Deutschland im Zeitalter der Reformation*. 3d ed. Göttingen: Vandenhoeck & Ruprecht, 1988.

Molendijk, Arie L. *Zwischen Theologie und Soziologie: Ernst Troeltschs Typen der christlichen Gemeinschaftsbildung: Kirche, Sekte, Mystik*. Gütersloh: Gütersloher Verlagshaus, 1996.

Mollat, Guillame, ed. *Bernard Gui: Manuel de l'Inquisiteur*. Vol. 1. 1926. Reprint, Paris: Champion, 1980.

Mollat, Michel. *The Poor in the Middle Ages: An Essay in Social History*. New Haven: Yale University Press, 1986.

Mommsen, Wolfgang J. *Max Weber: Gesellschaft, Politik und Geschichte*. Frankfurt: Suhrkamp, 1974.

Mommsen, Wolfgang J., and Jürgen Osterhammel, eds. *Max Weber and His Contemporaries*. London: Allen & Unwin, 1987.

Montet, Éduard. *La Noble Leçon*. Paris: Fischbacher, 1888.

Moore, R. I. *The Birth of Popular Heresy*. London: Arnold, 1975.

————. *The Formation of a Persecuting Society: Power and Deviance in Western Europe, 950–1250*. Oxford: Blackwell, 1990.

————. *The Origins of European Dissent*. Rev. ed. New York: Blackwell, 1985.

Moore, R. Laurence. *Selling God: American Religion in the Marketplace of Culture*. Oxford: Oxford University Press, 1994.

Moorman, John. *The History of the Franciscan Order*. Oxford: Clarendon Press, 1968.

Morgan, John. *Godly Learning: Puritan Attitudes Towards Reason, Learning, and Education*. Cambridge: Cambridge University Press, 1988.

Morris, Colin. *The Discovery of the Individual, 1050–1200*. New York: Harper & Row, 1972.

Mulhern, Philip F. *The Early Dominican Laybrother*. Washington, D.C.: n.p., 1944.

Mumford, Lewis. *The Myth of the Machine*. Vol. 1. New York: Harcourt Brace Jovanovich, 1967.

Mundy, John Hine. *Europe in the High Middle Ages, 1150–1309*. 2d ed. New York: Longman, 1991.

————. *Liberty and Political Power in Toulouse, 1050–1230*. New York: Columbia University Press, 1954.

————. *Men and Women at Toulouse in the Age of the Cathars*. Toronto: Pontifical Institute of Mediaeval Studies, 1990.

————. *The Repression of Catharism at Toulouse: The Royal Diploma of 1279*. Toronto: Pontifical Institute of Mediaeval Studies, 1985.

Mundy, John Hine, Richard W. Emery, and Benjamin N. Nelson, eds. *Essays in Medieval Life and Thought Presented in Honor of Austin Patterson Evans*. New York: Columbia University Press, 1955.

Murray, Alexander. "Missionaries and Magic in Dark-Age Europe." *Past and Present* 136 (1992): 186–205.

————. *Reason and Society in the Middle Ages*. Rev. ed. Oxford: Clarendon Press, 1985.

Nagel, Peter. *Die Motivierung der Askese in der alten Kirche und der Ursprung des Mönchtums*. Berlin: Akademie, 1966.

Neill, Stephen C., and Hans-Ruedi Weber, eds. *The Layman in Christian History*. Philadelphia: Westminster Press, 1963.

Nelli, René. *Les cathares ou l'éternel combat*. Paris: Grasset, 1972.

Nelson, Benjamin. "Max Weber's 'Author's Introduction' (1920): A Master Clue to His Main Aims." *Sociological Inquiry* 44 (1974): 269–78.

Neusner, Jacob, Ernest S. Frerichs, and Paul V. McCracken Flesher, eds. *Religion, Science, and Magic in Concert and in Conflict*. New York: Oxford University Press, 1989.

Nichols, John A., and Lillian Thomas Shank, eds. *Medieval Religious Women*. Vol. 1. Kalamazoo, Mich.: Cistercian Publications, 1984.

Nickson, Margaret. "The 'Pseudo-Reinerius' Treatise, the Final Stage of a Thirteenth Century Work on Heresy from the Diocese of Passau." *Archives d'histoire doctrinale et littéraire du Moyen Âge* 34 (1967): 294–303.

Nielsen, Donald A. "Rationalization in Medieval Europe: The Inquisition and Sociocultural Change." *Politics, Culture, and Society* 2 (1988): 217–41.

Nietzsche, Friedrich. *Basic Writings of Nietzsche*. Edited and translated by Walter Kaufmann. New York: Modern Library, 1992.

Nuccio, Oscar. *Il pensiero economico italiano, 1: Le fonti (1050–1450): L'etica laica e la formazione dello spirito economico*. 3 vols. Sassari: Edizioni Gallizzi, 1984–87.

Oakes, Guy. "Farewell to *The Protestant Ethic*?" *Telos* 78 (1988–89): 81–94.

————. *Weber and Rickert: Concept Formation in the Social Sciences*. Cambridge: MIT Press, 1988.

Oakley, Francis. *The Western Church in the Later Middle Ages*. Ithaca: Cornell University Press, 1979.

O'Dea, Thomas F. "Five Dilemmas in the Institutionalization of Religion." *Social Compass* 7 (1960): 61–67.

Oediger, Friedrich Wilhelm. *Über die Bildung der Geistlichen im späten Mittelalter*. Leiden: Brill, 1953.

Ordericus Vitalis. *The Ecclesiastical History of Orderic Vitalis*. Vol. 4. Translated by Marjorie Chibnall. Oxford: Clarendon Press, 1973.

Osborne, Kenan B. *Ministry: Lay Ministry in the Catholic Church, Its History and Theology*. New York: Paulist Press, 1993.

Osheim, Duane J. "Conversion, *Conversi*, and the Christian Life in Late Medieval Tuscany." *Speculum* 58 (1983): 368–90.

Ovitt, George, Jr. "The Cultural Context of Western Technology: Early Christian Attitudes Toward Manual Labor." *Technology and Culture* 27 (1986): 477–500.

———. *The Restoration of Perfection: Labor and Technology in Medieval Culture*. New Brunswick, N.J.: Rutgers University Press, 1987.

Owen, David. "Autonomy and 'Inner Distance': A Trace of Nietzsche in Weber." *History of the Human Sciences* 4 (1991): 79–91.

Owst, Gerald R. *Preaching in Medieval England*. Cambridge: Cambridge University Press, 1926.

Ozment, Steven. *The Age of Reform, 1250–1550: An Intellectual and Religious History of Late Medieval and Reformation Europe*. New Haven: Yale University Press, 1980.

———. *Protestants: The Birth of a Revolution*. New York: Doubleday, 1993.

———. *The Reformation in the Cities: The Appeal of Protestantism to Sixteenth-Century Germany and Switzerland*. New Haven: Yale University Press, 1975.

Pales-Gobilliard, Annette. *L'Inquisiteur Geoffroy d'Ablis et les cathares du comté de Foix (1308–1309)*. Paris: Éditions du Centre national de la recherche scientifique, 1984.

Paolini, Lorenzo. "Domus e zona degli eretici: L'esempio di Bologna nel XIII secolo." *Rivista di storia della Chiesa in Italia* 35 (1981): 371–87.

———. *L'eresia a Bologna fra XIII e XIV secolo*. Vol. 1, *L'eresia catara alla fine del duecento*. Rome: Istituto storico italiano per il Medio Evo, 1975.

Paolini, Lorenzo, and Raniero Orioli. *Acta S. Officii Bononie ab anno 1291 usque ad annum 1310*. 3 vols. Rome: Istituto storico italiano per il Medio Evo, 1982–84.

Paton, Bernadette. *Preaching Friars and the Civic Ethos: Siena, 1380–1480*. London: Centre for Medieval Studies, 1992.

Patschovsky, Alexander. *Der Passauer Anonymus: Ein Sammelwerk über Ketzer, Juden, Antichrist aus der Mitte des 13. Jahrhunderts*. Stuttgart: Hiersemann, 1968.

———. *Quellen zur Böhmischen Inquisition im 14. Jahrhundert*. Weimar: Böhlau, 1979.

———. "Waldenserverfolgung in Schweidnitz 1315." *Deutsches Archiv für Erforschung des Mittelalters* 36 (1980): 137–76.

———. "Zur Ketzerverfolgung Konrads von Marburg." *Deutsches Archiv für Erforschung des Mittelalters* 37 (1981): 641–93.

Patschovsky, Alexander, and Kurt-Victor Selge, eds. *Quellen zur Geschichte der Waldenser*. Gütersloh: Mohn, 1973.

Paul, Jacques. "Jacques Fournier inquisiteur." *Cahiers de Fanjeaux* 26 (1991): 39–67.

———. "La procédure inquisitoriale à Carcassonne au milieu du XIIIe siècle." *Cahiers de Fanjeaux* 29 (1996): 361–96.

Paulus, Nikolaus. "Die Wertung der weltlichen Berufe im Mittelalter." *Historisches Jahrbuch* 32 (1911): 725–55.

————. "Zur Geschichte des Worts Beruf." *Historisches Jahrbuch* 45 (1925): 308–16.

Pazzelli, Raffaele. *St. Francis and the Third Order: The Franciscan and Pre-Franciscan Penitential Movement*. Chicago: Franciscan Herald Press, 1989.

Pelikan, Jaroslav J. *The Christian Tradition: A History of the Development of Doctrine*. Vols. 1–3. Chicago: University of Chicago Press, 1978.

Pellicani, Luciano. "Weber and the Myth of Calvinism." *Telos* 75 (1988): 57–85.

Persecution and Liberty: Essays in Honor of George Lincoln Burr. New York: Century, 1931.

Peters, Edward, ed. *Heresy and Authority in Medieval Europe: Documents in Translation*. Philadelphia: University of Pennsylvania Press, 1980.

————. *Inquisition*. Berkeley and Los Angeles: University of California Press, 1989.

————. *The Magician, the Witch, and the Law*. Philadelphia: University of Pennsylvania Press, 1978.

Pètrement, Simone. *Le dualisme dans l'histoire de la philosophie et des religions: Introduction à l'étude du dualisme platonicien, du gnosticisme et du manichéisme*. Paris: Gallimard, 1946.

Petrus Sarnensis. *Petri Vallium Sarnaii monachi Hystoria albigensis*. Edited by Pascal Guébin and Ernest Lyon. 3 vols. Paris: Champion, 1926–39.

Philipps-Universität Marburg, ed. *Sankt Elisabeth: Fürstin, Dienerin, Heilige*. Sigmaringen: Thorbecke, 1981.

Platt, Colin. *The Parish Churches of Medieval England*. London: Secker & Warburg, 1981.

Portal, Charles. *Histoire de la ville de Cordes en Albigeois (1222–1799)*. 3d ed. Toulouse: Privat, 1984.

Pounds, N.J.G. *An Economic History of Medieval Europe*. New York: Longman, 1974.

Préaux, Jean, ed. *Problèmes d'histoire du christianisme 5*. Brussels: Éditions de l'Université de Bruxelles, 1974–75.

Preger, Wilhelm. "Beiträge zur Geschichte der Waldesier im Mittelalter." *Abhandlungen der königlich bayerischen Akademie der Wissenschaften, 3. Klasse* 13/1 (1875): 181–250.

————. "Der Tractat des David von Augsburg über die Waldesier." *Abhandlungen der königlich bayerischen Akademie der Wissenschaften, Historische Klasse* 14/2 (1878): 183–235.

Pressouyre, Léon, ed. *L'espace cistercien*. Paris: Comité des travaux historiques et scientifiques, 1994.

Prinz, Friedrich. *Askese und Kultur: Vor- und Frühbenediktinisches Mönchtum an der Wiege Europas*. Munich: Beck, 1980.

Pullan, Brian S. *A History of Early Renaissance Italy: From the Mid–Thirteenth to the Mid-Fifteenth Century*. London: Lane, 1973.

Raftis, James A., ed. *Pathways to Medieval Peasants*. Toronto: Pontifical Institute of Mediaeval Studies, 1981.

Ranft, Patricia. *Women and the Religious Life in Premodern Europe*. New York: St. Martin's Press, 1996.

Rapp, Francis. *L'Église et la vie religieuse en Occident à la fin du Moyen Âge*. Paris: Presses Universitaires de France, 1971.

Reinburg, Virginia. "Liturgy and the Laity in Late Medieval and Reformation France." *Sixteenth-Century Journal* 23 (1992): 526–47.

Renz, Horst, and Friedrich Wilhelm Graf, eds. *Troeltsch-Studien*. Vol. 3, *Protestantismus und Neuzeit*. Gütersloh: Mohn, 1984.

Reynolds, Susan. *Kingdoms and Communities in Western Europe, 900–1300*. Oxford: Clarendon Press, 1984.

Riché, Pierre. *Ecoles et enseignement dans le Haut Moyen Âge*. Paris: Picard, 1989.

———. *Instruction et vie religieuse dans le Haut Moyen-Âge*. London: Variorum Reprints, 1981.

Riesebrodt, Martin. "Ideen, Interessen, Rationalisierung: Kritische Anmerkungen zu F. H. Tenbrucks Interpretation des Werkes Max Webers." *Kölner Zeitschrift für Soziologie und Sozialpsychologie* 32 (1980): 111–29.

Ritschl, Albrecht. *Geschichte des Pietismus*. 3 vols. Bonn: Marcus, 1880–86.

Roach, Andrew. "The Cathar Economy." *Reading Medieval Studies* 12 (1986): 51–71.

Robinson, I. S. *The Papacy, 1073–1198: Continuity and Innovation*. Cambridge: Cambridge University Press, 1990.

Rondeau, Jennifer Fisk. "Lay Piety and Spirituality in the Late Middle Ages: The Confraternities of North-Central Italy, ca. 1250 to 1348." Ph.D. diss., Cornell University, 1988.

Roquebert, Michel. *Cathar Religion*. Portet-sur-Garonne: Éditions Loubatières, 1988.

———. "Le catharisme comme tradition dans la 'Familia' languedocienne." *Cahiers de Fanjeaux* 20 (1985): 221–42.

———. *L'épopée cathare: 1198–1212: L'invasion*. Toulouse: Privat, 1970.

———. *L'épopée cathare: Mourir à Montségur*. Toulouse: Privat, 1990.

Rösener, Werner. *Peasants in the Middle Ages*. Translated by Alexander Stutzer. Urbana: University of Illinois Press, 1992.

Rosenwein, Barbara H. *Rhinoceros Bound: Cluny in the Tenth Century*. Philadelphia: University of Pennsylvania Press, 1982.

———. *To Be the Neighbor of Saint Peter: The Social Meaning of Cluny's Property, 909–1049*. Ithaca: Cornell University Press, 1989.

Rosenwein, Barbara H., and Lester K. Little. "Social Meaning in the Monastic and Mendicant Spiritualities." *Past and Present* 63 (1974): 4–32.

Roth, Guenther, and Wolfgang Schluchter. *Max Weber's Vision of History: Ethics and Methods*. Berkeley and Los Angeles: University of California Press, 1979.

Rottenwöhrer, Gerhard. *Der Katharismus*. Vol. 1, *Quellen zum Katharismus*. Bad Honnef: Bock & Herchen, 1982.

———. *Der Katharismus*. Vol. 2, *Der Kult, die religiöse Praxis, die Kritik an Kult und Sakramenten der Katholischen Kirche*. Bad Honnef: Bock & Herchen, 1982.

———. *Der Katharismus*. Vol. 4, *Glaube und Theologie der Katharer*. Bad Honnef: Bock & Herchen, 1993.

Rubin, Miri. *Corpus Christi: The Eucharist in Late Medieval Culture*. Cambridge: Cambridge University Press, 1991.

Runciman, Steven. *The Medieval Manichee: A Study of the Christian Dualist Heresy*. 1947. Reprint, Cambridge: Cambridge University Press, 1960.

Russell, J. C. "Bevölkerung. B. Nord-, Mittel-, West- und Südeuropa." In *Lexikon des Mittelalters*, vol. 2, edited by Robert-Henri Bautier, cols. 11–14. Munich: Artemis, 1983.

Russell, Jeffrey Burton. *Dissent and Order in the Middle Ages: The Search for Legitimate Authority*. New York: Macmillan, 1992.

———. *Dissent and Reform in the Early Middle Ages*. Berkeley and Los Angeles: University of California Press, 1965.

———. "Interpretations of the Origins of Medieval Heresy." *Mediaeval Studies* 25 (1963): 26–53.

Šanjek, Franjo. "Le rassemblement hérétique de Saint-Félix-de-Caraman (1167) et les églises cathares au XIIe siècle." *Revue d'histoire écclésiastique* 67 (1972): 767–99.

———. "Raynerius Sacconi, O.P., *Summa de Catharis*." *Archivum Fratrum Praedicatorum* 44 (1974): 31–60.

Scaff, Lawrence A. *Fleeing the Iron Cage: Culture, Politics, and Modernity in the Thought of Max Weber*. Berkeley and Los Angeles: University of Berkeley Press, 1989.

Scheeben, Heribert C. "Libellus de principiis ordinis Praedicatorum auctore Iordano de Saxonia." *Monumenta Ordinis Praedicatorum Historica* 16 (1935): 1–88.

Schieder, Wolfgang, ed. *Volksreligiosität in der modernen Sozialgeschichte*. Göttingen: Vanderhoeck & Ruprecht, 1986.

Schlatter, Richard B. *The Social Ideas of Religious Leaders, 1660–1688*. London: Oxford University Press, 1940.

Schluchter, Wolfgang. *Paradoxes of Modernity: Culture and Conduct in the Theory of Max Weber*. Translated by Neil Solomon. Stanford: Stanford University Press, 1996.

———. *Rationalism, Religion, and Domination: A Weberian Perspective*. Translated by Neil Solomon. Berkeley and Los Angeles: University of California Press, 1989.

———. *The Rise of Western Rationalism: Max Weber's Developmental History*. Translated by G. Roth. Berkeley and Los Angeles: University of California Press, 1981.

———, ed. *Max Webers Sicht des antiken Christentums*. Frankfurt: Suhrkamp, 1985.

———. *Max Webers Sicht des Islams*. Frankfurt: Suhrkamp, 1987.

———. *Max Webers Sicht des okzidentalen Christentums*. Frankfurt: Suhrkamp, 1988.

———. *Max Webers Studie über das antike Judentum*. Frankfurt: Suhrkamp, 1981.

———. *Max Webers Studie über Hinduismus und Buddhismus*. Frankfurt: Suhrkamp, 1984.

———. *Max Webers Studie über Konfuzianismus und Taoismus*. Frankfurt: Suhrkamp, 1983.

Schmidt, Charles. *Histoire et doctrine de la secte des cathares ou albigeois*. Paris: Cherbuliez, 1849.

Schmitt, Jean-Claude. *The Holy Greyhound: Guinefort, Healer of Children Since the Thirteenth Century*. Translated by Martin Thom. Cambridge: Cambridge University Press, 1983.

Schmitz-Valckenberg, Georg. *Grundlehren katharischer Sekten des 13. Jahrhunderts*. Munich: Schöningh, 1971.

Schneider, Martin. *Europäisches Waldensertum im 13. und 14. Jahrhundert: Gemeinschaftsform–Frömmigkeit–sozialer Hintergrund*. Berlin: de Gruyter, 1981.

Schönbach, Anton E. *Studien zur Geschichte der altdeutschen Predigt, III: Das Wirken Bertholds von Regensburg gegen die Ketzer*. 1904. Reprint, Hildesheim: Olms, 1968.

Schreiber, Georg. *Gemeinschaften des Mittelalters*. Münster: Regensberg, 1948.

Schroeder, Ralph. *Max Weber and the Sociology of Culture*. London: Sage, 1992.

Scribner, Robert W. *Popular Culture and Popular Movements in Reformation Germany*. London: Hambledon Press, 1987.

———. "The Reformation, Popular Magic, and the 'Disenchantment of the World.'" *Journal of Interdisciplinary History* 23 (1993): 475–94.

Seaver, Paul S. *Wallington's World: A Puritan Artisan in Seventeenth-Century London*. Stanford: Stanford University Press, 1985.

Seeberg, Reinhold. *Thomasius' Dogmengeschichte des Mittelalters und der Neuzeit*. Erlangen: Deichert'sche Verlagsbuchhandlung, 1889.

Segl, Peter. *Ketzer in Österreich: Untersuchungen über Häresie und Inquisition im Herzogtum Österreich im 13. und beginnenden 14. Jahrhundert*. Paderborn: Schöningh, 1984.

———, ed. *Die Anfänge der Inquisition im Mittelalter*. Vienna: Böhlau, 1993.

Selge, Kurt-Victor. "Die Erforschung der mittelalterlichen Waldensergeschichte." *Theologische Rundschau*, n.s., 33 (1968): 281–343.

———. *Die ersten Waldenser*. 2 vols. Berlin: de Gruyter, 1967.

Sheils, W. J., ed. *The Church and War*. Oxford: Blackwell, 1983.

———. *Monks, Hermits, and the Ascetic Tradition*. Oxford: Blackwell, 1985.

Sheils, W. J., and Diana Wood, eds. *The Church and Wealth*. Oxford: Blackwell, 1987.

———. *Women in the Church*. Oxford: Blackwell, 1990.

Silber, Ilana Friedrich. "Dissent Through Holiness: The Case of the Radical Renouncer in Theravada Buddhist Countries." *Numen* 28 (1981): 164–93.

———. "Gift-Giving in the Great Traditions: The Case of Donations to Monasteries in the Medieval West." *European Journal of Sociology* 36 (1995): 209–43.

———. "Monasticism and the 'Protestant Ethic': Asceticism, Ideology, and Wealth in the Medieval West." *British Journal of Sociology* 44 (1993): 103–23.

————. *Virtuosity, Charisma, and Social Order: A Comparative Sociological Study of Monasticism in Theravada Buddhism and Medieval Catholicism.* Cambridge: Cambridge University Press, 1995.

Simmel, Georg. *The Philosophy of Money.* [1902]. Translated by Tom Bottomore and David Frisby. 2d ed. London: Routledge, 1990.

Skocpol, Theda, ed. *Vision and Method in Historical Sociology.* Cambridge: Cambridge University Press, 1984.

Smith, Morton. *Jesus the Magician.* San Francisco: Harper & Row, 1978.

Söderberg, Hans. *La religion des cathares: Étude sur le gnosticisme de la basse antiquité et du Moyen Âge.* 1949. Reprint, New York: AMS Press, 1978.

Sombart, Werner. *Der Bourgeois: Zur Geistesgeschichte des modernen Wirtschaftsmenschen.* Munich: Duncker & Humblot, 1913.

————. *Der moderne Kapitalismus.* 2 vols. Leipzig: Duncker & Humblot, 1902.

Sombart, Werner, Max Weber, and Edgar Jaffé. "Geleitwort." *Archiv für Soziale Gesetzgebung und Statistik* 19 (1904): i–vii.

Southern, Richard W. *Western Society and the Church in the Middle Ages.* Harmondsworth, Middlesex: Penguin Books, 1970.

Sprondel, Walter M., and Richard Grashoff, eds. *Alfred Schütz und die Idee des Alltags in den Sozialwissenschaften.* Stuttgart: Enke, 1979.

Spufford, Peter. *Money and Its Use in Medieval Europe.* Cambridge: Cambridge University Press, 1988.

Stark, Rodney. *The Rise of Christianity: A Sociologist Reconsiders History.* Princeton: Princeton University Press, 1996.

Stock, Brian. *The Implications of Literacy: Written Language and Models of Interpretation in the Eleventh and Twelfth Centuries.* Princeton: Princeton University Press, 1983.

————. *Listening for the Text: On the Uses of the Past.* Baltimore: Johns Hopkins University Press, 1990.

Strathmann, H. "Askese I (nichtchristlich)." In *Reallexikon für Antike und Christentum*, edited by Theodor Klauser, vol. 1, cols. 749–58. Stuttgart: Hiersemann, 1950.

Strauss, Gerald. *Luther's House of Learning: Indoctrination of the Young in the German Reformation.* Baltimore: Johns Hopkins University Press, 1978.

Strayer, Joseph R. *The Albigensian Crusades.* 1971. Reprint, Ann Arbor: University of Michigan Press, 1992.

Stroumsa, Gedaliahu G. "Ascèse et gnose: Aux origines de la spiritualité monastique." *Revue thomiste* 81 (1981): 557–73.

Sumption, Jonathan. *Pilgrimage: An Image of Mediaeval Religion.* Totowa, N.J.: Rowman & Littlefield, 1975.

Swanson, Ronald N. *Religion and Devotion in Europe, c. 1215–c. 1515.* Cambridge: Cambridge University Press, 1995.

Sweeney, James R., and Stanley Chodorow, eds. *Popes, Teachers, and Canon Law in the Middle Ages.* Ithaca: Cornell University Press, 1989.

Tabuteau, Emily Zack. *Transfers of Property in Eleventh-Century Norman Law.* Chapel Hill: University of North Carolina Press, 1988.

Tambiah, Stanley J. *Magic, Science, Religion, and the Scope of Rationality.* Cambridge: Cambridge University Press, 1990.

———. *World Conqueror and World Renouncer: A Study of Buddhism and Polity in Thailand Against a Historical Background.* Cambridge: Cambridge University Press, 1976.

Tanz, Sabine, ed. *Mentalität und Gesellschaft im Mittelalter: Gedenkschrift für Ernst Werner.* Frankfurt: Lang, 1993.

Tardif, Ad. "Document pour l'histoire du *processus per inquisitionem* et de l'*inquisitio heretice pravitatis.*" *Nouvelle revue historique du droit français et étranger* 7 (1883): 669–78.

Taylor, Larissa. *Soldiers of Christ: Preaching in Late Medieval and Reformation France.* Oxford: Oxford University Press, 1992.

Tentler, Thomas N. *Sin and Confession on the Eve of the Reformation.* Princeton: Princeton University Press, 1977.

Teske, Wolfgang. "Laien, Laienmönche und Laienbrüder in der Abtei Cluny [I]." *Frühmittelalterliche Studien* 10 (1976): 248–322.

———. "Laien, Laienmönche und Laienbrüder in der Abtei Cluny [II]." *Frühmittelalterliche Studien* 11 (1977): 288–339.

Thomas, Keith. "An Anthropology of Religion and Magic, II." *Journal of Interdisciplinary History* 6 (1975): 91–109.

———. *Religion and the Decline of Magic.* New York: Charles Scribner's Sons, 1971.

———. "Work and Leisure in Pre-Industrial Society." *Past and Present* 29 (1964): 50–62.

Thompson, E. P. "Time, Work-Discipline, and Industrial Capitalism." *Past and Present* 38 (1967): 56–97.

Thouzellier, Christine. *Catharisme et valdéisme en Languedoc à la fin du XIIe et au début du XIIIe siècle.* 2d ed. Louvain: Nauwelaerts, 1969.

———. "La Bible des cathares languedociens et son usage dans la controverse au début du XIIIe siècle." *Cahiers de Fanjeaux* 3 (1968): 42–57.

———. *Une somme anti-cathare: Le "Liber contra Manicheos" de Durand de Huesca.* Louvain: Spicilegium sacrum Lovaniense, 1964.

Tilly, Charles. *Big Structures, Large Processes, Huge Comparisons.* New York: Sage, 1984.

Toepfer, Michael. *Die Konversen der Zisterzienser.* Berlin: Dunker & Humblot, 1983.

Toussaert, Jacques. *Le sentiment religieux en Flandre à la fin du Moyen-Âge.* Paris: Librairie Plon, 1963.

Traugott, Mark. *Armies of the Poor: Determinants of Working-Class Participation in the Parisian Insurrection of June 1848.* Princeton: Princeton University Press, 1985.

Treiber, Hubert, and Heinz Steinert. *Die Fabrikation des zuverlässigen Menschen: Über die "Wahlverwandtschaft" von Kloster- und Fabrikdisziplin.* Munich: Moos, 1980.

Tremel, Ferdinand. *Wirtschafts- und Sozialgeschichte Österreichs.* Vienna: Deuticke, 1969.

Tribe, Keith, ed. *Reading Weber*. London: Routledge, 1989.

Troeltsch, Ernst. *Augustin, die christliche Antike und das Mittelalter*. 1915. Reprint, Aalen: Scientia Verlag, 1963.

———. "Die Bedeutung des Protestantismus für die Entstehung der modernen Welt." *Historische Zeitschrift* 97 (1906): 1–66.

———. *Gesammelte Schriften*. Vol. 4, *Aufsätze zur Geistesgeschichte und Religionssoziologie*. Edited by Hans Baron. Tübingen: Mohr, 1925.

———. *Protestantism and Progress: A Historical Study of the Relation of Protestantism to the Modern World*. Translated by W. Montgomery. Boston: Beacon Press, 1966.

———. "Religion und Kirche." *Preußische Jahrbücher* 81 (1895): 215–49.

———. Review of *Lehrbuch der Dogmengeschichte: Zweite Hälfte: Die Dogmengeschichte des Mittelalters und der Neuzeit*, by R. Seeberg. *Göttingische gelehrte Anzeigen* 163 (1901): 15–30.

———. *The Social Teaching of the Christian Churches*. [1912]. Translated by O. Wyon. New York: Macmillan, 1956.

Turner, Stephen P. *The Search for a Methodology of Social Science: Durkheim, Weber, and the Nineteenth-Century Problem of Cause, Probability, and Action*. Dordrecht: Reidel, 1986.

Tyrell, Hartmann. "Potenz und Depotenzierung der Religion: Religion und Rationalisierung bei Max Weber." *Saeculum* 44 (1993): 303–25.

———. "Protestantische Ethik—und kein Ende." *Soziologische Revue* 17 (1994): 397–404.

———. "Worum geht es in der 'Protestantischen Ethik'? Ein Versuch zum besseren Verständnis Max Webers." *Saeculum* 41 (1990): 130–77.

Università degli studi di Perugia, ed. *Lavorare nel Medio Evo: Rappresentazioni ed esempi dall'Italia dei secc. X–XVI, 12–15 ottobre 1980*. Todi: Presso l'Accademia Tudertina, 1983.

Van Engen, John. "The 'Crisis of Cenobitism' Reconsidered: Benedictine Monasticism in the Years 1050–1150." *Speculum* 61 (1986): 269–304.

Vauchez, André. *The Laity in the Middle Ages: Religious Beliefs and Devotional Practices*. Translated by Margery J. Schneider. Notre Dame, Ind.: University of Notre Dame Press, 1994.

———. *La sainteté en Occident aux dernièrs siècles du Moyen Âge d'après les procès de canonisations et les documents hagiographiques*. Paris: Boccard, 1983.

———. *The Spirituality of the Medieval West: From the Eight to the Twelfth Century*. Translated by Colette Friedlander. Kalamazoo, Mich.: Cistercian Publications, 1993.

Vicaire, Marie-Humbert. *Dominique et ses prêcheurs*. 2d ed. Fribourg: Éditions Universitaires, 1977.

———. *Histoire de Saint Dominique: Un homme évangélique*. 2 vols. 2d ed. Paris: Cerf, 1982.

———. "L'action de l'enseignement et de la prédication des mendiants vis-à-vis des cathares." *Cahiers de Fanjeaux* 20 (1985): 277–304.

———. "Le modèle évangélique des apôtres à l'origine de l'ordre de saint Dominique." *Heresis* 13/14 (1989): 323–40.

Volpe, Gioacchino. *Movimenti religiosi e sette ereticali nella società medievale italiana (secoli XI–XIV)*. [1922]. 5th ed. Florence: Sansoni, 1977.

Wagner, Gerhard, and Heinz Zipprian, eds. *Max Webers Wissenschaftslehre: Interpretation und Kritik*. Frankfurt: Suhrkamp, 1994.

Wakefield, Walter L. "The Family of Niort in the Albigensian Crusade and Before the Inquisition." *Names* 18 (1970): 97–117, 286–303.

———. *Heresy, Crusade, and Inquisition in Southern France, 1100–1250*. Berkeley and Los Angeles: University of California Press, 1974.

———. "Heretics and Inquisitors: The Case of Auriac and Cambiac." *Journal of Medieval History* 12 (1986): 225–37.

———. "Inquisitors' Assistants: Witness[es] to Confessions in Manuscript 609." *Heresis* 20 (1993): 57–65.

———. "The Treatise Against Heretics of James Capelli: A Study of Medieval Writing and Preaching Against Catharan Heresy." Ph.D. diss., Columbia University, 1951.

Wakefield, Walter L., and Austin P. Evans. *Heresies of the High Middle Ages: Selected Sources, Translated and Annotated*. New York: Columbia University Press, 1969.

Walsh, Katherine, and Diana Wood, eds. *The Bible in the Medieval World: Essays in Memory of Beryl Smalley*. Oxford: Blackwell, 1985.

Ward, Benedicta. *Miracles and the Medieval Mind: Theory, Record, and Event, 1000–1215*. Rev. ed. Philadelphia: University of Pennsylvania Press, 1987.

Wattenbach, Wilhelm. *Kleine Abhandlungen zur mittelalterlichen Geschichte*. 1886. Reprint, Leipzig: Zentralantiquariat der Deutschen Demokratischen Republik, 1974.

Waugh, Scott L., and Peter D. Diehl, eds. *Christendom and Its Discontents: Exclusion, Persecution, and Rebellion, 1000–1500*. Cambridge: Cambridge University Press, 1996.

Weber, Eugene. *Peasants into Frenchmen: The Modernization of Rural France, 1870–1914*. Stanford: Stanford University Press, 1976.

Weber, Marianne. *Max Weber: A Biography*. [1926]. Translated by Harry Zohn. New Brunswick, N.J.: Transaction, 1988.

Weber, Max. *Agrarian Sociology of Ancient Civilizations*. Translated by R. I. Frank. London: Verso, 1988.

———. *Ancient Judaism*. [1917–20]. Edited and translated by Hans H. Gerth and Don Martindale. Glencoe, Ill.: Free Press, 1952.

———. "Anticritical Last Word on *The Spirit of Capitalism*." [1910]. Translated by W. Davis. *American Journal of Sociology* 83 (1978): 1110–30.

———. *Briefe 1906–1908*. Edited by M. Rainer Lepsius and Wolfgang J. Mommsen in collaboration with Birgit Rudhard and Manfred Schön. Tübingen: Mohr, 1990.

———. *Briefe 1909–1910*. Edited by M. Rainer Lepsius and Wolfgang J. Mommsen in collaboration with Birgit Rudhard and Manfred Schön. Tübingen: Mohr, 1994.

———. "'Churches' and 'Sects' in North America: An Ecclesiastical Socio-Political Sketch." [1906]. Translated by C. Loader. *Sociological Theory* 3 (1985): 7–13.

———. *Die protestantische Ethik, II: Kritiken und Antikritiken.* Edited by Johannes Winckelmann. 5th ed. Gütersloh: Mohn, 1987.

———. *Die protestantische Ethik und der "Geist" des Kapitalismus.* Edited by Klaus Lichtblau and Johannes Weiß. Bodenheim: Athenäum Hain Hanstein, 1993.

———. "Die protestantische Ethik und der 'Geist' des Kapitalismus, I: Das Problem." *Archiv für Sozialwissenschaft und Sozialpolitik* 20 (1904): 1–54.

———. "Die protestantische Ethik und der 'Geist' des Kapitalismus, II: Die Berufsidee des asketischen Protestantismus." *Archiv für Sozialwissenschaft und Sozialpolitik* 21 (1905): 1–110.

———. *Die Wirtschaftsethik der Weltreligionen: Konfuzianismus und Taoismus: Schriften 1915–1920.* Edited by Helwig Schmidt-Glintzer in collaboration with Petra Kolonko. Tübingen: Mohr, 1989.

———. *Economy and Society.* Edited by Claus Wittich and Guenther Roth. Berkeley and Los Angeles: University of California Press, 1978.

———. *From Max Weber.* Edited by Hans H. Gerth and C. Wright Mills. New York: Oxford University Press, 1958.

———. *General Economic History.* [1923]. Translated by F. Knight. New Brunswick, N.J.: Transaction, 1981.

———. *Gesammelte Aufsätze zur Religionssoziologie.* Vol. 3. 1921. Reprint, Tübingen: Mohr, 1988.

———. *Gesammelte Aufsätze zur Sozial- und Wirtschaftsgeschichte.* Tübingen: Mohr, 1988.

———. *Grundriss zu den Vorlesungen über Allgemeine ("theoretische") Nationalökonomie.* 1898. Reprint, Tübingen: Mohr, 1990.

———. "'Kirchen' und 'Sekten.'" *Frankfurter Zeitung,* 13 April 1906.

———. "'Kirchen' und 'Sekten' in Nordamerika: Eine kirchen- und sozialpolitische Skizze." *Die christliche Welt* 20, no. 24 (14 June 1906): cols. 558–62; no. 25 (21 June 1906): cols. 577–83.

———. *The Methodology of the Social Sciences.* Edited and translated by Edward A. Shils and Henry A. Finch. Glencoe, Ill.: Free Press, 1949.

———. *The Protestant Ethic and the Spirit of Capitalism.* Translated by T. Parsons. New York: Charles Scribner's Sons, 1976.

———. *The Religion of China: Confucianism and Taoism.* [1915]. Edited and translated by Hans H. Gerth. New York: Free Press, 1964.

———. *The Religion of India: The Sociology of Hinduism and Buddhism.* [1916–17]. Edited and translated by Hans H. Gerth and Don Martindale. Glencoe, Ill.: Free Press, 1960.

———. "Some Categories of Interpretive Sociology." [1913]. Translated by Edith Graber. *Sociological Quarterly* 22 (1981): 151–80.

———. *Wissenschaft als Beruf: 1917/1919; Politik als Beruf: 1919.* Edited by Wolfgang J. Mommsen and Wolfgang Schluchter in collaboration with Birgitt Morgenbrod. Tübingen: Mohr, 1992.

———. *Zur Psychophysik der industriellen Arbeit: Schriften und Reden 1908–1912.* Edited by Wolfgang Schluchter in collaboration with Sabine Frommer. Tübingen: Mohr, 1995.

————. *Zur Russischen Revolution von 1905: Schriften und Reden 1905–1912*. Edited by Wolfgang J. Mommsen in collaboration with Dittmar Dahlmann. Tübingen: Mohr, 1989.

Weinstein, Donald, and Rudolph M. Bell. *Saints and Society: The Two Worlds of Western Christendom, 1000–1700*. Chicago: University of Chicago Press, 1986.

Weiß, Johannes. *Max Webers Grundlegung der Soziologie*. Munich: Verlag Dokumentation, 1975.

Wemple, Suzanne Fonay. *Women in Frankish Society: Marriage and the Cloister, 500 to 900*. Philadelphia: University of Pennsylvania Press, 1981.

Wenglinsky, Martin. "The Economic Meaning of the Parables." Paper presented at the annual meeting of the Association for the Sociology of Religion, Washington, D.C., 1995.

Wenzel, Siegfried. *The Sin of Sloth: Acedia in Medieval Thought and Literature*. Chapel Hill: University of North Carolina Press, 1967.

Werner, Ernst, and Martin Erbstösser. *Ketzer und Heilige: Das religiöse Leben im Hochmittelalter*. Vienna: Böhlau, 1987.

White, Stephen D. *Custom, Kinship, and Gifts to Saints: The "Laudatio Parentum" in Western France, 1050–1150*. Chapel Hill: University of North Carolina Press, 1988.

Wimbush, Vincent L., and Richard Valantasis, eds. *Asceticism*. Oxford: Oxford University Press, 1995.

Winckelmann, Johannes. "Die Herkunft von Max Webers 'Entzauberungs'-Konzeption." *Kölner Zeitschrift für Soziologie und Sozialpsychologie* 32 (1980): 12–53.

————. *Erläuterungsband zu "Wirtschaft und Gesellschaft."* Tübingen: Mohr, 1976.

————. *Max Webers hinterlassenes Hauptwerk: Die Wirtschaft und die gesellschaftlichen Ordnungen und Mächte*. Tübingen: Mohr, 1986.

Wischermann, Else M. *Marcigny-sur-Loire: Gründungs- und Frühgeschichte des ersten Cluniacenserinnenpriorates (1055–1150)*. Munich: Fink, 1986.

Wisskirchen, Rotraut. "Das monastische Verbot der Feldarbeit und ihre rechtliche Gestaltung bei Benedikt von Nursia." *Jahrbuch für Antike und Christentum* 38 (1995): 91–96.

Wittberg, Patricia. *The Rise and Fall of Catholic Religious Orders: A Social Movement Perspective*. Albany: State University of New York Press, 1994.

Wolff, Philippe, and Frédéric Mauro. *Histoire générale du travail*. Vol. 2, *L'age de l'artisanat (Ve–XVIIIe siècles)*. Paris: Nouvelle Librairie, 1960.

Wright, Anthony D. *The Counter-Reformation*. New York: St. Martin's Press, 1982.

Wuthnow, Robert. *Communities of Discourse: Ideology and Social Structure in the Reformation, the Enlightenment, and European Socialism*. Cambridge: Harvard University Press, 1989.

Zanoni, Luigi. *Gli Umiliati nei loro rapporti con l'eresia, l'industria della lana ed i communi nei secoli XII e XIII*. Milan: Hoepli, 1911.

Zaret, David. *The Heavenly Contract: Ideology and Organization in Pre-Revolutionary Puritanism*. Chicago: University of Chicago Press, 1985.

Zerfaß, Rolf. *Der Streit um die Laienpredigt*. Freiburg: Herder, 1974.

Zarnecki, George. *The Monastic Achievement*. New York: McGraw-Hill, 1972.

Zeeden, Ernst Walter. *Die Entstehung der Konfessionen*. Munich: Oldenbourg, 1965.

Zerubavel, Eviatar. "The Benedictine Ethic and the Modern Spirit of Scheduling: On Schedules and Social Organization." *Sociological Inquiry* 50 (1980): 157–69.

Zink, Michel. *La prédication en langue romane avant 1300*. Paris: Champion, 1976.

Zöllner, Erich, ed. *Wellen der Verfolgung in der österreichischen Geschichte*. Vienna: Österreichischer Bundesverlag, 1986.

INDEX

Page references followed by "." or "nn." refer to information in notes. Page references followed by "t" refer to tables. With some exceptions, medieval names are indexed by first name.

The Protestant Ethic and the Spirit of Capitalism (PE) (Weber), 13–25. *See also* Weber, Max
  on ascetic rationalism, 13–16, 23–25
  comparative cases in, 25, 41
  differences between original and revised editions of, 47–50
  on heterodox asceticism, 23–25
  on medieval monasticism, 18–21
  on mysticism, 22–23, 23 n. 50
  on orthodox laity, 21–22
  sects in, 55
  Weber's expansion of, 4, 16–18, 17 n. 19, 28, 30–31, 30–31 n. 76, 45, 49
Protestantism
  contrast of medieval Catholicism with, 53
  forerunners of ascetic, 12, 14, 17–18, 38, 54–55, 125
  and magic, 103
  and rationalism (*see* rationalism)
  Troeltsch on, 31–41
  Weber materialist analysis of, 17–18
"The Protestant Sects" (Weber), 45
Prouille, 188
Purgatory, and intercession, 68–69
Puritanism, revisionist historians on economic activities of, 77, 170–71, 173 n. 150

Quakers, 18 n. 26

Rachfahl, Felix, 26, 36, 40, 41, 41 n. 112
Rainerius Sacconi, 180 n. 14, 181 n. 15, 183, 185, 197
rationalism. *See also* self, empowerment of
  ascetic, 13–16, 18–21, 23–25, 40, 43–44, 192, 226–27
  and bourgeoisie, 38
  and calculability, 14–15
  emergence of lay, 5–6

  and literacy, 124
  and magic, 114–15
  and Protestantism, 14–15
  relationship to religion, 226–27
  religion role in, 44–45
  role of literacy in, 124
  and Rule of St. Benedict, 20
  Weber on, 13–16, 18–21, 40, 43–44, 192, 226–27
  Weber's typology of, 43–44
Raymunda de Rodesio, 189–90
Raymunda Gondaubou, 188
Raymunda Jotglar, 208
Reconciled Poor, 147 n. 58
Reformation
  disenchantment after, 102–6
  economic activities before, 228 n. 7
  literacy and success of, 123–24
Regula bullata, 84
Regula non bullata, 84
"Relationship of Protestantism to the Middle Ages" (Troeltsch), 38 n. 101
relics, of saints, 109–10
Religion and the Decline of Magic (Thomas), 103
Renous de Plassac, 190
rentier landlordship, Cistercians, 79–80
revisionist interpretations, of medieval asceticism, 61–62, 62t, 66 n. 15, 77, 94, 170–71, 173 n. 150, 196–201
Ritschl, Albrecht, 22–23
Robert of Arbrissel, 121
Robert of Molesme, 75
Rosenwein, Barbara H., 74 n. 31
Rottenwöhrer, Gerhard, 178 n. 9
Rule of St. Benedict, 5, 20, 96–97
  influence on Franciscans of, 84
  as organizational structure in monastic asceticism, 63–67, 73

sacerdotalism, 114, 118, 119, 161 n. 117. *See also* anticlericalism; priests; sacramentals

THANK
YOU
INDIA